# HUT to HUT USA

# HUT to HUT USA

LAUREL BRADLEY
& SAM DEMAS

**MOUNTAINEERS BOOKS** is dedicated to the
exploration, preservation, and enjoyment of outdoor
and wilderness areas.

1001 SW Klickitat Way, Suite 201, Seattle, WA 98134
800-553-4453, www.mountaineersbooks.org



Printed in China
Distributed in the United Kingdom by Cordee, www.cordee.co.uk
First edition, 2021

Copyeditor: Jennifer Zaczek Kepler
Design and layout: McKenzie Long
Cartographer: Lohnes+Wright
All photographs by the authors unless credited otherwise
Photograph and woodcut on page 18 copyright © Curt Carpenter
Front cover photographs, clockwise from upper left: *Trail through lush Maine woods, Maine Huts and Trails; Friends Hut at sunset in the American Prairie Reserve* (Photo by Reid Morth); *On the trail in the Three Sisters Backcountry* (Photo by Jonas Tarlen); *Juneau Lake Cabin on Resurrection Pass Trail*
Back cover photographs, left to right: *Mom biking with baby in tow toward Trout Lake on Resurrection Pass Trail in Alaska; The Rendezvous Hut in Washington's Methow Valley has sweeping views; Paddling Browns Tract near Raquette Lake in Adirondack Park* (Photo by John DiGiacomo)
Frontispiece: *Huts, like this Southwest Nordic Center yurt, offer comfort and solitude in the wilderness.*

Disclaimer: The authors acknowledge the emergence of the novel coronavirus during the final stages of research and writing. This guide is a snapshot of the hut systems' pre-pandemic policies and practices. Readers should be aware that many of the huts' policies, prices, and features may have changed. Always check the specific hut system website for the latest information, and call ahead before making plans.

The background maps for this book were produced using the online map viewer CalTopo, caltopo.com.

Library of Congress record is available at https://lccn.loc.gov/2021008628, and ebook record available at https://lccn.loc.gov/2021008629.

Printed on FSC®-certified materials

ISBN (paperback): 978-1-68051-268-7
ISBN (ebook): 978-1-68051-269-4

# CONTENTS

*As the cricket's soft autumn hum*
*is to us,*
*so are we to the trees*
*as are they*
*to the rocks and the hills.*

—Gary Snyder, excerpt from "Little
Poems for Gaia," *Axe Handles*

US HUT SYSTEMS
CANADA
PACIFIC OCEAN
Rendezvous Huts
Washington
Mount Tahoma Trails
American Prairie Reserve
North Dakota
Oregon
Sun Valley Mountain Huts
Montana
Three Sisters Backcountry
Idaho
Idaho State University Portneuf Yurts
South Dakota
Wyoming
Sierra Club Donner Pass Huts
Never Summer Nordic
Nebraska
Nevada
Utah
Tenth Mountain Division Hut System
California
Colorado
Kansas
San Juan Huts
Yosemite High Sierra Camps
Southwest Nordic Center
Arizona
New Mexico
Oklahoma
Texas
MEXICO
White Mountains NRA
Alaska
Delta Range Huts
Nancy Lake SRA
Bomber Traverse
Resurrection Pass Trail
Eklutna Traverse
Haleakala National Park Huts
Hawaii

8

Boundary Country Trekking
Porcupine Mountains Wilderness State Park
CANADA
AMC Maine Wilderness Lodges
Maine
Maine Huts and Trails
Vermont Huts Association
AMC Huts
Adirondack Hamlets to Huts
Vermont
New Hampshire
Minnesota
Wisconsin
Michigan
New York
Massachusetts
Rhode Island
Connecticut
Iowa
Pennsylvania
New Jersey
Ohio
Maryland
Delaware
Illinois
Indiana
West Virginia
Virginia
Missouri
Kentucky
ATLANTIC OCEAN
North Carolina
Tennessee
Arkansas
South Carolina
Mississippi
Alabama
Georgia
Louisiana
Florida
Gulf of Mexico
featured huts
bonus huts
N
0        200 MILES
0        400 KILOMETERS

# AN INVITATION TO DREAM

**MY HUT DREAMS BEGAN DURING** a life-changing, forty-two-day, hut-to-hut walk in the European Alps. Years later, beginning a deep dive into where huts are located and how they operate, I was corresponding with Swiss hut specialist, mountain guide, writer, and photographer Marco Volken and wrote about how much we in America had to learn from the Swiss about huts. Marco replied, "Sure, if you want to study how huts developed in the nineteenth century, come to the Alps. But we Europeans can't wait for Americans to get into huts and show us what twenty-first-century huts will look like."

As my partner, Laurel, and I started seriously hiking, skiing, and biking US hut systems, Marco's words suddenly turned into an epiphany. We began to see disconnected US hut initiatives as a series of creative impulses. Americans are indeed beginning to think broadly and act imaginatively about huts as local, educational, affordable, and environmentally sensitive infrastructure for building community and engaging young people with conservation. *Hut to Hut USA: The Complete Guide for Hikers, Bikers, and Skiers* is an invitation to sample the variety, pleasures, and creativity of American huts—in your armchair and on the trail. We also hope it will stimulate you to envision your own hut dreams, and to join the emerging conversation about huts in the US.

Desperate to connect with nature, we hike, bike, ski, and paddle to the far corners of the earth in search of adventure and authenticity. Meanwhile, a rising tide of overnighters

OPPOSITE: *A unique hut can draw you into high wild places, like this one on the Bomber Traverse in Alaska's Talkeetna Mountains.* (Photo by Seth K. Hughes)

*Aurora borealis over a backyard hut in Fairbanks, Alaska (Photo by Ken Tape)*

in the wild threatens to overwhelm trails, campsites, and beloved biomes; we are steadily loving wild places to death. Are huts and hut systems perhaps part of the solution?

US hut systems, still few in number, are extremely popular. Grassroots hut initiatives are springing up, and huts seem poised for significant growth. As hut-to-hut travel gains popularity, land managers and recreation professionals are beginning to pay attention. Should the US have more huts? Where are existing huts, and where might we build more in the future? Are simple huts compatible with American culture and values, or will we commercialize them as glamping? Can we use huts to expand access to nature while reducing human impact, to cultivate a sense of reciprocity with the natural world, and to help protect and restore ecosystems through conservation endeavors?

Join us in imagining possible futures for hut-to-hut travel in America. Plan, trek, question, dream . . . and share your hut dreams. How can US hut systems continue as simple and sustainable forces for the greater good?

# INTRODUCTION: HUTS FOR THE BODY AND SOUL

**ANTS DIG TUNNELS, SPIDERS WEAVE** webs, birds build nests, bears occupy dens, and humans build huts. Embodying the primitive roots of architecture, huts carry symbolic resonance. They represent shelter at its most essential. Just as the primitive hut invokes the earliest stages of human civilization, huts evoke childhood. Children love to build tiny dwellings; they construct sprawling forts in the backyard or with the table and chairs in the dining room. Filled with stuffed animals or imaginary friends, these diminutive structures become spaces for social experiments.

It is no wonder that huts exert a magical draw on backcountry travelers. When a tiny cabin, yurt, or spacious lodge comes into view, it promises comfort and company but also something more basic. It connects the modern traveler back to times when shelter was not taken for granted, and being inside a hut shapes and celebrates human interaction. Hut visitors revel in the utopian social and domestic possibilities of the backcountry hostelry. Starting afresh in a compact, well-organized—if temporary—community brings out the best in individual travelers, friends, or family members.

Huts cultivate the innate human capacity to connect and cooperate, even with complete strangers. A few days in these rustic structures, where daily rituals are reduced to the essentials, can deepen commitments to sustainable living back home. And the

remote hut, enmeshed in a deep forest or perched on a mountain ridge, is a sanctuary for humans seeking healing in nature.

Huts are unique overnight venues. But the daily trek between huts—relying on the human body to move forward day after day—adds a meditative magic to the experience. Hut-to-hut travel is about not only the destination but also the journey. Traveling long distances under our own muscle power transforms us into nature pilgrims. Days spent outdoors in repetitive motion free the senses to absorb gentle breezes, birdsong, towering trees, and freezing rain; strengthen the body; and release the mind from habitual worries and preoccupations.

After connecting in a small midwestern college town, we began to plan vacations around our passion for hiking in general and hut-to-hut in particular. At first, the appeal of long-distance travel on foot was bound up with the charm of international destinations. We spent two weeks hiking the Haute Route in Switzerland. Not only did we relish the stunning alpine landscapes and convivial hut life, but we also felt more deeply the transformative potential of a long walk. A few years later, we ventured away from the Alps and its well-trodden hut-to-hut paths and headed east. On a walking sojourn in northern Greece, there were few classic huts in the Pindus Mountains, and so we walked village to village, staying in wonderful little hotels and guesthouses. In Slovenia, on the other hand, we encountered an unusual abundance of huts; a walker can traverse the entire country and hit two huts a day—one for lunch and another to stay in overnight. We embarked on walking adventures in Ireland and the UK where there are no huts. Beyond Europe, we spread our wings and journeyed to the Southern Hemisphere, tasting hut life in Chile, and later spent three months studying huts in New Zealand.

But America the beautiful continued to call; we soon began actively seeking out US hut systems. Shocked by how little was known and written, I (Sam) started visiting US hut systems; interviewing the owners, operators, and guests; and scouring the literature. I eventually developed www.hut2hut.info to share what I learned, including more than 160 trip reports and articles; a map of hut system locations in North and South America; photo galleries; a series of "operational profiles" containing information for people designing, building, and running hut systems; and more.

While there are good publications (see Resources) on some hut systems in the US, none paint a complete picture of hut-to-hut travel opportunities or illuminate the larger situation of huts in America. And while Laurel enthusiastically joined this project, the label "hut nut" applies to me alone.

*Hut to Hut USA* introduces the idea of huts to American audiences and helps trekkers plan hut adventures in the US. To provide context, we survey hut-to-hut opportunities worldwide and explore the halting history of huts in America. We then summarize the situation of US huts and emerging trends.

OPPOSITE: *The Gazebo, a memorial to a dedicated Mount Tahoma Trails volunteer, offers shelter and views for quiet contemplation.*

*At the AMC's White Mountains huts, you might be awakened by a morning serenade.*

Next, we address how to plan a hut trip, and then present sixteen featured hut systems. This book focuses on opportunities for multiday, hut-to-hut backcountry travel in the US, profiling systems that conform to a very specific definition: three or more huts spaced a day's walk, ski, or bike apart. The trails linking them are designed to be walked, skied, or biked in a traverse or circuit that lasts at least four days. Ideally, the journey lasts long enough for the traveler to become immersed in place and to experience the recuperative power of nature.

Although we started the project with a carefully honed definition of huts and hut systems, we ended up selectively modifying that definition along the way, adding a few shorter itineraries (two huts over three days and two nights) in order to best represent the options. With the sixteen featured hut systems, we aimed to include as many areas of the US as possible, to acknowledge changing use patterns, and to highlight experiments and new trends.

There are thousands of huts, cabins, yurts, lodges, shelters, tent camps, treehouses, trailers, and other forms of rustic accommodations in the US. But only a few are connected to support long-distance backcountry travel. To honor the rich possibilities beyond the featured systems, we present hut clusters and individual huts in Bonus Hut Opportunities. If we had learned about a few of these options in time or stretched definitions differently, some might have become featured systems.

This is the first book to present the full range of US hut-to-hut opportunities and within a broad context, and we may have missed a few. While huts are not new, they are not well understood in the US. We hope to fill this gap by providing the bigger picture of how hut-to-hut travel fits into the US recreational opportunity spectrum.

The primary audience is hikers, skiers, and bikers dreaming about hitting the trail. This book is for folks of above-average fitness, possessing a spirit of adventure and solid backcountry skills. Another key audience is folks seeking to understand the past, present, and possible futures of huts in America, including the primary audience of outdoor enthusiasts, along with hut operators, land management officials, recreation planners, environmentalists, and people dreaming about future hut systems. We aim to provide a substantive overview to inform an emerging national conversation about huts in the US.

We love to walk and ski but, honestly, are less engaged with biking. There is only one existing system with routes aimed exclusively at two-wheeled adventurers, but we highlight additional bike-friendly systems. To focus our research, we opted not to cover modes of human-powered or human-plus-animal-powered travel such as paddling, horseback riding, mushing, llama and burro packing, and e-biking. The sixteen featured hut systems do not require advanced backcountry or mountaineering skills and gear, since systems of that nature are potentially beyond the capability of our target audience, but we profile four great hut-to-hut systems requiring advanced skills in Bonus Hut Opportunities.

*The joys of breaking trail through deep powder*

Over the course of two years, we hiked, skied, or otherwise traversed all sixteen featured systems for a total of 599 miles—every description and itinerary is based on direct experience (except one!). The one exception is Adirondack Hamlets to Huts, which opened during the pandemic, meaning and we were unable to visit due to travel restrictions. In many cases, we visited these systems a second or third time, depending on our knowledge of and experience with them. We talked with owners, staff, and land agency officials; conversed with other guests; avidly read logbooks; and took a lot of pictures. Nearing the end of the project, we realized we may be the only two people who have walked, skied, or biked sixteen US hut-to-hut traverses (some multiple times), a modest accomplishment and a splendid journey.

NEXT PAGE: *The promise of warmth and companionship draws the backcountry traveler to mountain huts.* (Woodcut of Fowler-Hilliard Hut on rice paper, Curt Carpenter)

# HUT CULTURE

# THE ORIGINS OF HUTS

**THE TERM *HUT*, REFERRING TO** rustic or primitive forms of human shelter, is remarkably vague and encompassing, and its meanings continue to evolve. Nomadic peoples and workers such as shepherds, herders, foresters, miners, stockmen, hunters, and fishers have traditionally used huts as shelters. Included in this architectural type are variations almost too numerous to count, including barracks, bivouacs, bothies, cabanas, cabins, casitas, follies, hermitages, hostels, lean-tos, lodges, platform tents, shacks, sheds, shanties, shelters, storage buildings, teahouses, tepees, writers' retreats, and yurts.

The hut is not only associated with rustic lifestyles, remote locales, local materials, and simple construction methods. Referred to as "the taproot of inhabiting" by French philosopher Gaston Bachelard, the hut also figures in musings about the origins of architecture and metaphysical notions of shelter. The primitive hut was an object of fascination among eighteenth-century Enlightenment thinkers. In his 1755 *An Essay on Architecture*, Abbé Marc-Antoine Laugier identified huts as the original human architecture, constructed by primitive societies as protection from the elements. While Laugier's hut—a vine-covered templelike structure (see illustration, next page)—is rather fanciful, archaeological evidence demonstrates that purpose-built wooden shelters date back more than ten thousand years. The primitive hut remains a touchstone of architectural thought and aspirations. Gaston Bachelard wrote compellingly in *The Poetics of Space* (1958) about modern humanity's recurring "hut dreams": "We hope to have elsewhere, far from the over-crowded house, far from city cares . . . the primitive hut, of prehistoric men." The ideal hut embodies the values of simplicity, authenticity, human

OPPOSITE: *Iconic Mont Blanc rises behind the Refuge du Couvercle above Chamonix, the center of European alpinism since the nineteenth century.* (Photo by Jerome Bon, Creative Commons, Wikimedia)

*This fanciful evocation of the origins of human architecture, an illustration by Charles Eisen, was the frontispiece in a 1755 edition of an* Essay on Architecture *by Marc-Antoine Laugier.*

scale, and a light imprint on the earth. There are echoes of Bachelard's hut dreams in many people's fascination with the tiny house lifestyle and publications such as *Cabin Porn* in the twenty-first century.

English walkers began to use the term *hut*, derived from the German *hütte*, in the nineteenth century to describe shelters adapted or constructed to support long-distance walking. Each alpine region has drawn still widely used equivalent terms from its local language: *hytte, refugio, cabane, capanna, dom,* and *chamanna.* Walt Unsworth's *Encyclopaedia of Mountaineering* offers a more specialized definition: "A mountain hut is a purpose-built refuge situated at some strategically high place in the mountains so that one or more peaks are readily accessible from it. It may vary in size from a simple bivouac shelter to something resembling a small hotel in size and facilities."

For centuries, European pilgrims and traveling merchants took shelter in rustic local accommodations—huts, hostels, taverns, or hotels. Beginning in the Middle Ages, the popularity of religious pilgrimages stimulated the development of specialized hostels (*alberges*, or auberges) to support long-distance walkers. Alpinists, first in Switzerland and then elsewhere, began to use cowsheds to stage early morning peak-bagging forays. Romantic-era walkers, seeking prolonged immersion in remote and beautiful mountains, also took advantage of climbers' huts; like mountaineers, they paid local farmers to shelter in rustic outbuildings. Alpine clubs, which arose in the 1860s to support climbers and soon embraced hikers, developed hut networks by identifying existing rustic shelters and organizing construction of new huts.

As walkers began to use huts, trail networks developed, often based on ancient pilgrimages or military and mercantile paths. When these routes passed through villages, walkers stayed in existing hostels and hotels. In the mountains, they stayed in purpose-built huts.

Thus, hut-to-hut travel in Europe evolved as a mix of lodging types. Early recreational

# THE THERAPEUTIC BENEFITS OF A MULTIDAY TRAVERSE

Hut-to-hut journeys can be transformative. Research shows that even a few hours in nature offer a balm for the spirit. In our experience, it takes three to four days to *begin* to feel the longer-lasting therapeutic effects of a human-powered trek. Here are some of the ways that a hut-to-hut journey works on your body and soul.

**Escape from the day-to-day.** Travel is a time-honored method of escaping from normal routines. Hut-to-hut trips are an effective way of breaking free from the claustrophobic web of stale habits, work and family pressures, anxiety, and the ubiquitous media.

**Establish a new daily routine.** While changing location may start the shift away from "life as usual," the journey changes the pattern and cadence of life. The hut-to-hut traverse structures each day, imposing a meditative rhythm on essential tasks. The day is spent walking, looking, resting, and eating outdoors. At the hut, the traveler's task is to relax, prepare and enjoy a meal, join in conversation, enjoy music or play games with others, and then sleep—life reduced to a set of simple acts.

**Enjoy the benefits of sustained exercise.** Moderate, sustained exercise for hours each day has a different impact than more concentrated workout routines we pursue at home and in the gym. For most people, long-distance human-powered travel is not a sport. You don't keep score. You are not training for something; you sink into the healing power of nature and enjoy the journey. Day after day of rhythmic exercise contributes to the potential for retraining neural networks and establishing new ways of being.

**Go on an accessible adventure.** Hut-to-hut adventures present a host of challenges. Even a four-to-seven-day journey is full of problems to solve—adverse weather, wayfinding, small medical emergencies, and fatigue. Hut logbooks are full of stories about personal growth and jubilant exclamations: "It was the one of the hardest things—and one of the best things—I've ever done."

**Experience a sense of renewal.** The first days are taxing; the muscles ache. Alone with your thoughts for days on end, you begin to recognize long-established, ruminative patterns. Soon the body begins to grow stronger, and the mind begins to clear. Historically, many great thinkers have found walking to be a powerful spur to creativity and mental clarity. We can all access this form of transcendence on long treks, seeing our life choices more clearly and reordering our priorities to achieve greater balance. Chinese traditional medicine calls this balancing the chi (energy) or life force; in the West, this is an aspect of mind-body medicine.

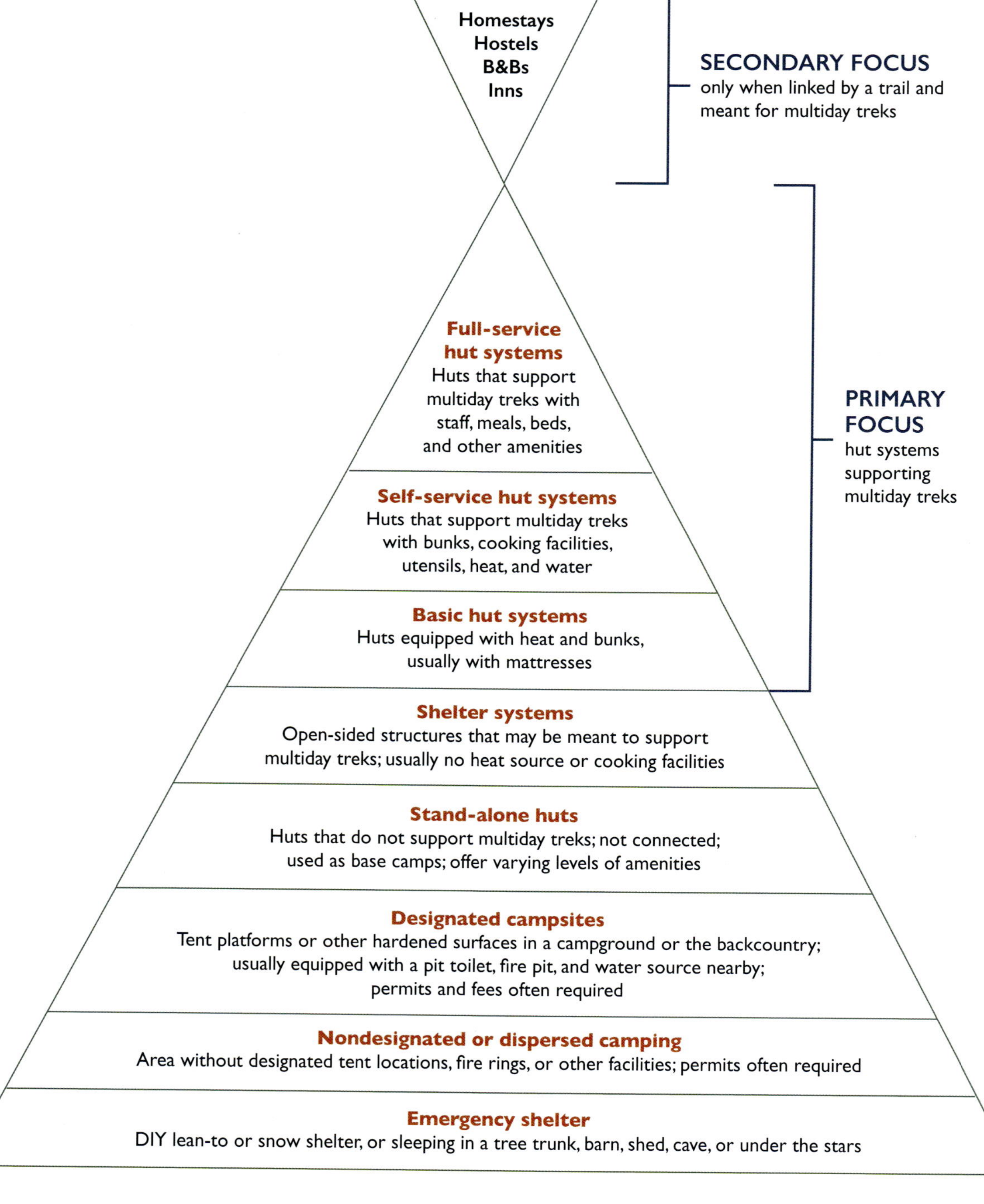


*The primary focus of this book is hut systems accessible via multiday treks, but it also describes some systems where inns, hostels, and B&Bs are linked via a trail.*

huts were quite primitive—both structurally and in terms of amenities. Expectations of comfort grew throughout the twentieth century, and new huts became larger and offered more services, a trend that continues.

## DEFINING HUTS AND HUT SYSTEMS

In the context of American recreation, people define *hut* differently in different regions. While the term is fluid, for the purpose of this book, all huts have the following characteristics: an enclosed structure with a roof, a floor, and walls; some kind of heat source; bunks or sleeping platforms, usually with a mattress; a water source; and an outhouse or other toilet facility.

Beyond these basic criteria, amenities vary. *Basic* huts are effectively wooden tents; users must carry everything except the tent for a comfortable overnight. *Self-service* huts provide bunks and mattresses, cookstoves and utensils, heating stoves, and a table with seating. *Full-service* huts are staffed, serve meals, and offer common gathering spaces. The diagram on the facing page situates hut systems designed to support multiday treks—the focus of this book—in the broader array of backcountry shelter options.

Hut systems comprise three or more backcountry huts that are spaced a day's walk, ski, or bike apart; designed to be traveled in sequence; and connected by a trail system supporting a traverse or circuit over a period of days or weeks. This mode of travel engages not only the body but also the soul. More than an overnight recreational activity or vacation interlude, the multiday hut-supported traverse is an opportunity for average folks to become pilgrims, to settle into the rhythm of a long-distance, human-powered journey, to voluntarily simplify life, and to connect with the healing powers of nature (see "The Therapeutic Benefits of a Multiday Traverse").

We describe sixteen hut-to-hut systems throughout the US. Several do not meet all our criteria, but in some cases, they are the only viable option in a region. Some provide an optimum experience with fewer huts, and others spotlight innovative approaches to hut-to-hut travel. Excluded are hut systems that traverse avalanche-prone terrain or require technical mountaineering or skiing skills and equipment. Our very specific definition and emphasis on hut systems excludes many rustic, hut-like overnight accommodations. In Bonus Hut Opportunities, we give passing attention to some of the many single, isolated huts and cabins and small clusters of backcountry huts not designed to support multiday travel; we also mention the remarkable system of more than 250 open-sided backpacking shelters along the Appalachian Trail and other open shelters along long-distance paths. Because the book focuses on human-powered modes of travel, we exclude road-accessible hostelries, cabins, yurts, and other huts, and we skip over huts that are accessible only via helicopter or snowcat.

# HUT SYSTEMS AROUND THE WORLD

**WHILE STILL IN THE EARLY** stages of development in the US, hut-to-hut systems exist worldwide and are especially well established in Europe and New Zealand. A quick worldwide survey shows that huts are not uniform or commodified, but rather expressions of specific cultures and hospitality traditions. The following "tour" not only underlines features common around the world but also demonstrates how huts reflect local recreational practices, accommodation preferences, regional architecture, and trail systems.

## EUROPE

With more than forty nations operating thousands of huts, Europe is the epicenter of hut culture. Many American hut enthusiasts first hike hut-to-hut in Europe. And indeed, the European-style hut embodies a specific ideal of shelter, service, and conviviality that is a model all around the world. One of the most prolific writers on hut-to-hut treks, Kev Reynolds opens *The Mountain Hut Book* with a celebration of alpine huts, each "unique in respect to location, architectural style and ambience." Reynolds writes, "It's a bit like a youth hostel, offering simple, reasonably priced accommodation and meals in a magical setting for visitors taking part in mountain activities."

European huts are concentrated in the Alps and other mountainous regions including the Pyrenees, where weather conditions can be capricious and life-threatening. Once Europeans began to seek out sublime mountain heights and wild

OPPOSITE: *The new Monte Rosa Hut embodies Swiss elegance in hut design and functionality.* (Photo courtesy of LafargeHolcim Foundation, Marcus Gerber)

nature for leisure, a system of shelters began to evolve. Alpine clubs, founded around Europe and in England beginning in the 1860s, began building and tending huts so members could pursue their passion for mountaineering safely and find community. Most clubs quickly expanded their scope to embrace walkers and skiers. It is no wonder that European hut life caters to group experience and celebrates new friendships forged by shared interests.

Today, alpine clubs provide much of the crucial organizational infrastructure that supports huts and hut users. Clubs operate at least 1300 huts in Europe and often receive forms of government support. Private huts are fully integrated into national and regional networks. There is a tradition of cooperation and reciprocal privileges among national clubs. Clubs build shelters beyond the borders of their home country; Germany operates 185 huts in Austria, and France oversees five in Morocco. Demonstrating the expansive scope of such organizations, the quasi-governmental German Alpine Club—the world's largest with 1.3 million members—boasts a host of initiatives including educational and advocacy programs, in addition to work in mountain cartography, safety protocols, and conservation efforts.

Hut-to-hut travel requires a network of trails. Continuously inhabited for mill-

*Capanna d'Alzasca, a Swiss Alpine Club hut staffed in summer, is modest in scale and features local stonework.* (Photo by Marco Volken)

# SWITZERLAND, THE BIRTHPLACE OF HUTS

Switzerland's national identity is bound up with rugged mountains, scattered alpine villages, and sporting activities favoring steep slopes, snow, and ice. Mountain walking and skiing are cherished pastimes. The Swiss Alps and the mountains around Chamonix, France, were *the* destinations in the early days of alpinism.

Switzerland planted the seeds that gave rise to huts throughout the Alps and Europe. The country's approximately four hundred huts (more than 9200 beds) reflect the free-market economy, strong local governments, and hospitality traditions. About half are privately owned, and local chapters of the Swiss Alpine Club operate the others. Two-thirds of Swiss huts are full-service in season. The geography and transportation system of Switzerland, a small country, make the mountains easily accessible recreational destinations. Because national railroads, buses, and cable cars are seamlessly coordinated, citizens and guests can escape town for a daylong hike to a mountaintop, catch a cable car down, hop on the waiting bus, and then take the train home.

Constructed by members of the Swiss Alpine Club in 1863, the year the club was founded, the Grünhornhütte was among the first purpose-built recreational huts in the world. Switzerland has preserved its first hut as a kind of museum and continues to be an innovator in hut construction and design. The 2009 New Monte Rosa Hut near Zermatt, for example, is remarkable not only for its complex crystalline form but also for its technological innovations. Nicknamed the Mountain Crystal, this five-story, 125-person-capacity hut generates all its own power and models other green building systems for remote settings.

ennia, the European continent is etched with ancient, interconnected walking paths. Each European country has thousands of miles of waymarked local and national trails maintained by government entities and private organizations. These trails in turn connect across national boundaries to form a Pan-European system. The European Ramblers' Association (ERA) organizes support for nearly 45,000 miles of trails, divided into twelve European Long-Distance Walking Paths, or E-paths, which extend from Norway's North Cape to Crete, and from the Atlantic Ocean to the Carpathians and the Black Sea. According to the ERA website, E-paths "are the backbone of Europe's walking trails. . . . and provide intercultural experiences across the borders. E-paths connect people and are the paths for peace, understanding and unity."

The very best trails, according to the ERA's Leading Quality Trails certification system,

*Resembling a lunar module, Bivouac du Dolent-La Maye offers overnight shelter to mountaineers heading up Mount Dolent in Switzerland.* (Photo by Marco Volken)

provide a mix of natural features and cultural attractions, passing through villages and towns as well as mountains and forests. And good trails connect easily with public transportation.

The European hut, with its basic but welcome creature comforts, protects guests from the elements and protects nature from human impacts. Huts, by concentrating use, help protect the natural surroundings that attract walkers and other nature pilgrims. Due to population pressure and limited wildlands, camping is strictly controlled in much of Europe and mostly restricted to crowded campgrounds in the lowlands. Huts, then, are the favored method for overnight trips in wild mountain heights across the continent.

In Europe, the sheer number of huts and the existence of long-established footpaths, arrayed across relatively compact mountain ranges, create extensive opportunities for traverses. While many huts in the Alps, for example, were not originally part of a system, patterns of use over time have linked individual huts into traverses of varying lengths. Some European hut wardens have actively encouraged links and the formal naming of specific hut-to-hut routes in order to attract hikers; walkers are a more reliable and profitable clientele than climbers, who tend to stay in a single hut to prepare for their trip up a given peak. In the US by comparison, with vast landscapes and a small number of huts, each hut system is a distinct entity, unconnected to others.

The European Alps, spanning seven European countries—Austria, Germany, France, Switzerland, Italy, Liechtenstein, and Slovenia—are home to the largest number of huts and most extensive network of long-distance hiking routes. Among the best known are the Haute Route, stretching from Chamonix, France, to Zermatt, Switzerland—home of the Matterhorn—and the Tour du Mont Blanc, circling an iconic peak that straddles three countries. The longer treks, punctuated with both huts and village lodgings, stretch across multiple countries. The Grande Randonnée Cinq (GR5), for example, takes a hiker from the Netherlands, through Belgium and Luxembourg, and then all the way across France, north to south, to Nice on the Mediterranean Sea. For a great overview of classic European hut routes, check out Kev Reynold's *The Mountain Hut Book* (see Resources).

The Western Balkans are also connected by a continuous spine of mountains. While alpinism and recreational walking came later to this region than to western Europe, there are hut-to-hut opportunities in Slovenia, Croatia, Bosnia and Herzegovina, Serbia, Montenegro, Bulgaria, Macedonia, and Greece. In 2010, the Via Dinarica Alliance was established to promote a long-distance trail across eight Western Balkan nations. The Alpine Association of Slovenia, which manages 177 alpine lodges, mountain huts, refuges, and bivouacs, hosts a website (www.mountain-huts.net) with an interactive map and information about the 668 huts in the larger region maintained by national alpine clubs.

## SCANDINAVIA

Scandinavian culture celebrates winter sports and rugged mountain terrain. In Norway, the passion for Nordic skiing is reflected in an extensive hut system; the Norwegian Trekking Association (DNT), with 260,000 members, operates a network of about 550 cabins on about 4375 miles of ski trails and 13,750 miles of marked hiking trails. Accommodations range from staffed lodges to no-service cabins. Self-service options with well-stocked pantries are also available. The Swedish Tourist Association operates forty-three staffed mountain cabins nationwide, including sixteen with saunas along the 270-mile Kungsleden Trail (King's Trail) in Swedish Lapland. Finland has about seventy self-service wilderness huts, many built originally to shelter hunters and anglers.

## THE UNITED KINGDOM AND REPUBLIC OF IRELAND

The very first alpine club, founded in England in 1857, contributed mightily to mountaineering but never embraced walking. The Alpine Club, based in London, has historically focused on climbing on the Continent and in Asia. Nevertheless, the United Kingdom and Ireland have extraordinarily robust rambling (recreational walking) cultures, supported by many organizations. The Ramblers, founded in the 1930s, celebrates walking as a common good and advocates for trails and public rights-of-way. And yet England, and indeed the entire UK and Ireland, has

*A volunteer crew at work on Coire Fionnaraich bothy in the Scottish Northern Highlands (Photo by John Mitchell, Mountain Bothy Association)*

almost no hut systems. This is because, except for some parts of Wales and Scotland, England lacks the rugged mountain ranges that resist settlements. Long-distance walkers stay in village hostels, bed-and-breakfasts, inns, and small hotels.

Bothies—simple rural stone cottages—are an exception. Since 1965, the Mountain Bothies Association has worked to save abandoned farm dwellings and maintain them as remote shelters "for the use and benefit of all who love wild and lonely places." More than one hundred bothies, mostly in Scotland, welcome hikers on a first-come, first-served basis with only a roof and walls. Walkers bring along everything else they need.



## CANADA

An enormous country in landmass, Canada has a modest number of hut-to-hut traverses. The Wapta Icefield Traverse near Lake Louise is perhaps the premier multi-day backcountry ski traverse in the Canadian Rockies. Its five capacious huts are maintained by the Alpine Club of Canada (ACC). In the Selkirk Mountains, the British Columbia Ministry of Forests and the Kootenay Mountaineering Club partner to support the four small huts of the Bonnington Traverse, open in both winter and summer.

Similar to alpine clubs in Europe, the ACC plays an important role in building and maintaining huts. In addition to the huts along mountain traverses, the ACC offers four full-service, frontcountry lodges and hostels and more than thirty-six stand-alone, self-service huts, almost all in the mountainous west. Backcountry hostelries range from fly-in ski lodges to cozy cabins to climbers' refuges, and there is even one in the US Adirondack Mountains! In Canada, huts are considered environmental stewardship tools. Canadian national parks, including Yoho, Banff, and Kootenay, have welcomed them.

In addition to club-supported hut systems, western Canada has hut systems run by private businesses and nonprofits. Jim Scott's *Backcountry Huts and Lodges of the Rockies and Columbias* (see Resources) lists 114 backcountry hostelries, some connected as traverses. Wells Gray Adventures has operated a full-service three-hut system for skiing and hiking in the Trophy Mountains in eastern British Columbia for decades. Closer to Vancouver, local nonprofits run two all-volunteer hut systems as a labor of love: the fourteen Sunshine Coast Trail huts in the Powell River region and four linked huts in Tetrahedron Provincial Park. Three large, high mountain huts are being constructed for hikers and skiers along the Spearhead Traverse in Garibaldi Provincial Park near Whistler Blackcomb Ski Resort.

Eastern Canada also provides hut-to-hut trekking and skiing opportunities. Quebec Province, with its deep connections to French culture, has developed hut systems in many of its national parks. The 65-mile Charlevoix Traverse, with six self-service huts and optional luggage service, passes through a forested UNESCO World Biosphere Reserve. Gaspésie National Park operates more than a dozen rustic huts, with several different loops for backcountry skiers to choose from.

The Sentiers de l'Estrie (Eastern Townships Trail) starts near the top end of Vermont's Long Trail and heads north to form a 124-mile footpath, punctuated with huts, through nature reserves and Mont-Orford National Park. Farther east, along the northern cape of Cape Breton Island, a nonprofit organization is building a five-hut system along the 30-mile Seawall Trail.

## AUSTRALIA AND NEW ZEALAND

Australia and New Zealand, both colonized by the British, differ in terms of hut-to-hut opportunities and infrastructure. Australia, vast and sparsely populated, has a few hundred recreational huts, primarily in the mountainous areas of Victoria and New South Wales. Most were originally built for workers—stockmen, graziers, gold miners, and foresters—and provide only very basic shelter for hikers or skiers. Planned hut-to-hut routes are rare, but it is possible to stitch together traverses in the Victorian Alps. The Australian Alpine Club, which defines itself as a snow sports club, maintains several huts in this region that visitors can ski between. Tasmania, an island state off the mainland, has developed several world-class walking trails punctuated with huts that compare favorably with the New Zealand system. The Overland Track features a new generation of upscale, full-service huts designed to blend harmoniously

*Welcome Flat Hut in Westland Tai Poutini National Park features the practical design typical of New Zealand's Department of Conservation.* (Photo by Geoff Spearpoint)

with the landscape and employ the latest green technology.

Arguably the hut capital of the world, New Zealand offers a vibrant case study in how huts fit into a nation's history, culture, terrain, and ecological future. The British sought to transform this rugged land into a pastoral "England of the South Seas." Thick natural vegetation—bush—was replaced, where practical, with pastureland. But many mountainous areas were impossible to tame, especially in places such as the Southern Alps on the South Island and the Tararua Range just north of Wellington on the North Island. As early as the 1880s, European adventurers recognized the Southern Alps in particular as fertile ground for mountaineering. Under British influence, the New Zealand Alpine Club started out in 1891 as an elite organization dominated by a wealthy few, but Kiwis (New Zealanders) quickly democratized it.

Walking—or tramping, as the Kiwis call it—also developed as a recreational pursuit beginning in the late nineteenth century. Rooted in practicality (many areas were too rugged to explore on horseback), tramping also resonated with the egalitarian ethos of New Zealand and was made accessible to everyone. After the British introduced deer to this land without mammals and imported trout to the streams and lakes, hunters and anglers were drawn into the bush on foot. Tramping clubs sprang up in urban areas and on university campuses, promoting the healthful benefits of walking and organizing outdoor adventures.

New Zealand's extensive system of huts and trails was born of both the embrace of tramping as a national pastime and the need for shelter from the storm in a maritime nation with rugged terrain. Initially, hikers took refuge in remote sheep sheds, primitive farm buildings, and huts built for miners and for hunters tasked with culling invasive mammals. In the late nineteenth century, New Zealand established the fourth national park in the world and began to construct purpose-built tracks and huts for tourists. Beginning in the 1950s, the government ramped up the building of recreational huts as the number of national parks rapidly increased. In 1987, the Department of Conservation (DOC) was established to protect the "conservation estate," natural lands that make up about a third of the nation, and to promote sustainable recreation. The DOC began to manage a nationwide inventory of about 960 public backcountry huts. In the 2000s, the DOC began its own hut-building phase, creating new huts with modern features, such as insulation and double-glazed windows.

With the Great Walks, branded in 1993, the DOC sought to advertise the best-known hiking and hut system to international audiences and to make some of the most popular tracks suitable for beginners and families. Many of the huts along these featured tracks, which include the Tongariro Northern Circuit on the North Island and the Abel

Tasman Coast Track on the South Island, were upgraded. The Great Walks campaign has been so successful that foreign visitors tend to outnumber Kiwis in these huts. Advance booking is a must, and the nightly cost per bunk is at least double that of non–Great Walks huts. The DOC is developing practices and policies to ensure locals have affordable access to these huts. They are also expanding the number of Great Walks while encouraging Kiwis and international visitors to take advantage of hundreds of other options in the vast network.

Some counts put New Zealand huts at more than 1400. In addition to the DOC huts, there are huts operated by local clubs, farmers, and regional nonprofits. Private businesses also contribute to the rich hut-to-hut options in New Zealand. We hiked the Banks Track near Christchurch on the South Island, traversing gorgeous maritime headlands and farm fields, then sheltering in quaint, quirky farm buildings. This system represents a partnership between multiple agricultural landowners seeking an additional revenue stream beyond farming. Farther south, a private outfitter provides luxury lodging and guides on two of the Great Walks: the Routeburn and Milford Tracks.

Kiwi youngsters are introduced to huts early in life; from overnight hut stays with family or youth groups, they learn responsible group behavior and sensitivity to nature and the environment. Far from the settled routines of home, they experience how random encounters can develop into friendships. New Zealanders, many belonging to tramping clubs, use their huts with

regularity and enthusiasm. *Hut bagging* is the term used for the friendly competition among hut enthusiasts (see www.hutbagger .co.nz). Hunters, fishers, and mountain bikers, in addition to hikers, depend on the system for shelter. Even while the DOC is creating a subset of higher-amenity huts, most Kiwis prefer little more than "wooden tents"—sturdy shelters with four walls, a roof to keep out the rain, picnic tables, counters for food preparation, bunks with mattresses, and a wood-burning stove.

Not only are huts well-used, practical features of the New Zealand landscape, but they are also vessels of national identity and nostalgia worth preserving. The DOC has a heritage hut unit that focuses on hut restorations and documentation of historic sites. In *Shelter from the Storm*, Shaun Barnett, Rob Brown, and Geoff Spearpoint provide an overview of the history, variety, and extent of New Zealand huts (see Resources). Their work enhanced appreciation of hut heritage and helped spawn the Backcountry Trust, which supports a wide range of voluntary efforts to restore remote huts and tracks.

New Zealand's dynamic hut heritage sets the stage for fascinating future possibilities. In the wake of greater recognition of indigenous rights and the role of Māori in land stewardship, it is worth watching what develops at Te Urewera, a former national park now managed by the local Tūhoe *iwi* (tribe). Not only has New Zealand accorded human rights to the central mountain, but it is also transitioning management of the park and its huts to the Māori. It will be interesting to see how indigenous values, celebrating the interconnectedness of all things, shape the administration and use of this beautiful area.

As environmental historian Geoff Park sets forth, "New Zealand's fertile plains were the last that Europeans found before the Earth's supply revealed itself as finite. . . . [We] have exploited these islands' richest ecosystems with all the violence that modern science and technology could summon . . . . [We] must live with the rest of nature or die with the rest of nature."

Mick Abbott, hard-core tramper, landscape architect, and professor at Lincoln University, has some fruitful ideas. Noting that conservation—that is, "planting, trapping, citizen science, drawing kids into the wild"—is the fastest-growing form of outdoor recreation in New Zealand, he suggests that properly sited and designed huts can activate citizens and tourists as conservation workers. Abbott sees a reenvisioned hut experience as one path toward an economy based on reciprocal relationships with nature. He boldly proposes that Kiwis and international visitors alike "pay for" hut stays by working on conservation projects—a special form of sweat equity.

## LATIN AMERICA

Rich in high mountain ranges, South America attracts mountain climbers, trekkers,

OPPOSITE, TOP:  *Meg Hut in Central Otago, New Zealand, was originally used by sheep musterers.*
BOTTOM:  *Eclectic accommodations welcome trampers on the private Banks Track in New Zealand.*

*Ecotourism guest huts in Chiang Mai province, Thailand*

hikers, and skiers. The few hut-to-hut traverses are widely scattered across the continent. Treks in Patagonia, encompassing Chile and Argentina, are the best known. Torres del Paine National Park in southern Chile offers two very popular overlapping multiday treks: the W trek, which takes three to five days and is fully served by huts, and the full circuit, or O route, which takes seven to nine days and requires some camping. In addition to large full-service huts, there are campsites and cooking facilities for backpackers. The Smugglers Trail in Patagonia has a five-hut guided walk.

Bariloche, Argentina, on the Chilean border, offers a popular five-day alpine hut-to-hut traverse. And a five-hut system is under development in Argentina's Perito Moreno National Park.

## JAPAN AND SOUTH KOREA

Asia has comparatively few huts, with the exception of Japan. Japanese culture embraces a deep spiritual connection with mountains, and with both animate and inanimate beings, rooted in Shinto religion. The 221 full-service huts in the Japanese Alps, with some connecting to form multiday traverses, are open during the mountain climbing season. These simple shelters, with capacities ranging from ten to five hundred, are especially popular when located near hot springs.

The northern island of Hokkaido is home to twenty-nine backcountry huts mostly operated by local mountain clubs for hikers and skiers. Ancient pilgrimage walks, such as the route around the small island of Shikoku or the Kumano Kodo, continue to draw walkers on multiday, meditative treks; pilgrims stay in temples and *ryokans* (traditional country inns) but not huts per se.

Hiking is a national craze in South Korea. Because there are few huts or backcountry cabins, trekkers committed to long walks rely on village accommodations. The 262-mile Jeju Olle Trail, which follows the coastline of an island with Korea's highest mountain, is among the best-known inn-to-inn walks in the country.

## OTHER PARTS OF THE WORLD

Hut systems and related inn-to-inn or guesthouse networks support long-distance human-powered travel in Bhutan, Iceland, Nepal, Morocco, and many more nations. Village-based guesthouse options are expanding rapidly as ecotourism spawns multiday treks in mountainous and forested regions around the world. And of course, climbers' huts are available to support mountaineers in major mountain ranges around the world, from the Andes, the Atlas, the Caucasus, and the Himalaya to peaks in Mexico and Tanzania.

# HUT SYSTEMS IN THE US

**HUTS HAVE NEVER PLAYED** a major role in sheltering backcountry travelers in the US. Yet since the 1980s, more huts have been developed and built as Americans embrace and adapt these shelter systems, which encourage and facilitate access to wild places by diverse user groups.

## HISTORY

Until the advent of car camping in the 1930s and the backpacking revolution of the 1970s, spending the night in the US backcountry involved either very rugged camping excursions or guided hunting and fishing expeditions, usually supported by horses. After two successful efforts (in 1888 and 1916) to bring the European full-service hut model to America, hut development halted for nearly two generations. The story of US hut systems was revived in the 1980s with western ski huts. New experiments continue into the twenty-first century. The table on the next page provides a chronology of US hut systems.

There is no doubt that the extensive European hut system influenced the development of huts in the US. However, our vast countryside, patterns of land ownership, economic norms, and attitudes toward nature and personal freedom have all affected how US hut systems are developed, where they exist, and how they operate.

The Appalachian Mountain Club (AMC), established in 1876 in Boston and explicitly patterned on European alpine clubs, built the very first hut system in this country. Instead of the Alps, members gravitated to

OPPOSITE: *Montana's American Prairie Reserve has clusters of spacious yurts.*

# CHRONOLOGY OF US HUT SYSTEMS

| DATE | SYSTEM | STATE |
|---|---|---|
| 1888 | Appalachian Mountain Club (AMC) Huts* | NH |
| 1913 | Glacier National Park chalets (most no longer exist) | MT |
| 1916 | Yosemite High Sierra Camps* | CA |
| 1937 | Haleakala National Park | HI |
| 1938 | Sierra Club Donner Pass area huts | CA |
| 1945 | Porcupine Mountains Wilderness State Park cabins* | MI |
| 1953 | Alfred A. Braun Hut System | CO |
| 1964 | Eklutna Traverse | AK |
| 1964 | Delta Range mountaineering huts | AK |
| 1968 | Pinnell Mountain National Recreational Trail | AK |
| 1971 | Bomber Traverse | AK |
| 1973 | Resurrection Pass Trail* | AK |
| 1981 | Rendezvous Huts* | WA |
| 1982 | Sun Valley Mountain Huts* | ID |
| 1982 | Tenth Mountain Division Hut Association* | CO |
| 1983 | Idaho State University Portneuf Range Yurt System | ID |
| 1984 | Boundary Country Trekking* | MN |
| 1985 | Nancy Lake State Recreation Area | AK |
| 1985 | White Mountains National Recreation Area | AK |
| 1986 | Never Summer Nordic* | CO |
| 1987 | San Juan Huts* | CO |
| 1987 | Southwest Nordic Center* | CO |
| 1987 | Summit Huts | CO |
| 1989 | Bear River Outdoor Recreation Alliance | WY |
| 1990 | Mount Tahoma Trails Association* | WA |
| 1992 | Hinsdale Haute Route | CO |
| 2003 | AMC Maine Wilderness Lodges | ME |
| 2007 | Cascade Huts (no longer operational) | OR |
| 2007 | Maine Huts and Trails* | ME |
| 2008 | Stehekin Outfitters | WA |
| 2011 | San Juan Haute Route | CO |
| 2012 | Alaska Huts Association | AK |
| 2014 | Three Sisters Backcountry* | OR |
| 2018 | American Prairie Reserve* | MT |
| 2020 | Adirondack Hamlets to Huts* | NY |
| 2020 | Vermont Huts Association | VT |

*Note:* Date listed is when the first hut in the system was built; some dates are approximate. Asterisk (*) indicates a hut system featured in this book.

*The AMC Carter Notch Hut, which opened in 1914, is the oldest hut in the US.* (Photo courtesy of AMC Library and Archives)

the White Mountains in New Hampshire. Madison Spring Hut, the AMC's first, completed in 1888, was built as a safe and convenient base for both hikers and climbers. Other huts, some planned as emergency shelters in response to accidents, followed. By the late 1930s, seven of the current eight huts were in place, offering comfortable accommodations along the rugged trail through the Presidential Range. The AMC hut system was the first and last to be built by a US conservation organization until the American Prairie Reserve huts opened in 2018.

Various other organizations promoted hiking and skiing in early twentieth-century America and helped, directly or indirectly, create backcountry lodging opportunities. Among conservation and outdoor recreation organizations established around 1900 were the Sierra Club (1892), the Mazamas (1894), and The Mountaineers (1906); the Adirondack Mountain Club was founded in 1922. None of their lodgings, though, were built to support hut-to-hut. The traverse just wasn't an American thing.

Two trail-related shelter systems did flourish in the early twentieth century. The Green Mountain Club of Vermont, established in 1910, promoted the vision of a long-distance trail, punctuated with shelters, traversing the entire north–south axis of the state. This project inspired the even more ambitious Appalachian Trail (AT).

In 1921, Benton MacKaye published "An Appalachian Trail: A Project in Regional Planning," proposing that a trail with a network of shelter camps, "with proper facilities and protection, could be made to serve as the breath of a real life for the toilers in the bee-hive cities along the Atlantic seaboard and elsewhere." His idea of shelter camps, providing both comfortable accommodations and educational and nature immersion opportunities, was ultimately deemed impractical; instead, three-sided rustic shelters were positioned every 8 to 12 miles along the trail.

The AT offers day hikers and section hikers opportunities to commune with nature and, for the really adventurous, the grand structure of a rugged, long pilgrimage. But without the comfort and convenience of huts, the AT is not accessible to the full spectrum of Americans envisioned by MacKaye. Subsequent US long-distance trails, such as the Pacific Crest Trail, the Continental Divide Trail, and the North Country Trail, were designed for backpackers and have not, for the most part, included shelters or huts.

While Europe gave rise to alpine clubs and built a system of recreational mountain huts, America was leading the world in preserving wild natural lands. In the nineteenth and early twentieth centuries, conservationists articulated the positive value of wilderness for humanity. They lobbied for protecting wildlands, some pristine and

*Built in Yosemite National Park by the Civilian Conservation Corps, Ostrander Ski Hut opened in 1941.* (Yosemite Historic Photos Collection)

some already spoiled by logging and mining. Clubs, including the AMC and the Sierra Club, joined the campaign to save wildlands and to prevent further devastation through uncontrolled resource extraction. The National Park System grew out of these efforts. Early conservationists, including John Muir and President Theodore Roosevelt, foregrounded the concept of "wilderness," that is, areas of the earth untouched by man. The distinctive American celebration of wilderness has dramatically shaped the international conservation discourse and US values related to the outdoors—and it has conditioned attitudes about manmade structures in the backcountry.

In 1916, the National Park Service established the Yosemite High Sierra Camps, the second US hut system, to promote use of the park and access to the sublime high country. The High Sierra Camps (initially three, now five) were based on the Sierra Club tradition of an annual high trip. Members, invited to spend a month each summer in Yosemite's high meadows, were treated to comfortable overnight lodgings and hot meals in tent encampments, with supplies hauled up by mule train. Today, Yosemite is the only US national park with a fully operational hut system.

Two other national parks—Montana's Glacier and Haleakala in Hawaii—also created backcountry lodging early in the twentieth century. Between 1910 and 1915, the Great Northern Railway set up nine chalet encampments, spaced a day's horseback ride apart, in Glacier National Park to offer comfortable overnight accommodations to visitors traveling by horse. These chalets flourished until the Great Depression. After World War II, with the private automobile having replaced the train for most long-distance travel and with roads penetrating the park's interior, all but two of the chalets were decommissioned. The two still in operation—Sperry and Granite Park Chalets—attracted hikers beginning in the 1950s; the chalets are now so popular that reservations are awarded via a lottery. Sperry Chalet dormitory was destroyed by fire in 2017 and has been rebuilt.

In 1916 in Hawaii, long before statehood, Haleakala Crater was designated part of Hawaii National Park. In the mid-1930s, the Civilian Conservation Corps embarked on extensive trail-building projects and constructed three backcountry cabins, which may be linked on a multiday journey.

In Michigan, an extensive backcountry cabin system in the Porcupine Mountains showed that hut-to-hut travel could take root on state as well as federal lands. In 1945, what is now called Porcupine Mountains Wilderness State Park was established to conserve the largest stand of old-growth northern hardwood forest in the Upper Midwest. Twelve backcountry cabins offered rustic shelter to hikers and skiers seeking either single-destination getaways or hut-to-hut opportunities. The Porkies, arguably the most expansive network of its day, remains one of the oldest and largest hut systems.

Yosemite National Park almost became home to a hut-to-hut ski system. In the 1930s, Yosemite developed a ski resort at Badger Pass and drew up plans for at least two backcountry huts to shelter ski touring enthusiasts overnight. Only Ostrander Ski Hut, which opened in 1941, was built. Initially run by a National Park Service concessionaire, it is now managed by a private foundation.

Skiing was gaining momentum in America across the 1920s and 1930s. While downhill skiing ultimately came to dominate, ski touring drew an enthusiastic following. Here and there, in the 1930s and early 1940s, infrastructure was created to shelter backcountry skiers—for example, ski school cabins associated with the Sun Valley Resort in Idaho and the first of several Sierra Club huts near Donner Pass in California.

Publications affiliated with the National Ski Association of America advocated for better ski mountaineering skills and for European-style huts in the US. In the 1942 *American Ski Annual*, James Laughlin's "A Plea for Huts in America" called out to the association to get involved in setting up a chain of huts, enabling "the cream of skiing," that is, multiday ski tours. Also in 1942, David Brower, who later became the executive director of the Sierra Club (1952–69), compiled the *Manual of Ski Mountaineering* in collaboration with other Sierra Club ski mountaineers from the San Francisco Bay region at the request of the association. The slim book proved useful as a training manual for the Tenth Mountain Division, the Colorado-based World War II army division (which included Brower) that specialized in mountain warfare and is now memorialized in the largest US hut system!

The Alfred A. Braun Huts were the third US system and the nation's first ski hut system. In 1953, under the auspices of the National Ski Association, Aspen-based ski enthusiasts rebuilt an old miners' cabin for overnights in the backcountry and called it Tagert Hut. Additional huts were added in the late 1950s and early 1960s. In 1967, Alfred A. Braun was designated manager of the system and oversaw the construction of three additional huts, bringing the total to seven. This hut system, now managed by a nonprofit, is named for the charismatic and opinionated Braun. The huts, for winter use only, cater to expert skiers trained to navigate in avalanche-prone terrain mostly above tree line. The Braun huts are simple, low-amenity structures situated on government land—in this case, US Forest Service (USFS) holdings. The small size, reminiscent of mountaineering bivvies, is best suited to a single party.

Alpine clubs organized shelter systems for mountaineers in Alaska. Beginning in the 1960s, not long after the Braun huts were established for expert backcountry skiers in Colorado, the Mountaineering Club of Alaska (MCA) and the Alaska Alpine Club (AAC) got to work. Over successive decades, the AAC built three huts in the glacier-rich Delta Range, not far from Wrangell–St. Elias National Park and Preserve. The MCA also put together a trio of huts across the Eklutna Traverse northeast of Anchorage in the Chugach Mountains. This organization also orchestrated a chain of huts across the Bomber Traverse in the Talkeetna Mountains between 1971 and 2018, one of which is operated by the American Alpine Club. All these club huts are aimed at expert hikers and skiers primed to cross glaciers and navigate rough, unmarked terrain.

*The Sperry Chalet, one of two popular backcountry lodges in Glacier National Park, burned in 2017 but reopened three years later after being fully restored. (Photo courtesy of Glacier National Park)*

With the construction of an extensive Interstate Highway System in the 1950s and 1960s, car camping became *the* American way to experience nature. Campsites on county, state, federal, and private lands, with picnic tables, fire rings, and toilet facilities, provided modest comforts and safety for families seeking inexpensive overnights in the great American outdoors. In the 1970s, the backpacking boom emerged as a complement and corrective to car camping. Backpacking, fueled by the environmental movement, youth culture, and innovations in lightweight and waterproof gear, offered young people and wilderness seekers opportunities to journey far from roads and crowded campgrounds. Throughout the 1960s and 1970s, increasing numbers aspired to take multiday journeys in wild natural areas. The backpacker's ethos is straight out of the American rugged individualism playbook, celebrating solitude in nature, making do with little, and stoic survival rather than comfort. Huts, with associations of comfort and conviviality, were alien to the hard-core backpacker mindset. Even so, huts figured in conversations about how to best accommodate new waves of walkers and nature enthusiasts in the backcountry.

William E. Reifsnyder, a Yale professor and member of the AMC's hut committee, had extensive experience with European huts. He advised the American Youth Hostel Association to consider huts in relation to hostel development in the US. And in the late 1970s, he wrote *High Mountain Huts: A Planning Guide* for the Colorado Mountain Trails Foundation in cooperation with the USFS (see Resources). In this substantial pamphlet, Reifsnyder presented detailed guidelines for a hypothetical hut and trail system in the mountain West, catering to both walkers and skiers. His closing sentence, "Huts are an idea whose time has come," was prescient.

During the 1980s, ten new hut systems—all catering to Nordic skiers—came into being in the American West. These systems define a distinctly American approach to huts. New operations in Colorado, Washington, Idaho, Wyoming, and Minnesota were each locally driven by small private businesses, nonprofits, and one university outdoor program; the huts—all self-service—are situated on public land. Even though a hut operation may claim to be a backcountry adventure without the weight, clients must carry their own food in almost all cases.

All these hut-to-hut ski systems take advantage of public lands through special use permits. Technically they are all concessionaires and pay a percentage of revenue to their government "landlords." Eight are on USFS land and two are on state parks property. Every new hut system targeting USFS land, whether a for-profit or a nonprofit initiative, must negotiate with the district office and go through mandated assessment and review. In most of these early cases, permits were initially granted for seasonal structures only. Huts, built to be removed in the late spring and reassembled in the fall, tended to be small and relatively portable. Yurts proved a popular solution to this design challenge (see "Yurts as Huts"). As USFS district officials developed confidence in individual concessionaires over time, permission to leave the huts up year-round was usually granted. In a unique partnership, the USFS (along with the Colorado Historical Society) operates two historic railroad structures—Ken's Cabin and the Section House—as an interpretive center in summer and through a special use permit allows Summit Huts to welcome backcountry skiers in winter. The two systems on state lands, Never Summer Nordic in Colorado and the Mount Tahoma Trails Association in Washington, must also periodically renegotiate their permits.

The Mount Tahoma Trails Association and Colorado's Tenth Mountain Division Hut Association and Summit Huts were created by local outdoor enthusiasts committed to creating systems to support their own recreational pursuits, and also to invite others to enjoy the same pleasures. They are run by nonprofits with a relatively narrow focus, in contrast to the much broader missions of the AMC and the Sierra Club, who established some of America's very first backcountry huts. The exemplary Tenth Mountain Division Hut Association is notable for its scale, the design and structural integrity of its huts, and professionalism in management and operations. This is due in part to the standards of its founders, its premier ski country location, and the deep pockets of its patrons.

Private business drove the creation of most new hut systems in the 1980s. From

# YURTS AS HUTS

Yurts entered American consciousness in the 1960s and 1970s in the wake of the counterculture's embrace of simple building types worldwide. Originating in central Asia among nomadic pastoralists, these cylindrical dwellings were pictured in a widely read 1962 article in *National Geographic*, "Journey to Outer Mongolia" by Supreme Court Justice William O. Douglas. Yurts were among the elemental home types highlighting natural materials and "human resourcefulness" celebrated in *Shelter*, a 1973 publication by one of the editors of *The Whole Earth Catalogue*. Yurts became an affordable backcountry shelter option and a business opportunity across the country. Inspired by Douglas's article, private school teacher Bill Coperthwaite established the Yurt Foundation, which became a national source for creative yurt designs and DIY ideas.

In the early 1970s, *National Geographic* photographer Dean Conger joined a backcountry trip near Sun Valley, Idaho, with Leonard Expeditions, a new guide outfit employing canvas wall tents. Conger suggested to owner Joe Leonard that a yurt might make a good remote shelter. By mid-decade, Leonard had built a yurt based on Conger's sketches—arguably the first high mountain yurt in the US.

Kirk Bachman, who guided for Leonard, went off to develop his own yurt business in Jackson, Wyoming. The company provided yurts for a hut system at his alma mater, Idaho State University. In the early 1980s, an article touting Bachman's yurts in *Cross Country Skier* magazine inspired the Youngs in northern Minnesota to order and assemble a yurt kit, which they set up that same winter, establishing Boundary Country Trekking's yurt-to-yurt ski system.

In 1986, Rodney Ley launched Never Summer Nordic in northern Colorado with one Bachman yurt and another two from Pacific Yurts (a company founded in 1978 in Oregon). The founder of the Southwest Nordic Center in southern Colorado visited Never Summer Nordic's yurts in 1987 before opening his first homemade yurt. Today, yurts are everywhere in the backcountry. They can be disassembled with ease, making them ideal seasonal shelters.

Washington to Idaho, Colorado to Minnesota, energetic individuals and couples saw opportunity in the Nordic skiing boom. The Rendezvous Huts may have been the first of this wave of huts to open. Huts were a vehicle for making a living and pursuing a labor of love. These small enterprises developed organically over time, sometimes in conjunction with related enterprises. The Boundary Country Trekking folks were also

*Hut-to-hut via fat-tire bike is on the rise.* (Photo by Madi McConnell)

in the guiding, dogsledding, and lodging business; huts were an outgrowth of Sun Valley Trekking guiding activities. As local entrepreneurs, hut system owners could get things done without fuss and react to emerging trends. The Southwest Nordic Center founder, after observing the Never Summer Nordic yurts, collaborated with a carpenter friend to design and build the system's yurts. In 1987, San Juan Huts developed a ski—and then hike—hut system, and later responded to new recreational trends with the nation's first hut-to-hut routes exclusively for mountain bikers.

Ten hut systems have emerged so far in the twenty-first century. In addition, most of the nation's hut systems have expanded operations, embracing more travel modes and seasons; on top of hiking, skiing, and biking, a few have also added paddling options.

In 2003, the AMC embarked on a multipronged Maine Woods Initiative in the 100-Mile Wilderness near Mount Katahdin. The AMC purchased 70,000 acres and established 120 miles of trails in service to land conservation. Lodges and cabins included in the purchase draw people to the reserve; programs support hiking and lodge-to-lodge recreational skiing as low-impact ways of enjoying the Maine woods.

Four years after the launch of that initiative, a new nonprofit inaugurated an ambitious huts and trails system in another economically depressed region of the state. Maine Huts and Trails built four high-end huts, and a trail system, to welcome hikers, bikers, and skiers. Despite energetic programming, the full-service offerings proved unsustainable; in 2019, Maine Huts and Trails shifted to a self-service model with greater reliance on volunteer staff.

In Oregon, local entrepreneurs created a couple of new hut systems near well-established downhill ski areas. Cascade Huts opened in 2007 in the shadow of Mount Hood with three small plywood cabins. Unfortunately, this operation has gone dormant since 2018. Farther south, not far from Mount Bachelor, Three Sisters Backcountry offers a two-night Nordic traverse. This family business, opened in 2014, operates on an enhanced self-service model, with a fully stocked pantry of ingredients ready to inspire visitors to cook tasty meals. They modeled this practice on the San Juan Hut Systems bike huts in Colorado.

In 2018, American Prairie Reserve, a private landscape-scale project in Montana, opened the first of three huts in a projected ten-hut system. The organization aims to become the largest nature reserve in the continental US. This is the second US hut system not located in the mountains (the other is in Minnesota). Hut manager Mike Kautz, a veteran of the AMC's White Mountains hut system, introduced huts as a means to welcome visitors to the area.

The Vermont Huts Association inaugurated a four-hut traverse in 2020, linking existing huts to support skiing from Camels Hump to the Bolton Valley. This organization coordinates eight dispersed huts throughout the state, and aims to create an extensive network of backcountry accommodations as a means of stitching together Vermont's myriad trail systems.

Adirondack Hamlets to Huts (AHH) also opened in 2020, using the hut-to-hut idea to organize nature-based travel in Adirondack Park, encompassing six million acres of wildlands and 102 towns and villages. This nonprofit orchestrates routes combining hiking and paddling, or other travel modes, with overnights in existing hostelries. Hut-to-hut, in this case, is close to the European experience of village-to-village travel. To drive economic development, and to serve recreational and conservation goals, AHH has identified, analyzed, and prioritized twenty-six routes in the region. New huts may be constructed in the future to fill in gaps between existing accommodations.

## US HUT SYSTEMS TODAY

This overview of US hut systems reflects our six years of research. The information presented is based on the sixteen featured hut systems (see "Featured Hut Systems at a Glance" in Part III) and the additional ten listed in "More Hut-to-Hut Traverses" in Bonus Hut Opportunities. These twenty-six hut systems come closest to meeting our definition of a hut system, which focuses on supporting multiday hut-to-hut traverses.

### LOCATION AND GEOGRAPHY

Hut systems, concentrated in the West and the Northeast, are almost all located in mountainous regions rich in scenery and recreational activities. Colorado, with more than six hut systems, is the epicenter. Many American huts were established to shelter cross-country skiers, and hut systems crop up in such winter playgrounds as the Vail, Breckenridge, and Aspen area in Colorado; Sun Valley in Idaho; and west-central Maine.

You can't have huts without trails. Almost every US hut system is located on an existing, signed trail network maintained by a land management agency or a local nonprofit. Hut system managers and community volunteers help with trail maintenance; local snowmobile clubs may help groom trails. On average, the distance between huts is 6 to 8 miles. Long-distance trails, which are central to the European hut-to-hut experience, play almost no role in American hut life. The eight AMC huts on the Appalachian Trail in the White Mountains of New Hampshire and four of the Porcupine Mountains cabins on the North Country Trail are the exceptions.

US hut systems, with a few exceptions, are situated on federal lands—managed by the USFS, the Bureau of Land Management, and the National Park Service—and on state lands. US huts attract nature lovers because of proximity to wild places and wilderness

*A gathering of skis at a Maine Huts and Trails hut* (Photo by John Orcutt)

areas in particular. The huts themselves are never in federally designated wilderness areas; the Wilderness Act of 1964, with very few exceptions, forbids manmade structures, roads, and the use of motorized vehicles and tools. In some hut systems, public lands are mixed with private holdings including conservation trusts, timber company leases, and tribal territories.

## MODES OF TRAVEL AND EXTENT OF TRAILS

The very first US hut systems catered to hikers. The next wave, established between the 1960s and 1980s, mostly accommodated skiers. Since the 1990s, hut systems have begun to diversify modes of travel on their trails in a move to increase revenues in the former off-seasons. Today, about two-thirds of the nation's twenty-six hut systems support more than one mode of hut-to-hut travel. Bicycling is on the rise, even in winter, with the advent of fat-tire bikes. The newest hut systems, including American Prairie Reserve and Adirondack Hamlets to Huts, have embraced multiple modes from the outset. The Adirondack Hamlets to Huts routes incorporate paddling and hiking; the system is also open to e-bikes. As American Prairie Reserve adds huts and connecting routes, paddling will join the list of modalities along with hiking and biking. While our sixteen featured itineraries cover nearly 600 miles, all the US hut systems add up to approximately 1870 miles, not all of which support traverses.

## RESERVATION FORMATS

Huts around the world, notably in Europe and New Zealand, are rented mostly by the bunk, meaning that you share the hut with folks you don't know. With exclusive-use rentals, you rent all the beds in the hut, whether you use them or not. In the US, about half the huts are shared, and the other half are primarily exclusive use. Two of the three systems in the eastern US are by the bunk. The two systems in the Midwest are exclusive use. Sixty-two percent of the systems in the West rent the entire hut, cabin, or yurt to a single party. The largest hut systems—the Appalachian Mountain Club and the Tenth Mountain Division Hut Association—follow Europe and New Zealand, inviting visitors to share space and to connect socially. These two systems combined have more than one-third of the total hut beds: 417 in the thirty-four huts in the Tenth Mountain Division Hut Association and 414 in the AMC's eight huts in the White Mountains.

## HUT USERS

While huts as a recreational option are not well known in the US, every hut system we visited is very popular, with 70 to 80 percent occupancy typical during the high season. Friends and families gather in huts for sustained togetherness. Visitors to each system tend to be fairly local, traveling within their state or region, and some make it an annual event. By contrast, in Europe and New Zealand, huts draw huge numbers of international tourists.

Hut-to-hut traverses are great for vacation getaways and long weekends. Logbook entries testify to the popularity of marking special occasions including birthdays and anniversaries. All across the country, we encountered women's groups enjoying the pleasure of each other's company away from the distractions of daily life. America's huts are generally family friendly but require parents to match their children's strength, skill level, and capacity for communal living to the demands of the traverse and accommodations. The two AMC huts with access trails under 3 miles swarm with parents and children; kids grab upper bunks, reveling in a sleep-play arrangement resembling a jungle gym, and spill off front porches to nearby lakes, streams, and waterfalls. Most hut systems offer reduced rates for children. Other users include youth, school, and church groups, outdoor clubs, and hut-based education and therapeutic programs (see "Huts for Education and Therapy").

Hut users, especially at the larger huts rented by the bunk with shared cooking and common areas, are a cooperative and communal bunch. At the Tenth Mountain Division Hut Association huts, you might find a few friend groups consisting of two or three couples, another couple on their own, an extended family group celebrating a significant birthday, and a party of young men. In the AMC huts, which accommodate between thirty-six and ninety-two hikers, overnighters strike a balance between respecting the privacy of others and engaging with fellow travelers in games and conversations during and after meals.

Exclusive-use huts, with capacities ranging from two to twelve, are perfect for existing groups including families, friends, and groups bonded by their mutual love of hiking, skiing, or biking and the great outdoors. In our case, since we are just two, we invite along friends, family, and acquaintances to share the adventure and cozy spaces.

## AMENITIES AND SIZE

On the most basic level, the hut is an enclosed shelter with a roof, a floor, a heat source, basic furniture for eating and sleeping, a logbook, a water source, and a toilet facility. Huts are further defined by their amenities, size, and capacity. What comes with the hut? How much does the visitor have to carry, and how much work is required to ensure a comfortable night? How many will share the hut, and how will capacity shape the experience?

In the US, huts are predominantly self-service, with notable full-service exceptions being the AMC huts and the Yosemite High Sierra Camps—the oldest systems. We developed a shorthand code for hut amenity levels: basic, self-service, self-service+, and full service (see How to Use This Guide). We were surprised to find that every hut in the US has more amenities than almost every DOC hut in New Zealand, the hut capital of the world. Nearly all self-service huts in the US incorporate one or more gas burners or a stove in the kitchen area, and plastic-covered mattresses on the bunks. Kitchens come fully equipped with pots and pans, dishes and utensils, and some kind of dishwashing tubs. Contrast this to New Zealand, where only Great Walks huts have gas cookers and hikers carry their own dishes and utensils. US operators add extra touches such as playing cards, puzzles, and small libraries. Increasingly, huts have solar lighting fixtures and a charging station. Wood-fired saunas are a welcome, if uncommon, feature. The only US hut systems offering showers are the Yosemite High Sierra Camps and Maine Huts and Trails.

Most American hut-to-hut travelers, like backpackers, carry their own food, clothing, and more. Some hut systems provide sleeping bags and pillows; others supply only pillows. The self-service+ huts—the San Juan Hut System for bikers and the Three Sisters Backcountry huts—provide stocked pantries, allowing visitors to carry very little weight en route. This compares directly with some huts in Norway, where overnight visitors pay for pantry provisions on the honor system. A few US traverses require users to carry just about everything with them. In Alaska, the backcountry cabins are very basic; while log structures on both state and federal land are spacious and well built, the interiors have counters but no cookstoves or utensils, and the bunks are bare sheets of plywood. Hikers, bikers, and skiers carry everything except a tent; in winter, you might also need to haul firewood on a sled.

Compared with Europe, where huts typically house forty to eighty people, American huts are small. While the AMC huts are built roughly on the scale of European huts, the US national average is about fourteen beds per hut across all 166 huts. Several owners have speculated in informal shoptalk that economies of scale begin at about fourteen beds per hut; small-capacity huts are expensive to operate.

Huts in the American West tend to be small, with an average of twelve beds; mountaineering huts in Alaska can accommodate as few as four, while the yurts in backcountry ski systems in the Lower 48 usually hold between six and twelve. The Tenth Mountain Division Hut Association,

CLOCKWISE FROM TOP: *The huts run by the Mount Tahoma Trails Association feature well-stocked kitchens. The wood-fired sauna is a welcome amenity at Sun Valley's Boulder Yurt. Travelers can access the outhouse at the Sierra Club Peter Grubb Hut even when the snow deepens in winter.*

# THE ENVIRONMENTAL IMPACT OF HUTS

Until recently, there has been no definitive research proving the common wisdom that huts concentrate use, thereby reducing the impact of backcountry travelers on the places they visit. When I (Sam) advocated for such research with hut managers, many shrugged, suggesting there was no need to study the obvious. Dr. Jeff Marion, a leading recreation ecologist and author of *Leave No Trace in the Outdoors*, is the first scholar to conduct research in this arena. Dr. Marion and doctoral student Johanna Arredondo found Mount Assiniboine Provincial Park and Banff National Park in Canada to be ideal sites for their study. Assiniboine is a roadless backcountry park offering rustic one-room huts, a lodge with associated cabins, and campsites. Banff National Park is a similar neighboring park with traditional backpacking campsites and a new type of campsite featuring constructed, well-defined tent pads. Usage data is available for both parks and each form of overnight accommodation, allowing the team to analyze environmental impacts on a per capita basis, research that Dr. Marion summarized for us in personal correspondence.

To gauge adverse visitor impact, the researchers evaluated the total area of vegetation and soils trampled at each site, measuring indicators such as area of intensive trampling, vegetation loss, and exposed soil. With the huts, Dr. Marion and his team found "exceptionally little trampling-related impact beyond their 'design footprint' which was reasonable and small." As he explained, "We saw exceptionally few informal 'visitor-created' trails or trampled spots—most visitors were using the formal trails provided." By contrast, both the traditional and tent-pad campsites showed greater signs of human impact, larger affected areas, and more vegetation loss and exposed soil. A much larger area around the lodge complex, including its cabins, was affected.

The data demonstrates that huts are remarkably effective in minimizing the extent of visitor impacts (the design footprint and additional visitor use impact). On average, the area of impact for 100 visitors was 7.9 square meters for huts compared with 45.1 for traditional campsites, 46.6 for campsites with developed tent pads, and 58.4 for lodge and cabin guests. Dr. Marion attributes the findings to "the spatial concentration and containment of visitor activity to the huts, decks, dining facility, and formal trails provided by the hut facilities." In evaluating the study findings, he went on to proclaim, "As a recreation ecologist I have essentially no comments or suggestions for further improvement of their hut operations (this is exceedingly rare!)." Huts, it turns out, do indeed reduce human impacts.

*Scholar Jeff Marion and associates found that campers pitching tents on tent pads like this one in Banff National Park have a greater impact on the places they visit than hut visitors do. (Photo by Jeffrey Marion)*

the nation's largest, has an average of twelve beds per hut.

America's full-service hut systems serve between thirty-five and one hundred guests; these include the AMC's White Mountains huts and Maine lodge-to-lodge system, and also the Yosemite High Sierra Camps. They offer hot meals, bedding, and some house-keeping; the facilities are more spacious and may comprise several structures includ-ing separate bunk- and bathhouses. At the Maine lodges, visitors can opt for shared accommodations in the bunkhouse or a pri-vate cabin shared with their trail compan-ions. The five backcountry Yosemite High Sierra Camps welcome visitors with an array of mostly seasonal structures includ-ing a dozen or more platform tents, toilet and shower enclosures, and the stone-and-canvas dining hall. The small tents, with capacity for two to six, offer some privacy in these encampments serving between thirty-two and sixty guests.

## ARCHITECTURE AND DESIGN

Architecturally, huts in the US range from large to small, primitive to elaborate. Maine Huts and Trails offers beautifully designed lodges made of wood and stone with spacious, light-filled public rooms and indoor toilets. Typically, Colorado's Tenth Mountain Division Hut Association huts are sturdy log or wood-frame structures, topped by a peaked gable, with a detached outhouse nearby. The San Juan Huts are simple, roofed, rectangular plywood boxes.

# EYES WIDE OPEN: THE CASE AGAINST HUTS

*All conservation of wilderness is self-defeating, for to cherish we must see and fondle, and when enough have seen and fondled, there is no wilderness left to cherish.*

—Aldo Leopold, *A Sand County Almanac*

In managing wildlands, what is the right relationship of people to the land? Ardent backpackers and preservationists Guy and Laura Waterman argue that structures in the wild, including huts, violate the spirit of wilderness by their mere existence. In *Forest and Crag: A History of Hiking, Trail Blazing, and Adventure in the Northeast Mountains*, they root this argument in the early conflicting values of "improvements" (building trails and shelters to enhance use, i.e., for human enjoyment of the experience) and "explorations" (preserving terrain hitherto unexplored, untainted). They argue that all human "improvements" are sacrilege. This fundamental tension between preservation and use embodies the human condition. People say they are committed to preserving the environment, and yet they love their conveniences. Huts create a slippery slope to destruction of what we cherish.

American ideas about how to manage wilderness are a touchstone of outdoor ethics worldwide. While everyone agrees that huts do not belong in federally designated wilderness areas, when should this prohibition extend to other back- and frontcountry wildland? Decisions are currently made on a case-by-case basis by local, state, and federal environmental review processes. Key criteria include environmental impacts, aesthetic considerations, and how the structure might affect the quality of the outdoor experience. In these contexts, the arguments against huts can be summed up in three major points:

The Three Sisters Backcountry huts are also small wooden structures, built with frames crafted from welded metal to allow for disassembly and seasonal removal (no longer required) and embellished with custom-welded decorative flourishes. Systems generally aim for design consistency across multiple sites, in part to simplify maintenance. Surprisingly, rainwater collection from roofs—used extensively in New Zealand—is not widespread in the US. Solar energy is employed for lighting in most US hut systems.

Yurts, common in western hut systems, combine coated canvas walls with steel or wooden interior supports. Yurts come in twelve-, sixteen-, twenty-, and thirty-foot-diameter models. These round buildings fit harmoniously into almost any setting. Yurts, popular in some of the snowiest landscapes, are often elevated on a wooden deck, which also provides welcome

**Environmental impacts.** Huts enable greater access and encourage larger group size; more people in the wild cause more environmental destruction, particularly in fragile zones. Negative effects include trail erosion, soil compaction, and vegetational trampling. Improper handling of human waste of all kinds can result in degraded air and water quality. Cutting firewood, smoke from wood fires, and human scent and noise disturb wildlife habitat.

**Aesthetic disruption.** More people can mean visual annoyances (e.g., more frequent and obtrusive trail markings), more noise (talking, shouting, music, helicopters, and motorized vehicles stocking and maintaining huts), and less solitude, a key value for seekers of remoteness. Backcountry skiers and hikers don't generally want a lot of other people in their favorite areas.

**Commodification of the experience.** As visitor numbers and amenity levels increase, the experience is diminished, and potentially commercialized. If it is too easy to get into the backcountry, people lacking requisite skills are attracted, and safety becomes a concern. Affordability and elitism are concerns; for example, some Appalachian Trail through-hikers skeptically view the AMC's White Mountains huts as privileged sanctuaries for city folks. In New Zealand, some trampers complain that the Great Walks are marketed to tourists.

outdoor living space. Firewood and the propane tank are sometimes stored under the deck. Wall tents are used by Sun Valley Mountain Huts.

Huts aim to minimize human impact on wild places (see "The Environmental Impact of Huts"). Building footprints are modest and interior organization compact and functional. Most combine bunks and cooking and living areas into a single room. In the two-story huts, the sleeping quarters are usually upstairs. Look for special features: a mudroom provides welcome space to change out of heavy boots and wet raingear; a covered walkway makes for a dry passage between the hut and the outhouse or firewood depot. Even in the Alaska backcountry cabins, remarkably consistent in design and materials, we found fanciful flourishes in the interior woodwork. Backcountry construction is a niche market. Some systems receive donations to cover the cost of hut construction (often memorial huts) and require maintenance endowments.

## BUSINESS MODELS AND PRACTICES

Hut systems in the US are run by a variety of nonprofits, government entities, and small private businesses, with the exception of Yosemite High Sierra Camps, which is run by a large corporation. Overall, eight of the twenty-six traditional hut systems are privately operated business enterprises, twelve are nonprofits, and four are government operated. There is no dominant model, and this mix reflects ongoing experimentation in an evolving business sector.

Regional not-for-profits, including the Tenth Mountain Division Hut Association, Summit Huts System, and Alfred A. Braun Hut System in Colorado; the Mount Tahoma Trails Association in Washington; American Prairie Reserve in Montana; and Maine Huts and Trails, are a uniquely American structure for supporting hut-to-hut enterprises. This category includes some clubs—the AMC, the American Alpine Club, and the Mountaineering Club of Alaska. The charitable model taps into generous donations of money and time from passionate users and keeps operations focused not only on practical management issues but also on the larger mission. All four hut systems in the Northeast operate as nonprofits.

By contrast, for-profit hut systems dominate in the American West (seven of the eleven systems), and they are all run by small family businesses, with the exception of the Yosemite High Sierra Camps, which is operated by Aramark, a corporate concessionaire. The mom-and-pop shops rose out of the 1980s boom in Nordic skiing and backcountry adventure. Several of these small businesses are on their second or third owners. These operations demonstrate that, with favorable terrain, solid management, hard work, and good luck, a hut-to-hut operation can support a family, especially when owners are firmly committed to the area and an outdoor lifestyle.

Government support for US huts is critical. Twenty of the twenty-six hut systems are sited on public lands (federal and state) and operate as permitted concessions. Equally important, the trails connecting most of these huts are built and managed by state and federal government agencies. Interestingly, since more than 90 percent of trail maintenance in the US is performed by volunteers, volunteers contribute a significant amount of labor to hut systems.

With few exceptions, including in Alaska, Hawaii, and Michigan, government agencies do not operate hut systems in the US. In Alaska, hundreds of backcountry cabins—a few with multiday traverse potential—are not only situated on state and federal lands but also administered by the Alaska Department of Natural Resources, US Forest Service, and Bureau of Land Management. Cabins in Michigan's Porcupine Mountains are operated by the state park. In national parks, hut systems exist as a concession in Yosemite and are operated by the National Park Service in Haleakala.

A new business model is emerging with Adirondack Hamlets to Huts (AHH), which

# HUTS FOR EDUCATION AND THERAPY

Huts, located in wild and beautiful settings, are ideal sites for educational and therapeutic programs centered around nature and the environment. In 2018, several hut operators joined us in conducting a survey of US hut systems to learn more about what programs are on offer. Data reveals that 17 percent (nearly 20,000) of the 115,000 annual visitors to American huts participate in some kind of guided activity. Outdoor clubs, schools and universities, military and veterans' organizations, church and youth groups, and corporations find that huts are conducive environments for workshops, classes, and training sessions.

Some systems have robust educational programming. For example, the Appalachian Mountain Club (AMC) huts each have a naturalist on staff, offering daily nature walks, talks, and a Junior Naturalist program. Across the nation, hut talks and interpretive materials cover natural history; cultural, military, and American Indian history; mining; and forestry. Maine Huts and Trails visitors learn about the green technology behind the waste systems in these "eco-lodges" through daily tours. Each American Prairie Reserve hut is defined by a theme tied to the locality; visitors can informally explore ideas through specially designed signage and the selection of books in the bookcase-sized library.

Huts are perfect places to teach outdoor skills, through programs ranging in duration from half a day to a long weekend or an entire week. Several times each winter, the Tenth Mountain Division Hut Association's Sangree M. Froelicher Hut—built for educational programming—houses a group pursuing wilderness first-aid certification with a special emphasis on winter conditions. Remote high mountain huts and yurts are great settings for avalanche safety training and for orienteering and map and compass courses. In addition, huts hold workshops on photography and writing, natural history, ecology, wildflowers, geology, biodiversity, and stargazing. Huts make excellent base camps for work parties engaged in trail maintenance, conservation, and citizen science projects.

Veterans' groups have recognized the superb match between huts and nature-based therapy in the Tenth Mountain Division and elsewhere. Huts for Vets, based in Aspen, Colorado, stages weeklong programs that combine wilderness therapy, philosophical discussions, physical challenges, and career advice for veterans and active-duty service members. San Juan Huts is central to LEADS Serves, which organizes healing outdoor opportunities for veterans and their families, youth, and athletes with adaptive needs. And the Wounded Warrior Project stages therapeutic odysseys at select AMC huts.

is both public and private. AHH is *not* a hut system in the brick-and-mortar sense, but rather an entity that promotes this scenic region by connecting visitors who hike, bike, paddle, snowshoe, or ski with a network of existing routes and lodgings (motels, camps, and inns). AHH acts as coordinator and publicist, encouraging participation in European-style village-to-village journeys in upstate New York. The initiative has been partially funded by the state, aspiring to draw a few of the millions of annual international visitors to New York City and Niagara Falls farther north to this six-million-acre park. This model, using huts and trails to drive economic development, has broad appeal and also drives several hut-to-hut initiatives currently under development.

## CHALLENGES

Most hut systems are doing well financially, as demand far outstrips supply. Marketing costs are virtually nonexistent, as systems rely on word of mouth and social media. That said, the costs and complications of setting up and operating a new hut system are considerable. While US hut operations are—across all types—financially viable, systems can fail and must adapt to harsh fiscal realities. Cascade Huts in Oregon, founded in 2007, has posted "closed until further notice" on Facebook. Maine Huts and Trails (MHT), also established in 2007 as a regional nonprofit, took on the task of constructing and maintaining most of the trails. In 2019, citing difficulties in attracting seasonal help and the high cost of building and trail maintenance, MHT shifted from a full-service to a self-service model of operations and now relies on volunteer staff during busy weekends.

Establishing a new hut system requires permits and negotiations with federal or state agencies, money, and a building plan. Current owners and managers cite interactions with agency officials and bureaucratic procedures as their greatest frustration. High turnover in district offices makes it difficult for the USFS to establish long-term, productive working relationships. New systems must successfully undergo site and building plan review, and the National Environmental Policy Act requires an environmental impact statement or, in cases with less potential impact, an environmental assessment for actions "significantly affecting the quality of the human environment." These lengthy and costly processes can be difficult for a small operator. Plans must also comply with regulations related to insurance, health and safety, and fire and building codes. Some operators struggle to get designs past local inspectors, as building codes tend to be written to city and town standards and are difficult to adapt to the backcountry. Siting and construction of huts can be tricky, and there are no clear guidelines available. Backcountry construction is expensive, especially when materials must be transported by helicopter to sites inaccessible by road. A new generation of prefabricated huts on the horizon may simplify construction in the future.

Running a hut system involves a lot of hard work, mostly invisible to the visitor. Tasks run the gamut from reservations to resupply, and from maintenance to managing staff. In a few cases (the Mount Tahoma Trails

Association and Alaska Alpine Club huts), volunteers not only administer the system but also provide all the labor to maintain the huts (and trails). The owner of the Southwest Nordic Center hut system manages to do all the supply, maintenance, and reservations tasks himself. Only the larger nonprofits—for example, the Tenth Mountain Division Hut Association, the AMC, Maine Huts and Trails, and San Juan Huts—hire full-time, year-round staff. But most outfits get the jobs done with seasonal help. Hut owners and managers must find and retain good part-time workers in remote rural areas. Full-service systems leverage tradition and location to recruit summer staff. The opportunity to work in the Yosemite backcountry will always prove irresistible to enough folks to fill the staff rosters each year at the High Sierra Camps. The AMC model of staffing huts in the White Mountains with college students lives on as a cherished tradition and powerful recruiting engine.

## NEW DIRECTIONS AND TRENDS FOR US HUTS

As hut systems expand, several trends are now clear. Hut systems are under development not only in the mountains but also at lower elevations and closer to towns and urban centers. Hut systems, new and old, continue to embrace multiple modes of travel. And projects that leverage hut-to-hut for explicit tourism and economic development goals are on the rise. Six new systems are in the planning and implementation phases, and five more are farther out on the horizon. If all of these initiatives come to fruition in the next decade, the overall growth curve of US hut systems will be as steep as that of the 1980s ski hut boom.

*Imagine a hut system where you can stay overnight in a converted shepherd wagon like this working wagon in the Pioneer Mountains in Idaho.*

*The AMC Harriman Outdoor Center, an hour from New York City, allows urban dwellers to enjoy nature relatively close to home.* (Photo courtesy of Appalachian Mountain Club)

Existing hut systems continue to establish new huts, routes, and programs. The American Prairie Reserve, which opened three huts between 2018 and 2020, is beginning work on another of the projected ten huts. Adirondack Hamlets to Huts launched its first season in 2020 with four routes and has plans to expand. Two Colorado hut systems, allied under the Tenth Mountain Division umbrella, are moving forward with long-range plans. The Grand Huts Association, now operating only one of seven projected huts, has funding for a second. The Summit Huts Association opened a fifth hut in 2019, and as part of its master plan, the association is actively exploring options for both building new backcountry structures and repurposing existing structures. The Tenth Mountain Division Hut Association has completed a facility in Leadville, Colorado, to house seasonal staff, vehicles, equipment, and supplies supporting field operations.

Like Adirondack Hamlets to Huts, two other initiatives embrace the European village-to-village model, which relies on existing infrastructure for lodging and meals. LandPaths, an innovative land trust in Sonoma County, California, is planning multiple treks designed to connect people with the land. Existing accommodations and newly built huts will serve as overnight shelter and as sites for environmental education and hands-on land stewardship activities. Since 2011, Friends of the Columbia Gorge has been working toward a 200-mile loop trail on both sides of the majestic Columbia River. Gorge Towns to Trails will promote multiday trekking adventures in this popular scenic area, with overnights in inns, motels, and bed-and-breakfasts in small towns renowned for local wine and beer.

Other emergent hut systems are focused on biking and skiing, with hiking sometimes in the mix. In Minnesota, Superior Highland Backcountry, an organization dedicated to expanding and protecting backcountry skiing opportunities in the northeastern part of the state, projects a network of huts above Lake Superior, along a ridge that stretches from Finland to Lutsen. In Oregon, mountain bikers can look forward to the completion of the 670-mile Oregon Timber Trail. The Oregon Timber Trail Alliance and Travel Oregon, the state tourism bureau, are working together to realize a route incorporating overnight stays in towns and, eventually, in purpose-built huts. The Alaska Huts Association, in collaboration with the USFS and Alaska Railroad, is raising funds for the Glacier Discovery Project, a three-hut hiking, biking, and skiing system with trailhead access by train.

Other initiatives, some only in the discussion phase, demonstrate how huts figure in the national conversation. Master plans for both Snowmass and Aspen ski areas include backcountry hut systems. Snowmass, where three huts are proposed for both winter and summer use, has won USFS approval for its master plan; the next step toward the proposed hut system is the required environmental review. In California, the Bay Area Ridge Trail Council, which has completed 380 miles of a 500-mile route following ridgelines around the bay, hopes to build a hut network. The Alaska Trails Initiative proposes a hut-to-hut network from Seward to Anchorage as part of an effort to entice more visitors, especially from cruise ships, to spend time experiencing the state's scenic wonders through human-powered journeys.

APX1, a company based in Sun Valley, Idaho, working with a group of investors, envisions a hut system extending from the US-Canada border to the US-Mexico border. This long-distance hut-to-hut route through Idaho, Utah, and Colorado will utilize existing trails and hut systems, and also build new trails and huts as needed. The reservation platform under development will be open source and optimized for hut system reservations, supporting both exclusive-use and by-the-bunk reservation models. The new huts will be owned and operated by APX1, while new trails will be built and maintained by a separate nonprofit.

Over the next several decades, US hut development will reflect past successes and respond to new needs and ideas. As the sector matures, American creativity may shape huts and hut-to-hut travel in ways that are surprising and uplifting.

## FUTURE POSSIBILITIES

*You can count the seeds in the apple, but you can't count the apples in the seeds.*

—Anonymous

Until the 1980s, hut systems were rare in the US. With the burst of initiatives and innovations over recent decades, huts have finally gained a firm foothold on American soil and in the public imagination. Predicting the future is perilous; nevertheless, we can't resist making some projections.

Huts, as a sector in American recreation and education, will begin to mature over the next decades. Some changes will be driven by economics, recreational trends, gear innovations, and climate change, while a commitment to rebalancing the human relationship with nature will drive other developments. We predict that biking will drive the next big thrust in hut system development. Long-distance bikers, on both gravel and single-track routes, represent an eager audience. Like it or not, as e-bikes proliferate in the backcountry, bringing hordes of new users to rugged places, huts—designed to meter and concentrate use—will be an environmentally sound response to help mitigate crowding and habitat disruption.

Climate change, which is negatively affecting destination ski resorts, adds incentives for these massive corporations, already struggling under unsustainable business models, to diversify into other activities. Ski resorts may try to leverage their extensive USFS permits and lobbying power to create upscale hut systems. Marketing campaigns will promote the joys of "uphill" and "side-country" skiing in winter, and tout the comforts of luxurious backcountry huts to affluent hikers in summer.

Another possible scenario: European-style inn-to-inn or village-to-village traverses will flourish, with trails serving as stepping stones from the city to the country. As in Europe, trekkers in the US will be able to reserve farm stays and lodging in picturesque small towns, consume local food and beverages, and visit cultural sites along the way. Reservation platforms, developed in cooperation with local tourism and economic development agencies, will proliferate. Under these hut-to-hut networks, affiliate accommodations might be branded as walker, biker, and/or skier friendly. In short, hut-to-hut travel will become a more familiar option for average, fit folks looking for outdoor adventure.

But what about some more radical, visionary scenarios? As "local" becomes a dominant travel theme, the next generation of huts may be situated close to where most people actually live. We envision a set of frontcountry huts, that we call "nearby nature" huts, at the urban and suburban edges, allowing urbanites to spend time in nature close to home. Public transportation increasingly provides access to the vast networks of trails that already exist in these settings. Frontcountry parks and trails provide affordable, low-barrier portals for urban communities to enter the natural world, to learn outdoor skills, and to experience the healing balm of trees, grass, rocks, and waterways.

The Appalachian Mountain Club (AMC), originator of the first US hut system, is working toward a version of this future. Rustic,

*Why not organize a hut system that accommodates skijorers and their dogs?* (Photo by Randi Hausken, Creative Commons, Wikimedia)

affordable frontcountry accommodations are under development in Averell Harriman State Park, 38 miles from the Bronx. AMC's Harriman Outdoor Center is reaching beyond the usual white, middle-class hut-to-hut user groups by developing cabins and bunkhouses for people without the gear and skills for camping and backpacking, as well as offering a variety of youth leadership and engagement programs. With the goal of providing comfort and offsetting fear of the unfamiliar, this program serves, among others, African American, Latino, Asian, and other groups currently underrepresented in our great wild places.

The title of E. O. Wilson's book *Half-Earth: Our Planet's Fight for Life* refers to how much of our world must be protected in order to ensure the level of species biodiversity needed for humans to thrive. About 30 percent of the terrestrial domain is at least theoretically under some kind of protection. *Half-Earth* proposes an umbrella project under which a global army

is mobilized to serve the planet and ensure our own survival. The troops will be eyes on the land, monitoring violations of legislated protections. Huts, designed to minimize human impacts, will house this new conservation corps. This army, composed of citizen scientists, academic researchers, and conservation workers, will repair ecosystems and restore landscapes. Some hut encampments will be temporary, relocated to new work sites as projects are completed and in response to overuse and climate change. These volunteer experiences will provide urban dwellers with respite from city life through opportunities for hands-on conservation work, while also connecting people dedicated to the restoration and preservation of the earth.

Just for fun, imagine new (and existing) hut systems supporting snowshoeing, skijoring, dogsledding, llama or burro packing, long-distance running, and paddling sports—or hut systems that support people who want to travel with their dogs. Portable

# LAND ETHICS FOR HUTS

*A thing is right when it tends to preserve the integrity, stability, and beauty of the biotic community. It is wrong when it tends otherwise.*
—Aldo Leopold, "The Land Ethic," in *A Sand County Almanac*

The community of practice for hut systems may decide someday to develop an ethics statement; this is our personal vision of the issues it should address. These ethics will inform the development of a set of best practices for the hut community, and will become one basis for clearly branding hut systems as exemplary stewards of the land.

As organizations building and operating on wildlands, we have a particular responsibility to set an example in preserving and protecting our biotic community. We voluntarily and wholeheartedly operate our hut systems as stewardship tools designed to concentrate and mitigate human impacts, and to preserve wildlands while making them accessible for recreation, education, and conservation. We creatively weave Leave No Trace principles into every aspect of our programs and operations, and we share resulting innovations with other hut systems as an evolving body of best practices.

Our commitment to our customers, to land owners and managers, and most of all to the land itself is to celebrate and care for the special spirit of the place—the *genius loci*—on which we operate. Over time, we pledge to leave the land in better ecological health than we found it. Our hut systems are places for experiencing, exploring, and understanding moral responsibility to nature. The land ethic drives our operational and business practices, and includes:

**Environmental protection.** The land is not ours; we are its stewards. We conform with and strive to exceed federal, state, and local regulations designed to protect

huts, including yurts, tents, sheep wagons, tiny houses on trailers, and camper vehicles, could be used to link existing huts to create new traverses. And somewhere, a kids'-scale hut system, with huts just a few miles apart, will expose children to the joys of hut life and the thrill of completing a "long-distance" trip.

Huts will become ever more powerful places for learning and healing, places that allow people to reimagine their lives and the society they live in. A hut traverse will become a recognized cure for "nature deficit disorder." Programs will teach simple green living skills that have application back home. Hut-to-hut will contribute to creating vegetation, soils, wildlife, and water and to ensure the overall environmental quality of the land we share with wild nature. We also work with regulatory agencies and legislatures to revise misguided regulations on huts.

**Environmental education and conservation.** We support use of huts for teaching and hands-on work advancing environmental protection, conservation, and restoration. We actively educate our clientele in low-impact outdoor skills and practices. We strive to keep huts affordable for young people, families, and like-minded organizations.

**Siting, design, and construction.** We strive to at least meet and, where feasible, exceed regulations and best practices designed to minimize the human impacts on the land. We will creatively adapt and apply Leave No Trace principles to guide the siting, design, construction, and maintenance of huts, trails, and associated amenities.

**Visitor management.** Staff proactively implement and monitor the results of our visitor management plan. This plan, articulating how we balance resource protection and recreation, uses a combination of persuasive communication strategies and necessary regulations to encourage hut users to minimize environmental impacts, and to ensure they do not degrade the quality of experience for others.

**Business ethics.** Whether the business model is nonprofit, for-profit, or government operated, we actively engage our communities and strive to provide locals with affordable overnight accommodations. We work to be financially viable while operating exemplary environmental enterprises. We act in accord with evolving principles and standards, such as those articulated by the B Corps community: meeting high standards of verified social and environmental performance, public transparency, and accountability to balance profit and purpose.

new generations of outdoor citizens, motivated to make healthy, earth-friendly lifestyle choices and promote environmentally sound policies. Huts will function as authentic, safe spaces, embracing travelers who work and live together with friends, family, and—imagine!—people they don't even know. Hut systems will become a new version of the summer camp, where young and old learn outdoor skills and natural history together, and experience the pleasures of steady physical movement through wild spaces day after day.

A pilgrimage is a long journey to some sacred place as an act of religious devotion or spiritual awakening. Hut systems will

*The Bomber Traverse in Alaska, which does not have reliable trail markers and crosses glaciers, is beyond the skill level of all but the hardiest hut seekers. (Photo by Tom Swift)*

function as innovation hubs for new generations of environmental pilgrims seeking to update ritual journeys of redemption and spiritual renewal, rites of passage, and vision quests. Perhaps we will develop a new set of distinctively American pilgrimage trails, with veneration of nature and personal reflection integrated into the hut-to-hut traverse.

Huts will be settings where conversations between polarized groups can begin. Hunters and hikers, for example, have largely diverged in recent generations. United by a love of the outdoors, folks from seemingly opposed camps could come together to rediscover common ground. After a day spent in shared recreation or on a service project, hikers and hunters, bikers and anglers, snowmobilers and environmentalists might forge lasting bonds over dinner in the sheltering warmth of the hut.

Finally, we believe America will slowly begin to place huts at regular intervals along at least one of its long-distance trails. Remember Benton MacKaye's vision for the Appalachian Trail? It may be too late to situate huts along parts of the 2200-mile-long AT, but perhaps the situation is ripe somewhere else. The North Country Trail, still under development through the populated heartland, will eventually cover 4600 miles. This trail, the longest, youngest, and least tradition-bound national long-distance trail, may be the most likely to innovate, building linked huts along a few sections of what may become a coast-to-coast path.

## US HUTS WILL COME OF AGE

The land management community will come to acknowledge huts and incorporate hut-to-hut travel into long-range planning on federal, state, and local levels. Because pressures on some iconic landscapes are threatening to destroy their ecological viability, drastic limitations on public access will be necessary in some places. As research in recreational ecology documents that huts minimize human impacts, hut systems will be deployed by land management agencies as a conservation strategy. Skillfully designed, managed, and monitored hut and trail systems will direct people away from fragile and overused areas toward other carefully selected and hardened sites. Portable huts will also be deployed in order to change front- and backcountry use patterns.

Public parks, including our most iconic national parks, are chronically underfunded with no substantial funding increases in sight. In the absence of adequate government support, we must leverage creativity to preserve our cherished places and to promote nature immersion for all. Robert Manning, a specialist in national parks, points to "parknerships" as one part of the solution. Financially stressed state and federal parks will partner with a wide range of nonprofit organizations, including new and existing hut systems. Hut systems with strong conservation programs might then get creative in their fee structures, trading overnights for work in the field. Outdoor clubs will partner with parks and develop hut systems operated by member volunteers to enhance lodging options on public lands.

As Americans learn to love their huts and as new systems rise, huts owners and operators will increasingly reach out to each other. The US Hut Alliance, comprised of hut system representatives and hut advocates, is coming together to exchange information, find common cause in operations, and speak with one voice on important topics. The alliance will articulate best practices and develop an ethics statement situating huts on the leading edge of environmentally sensitive recreation. See "Land Ethics for Huts" for an example of what this might look like. Finally, American land managers and hut operators can learn a lot from systems in Europe, Canada, and New Zealand. We believe land managers will begin to make study tours to see what is being done elsewhere, and that US systems will invite foreign hut specialists to hut-related conferences, workshops, and design charettes to generate promising ideas for the twenty-first century.

NEXT PAGE: *Challenge yourself to plan and execute a hut journey across unknown terrain, knowing that you will find shelter at day's end.*

# PLANNING A HUT-TO-HUT ADVENTURE

**LOCATED IN SPECIAL PLACES,** huts make backcountry overnights comfortable and accessible and provide special opportunities for conviviality. They also contribute to the conservation of natural places.

**Comfort and convenience.** Hut-to-hut hiking, skiing, and biking are sometimes touted as adventure without the weight. The hut-to-hut traveler carries much less than the backpacker. Arriving at a hut, travelers settle into an evening buoyed by simple comforts including places to sit, a bed to lie on, and a kitchen zone where meals can be prepared standing up! Come what may weather-wise, a hut provides reliable shelter. Huts, then, welcome folks to the backcountry who might not feel up to the rigors of backpacking, or just want to be comfortable. Huts are a great venue to introduce children to the pleasures of multiday nature immersion trips. Since many huts in the US require reservations, travelers know the daily distance and evening destination. With peace of mind, they focus on the day's journey, even as the vision of a cozy lodge, cabin, or yurt inspires forward motion.

**Conviviality.** Huts provide a rare opportunity in communal living, promoting cooperation among folks traveling together and instant overnight community. The hut experience can transform strangers into friends and erase social barriers. Coordination around cooking, eating, heating, sleeping, and cleaning stimulates fresh thinking and a sense of connection.

**Conservation.** Some rugged adventurers reject huts as too civilized and believe these permanent or semipermanent structures violate their pristine natural settings (see "Eyes Wide Open: The Case Against Huts" in Part I). In fact, huts are good for the environment! They are designed to concentrate and shape use, thereby minimizing the impacts of human travel, particularly in fragile environments. The experience of living in huts—even if only for a few days—might lead to a change in lifestyle back home and inspire adventurers to take steps to minimize their daily footprint on this beautiful earth.

*Kids love hut adventures—and a few hut systems even allow dogs!* (Photo by James Harnois)

# TYPICAL HUT EXPERIENCES

**AFTER A DAY ON THE TRAIL,** it is a thrill to catch sight of the hut nestled among tall trees or sitting in the open below an exposed ridge. A porch welcomes you, offering bench space to sit and remove your boots or skis. There will be hooks on the porch or in the mudroom, where you may also find an array of hut slippers and shelves to stash boots. Shuck off your outerwear, don some slippers, and enter your home for the night.

Your experience will vary depending on whether the hut is exclusive use or shared, self-service or full service. Let's say your hut is an **exclusive-use, self-service** yurt or cabin. Upon entering the hut, everyone claims a bunk. Spread out your sleeping bag and stow your pack. Find the hut manual and get familiar with recommended routines and resources. Someone gets wood and starts a fire; another gets the water supply going by filling the snowmelt pot or trekking to a nearby stream. Locate the outhouse, check the toilet paper supply, and shovel snow off the path if needed. The cooks gather provisions and make a dinner plan, perhaps offering snacks and a libation as the companions settle in. Then you all change into hut clothes and relax.

Evenings in small huts embody *hygge*, the Danish term for coziness and comfortable conviviality. Relaxation is as natural as breathing after a full day on the trail; the collective mood is buoyed by the day's exercise and sustained immersion in nature. Except on warm summer days, the glowing woodstove requires tending. This activity, along with meal prep and cleanup, is an opportunity for collaboration. Some hut trekkers haul fancy foodstuffs to make ambitious meals; others rely on dehydrated meals in a bag, which require only boiling water and time. After dinner, solitary

*The "croo" at the AMC Mizpah Hut take a break after preparing focaccia for dinner.*

tasks such as journaling and reading may draw individuals to their bunks or to a bench in the corner. Write or draw in the logbook. Someone may pull out a deck of cards—stashed in their pack or found in the hut—to play some games. A hut guitar or a harmonica may stir the group to song. The evening winds down to the soft sounds of people chattering and shuffling stuff. The fire crackles. Perhaps a coyote wails in the distance, or crickets chorus outside. Early bedtime is the norm for hut-to-hut travelers who must rise, make breakfast, pack, and hit the trail in the morning.

What about the **shared, self-service** hut that rents *by the bunk*? Experiences are much the same as in exclusive-use huts, but think of these as temporary cohousing.

## HUT ETIQUETTE

Hut stays demand our best behavior. The same rules of common courtesy that govern any group activity apply. There are also special expectations, tasks, and taboos particular to this mode of travel.

**Don't foul the nest.** Remove boots and wet gear before entering. Keep your personal gear, including sleeping bag and foodstuffs, orderly and stashed out of the way. Wash hands frequently. Wash your own dishes and any others within reach. Bring along a trash bag, and use it to contain and pack out food waste, recyclables, wrappers, and so on. Do not leave excess food behind in the hut, as it can attract pests.

**Share the space harmoniously.** Whether you are a self-contained group or find yourselves among unfamiliar fellow travelers, always consult with others to coordinate meal preparation and cleanup, orchestrate sleeping arrangements, and share common cabin duties.

**Enjoy yourselves—quietly!** Huts are especially cozy homes away from home. Everyone makes the effort to be friendly; even the most exhausted traveler can accept gestures of welcome with a smile, and shy people summon some extroverted cheer. Be ever mindful, though, that some hut visitors crave quiet or are seeking solitude. It's best to leave music players at home and silence cell phones if you bring one. A shared hut is not the place for rowdy late-night parties or boisterous conversations. Observe quiet times, which generally begin at ten o'clock at night and extend until seven in the morning. Bring earplugs to keep from being disturbed by fellow travelers. If you are traveling with a group to celebrate a special occasion, book the entire hut!

**Leave the hut cleaner than you found it.** The hut manual will articulate best practices for guests and will list cleaning tasks. Check the list twice and do it all. Leave the hut well supplied with kindling and other firewood, and observe water protocols.

**Practice good citizenship on the trail.** Etiquette extends to the trail. Stay on trail, avoid shortcuts, and yield to uphill travelers. When encountering horses or pack-trains, move to the downhill side of the trail; look to the rider for instructions. Minimize your noise imprint, and let nature's sounds prevail.

Communal living in a shared space requires communication and cooperation (see "Hut Etiquette"). Who will chop wood and stoke the fire? Keep the snowmelt pot full? Even hanging wet clothing can initiate interaction as overnighters spread stuff out on racks surrounding the woodstove or on lines strung above the porch. The kitchen is always the center of action—guests check with others to figure out who does what, where, and when, ensuring an easy flow of cooking, eating, and cleanup within the limited space.

Here's what to expect at a **shared, full-service** hut: You catch sight of the hut, noticing folks relaxing on the porch and enjoying the view. They call out greetings as you enter. You remove your boots or skis, sling off your pack, and seek out the staff host. Upon registration, you get a brief orientation to the spaces, schedule, and routines; make sure to clarify your dietary preferences at this point. Next, find a bunk room or go to your assigned platform tent. If you are lucky or arrive early, you get to choose your favorite—the bottom bunk makes trips to the toilet easier; a top bunk offers greater privacy. After organizing your stuff in the sleep space, reconnoiter. Is there a lounge area with comfortable seating? Or just a big room with picnic tables for meals and other pastimes including games, journaling, conversation, and more? Is the bathroom in a separate building or down the hall? Can you walk to a pretty lake, babbling brook, or stunning viewpoint?

As dinnertime approaches, you strike up conversations with fellow guests, trading trail notes and origin stories; you learn that some travelers are repeat visitors or that their parents visited the same hut on their honeymoon decades ago! Meals in full-service huts are served family style. Pick a table with sympathetic people, then enjoy a hearty, multicourse meal and lively service by staff. Conversation often drifts toward trail conditions, weather, the way ahead, and tales of favorite destinations. After dinner, the hut settles down to a quiet hum; check out the logbooks, investigate the hut library, or propose a game or puzzle with your companions and new acquaintances. Music happens; staff are often talented musicians; trekkers may bring a small instrument to play; occasionally there is a sing-along. And then, by ten o'clock, silence descends on the hut as tired travelers seek sleep.

Whether you end up in an exclusive-use or shared hut, mornings pass quietly as folks get up and prepare for the day on the trail. At full-service hut systems, you might get a wake-up song, with a staffer musically announcing dawn and breakfast in half an hour. Hut travelers tend to be seasoned hikers, skiers, or bikers who understand that an early start sets a good tempo for the day. Have breakfast. Stuff your sleeping bag into its sack, put raingear and snacks at the top of the pack, fill water bottles, and check the map. Gather useful information from your hut mates. Join in the group cleanup tasks. You are now ready to set off and enjoy the day's travel to the next hut.

## MORE NITTY-GRITTY HUT ROUTINES

When you arrive at the self-service hut, take care of a few important tasks before you settle in:

- Shovel out ashes from the stove and dump them in a designated area.
- Turn on the propane and electricity.
- Fill pots for melting snow outside in the "clean snow" area. Sometimes a special pee zone is indicated;

*Family time at the Chittenden Hut, Vermont Huts Association* (Photo by Marius Becker)

this area should be avoided when filling the melting pots. Use the wood-burning heat stove, not the propane burner, to melt snow.

After you settle in, here are some tips to ease your stay:

- Read the hut manual or posted notices in the kitchen area to master the best system to clean dishes, which may involve multiple dishpans to minimize water use, and follow pre-ferred gray water disposal routines.
- Some huts provide pillows. If the one you're staying in doesn't, make your own. Bring along a pillowcase or use an empty stuff sack, and fill it with extra clothing.
- Keep your headlamp handy. Many huts are equipped with propane or electric lanterns; some are equipped with solar chargers.

Before you leave, clean and secure the hut for future guests:

- Sweep the floors and wipe down the counters.
- Turn off the propane and electricity.
- Lock the door.

Treat the hut as your home. Honor the next visitors by leaving the hut clean and well-stocked.

FLEA

# HOW TO USE THIS GUIDE

**EACH FEATURED HUT SYSTEM CHAPTER** begins with essential information you need to plan your hut-to-hut adventure. Start by selecting a hut system and itinerary and then honing a plan geared to the group's interests, abilities, time frame, and geographical preferences. Would you prefer to hike, bike, or ski? The location and desired mode of travel will help you narrow your choices. This section leads you through the elements of the featured hut system chapters so that you will be well prepared to craft plans for excellent adventures.

## KEY HUT SYSTEM INFORMATION

Each hut system begins with key information trekkers need to evaluate whether it is suitable for them and their fellow travelers.

**Location** lists the name of the park, forest, or other land management agency, the nearest town(s), and the state. **Distance** includes the average distance between huts and the total mileage for the featured itineraries. **Elevation gain/loss** includes the total gain and loss (in feet) for the featured itineraries.

## DIFFICULTY RATINGS

This rating is an assessment of how challenging the route is, based on both quantifiable elements (including daily distance and elevation gain and loss, weather, and terrain) and our subjective experiences hiking, skiing, or biking each trail. The difficulty rating is necessarily imprecise, given that trails vary mile by mile and may become treacherous under adverse weather conditions. When rating trails, we assume reasonably good weather and that the trekker will be carrying a pack weighing at least

OPPOSITE: *Setting the table for dinner at the AMC Greenleaf Hut*

twenty-five pounds. The hiking ratings refer to the trails and terrain. For skiing, difficulty is calibrated in relation to the required skiing skills for the individual.

Most hikers already know what level of challenge is right. But if you need help with the self-evaluation, consider using ATG Oxford's online Fitness Test (see www.atg-oxford.co.uk/fitness-questionnaire). While this seven-question test is no substitute for self-knowledge, it will assign you a fitness level from 1 to 5.

We rate the hikes in this book as easy, moderate, or difficult.

**Easy.** These trails feature minimal elevation gain, clear-cut navigation cues, and a hardened, clearly defined treadway. Healthy folks who take walks and are accustomed to some exertion will enjoy these trails (ATG fitness levels 1 and 2). They are also suitable for children.

**Moderate.** These are trails of longer distance, with moderate elevation gain and loss (less than 3000 feet per day), and some rough footing, but should be fairly easy to navigate for alert trekkers. A good level of fitness is required (ATG fitness levels 3 and 4). These trails are suitable for strong children with previous backcountry hiking experience.

**Difficult.** These routes may be long (more than 6 to 8 miles per day), include considerable elevation loss and gain, and cross steep, rocky, or muddy terrain. Footing can be unstable or rough and trails difficult to navigate. These routes are for folks who have completed several multiday hiking or ski trips and are very fit (ATG fitness level 5), with stamina to keep going all day, and the mental toughness to solve problems on the trail.

Skiing difficulty ratings are based on required Nordic skiing skills and endurance in relation to distance, steepness, elevation change, and navigation challenges. Downhill or alpine skiers should not assume that their skills transfer directly. The skiing difficulty ratings assume moderate to good weather conditions. Proceed with additional caution after heavy fresh snowfall, in crusty or icy conditions, or with reduced visibility accompanying snowfall or heavy fog.

**Novice.** Skiers with more than beginner skills who have five to ten backcountry day trips under their belts. Novices should be competent in getting up from a fall, adjusting stride to terrain, gliding, kick turns, AVA turns, snowplowing, double poling, and skinning (when terrain requires). Novices are advised to team up with more advanced skiers and focus on routes with minimal elevation gain and loss.

**Intermediate.** Geared to very fit skiers who have participated in multiple hut-to-hut ski trips and are accustomed to carrying a heavy backpack in winter conditions. Skiers must be able to check speed and maintain balance on steep terrain. These routes may require the ability to execute turns on fairly steep slopes and transition from uphill skiing with skins to downhill runs. Elevation gain may be up to 3000 feet per day with distances up to 9 miles.

Advanced routes are not featured in this book because they are beyond the target audience.

## TERRAIN

Brief notes on the landscape, plus special features, are covered in this category.

# RENT A BUNK OR THE WHOLE HUT?

In countries with highly developed hut-to-hut cultures, huts are almost always communal shelters, where each guest claims a bunk and then shares all the other spaces and amenities. In the US, such communal hostelries represent a little less than half of the hut-to-hut options treated in this book. When you reserve hut space by the bunk, you can expect to find bunks stacked two high. Other huts may feature a sleeping room or loft with mattresses spread across the floor.

Unlike New Zealanders and Europeans, many Americans prefer to have the entire hut to themselves; the dominant model for hut occupancy in the western United States is exclusive use. When you rent the entire hut and control the guest list, you may avoid awkward encounters with incompatible strangers. But you also miss opportunities to meet new people and learn from fellow travelers. Some hut systems offer both by-the-bunk and exclusive-use options in different seasons or days of the week.

## MODES OF TRAVEL

Only human-powered modes—hiking, skiing, biking, and paddling, where relevant—are listed, in order corresponding to the seasons below. We traveled each system in the mode for which it is best known (hiking, skiing, or biking) and did not usually return to try other modes.

## SEASON

This category lists the season(s) of operation (exact dates vary from year to year), with the most popular season listed first.

## HUTS

This category lists the number and capacity of huts for the system as a whole; whether reservations are **by the bunk** (each person rents a bunk, and the hut is shared) or **exclusive use** (one group rents the whole hut); and the level of amenities. We use the following four amenity codes:

**Basic.** A hut with bunks plus mattresses (except in Alaska cabins), basic furnishings, a woodstove for heat, a water source, and an outhouse. Bring your own food, cookstove, fuel, utensils, and sleeping bag.

**Self-service.** Same as above plus a gas cookstove and dishes, utensils, and cooking pots. Some provide sleeping bags and/or pillows. Bring your own food and sleeping bag or sleep sheet, if needed.

**Self-service+.** Same as self-service huts but with a fully stocked pantry and cookbook for meal preparation.

**Full service.** Larger accommodations with separate dining and sleeping rooms, bunks with mattresses and bedding, running water, and indoor bathroom facilities (some exceptions). Meals (breakfast and dinner) are prepared and served by staff; pack lunches are available upon request. Full-service huts usually provide both indoor and outdoor areas to sit and socialize and offer books, magazines, and games. Only two featured hut systems offer showers.

## OVERVIEW AND AMENITIES

An overview of the hut system, its character, natural features, recreational opportunities, and history, this section highlights what makes the hut system special and key reasons for visiting it.

The amenities section focuses on hut design, spaces, amenities, setting, and special features in more detail. We list individual huts in a system, elevation for those not in the itinerary, and a few notes on location and other features. For systems with a large number of huts, we highlight only those included in the featured itineraries.

## PLANNING AND PREPARATION

Here you'll find practical information needed for planning and booking.

**Contact:** The hut system's website, phone number, and/or email.

**Booking:** Reservation methods, tips about lotteries, and other early booking procedures.

**Membership:** Membership costs and benefits, if applicable. Member discounts are often available, reducing the cost of overnight stays.

**Rates:** We use the following codes to indicate the price range of hut systems.

Refer to each system's website for exact prices. Prices change over time. The symbols listed below indicate the cost per person, per night. For exclusive-use rentals, the per person nightly rate is calculated by dividing the cost for renting the whole hut by the number of bunks in the hut.

- $: $10–$40 per night
- $$: $41–$80 per night
- $$$: $81–$170 per night

**Transportation:** How to get to the hut system office or area (directions to the trailhead are provided in the itinerary). Most people drive in a personal vehicle to access hut systems. Two cars are ideal when the beginning and ending trailheads are not the same. We indicate when there is a local shuttle or car relocation service, as well as any public transit options.

### MAPS

This section lists the maps and/or GPX files provided by the hut system and any recommended apps. Recommendations for additional paper maps and/or GPS options to purchase are included when applicable.

### PACKING TIPS

Items specific to the hut system that may not be included in the general packing lists (see "Packing" later in this chapter), and special reminders based on our experience. For ski trips, we list recommended ski equipment.

### OTHER TIPS

This catch-all section covers useful details on topics ranging from parking, permits, and road conditions to trail warnings, wildlife precautions, bug seasons, pet policies, gear shuttle services, items available for purchase, and more.

## ITINERARY

Here we identify the itinerary and indicate the total distance and number of days and nights. The overall itinerary is described, with notes about the trail marking system and a few comments on the trail experience. We aim, in the featured itinerary, to encompass the full hut system, and we indicate shorter or easier alternatives when applicable. A few very large systems cannot be represented by a single itinerary. In such cases, we highlight a few options that give a sense of the system as a whole.

The following information is provided for each travel day:

- Distance (in miles)
- Elevation gain/loss
- Difficulty
- Hut elevation
- Hut GPS coordinates (in decimal degrees) based on the WGS84 datum
- Trailhead (for day 1)
- Getting there (driving directions for day 1)

This information is followed by navigation directions. Mileage is indicated cumulatively for the day and starts over the next day. The more complicated the trail navigation and the more challenging the terrain, the more navigation detail is provided.

For each featured itinerary, a locator map depicts the entire route. Longer and more detailed itineraries include additional maps showing daily sections. Maps show intersecting trails and roads, which are helpful not only for wayfinding but also for planning emergency exit routes and plotting alternative routes due to trail damage or other issues. The maps in the book are suitable

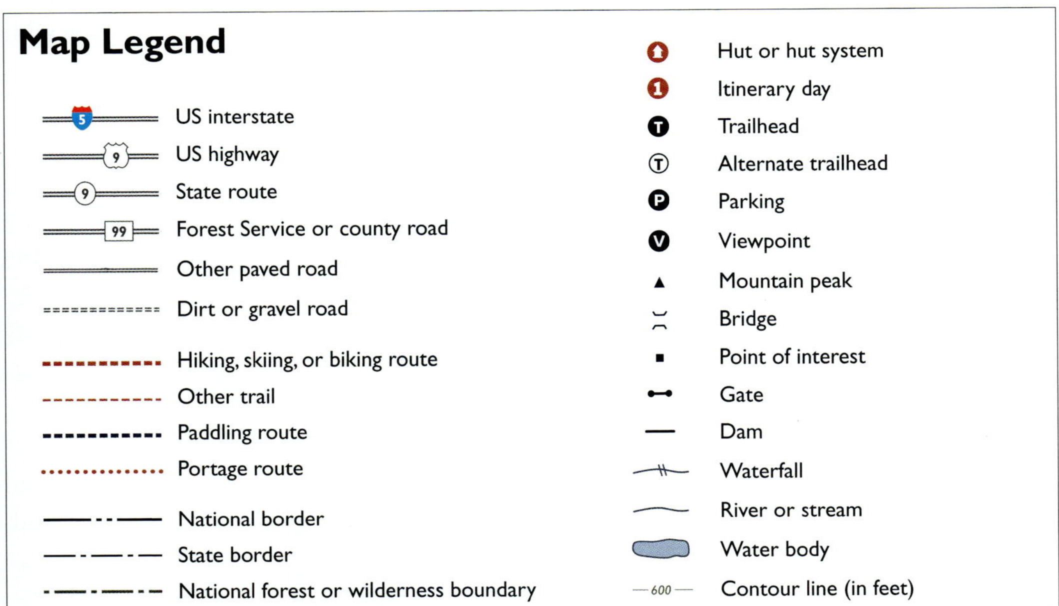

## Map Legend

| | |
|---|---|
| US interstate | Hut or hut system |
| US highway | Itinerary day |
| State route | Trailhead |
| Forest Service or county road | Alternate trailhead |
| Other paved road | Parking |
| Dirt or gravel road | Viewpoint |
| Hiking, skiing, or biking route | Mountain peak |
| Other trail | Bridge |
| Paddling route | Point of interest |
| Portage route | Gate |
| | Dam |
| National border | Waterfall |
| State border | River or stream |
| National forest or wilderness boundary | Water body |
| | Contour line (in feet) |

for field use for the easier, more straightforward systems. Hut systems usually provide paper maps to carry or GPX files to download. Under "Planning and Preparation," we indicate when travelers should acquire additional maps and GPX files.

## CHOOSING A HUT SYSTEM

Each hut system has a distinct character, shaped by a specific locale and the vision or unique energy of the host organization or founder. Some offer extensive networks of trails and lodgings, while others are confined to one route and only a few huts. Many are seasonal, welcoming skiers in winter or hikers and bikers in summer; others operate in multiple seasons. Hut accommodations can be really basic or almost luxurious; some systems provide tasty meals, while most expect their clients to carry and prepare their own food.

Spend time perusing this book with an open mind and active imagination. Read the introductory material and skim the pictures and chapters dedicated to specific hut systems. Begin to compile criteria for your journey. Check out the US Hut Systems map (near the beginning of the book) to get a sense of where opportunities exist. Make an initial list of appealing and appropriate hut systems. Once you have identified some options you find attractive, study the relevant itineraries.

### CHOOSE YOUR COMPANIONS

Before going too far down the planning road, be clear about who will share this adventure. While most folks travel hut-to-hut in small friend or family groups, some travel alone. The solo traveler will focus on hut systems that rent by the bunk. Groups—including couples—should define roles and discuss expectations, fears, and foibles early

*Kids enjoy a cookout at the Tenth Mountain Division Fowler-Hilliard Hut.* (Photo by Jenifer Blomquist)

# HUTS AND KIDS

Children love hut trips. These rustic adventures with family and friends often count among the most cherished memories of childhood. Some hut systems, including the Appalachian Mountain Club (AMC) huts, have special kids' activities, as well as evening nature programs. Most children find certain huts to be both playground and personalized camp. Hut trips can offer just the right bonding experience for families with teenagers. Some hut systems have age limits or guidelines about which huts are most appropriate for the youngest of children. Ask about the most kid-friendly huts during your pre-booking phone call with system staff. For example, the AMC strongly suggests that families with children under three stay only in the smaller huts. Ultimately, parents must determine when their child is ready for a hut trip and make plans that ensure safety and fun.

To travel under their own power to a hut, a child should already be a seasoned hiker or skier, at least for the distances in question. To prepare, get out on the trail for day trips to build familiarity and stamina.

Remember that small children cannot carry their full share of food and gear. Divide up the weight among others. Parents should also take extra care with emergency planning: prepare for the unexpected, and figure out who might carry the child if they can't make the distance. Focus on huts with short access hikes if your children are very young.

How your children act around others is particularly important for by-the-bunk hut systems. Their behavior will affect others. Make sure they are comfortable and considerate when sharing space with strangers. And be prepared to monitor their behavior as well. Keep them from romping around in stairwells, on woodpiles, and near woodstoves and from playing with dangerous tools such as saws and axes. Keep them out of a busy kitchen, unless they are part of your cook crew.

Renting an exclusive-use cabin with friends is a good way to start cultivating your kids' social skills related to communal living, sharing, and consideration for others.

in the planning process. Each group should have a leader who steers the planning process and attends to all the details. Will children be part of your group? (See "Huts and Kids.") Is your dog essential to all family outings, including hut trips? Be aware that few hut systems allow pets.

## ASSESS YOUR ABILITIES AND FITNESS LEVELS

Hut-to-hut adventures are not for beginners; hut travelers should build on their existing skills and trail experiences. The multiday hike, ski, or bike, with loaded packs, extends proven capabilities and intensifies known

# ADVENTURE WITHOUT THE WEIGHT

*All the paraphernalia of a journey can be such a hindrance, so I discard most every-thing, but then sleeping apparel, paper robe, and raincoat, inkstone, brush and paper, medicine, lunch basket, and so on, wrapping them all up and hoisting them onto my back—legs wobbly and body weak—I felt as if I was being dragged backwards and I barely made any headway at all, feeling nothing but misery.*

—Matsuo Bashō, "The Knapsack Notebook"

A major advantage of hut-to-hut travel is that you get the adventure without the weight. For most US hut trips, you do not need to bring a tent, a cookstove, fuel, cooking and eating utensils, or a sleeping pad. You can still expect to bear the weight of clothing, foul-weather gear, food, a sleeping bag, emergency supplies, and optional personal items.

To gauge how heavy the "weightless" hut trip might be, we weighed a backpack with everything needed for a four-day hiking trip staying in self-service huts. This pack included all the items on the Essential Gear and Essential Clothing packing lists, plus the first seven items on the Optional Gear and Clothing list. With ten pounds of food and two liters of water, the pack (capacity fifty-eight liters) weighed twenty-seven pounds. By comparison, a four-day trip in a full-service hut system eliminated the need for the sleeping bag and food; pack weight went down to less than twenty pounds and fit in a thirty-to-forty-liter pack.

Winter hut-to-hut travel requires a larger pack and heavier loads because of extra cloth-ing and emergency gear. We added all the essential items from the ski gear and clothing lists to the Essential Gear and Essential Clothing lists (along with the same seven optional extras), and the weight came to thirty-seven pounds and fit in a sixty-liter pack.

pleasures. When you plan for a group, make realistic assessments of each member's fitness level. As a rule of thumb, plan for the least fit or prepared among you. Consider how far you wish to travel each day, and factor in weather and hours of daylight. Winter days are short, especially in the northern reaches of the country. Review your experiences to date: Have you spent days on trail with a full pack? Do you need to institute a training regimen to get in shape? For winter backcountry ski trips, be brutally honest in evaluating your skills and comfort with risks posed by cold, capricious weather, altitude, and extreme terrain.

## CONSIDER PREFERENCES FOR COMFORT AND CONVIVILIATY

Keep in mind that not all hut systems are created equal when it comes to amenities. Look into your hearts; take the pulse of the group. Will you be happy overnighting in a simple plywood box with a roof, bunks, a wood-stove, a gas range to prepare meals, and an outhouse? Or do you seek a more roomy and comfortable shelter with indoor toilets, separate dining and sleeping rooms, and prepared meals? To help sort this out, pay close attention to the hut system amenities rating and descriptions. Backcountry hut travel offers wonderful opportunities for socializing on the trail and in the huts themselves. Sharing the kitchen and the common table and collectively keeping the fire burning bright contribute to a sense of community. If this sounds heavenly, focus on systems that rent by the bunk. If you prefer greater solitude or aim to rely on existing family and friendship ties for social magic, look for exclusive-use hut systems. (See "Rent a Bunk or the Whole Hut?")

## DECIDE WHERE, HOW, AND WHEN

When choosing a hut adventure, focus first on geography, travel modalities, and season. Hut systems in the US are mainly in the Northeast or the West. Some lucky souls will be able to go local, choosing a hut system by proximity to their home turf. But many of us must go a good distance to connect with the American hut-to-hut experience. What type of terrain draws you? While most hut systems are in the mountains, some are sited among gentle slopes, and others are perched atop steep inclines. Are you drawn to high-profile destinations such as Yosemite National Park, Mount Rainier, or New Hampshire's White Mountains? Will you answer the siren call of the Alaska wilderness? Or venture to the only two US hut

systems not in the mountains, Montana's American Prairie Reserve or Minnesota's Boundary Country Trekking?

How do you choose to travel hut-to-hut? Are you a hiker, skier, or biker? Or do you prefer snowshoes? Most hut systems were established to shelter either hikers or skiers. Biking has expanded operating seasons for many hut systems, and has stimulated the opening of at least one set of dedicated bike hostelries (see San Juan Huts in Part III). While a few hut systems operate year-round, most have a primary season: winter for systems most popular with skiers, and summer for systems inaugurated by hikers. Some have the conditions to support robust summer and winter seasons. Hut-to-hut travel opportunities can be very limited in late fall and in spring.

## DETERMINE HOW MUCH TIME YOU HAVE

Because our basic definition of a hut system comprises three or more connected huts, the itineraries in this book require more than a long weekend to execute, especially when factoring in travel to a site. This book provides options for journeys lasting five to ten days (including travel and rest days). You can almost always organize a shorter sojourn; just do part of the route. Or pick a short itinerary such as the Three Sisters Backcountry huts in Oregon. Remember to build in extra time to acclimate to altitude if you are focusing on a high mountain hut system.

## CONSIDER HOW MUCH YOU WANT TO SPEND

Costs vary a lot, depending on the system and amenities. Renting by the bunk can cost less than $20 a night. A night at a full-service hut system—meals included—will cost $100 or more per person. It is impossible to generalize except to state that costs vary by length of trip, size of group, travel costs to and from the locale, menu choices, and more.

## THINK ABOUT HIRING A GUIDE

Even moderately experienced hikers, skiers, and bikers are capable of planning every aspect of a hut-to-hut adventure on their own. But some may seek extra support to explore this arena of multiday human-powered travel. Look for guided group trips; some systems organize their own. The Yosemite High Sierra Camps offer a ranger-guided option, which garners rave reviews. The Appalachian Mountain Club hosts lodge-to-hut and hut-to-hut outings with expert guides in New Hampshire's White Mountains. There is a long-established tradition of backcountry outfitters and independent guides, especially in the American West. We hired guides for support in Colorado's Tenth Mountain Division system, because of challenges related to winter wayfinding and difficult terrain.

## HONING THE PLAN

Once you have identified a few attractive options for a hut-to-hut trip, consult not only the relevant itineraries in this book but also the hut system's website. Review operating season dates and reservation and cancellation procedures and policies. Expand your knowledge of the region by consulting books and other sources on geography, terrain, and natural and cultural history.

Prepare a list of questions to guide a telephone conversation with staff at your favored hut system. Consider logistics: Will you do a circuit returning to the same trailhead or a traverse requiring transportation at the end? Where will you stay before and after the trip? If the itinerary includes a rest day, what activities should not be missed—swimming, fishing, summiting nearby peaks, downhill powder runs?

Get in touch with the hut system. Find out about liability waivers, keys and access codes, necessary permits, policies on outdoor fires and pets, dates of hunting and fishing seasons, and safety provisions and precautions. Ask for relevant maps. See Resources for a list of books and articles useful for planning and dreaming.

## MAKING A RESERVATION

After you have completed the research phase of the planning process, it's time to make a reservation. Most hut systems in this book are very popular; weekend reservations can be difficult to come by. Newer systems including the American Prairie Reserve and Adirondack Hamlets to Huts are still building audiences and can be easier to book. The Tenth Mountain Division huts, Yosemite High Sierra Camps, and Mount Tahoma Trails Association use a lottery system to address greater demand than supply. Pay attention to advance booking provisions of each system and plan accordingly. For example, some of the Alaska backcountry huts can be booked six months in advance. We have heard stories of folks going online in the wee hours of the morning exactly 180 days before

*High mountain huts, like the Fowler-Hilliard Hut in the Tenth Mountain Division Hut System, beckon with the promise of warmth and comfort.*

their desired dates in order to maximize chances of getting what they want.

With reservations on the calendar, you can move on to checking your gear against packing lists and researching travel options. From here on out, preparing for the hut-to-hut adventure follows the same course as other trips. Enjoy!

## PACKING

The art of packing involves assembling clothing and gear sufficient to keep you comfortable and safe while avoiding unnecessary weight. Beyond certain essentials, what you carry depends on the hut system's level of amenities, terrain, weather, trip length, mode of travel, and personal choices (see "Adventure Without the Weight"). Each hut system's website details what is provided at the hut and what to bring. The packing lists we provide will help you decide what is essential and what is optional. While our lists are not ultralight in approach, they aim to minimize weight.

Start with our lists, then modify to suit your needs. Keep it simple; err on the side of less stuff. Unplug and don't bring electronic games, laptops, and music players. Most huts have cards and board games, and a few provide guitars. Consider bringing a harmonica or other compact instrument.

Start with a good pack, with a capacity tailored to your itinerary. Advanced gear design now provides impressive options in the backpack market; choose a lightweight pack with good suspension, sternum straps, and a padded waist belt. Don't forget the waterproof rain cover. We also recommend using a pack liner for extra protection.

# THE TEN ESSENTIALS

The Ten Essentials, a list developed by The Mountaineers, is a great place to start when packing—whether you're headed out for a day trip or a multiday adventure. The point of the Ten Essentials has always been to answer two basic questions: Can you prevent emergencies and respond positively should one occur, and can you safely spend a night—or more—outside? Use this list as a guide, and tailor it to the needs of your outing.

1. Navigation (map and compass)
2. Sun protection (sunglasses, sunscreen, hat)
3. Insulation (extra clothing and layers, including raingear)
4. Illumination (headlamp or flashlight)
5. First-aid supplies
6. Fire materials (firestarter and matches or a lighter)
7. Repair kit and tools including a knife or multitool
8. Extra food
9. Extra water
10. Emergency shelter

These packing lists are designed to work together in preparing for different forms of travel and in different seasons. The items on the first three lists form the basic kit for hiking trips. For a skiing or biking trip, add from the specific lists as needed. Within groups, divide shared items including the first-aid kit, emergency shelters, repair kits, cookstove, and pots among individuals. Adjustments to clothing lists will depend on mode and season of travel.

These first three lists are tailored for a typical hut-to-hut hiking trip in a basic or self-service hut from spring through fall. Pack all the items from the Essential Gear and Essential Clothing lists, and pack selectively from the Optional Gear and Clothing list.

## ESSENTIAL GEAR

The following list of critical gear includes the Ten Essentials, outlined in the sidebar above, as well as other items you will find essential:

- Sleeping bag
- Headlamp with extra batteries
- Topographic trail maps and compass
- Copy of your trip itinerary
- Key or combination to hut lock
- First-aid kit, including moleskin or other blister remedies
- Water and wide-mouth water bottles or hydration system (two liters per person)
- Food, including snacks
- Small pocketknife
- Nylon cord

- UV-protective sunglasses
- Sunscreen and lip balm
- Lighter or matches
- Whistle
- Duct tape
- Route description or guidebook
- Toilet kit: toothbrush, soap, comb, personal medications, washcloth or small towel
- Watch
- Bandana
- Hat
- Windbreaker or raincoat (with hood) and waterproof, breathable pants
- Firestarter
- Trash bag
- Emergency shelter

## ESSENTIAL CLOTHING

In addition to what you are wearing as you set out on the trail, including sturdy walking shoes or boots suited to the terrain, bring along the following items:

- One or two extra pairs of socks, depending on conditions and duration of trip
- One pair of pants and a long-sleeve shirt
- Extra underwear and a T-shirt, or a small amount of biodegradable laundry soap and a few clothespins
- Long underwear
- Insulating layer such as a wool sweater, down or fleece vest, or heavy wool shirt
- Wool hat
- Gloves or mittens
- Hut slippers or light shoes to use in hut and for trips to the outhouse

Clothing should be wool or wicking synthetic material appropriate to the terrain and weather. Cotton is not recommended except for optional hut wear. Unless you are out for more than four days, an extra pair of pants and extra shirt are generally not needed.

## OPTIONAL GEAR AND CLOTHING

These extras can come in handy, depending on your personal preference and your destination:

- Reading material
- Cell phone for camera, emergency use, and navigation apps
- External battery to charge cell phone
- Hut clothing (can be cotton)
- Trekking pole(s)
- Insect repellent
- Camera
- Pen or pencil and notebook
- Candle
- GPS device
- Earplugs
- Personal beacon (e.g., Garmin inReach or SPOT), to summon emergency rescue if needed
- Water treatment system (for trail and emergency use)
- Pillowcase
- Toilet paper, trowel, and hand sanitizer for trail use
- Head net
- Gaiters
- Swimsuit
- Brandy, candy, or other indulgences

## BIKING GEAR

The amount and type of clothing will vary by season. In addition to the items listed

*Bunks with mattresses are standard in every US hut system except Alaska's basic huts.*

above, the following items complete your kit for biking:

- Large-volume hydration pack (seventy to one hundred ounces)
- Panniers or bike bags (up to twenty liters total, assuming food and water are provided at the hut)
- Mountain bike, helmet, and bike repair kit
- Cycling shorts with chamois crotch
- Lightweight synthetic T-shirt or sleeveless shirt
- Riding gloves, cycling socks, and cycling shoes
- Windbreaker

For more detail, see *The Bikers' Bible* by the San Juan Hut Systems (see Resources).

## SKIING GEAR

Your skis and related gear will depend on the terrain, snow conditions, and whether the trails are groomed, or groomed and tracked. The variety of ski types on offer can be bewildering. We break these into three basic types: classic, metal-edged touring, and telemark or alpine touring skis.

**Classic cross-country skis.** Recommended for groomed and tracked routes, these are the most popular type of Nordic ski but not ideal for ungroomed backcountry conditions. Skate skis, requiring wide, groomed pathways, are not generally used for skiing hut-to-hut; Methow Trails in Washington provides one of the best and only opportunities to use skate skis on a hut adventure.

**Metal-edged touring skis.** These skis are recommended for groomed and ungroomed trails. Metal edges provide greater control in ungroomed conditions. Wider metal-edged skis are sometimes called backcountry skis.

**Telemark and alpine touring skis.** These skis are recommended for ungroomed trails and downhill slopes. Equipped with bindings that have both free-heel and locked-heel modes, these wide, short skis worn with heavy plastic boots are best suited to those who combine backcountry treks with thrilling downhill runs full of turns.

We recommend wide (at least 65 millimeters), no-wax, metal-edged touring or backcountry skis for most systems in this book. However, you should adopt the equipment that suits you best—which may be your own waxable skis. When selecting poles, choose a larger basket if you plan to venture into untracked territory and deep powder zones. Consult your local outdoor store for further guidance.

Experienced Nordic skiers will most likely choose to bring their own equipment on hut-to-hut adventures. If you plan to rent ski gear, research rental outlets near your target hut system in advance. Phone ahead to locate the proper equipment and inquire about costs and operating hours. Do not assume that a ski shop will carry Nordic or cross-country equipment; many only supply downhill ski gear. Ask detailed questions. Allow time for renting and returning equipment in your trip schedule.

The following gear and clothing (with adjustments for season and mode of travel) complete your kit for skiing. If these items are unfamiliar, you probably shouldn't be skiing hut-to-hut without a guide.

## Essential Ski Gear

Every skier should bring the following items:

- Skis, poles, and boots suited to the conditions of the hut system
- Sleeping bag, ideally rated down to at least 0 degrees Fahrenheit
- Warm hat(s); one thin and one thicker hat are more versatile and can be worn together

- Ski goggles
- Wax kit with cork and applicator (if using waxable skis)
- Climbing skins
- Emergency shelter: bivouac sack, foam pad, ground cloth, and backcountry snow shovel
- Signaling mirror
- Stove and pot for emergency use
- Knee-high gaiters
- One ski repair kit per group, including screwdrivers, binding screws, plumber's putty, zip ties, baling wire, extra binding, and spare cables for telemark bindings

## Essential Ski Clothing

Experienced skiers will know what works for them. Here's what we recommend:

- Parka or anorak
- Neck gaiter or balaclava
- One pair gloves or mittens
- One pair heavy over-mittens
- Ski touring pants (knickers, pants, or tights)
- Two to three pairs of extra wool socks
- Shell layers: waterproof hooded jacket and pants
- Long underwear (top and bottom)
- Hut slippers

## Optional Ski Gear and Clothing

These items depend in part on the terrain you will be skiing:

- Avalanche safety gear: beacon (transceiver), shovel, and probe pole
- Hut clothes (can be cotton)
- Day pack or fanny pack for day tours

- Thermos
- Altimeter (essential in remote mountain terrain)

## FOOD

Food is not only fuel but also entertainment, with snacks and meals highlighting each day. For full-service hut trips, you bring only snacks and sometimes also lunches. The self-service hut-to-hut journey requires menu planning and heavier loads of food. Some hut regulars haul fixings for hearty gourmet meals accompanied by wine and other libations. Others take their cues from tent-toting backpackers and rely on lightweight dehydrated meals. Make sure you get enough calories. Your food bag will get progressively lighter throughout the trip.

We suggest aiming somewhere between elaborate scratch cooking and freeze-dried meals. Pack light. Once you compose a menu and shop for provisions, eliminate bulky packaging and measure and repackage ingredients, including dry spices, salt, and pepper, in ziplock bags. We usually stick with oatmeal for breakfast, with daily servings premeasured and seasoned with dried fruit, salt, cinnamon, and a little sugar. Dump in some trail mix or nuts at the end of cooking for extra crunch and nutrients. Plastic bags can be washed and saved or used to hold garbage. Make lunch in advance, or take fixings easy to prepare on trail. Wraps and rye crackers are light and survive well in your packs. Simply slather with peanut butter, some cheese and mustard, or the contents of a flavored tuna pack. Dinner possibilities are limited only by your imaginations, weight tolerance, and

cooking experience. As almost all US huts are equipped with gas stoves, you don't have to limit yourselves to the quickest cooking options in order to conserve fuel. That said, everyone will be hungry, so plan meals that can be made without fuss.

Except in huts rated basic, kitchens are stocked with the pots, pans, and utensils needed for meal preparation, and dishes and cutlery for eating. There is always some kind of coffeemaker. Allow extra cooking time at high altitude.

## STAYING SAFE

Safety should anchor every step of trip preparation. Communication is key. With your group, review not only the itinerary but also wayfinding methods on trail. Make sure everyone is familiar with safety resources and procedures.

### PLAN AHEAD WITH YOUR GROUP

Traveling with others is generally safer than going solo. However, groups require an experienced leader, whose role is to make the final decision in the case of serious, risk-related circumstances. The leader, and ideally each member of the group, should have a realistic assessment—in advance—of the skills, fitness, and capabilities of each member of the party, and a good grasp of group dynamics. And each member should be prepared to help others as needed. Arrange for a guide if necessary to ensure safety.

Review the route in advance and engage everyone in wayfinding. Identify alternative routes, and be prepared to adjust your itinerary if things don't go according to plan.

*Maintaining the huts of the Southwest Nordic Center includes such invigorating tasks as snow removal, which the SWNC owner does regularly.*

On trail, assign a lead and a sweep who takes up the rear, and observe protocols for ensuring the group stays together.

## NOTIFY SOMEONE ABOUT YOUR PLANS

Be sure to leave a copy of your itinerary, including date and time of departure and return and emergency contact information, with a responsible person to initiate search efforts if you do not return as planned. Be sure to have emergency phone numbers (e.g., hut system and search and rescue), along with hut lock combinations or hut keys, with you on trail. Take a picture of keycodes and entry instructions with your phone or otherwise back up vital information.

## KNOW THE TRAIL MARKERS

Most, but not all, hut system trails are well marked with some combination of tree blazes, diamond-shaped markers, colored streamers affixed to trees, and cairns. A few, such as the Yosemite High Sierra Camps, feature trails so well worn that markers are not required. Man-made markers are discouraged in formally designated wilderness areas and largely absent on some trails. We provide more detailed navigation notes when systems pose wayfinding challenges. Before embarking, study the maps and navigation instructions to determine how and whether the trail is marked, and the nature of the terrain. On trail, train yourself to be vigilant in watching for markers; become familiar with the types, frequency, locations, and patterns of trail markers.

## BE READY TO NAVIGATE

Take maps, bring a compass, and read the navigation directions in advance. A GPS device can be very helpful and is specifically recommended for systems with few trail markings and/or confusing terrain. Where wayfinding is difficult, we include GPS

# A NOTE ABOUT SAFETY

Safety is an important concern in all outdoor activities. No guidebook can alert you to every hazard or anticipate the limitations of every reader. Therefore, the descriptions of roads, trails, routes, and natural features in this book are not representations that a particular place or excursion will be safe for your party. When you follow any of the routes described in this book, you assume responsibility for your own safety. Under normal conditions, such excursions require the usual attention to traffic, road and trail conditions, weather, terrain, the capabilities of your party, and other factors. Keeping informed on current conditions and exercising common sense are the keys to a safe, enjoyable outing.

—Mountaineers Books

coordinates in the itinerary descriptions. In exposed terrain with few or no trail markers, it may be necessary to use an altimeter; such cases are noted. When you download a map to a GPS app, double-check before you leave wireless range to ensure that the map is reliably available on your device. Also before departure, be sure to mark the precise locations of the destination huts on your paper and GPS maps. This will save you time and trouble when it comes to actually finding your day's destination!

Once on trail, focus on your surroundings. Be alert to the trail underfoot, landmarks, trail junctions, road crossings, and other markers. Pause to verify your location by map and compass at regular intervals, even on easy trails. It is good practice. GPS phone apps (with maps downloaded in advance) or dedicated GPS devices can be very helpful in determining precise location and in tracking progress. *But in the end, an electronic device should not replace the map and compass. Cultivate these skills!* If you use a GPS device, bring an external battery large enough to maintain power for the duration of a multiday trip. When on the trail, be prepared to stop and retrace your steps if it has been more than fifteen to twenty minutes (more or less depending on the pattern of markers) since you last sighted the well-trod way, a trail blaze, a diamond, or some other indication that you are on track. Better to take the time to verify the course sooner rather than later.

## PLAN FOR THE WORST-CASE SCENARIO

What will cause you to abort the trip? To turn back prematurely? As part of your preparations, discuss what might go wrong and how to adapt plans accordingly. When making the reservation, learn as much as possible from the hut system folks about the terrain, trail conditions, and special health and safety concerns. Are there difficult stream crossings? Is lightning an issue?

Discuss these and other contingencies in relation to your group's skill level during the pre-trip phone call. In winter, what do the hut system folks recommend if a blizzard strikes? Do you have the relevant emergency telephone numbers, and is there cell service anywhere? Does hut system staff run checks on guests when adverse weather sets in? Will loved ones feel more comfortable if you carry a communications device such as a Garmin inReach or a SPOT?

On the departure day, check the forecast one last time. Be prepared to change your plans if advisable. Weather, especially heavy rain, fog, and snow, can impair visibility and obscure landmarks, making it easier to get lost. Combined with the tendency of many folks to overestimate their skills and level of conditioning, poor weather conditions can make for dangerous situations. It is very common for less experienced backcountry travelers to underestimate travel time to the hut and to carry too much weight. Be aware and take care.

Winter hut-to-hut travel always skirts danger. Heavy snow, extreme cold, or icy conditions can quickly turn an easy trail into a difficult one. Wayfinding may become impossible during fog or blizzard conditions. Backcountry hut-to-hut skiing allows little margin for error. If you get lost or run out of daylight, be prepared to spend the night outdoors. (Always pack spare, charged headlamp batteries.) For most ski trips, pack emergency supplies including a shovel and shelter, or be prepared to build an emergency snow cave or trench. While this guide avoids hut and trail systems in avalanche terrain, or routes that require expert skiing or technical mountaineering skills, challenges can pop up anywhere in the backcountry.

## KNOW WHO TO CALL IN CASE OF AN EMERGENCY

Ideally, serious injuries on trail and at the huts are treated by search and rescue (SAR) teams, usually coordinated at the county level by the local sheriff's office. Consult with each hut system about regional SAR operations and contacts. Take along local SAR phone numbers in case an accident occurs when you are in cell phone range. When an accident occurs out of cell phone range, one or more members of the party might hike, ski, or bike to contact the SAR office by phone. More people are now using a personal beacon (e.g., Garmin inReach or SPOT) to call for help and pinpoint their position in case a rescue is needed.

SAR services are very expensive. To avoid exorbitant bills, research insurance options. Membership in the American Alpine Club includes a rescue benefit (see www.american alpineclub.org/rescue). Some states sell SAR cards, using the revenue to reimburse SAR teams after the fact. Two examples are the Colorado Outdoor Recreation Search and Rescue card (see https://cdola.colorado .gov/funding-programs/search-and-rescue -fund) and the New Hampshire Fish and Game Department's Hike Safe cards (see www.wildlife.state.nh.us/safe/).

NEXT PAGE: *With more than 350 public use cabins, Alaska has vast opportunities for hut trips. Devil's Pass Cabin is one of eight cabins along the Resurrection Pass Trail on the Kenai Peninsula.*

# FEATURED HUT SYSTEMS

**IN THIS SECTION**, we introduce sixteen hut systems across the US and present all the information you need to dream about and plan to visit them. Our definition of a **hut system** guided the selection: three or more backcountry huts spaced a day's walk, ski, or bike apart, designed to be traveled in sequence, and connected by a trail system supporting a traverse or circuit over a period of days or weeks. A few of the featured systems have only two huts; we opted to include them in order to represent more parts of the country, or because a

# FEATURED HUTS AT A GLANCE

| | STATE | NUMBER OF HUTS | BEDS IN SYSTEM | AMENITIES | RESERVATION FORMAT | | MILES IN FEATURED ITINERARY |
|---|---|---|---|---|---|---|---|
| | | | | | EXCLUSIVE USE | BY THE BUNK | |
| **NORTHEAST** | | | | | | | |
| Maine Huts and Trails | ME | 4 | 168 | SS | | ✓ | 42.7 |
| Appalachian Mountain Club Huts | NH | 8 | 414 | FS (in season) | | ✓ | 59.6 |
| Adirondack Hamlets to Huts | NY | N/A | N/A | FS and SS | ✓ | | 46.1 |
| **MIDWEST** | | | | | | | |
| Porcupine Mountains Wilderness State Park | MI | 13 | 54 | SS | ✓ | | 22.7 |
| Boundary Country Trekking | MN | 2 | 14 | SS | ✓ | | 20.8 |
| **COLORADO** | | | | | | | |
| Never Summer Nordic | CO | 3 | 24 | SS | ✓ | | 11.7 |
| Tenth Mountain Division Hut System | CO | 34 | 417 | SS | | ✓ | 13.3 or 26.3 |
| Southwest Nordic Center | CO | 4 | 24 | SS | ✓ | | 17.3 |
| San Juan Huts | CO | 16 | 128 | SS and SS+ | | ✓ | 29.5 or 142.7 |
| **WEST AND ALASKA** | | | | | | | |
| American Prairie Reserve | MT | 3 | 27 | SS | ✓ | | 19.7 |
| Sun Valley Mountain Huts | ID | 6 | 102 | SS | ✓ | ✓ | 14.8 |
| Rendezvous Huts | WA | 5 | 45 | SS | ✓ | | 21.3 |
| Mount Tahoma Trails | WA | 4 | 42 | SS | | ✓ | 25 |
| Three Sisters Backcountry | OR | 2 | 16 | SS+ | ✓ | ✓ | 21 |
| Yosemite High Sierra Camps | CA | 5 | 204 | FS | | ✓ | 48 |
| Resurrection Pass Trail | AK | 8 | 56 | B | ✓ | | 38.8 |

*Note:* This table includes data on huts located in traverses only; data does not include huts or beds that are not practical to link with others for a multiday traverse.

system offers a satisfying, if short, hut-to-hut experience. We made some other judgment calls in relation to public use cabins in Alaska and Michigan that we felt were worthy of inclusion in this guide. While these cabin-rich systems may not have been designed primarily for hut-to-hut travel, they work well for multiday human-powered journeys. We also highlight a few new experimental systems that expand our definition and perhaps represent ways in which hut travel could grow in the future.

| HIKE | BIKE | FAT BIKE | SKI | SNOWSHOE | PADDLE | DIFFICULTY | GEAR SHUTTLE | GUIDING AVAILABLE | HUTS STAFFED |
|---|---|---|---|---|---|---|---|---|---|
| ✓ | ✓ |  | ✓ | ✓ | ✓ | Easy to moderate | Yes | Yes | Volunteers |
| ✓ |  |  | ✓ | ✓ |  | Moderate to difficult | No | Yes | Yes |
| ✓ | ✓ |  | ✓ | ✓ | ✓ | Easy to difficult | Yes | Yes | N/A |
| ✓ |  |  | ✓ | ✓ |  | Easy | No | No | No |
|  |  | ✓ | ✓ | ✓ |  | Novice to intermediate | Yes | No | No |
| ✓ | ✓ |  | ✓ | ✓ |  | Novice | No | No | No |
| ✓ | ✓ |  | ✓ | ✓ |  | Novice to advanced | No | Yes | No |
|  |  |  | ✓ | ✓ |  | Intermediate | No | No | No |
| ✓ | ✓ |  | ✓ |  |  | Easy to difficult | No | No | No |
| ✓ | ✓ |  |  |  | ✓ | Easy | No | Yes | No |
| ✓ | ✓ |  | ✓ | ✓ |  | Novice to intermediate | Yes | Yes | No |
| ✓ | ✓ | ✓ | ✓ | ✓ |  | Novice to intermediate | Yes | No | No |
| ✓ | ✓ |  | ✓ | ✓ |  | Novice to intermediate | Yes | No | Volunteers |
|  |  |  | ✓ |  |  | Intermediate to advanced | No | No | No |
| ✓ |  |  |  |  |  | Moderate to difficult | No | Yes | Yes |
| ✓ | ✓ |  |  |  |  | Easy to moderate | No | No | No |

The amenities listings use several acronyms: B for basic; SS for self-service; SS+ for self-service+; FS for full service.

## MAINE HUTS AND TRAILS

*I do not know of any poetry to quote which adequately expresses this yearning for the Wild. . . . Mythology comes nearer to it than anything.*

—Henry David Thoreau, *Walking*

**Location:** Carrabassett Valley and Bigelow Range near Kingfield, Maine
**Distance:** Huts 7 to 12 miles apart; full traverse 42.7 miles
**Elevation gain/loss:** 3300 feet/3190 feet
**Difficulty:** Easy to moderate
**Terrain:** Low-lying mountain trails through forests and near lakes and rivers
**Modes of travel:** Winter skiing and snowshoeing; summer and fall hiking, paddling, and biking
**Season:** Year-round
**Huts:** Four eco-lodges (capacity 32 to 48), self-service, by the bunk

---

**MAINE HUTS AND TRAILS** (MHT) offers four large, comfortable huts along a well-planned traverse nestled in the High Peaks region of west-central Maine. Imagine a family-friendly summer camp offering beautifully designed, light-filled lodges with separate bunkhouses. This hut system is great for up to five days of hut-to-hut travel in summer, fall, and winter. The huts can also serve as woodsy base camps for friend groups, couples, or singles eager to take in mountain views, woodland plants, wildlife, and the waterfalls and waterways of the region.

One of the youngest systems in the US, MHT initially offered a European-style, full-service hut experience, with spacious lodgings and delicious meals (see "Founder's Story"). The four huts and connecting trails were the first step toward an eventual goal of twelve eco-lodges stretched along 180 miles of mostly new trail in the heart of Maine. Located midway between the Appalachian Mountain Club's eight huts in the White Mountain National Forest and Maine Wilderness Lodges near

OPPOSITE: *Adirondack Hamlets to Huts and others in the region incorporate both hiking and paddling in hut trips.* (Photo by John DiGiacomo)

Greenville, MHT could one day provide vital infrastructure for an extended hut-to-hut route across northern New England. Despite gorgeous lodges, good trails, and year-round operations, MHT has struggled. In 2019, this nonprofit shifted from full-service to self-service and replaced paid hut managers with volunteers.

West-central Maine, home to Sugarloaf ski resort, abounds in scenery and recreational opportunities. The High Peaks region boasts ten of Maine's fourteen mountains higher than 4000 feet. With West Peak (4150 feet) and Avery Peak (4090 feet) defining the horizon, trampers travel the same mountain chain as New Hampshire's White Mountains but without the crowds or high ridges. The MHT route through coniferous and mixed hardwood forests features special places including Grand Falls and Flagstaff Lake, a vast, watery expanse with intimate loon nesting sites.

Winter is a great season to visit these huts and trails, which are groomed and well suited for brisk ski treks with a few challenging ups and downs. Enjoy rhythmic glimpses of sky and open space through tall, columnar trees with each glide.

Summer and fall offer opportunities for hiking, paddling, and biking. Trails vary from wide paths flanked by towering evergreens, to narrow tracks on wooded hillsides, to fecund wetland boardwalks. The hiking is easy, so enjoy the seasonal wildflowers in summer and the technicolor foliage in fall. Following rainy periods, be prepared for wet or muddy footing through meadows and streambeds.

A paddling option was recently added to the summer season mix. Hikers leave Flagstaff Hut on foot, tramp about 4 miles, then switch to canoes or kayaks for a 6-mile paddle down the Dead River. Shortly before the river bursts into rapids, haul out the boats, pull on your boots, and hike the final 2 miles to reach Grand Falls Hut. This section of river is part of the 740-mile Northern Forest Canoe Trail, which begins in New York State and finishes in Fort Kent, Maine.

## HUTS AND AMENITIES

The huts within the MHT system embody the gold standard in design and comfort. All designed by architect John Orcutt in a style both woodsy and modern, the four huts elevate rustic shelter to eco-lodge status. The lodge buildings graciously accommodate relaxing, meal prepping, dining, socializing, and grooming and bathing. Features include vaulted great rooms, expansive windows, striking nature photographs, and woodstoves. Every hut offers a screened porch and a library with comfy couches, books, and games to pass evening hours and rest days. Bathrooms are equipped with green plumbing fixtures, including Nepon foam-flush composting toilets, and hot showers.

Separate bunkhouses provide private rooms for couples or groups of three, whereas larger parties and friendly strangers can choose from rooms for four, six, eight,

# FOUNDER'S STORY

Maine Huts and Trails (MHT) is a small nonprofit that opened its first three huts in 2008. Founder Larry Warren, a former president of Sugarloaf ski resort, proposed developing a hut-to-hut system in the 1970s to transform the region into a year-round tourist destination. By the 1990s, his vision began to attract attention, in part due to increasing development and threats by private landowners to eliminate long-cherished public access privileges. Warren devoted his prodigious energy and political connections to making the case for access, preservation, and land stewardship.

Even though he was originally inspired by the Appalachian Mountain Club's White Mountains hut system, Warren ultimately turned down the club's offer to fund his vision in order to keep revenue in the state. He sought support from organizations and philanthropists based in Maine or with significant operations in the region; L.L.Bean, the Chewonki Foundation, Outward Bound, New Balance, and private donors are prominently credited in each hut entryway. The 80 miles of trail, developed and maintained by MHT, are mostly on easements negotiated by Warren.

Located primarily on lands owned by MHT itself, as well as the Penobscot Nation and a number of timber companies, the Maine system reflects cooperation among landowners and a successful effort to maintain public recreational access to private lands. In keeping with Warren's vision, MHT encourages sustainable development and low-impact recreation in this economically challenged region. Partnerships are key to sustaining infrastructure and educational programs. The organization works with groups such as the Trust for Public Land, the Northern Forest Canoe Trail, the New England Mountain Bike Association, Sugarloaf, Colby College, and local businesses to organize volunteers, create special events, and collaborate on regional marketing campaigns.

or twelve. Bunks feature plastic-covered mattresses and pillows; guests provide their own sleeping bag and pillowcase. Underfloor radiant heat in the bunk rooms takes the edge off the winter cold, and insulation plus window screens prevents summer from feeling stifling. Three of the huts can operate off the grid, using solar and hydropower.

## STRATTON BROOK HUT

Stratton Brook Hut (sleeps forty-four) is close to Sugarloaf, the downhill ski resort at the heart of Maine's High Peaks region, and 3.6 miles by trail from the state's largest Nordic center, Sugarloaf Outdoor Center, where you can rent skis, snowshoes, and bikes. Guests enjoy great views of the

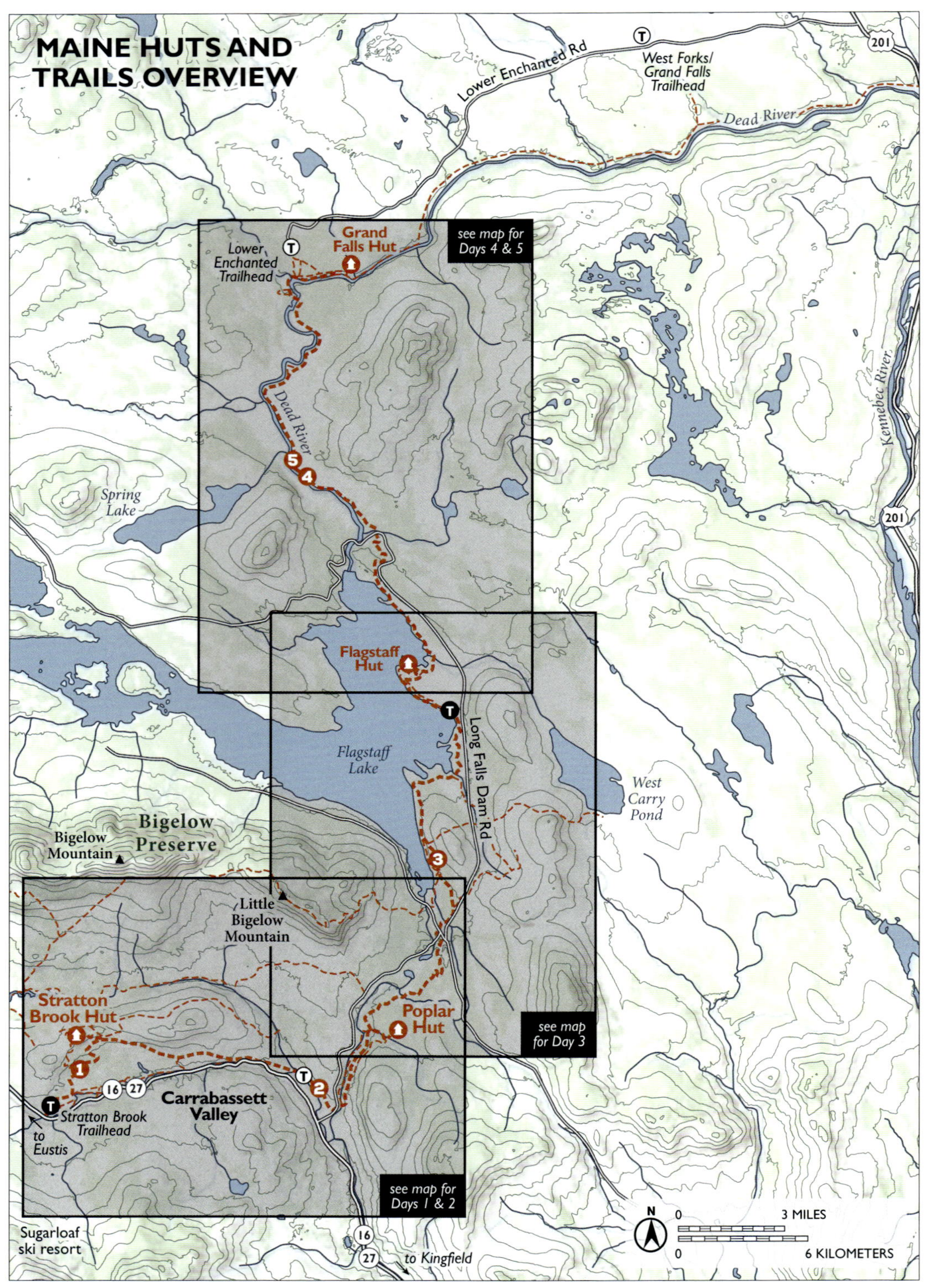
MAINE HUTS AND
TRAILS OVERVIEW
Lower Enchanted Rd
West Forks/
Grand Falls
Trailhead
201
Dead River
Grand
Falls Hut
see map for
Days 4 & 5
Lower
Enchanted
Trailhead
Kennebec River
201
Dead River
Spring
Lake
5 4
Flagstaff
Hut
T
Flagstaff
Lake
Long Falls Dam Rd
West
Carry
Pond
Bigelow
Preserve
Bigelow
Mountain
3
Little
Bigelow
Mountain
Stratton
Brook Hut
Poplar
Hut
see map
for Day 3
1
16 27
T 2
Carrabassett
Valley
T
Stratton Brook
Trailhead
to
Eustis
see map for
Days 1 & 2
Sugarloaf
ski resort
16
27
to Kingfield
N
0        3 MILES
0        6 KILOMETERS

Bigelow Range and Sugarloaf, and ambitious hikers can use the hut as a base camp for day or overnight backpacking visits to several nearby 4000-foot peaks. The newest, this hut embodies lessons learned about design and construction methods for these unique backcountry structures.

## POPLAR HUT

Poplar Hut, offering a tall, central building with separate bunkhouses, was the first built in the MHT system. It features a lovely library in the airy upstairs space, provides easy access to 50 miles of single-track mountain biking trails in Carrabassett Valley, and sleeps up to forty-four people. We recommend side trips to waterfalls with swimming holes.

## FLAGSTAFF HUT

Twisted driftwood accents add character to this handsome horizontal structure situated a short way up the wooded slope from Flagstaff Lake. Because of its proximity to a trailhead and lake access, this is the most popular of the MHT huts. Flagstaff Hut, which sleeps forty-eight, attracts a nearly equal number of visitors in winter and summer. Flagstaff Lake, the fourth largest in Maine, offers opportunities for swimming, boating, and bird-watching from a dock and viewpoints near the hut or along the shore. Canoes, kayaks, and paddleboards are available for free to MHT members; nonmembers can rent them for a nominal fee.

## GRAND FALLS HUT

Perched above the Dead River and a short distance from Grand Falls, this remote hut, the smallest in the MHT constellation (sleeps thirty-two), beckons to hikers, skiers, and anglers. Excellent fly-fishing creeks and the Dead River yield wild brook trout and salmon. Grand Falls Hut serves as a great overnight venue for whitewater enthusiasts braving the Dead River rapids between Grand Falls and the Forks.

## PLANNING AND PREPARATION

**Contact:** www.mainehuts.org; (207) 265-2400; lodging@mainehuts.org

**Booking:** Check availability and make reservations via website or by phone

**Membership:** Not required; individual and family memberships available; members receive a discount on lodging and other services

**Rates:** $; half rate for children age fifteen and under; inquire about additional rates for private rooms or full-hut rental

**Transportation:** Directions to trailheads and other details, including car relocation services and boat rental, available on website

## MAPS

MHT provides a detailed topographical map of the hut system and its trails.

## PACKING TIPS

Bring a pillowcase and sleeping bag. Pack a mosquito head net in summer. Classic skis are recommended in winter.

## OTHER TIPS

Pets are not allowed in huts, and electronic devices are discouraged. A gear shuttle, for packs weighing up to thirty-five pounds, is available by making arrangements before your trip.

*Designed by architect John Orcutt, the MHT huts offer gracious spaces and unique features. (Photo by John Orcutt)*



## ITINERARY: MAINE HUTS AND TRAILS FULL TRAVERSE

### 42.7 miles, five days, four nights

The recommended summer itinerary invites hikers on a five-day Maine woods outing. This route can also be accomplished by foot for the first three days, and by foot *and* canoe or kayak on days 4 and 5. Arrange for canoe or kayak rental in advance with MHT.

The directions for skiing this itinerary hut-to-hut are the same as for hikers, except for a winter diversion to Halfway Yurt, between Poplar Hut and Flagstaff Hut. Halfway Yurt is a perfect stopping place for lunch or a quick rest around a woodstove.

The trail connecting the four MHT huts is called the Maine Hut Trail and is marked with white-and-blue diamonds emblazoned with the organization's logo, as well as with blue paint blazes. A variety of other trails cross and/or join with the Maine Hut Trail, including side and loop trails, the Appalachian Trail (indicated by white blazes), and snowmobile and bike trails. Signs noting trail names and destinations with distances in miles are consistently placed at every junction to aid wayfinding.

## DAY 1: TRAILHEAD TO STRATTON BROOK HUT

**Distance:** 3.1 miles
**Elevation gain/loss:** 660 feet/150 feet
**Difficulty:** Easy to moderate
**Hut elevation:** 1880 feet
**Hut GPS:** 45.100°N, 70.300°W
**Trailhead:** Route 16/27 Stratton Brook Trailhead (45.081°N, 70.317°W)

### Getting There

From Kingfield, head north on State Route 16/27 for about 17 miles. At the intersection with Sugarloaf Access Road, continue straight on SR 16/27 and immediately begin looking on your right for the sign for the Route 16/27 Stratton Brook Trailhead. Overnight parking is permitted, and the trailhead has a vault toilet and kiosk.

### On the Trail

Setting out from the trailhead kiosk, head east on the trail for about 150 yards until it connects with the Narrow Gauge Pathway and turn left (north). After 250 yards, cross a bridge over the Carrabassett River, and then turn right (east) to continue on the Narrow Gauge Pathway for 0.6 mile, roughly paralleling the Carrabassett River.

At the junction with the Maine Hut Trail, turn left (north) and ascend gradually for 1.6 miles to the junction with the Newton's Revenge Trail. Turn left onto the Newton's Revenge Trail for a steep 0.5-mile climb. Look back along this section for some great views. Following trail signs, go left onto a service road for 0.1 mile to Stratton Brook Hut and enjoy fabulous views of Sugarloaf ski resort to the south and the Bigelow Range to the north.

## DAY 2: STRATTON BROOK HUT TO POPLAR HUT

**Distance:** 7.6 miles
**Elevation gain/loss:** 720 feet/1120 feet
**Difficulty:** Moderate
**Hut elevation:** 1314 feet
**Hut GPS:** 45.101°N, 70.185°W

# SHORT ITINERARIES

Since three of the four huts can be reached directly from a nearby trailhead, you might choose to visit only two or three huts, or settle into a single hut for several days.

- Hike Stratton Brook Hut to Poplar Hut, or Poplar Hut to Flagstaff Hut.
- Set up base camp at Stratton Brook Hut to summit Avery Peak and West Peak in the Bigelow Range.
- Set up base camp at Flagstaff Hut to enjoy swimming and canoeing or kayaking.
- Hike Flagstaff Hut to Grand Falls Hut, then raft down the Dead River (make reservations with a separate outfitter).

# DAYS 1 & 2

Little Bigelow Mountain
Appalachian Trail
Bigelow Preserve
Carriage Rd
Poplar Stream
3
service rd
Poplar Hut
Esker Trail
Houston Brook
Houston Brook Rd
Stratton Brook Pond
Mountain Trail
Newton's Revenge Trail
Stratton Brook Hut
Warren's Trail
Poplar Stream Falls
Larry's Trail
Maine Hut Trail
Crommet's Overlook
Carriage Rd
Oak Knoll Trail
Maine Hut Trail
South Brook
2
Carrabassett River
five-way junction
1
to Eustis
Narrow Gauge Pathway
16 27
Airport Trailhead
Sugarloaf Regional Airport
Stratton Brook Trailhead
Sugarloaf ski resort
16 27
Carrabassett River
16 27
to Kingfield
N
0   1 MILE
0   2 KILOMETERS

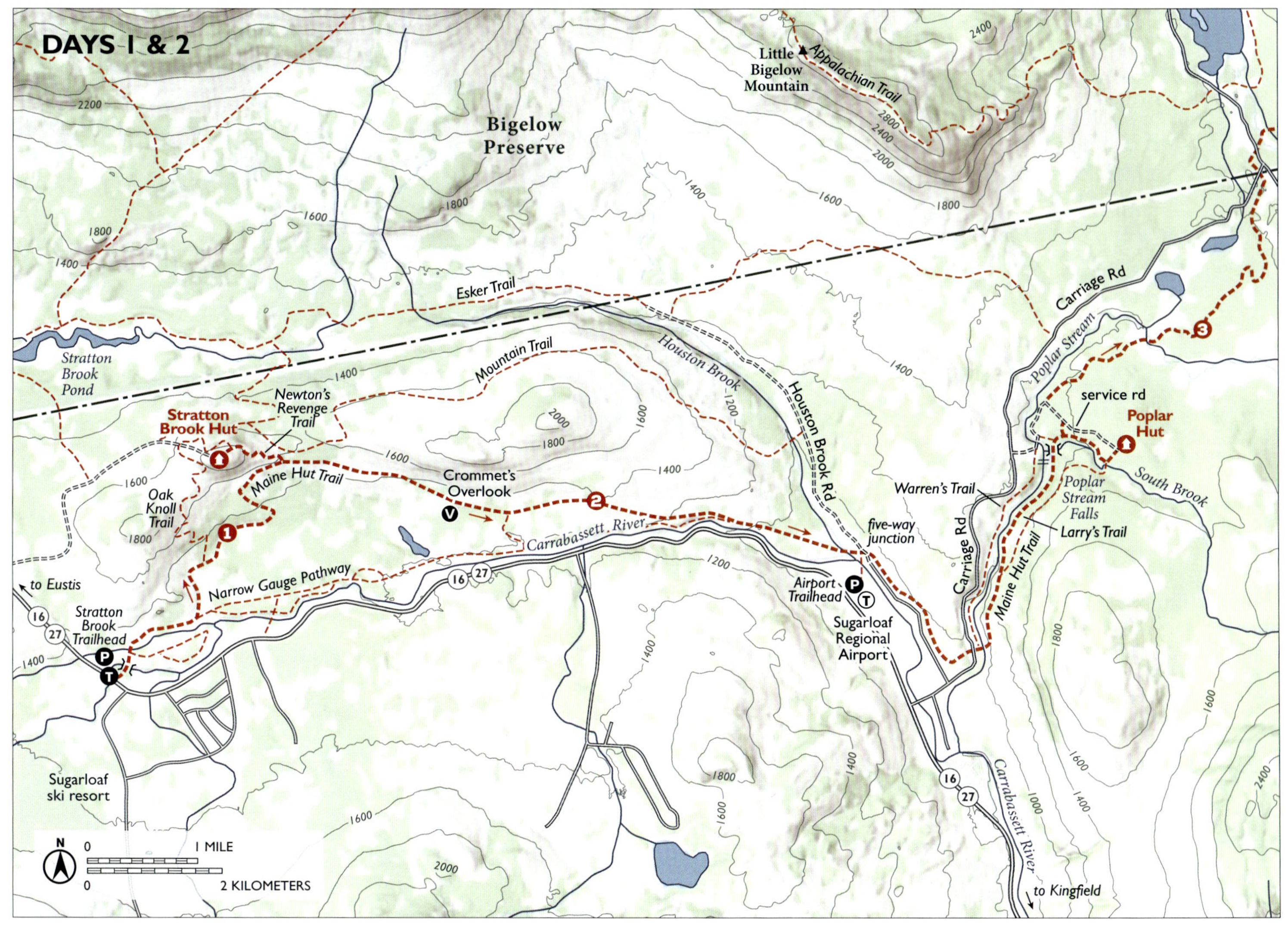

*Stratton Brook Hut looks cozy when the temperature dips below zero.* (Photo by John Orcutt)

Prepare for a steep descent and great views! Retrace yesterday's steps on the Newton's Revenge Trail to the junction with the Maine Hut Trail. Turn left (east) onto the Maine Hut Trail and head steadily downhill (and past an excellent view of Sugarloaf Mountain at Crommett's Overlook). After 3.1 miles, the trail merges with the Narrow Gauge Pathway and begins to level out.

In another 0.8 mile, you reach a five-way junction signed for the Airport Trailhead, Houston Brook Road, and the Narrow Gauge Pathway. This junction can be confusing; make sure to follow the Maine Hut Trail's white-and-blue diamond blazes and signs.

After about 0.7 mile, the trail turns from a southeast direction and heads northeast to cross Carriage Road. Continue across Carriage Road and soon reach a junction offering two routes to Poplar Hut: via the Maine Hut Trail or via Warren's Trail. We recommend continuing on the Maine Hut Trail for 0.7 mile, at which point you can bear left to leave the Maine Hut Trail and follow Larry's Trail, which is the most appealing route. The three trails (the Maine Hut Trail, Warren's Trail, and Larry's Trail) converge to take you to Poplar Hut.

Follow Larry's Trail for about a mile along the east side of Poplar Stream and then cross a wooden bridge over South Brook, just above its convergence with Poplar Stream. To the right, glimpse Poplar Stream Falls. The pool at the base is large enough for a cool plunge. Continue on Larry's Trail by ascending a set of steep steps and pass the junction with Warren's Trail. At the next trail junction, take a right onto the Poplar Stream Trail, which passes a tiny hydropower plant. At the intersection, turn left onto the Maine Hut Trail spur to reach Poplar Hut in about 200 yards.

*Option:* Poplar Hut can also be reached in 3.2 miles from the Airport Trailhead.

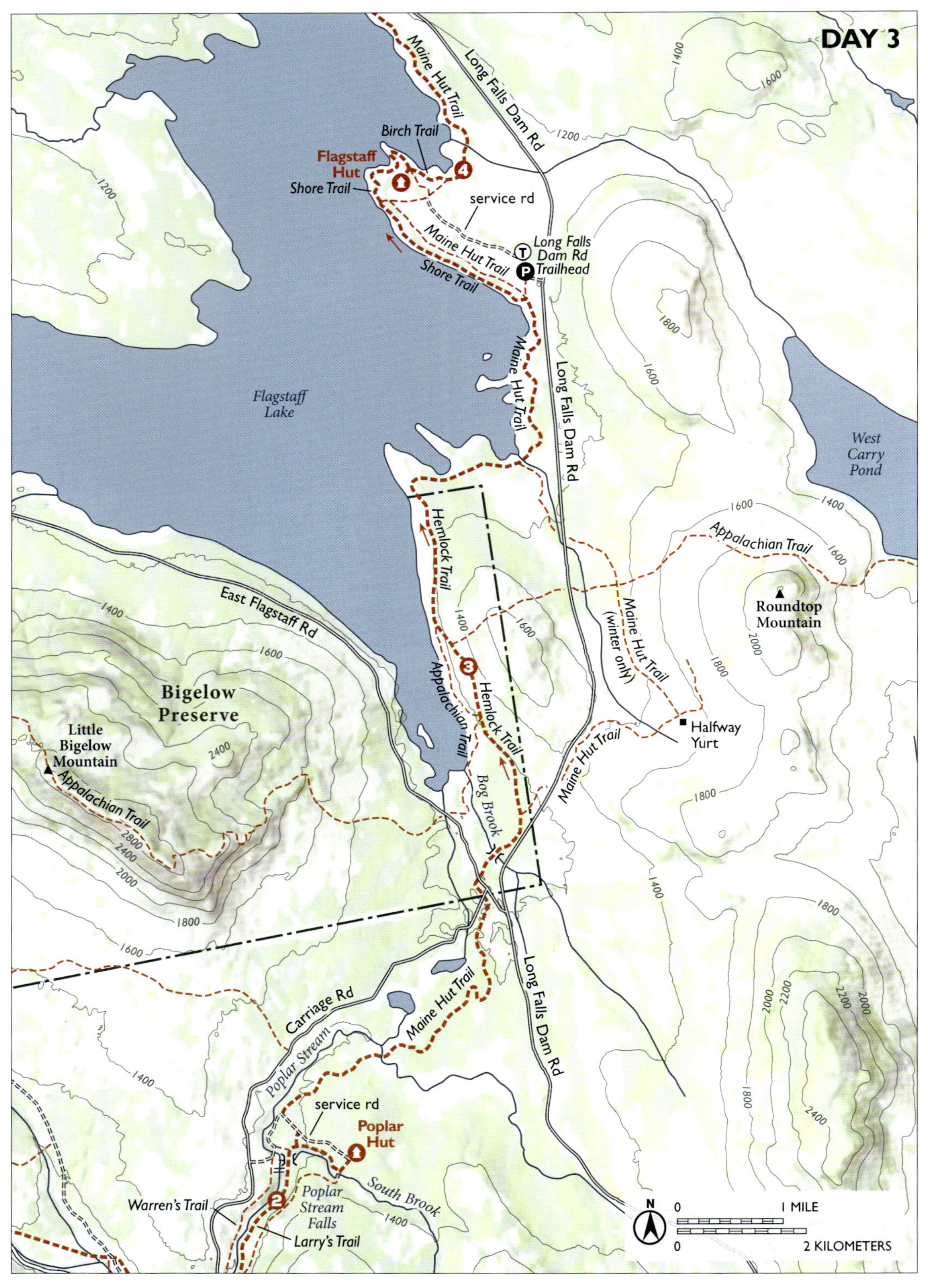
DAY 3
1400
1600
1200
Maine Hut Trail
Long Falls Dam Rd
Birch Trail
Flagstaff Hut
Shore Trail
service rd
Maine Hut Trail
Long Falls Dam Rd Trailhead
Shore Trail
Maine Hut Trail
Flagstaff Lake
1800
1600
West Carry Pond
1600
1400
Appalachian Trail
1600
East Flagstaff Rd
1400
1600
Hemlock Trail
Roundtop Mountain
2000
1800
Bigelow Preserve
Little Bigelow Mountain
Appalachian Trail
2400
Appalachian Trail
Hemlock Trail
Maine Hut Trail (winter only)
Halfway Yurt
1800
2800
2400
2000
1800
1600
Bog Brook
Maine Hut Trail
1400
Long Falls Dam Rd
2000
2200
2000
Carriage Rd
Poplar Stream
Maine Hut Trail
service rd
Poplar Hut
1800
2400
Warren's Trail
Poplar Stream Falls
South Brook
Larry's Trail
1400
N
0   1 MILE
0   2 KILOMETERS

*Early morning light on Avery Peak in the Bigelow Range across Flagstaff Lake* (Photo by John Orcutt)

## DAY 3: POPLAR HUT TO FLAGSTAFF HUT

**Distance:** 11.5 miles

**Elevation gain/loss:** 1090 feet/1090 feet

**Difficulty:** Easy

**Hut elevation:** 1162 feet

**Hut GPS:** 45.198°N, 70.177°W

Retrace your steps on the Poplar Stream Trail in the direction of the hydropower plant, past the junction to Larry's Trail. The trail joins the service road. Follow the service road for 0.2 mile to a T intersection about a half mile from Poplar Hut. The sign indicates a right turn toward Flagstaff Hut (about 11 miles from this point). At this T intersection, continue onto the Maine Hut Trail, now an old logging road, which veers northwest after 0.2 mile. The Maine Hut Trail crosses Carriage Road and then crosses East Flagstaff Road. Shortly after, you cross a footbridge over Bog Brook.

At 4.3 miles, reach a junction on the right for Halfway Yurt (winter route). Instead, bear left onto the Hemlock Trail, which is a separate trail but is marked with Maine Huts and Trails' white-and-blue diamonds. Along this stretch, you encounter the Appalachian Trail (AT) three times. At first, the two trails touch briefly but do not cross. On the second encounter, the trails run together for about 0.2 mile (you'll briefly see the white AT blazes painted on trees). At this point, the AT comes in from the west, bends south, follows the Hemlock Trail for 0.2 mile, and then branches off to the east. (See the Halfway Yurt inset on the map supplied by Maine Huts and Trails for details about these intersections with the AT.)

Continue straight (north) on the Hemlock Trail as it overlaps with the AT. The Hemlock Trail will soon begin to follow the shore of Flagstaff Lake before it rejoins the Maine Hut Trail in 1.8 miles from the final AT junction.

Even though the trail draws close to Flagstaff Lake for a good distance, lake access is

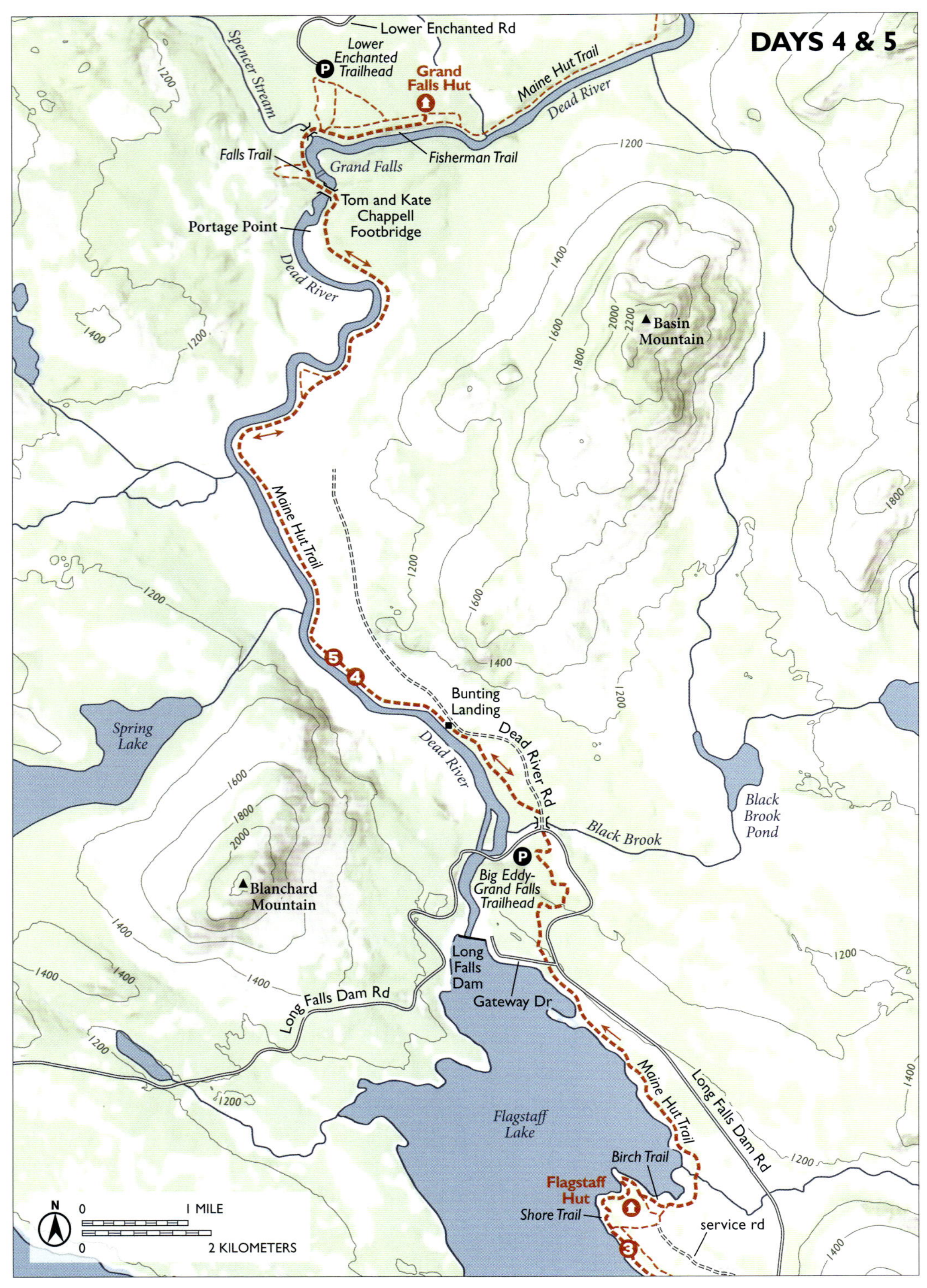
DAYS 4 & 5
Lower Enchanted Rd
Lower Enchanted Trailhead
Grand Falls Hut
Maine Hut Trail
Dead River
Spencer Stream
1200
Falls Trail
Grand Falls
Fisherman Trail
Tom and Kate Chappell Footbridge
Portage Point
Dead River
1200
1400
1200
1200
1400
1800
1600
1400
2200
2000
Basin Mountain
1600
1800
Maine Hut Trail
Spring Lake
1600
1800
2000
1400
5
4
Bunting Landing
Dead River
Dead River Rd
1200
Black Brook
Black Brook Pond
Blanchard Mountain
1400
1400
1400
Long Falls Dam Rd
1200
1200
Long Falls Dam
Gateway Dr
Big Eddy- Grand Falls Trailhead
1200
Flagstaff Lake
Maine Hut Trail
Long Falls Dam Rd
1200
1400
Birch Trail
Flagstaff Hut
Shore Trail
1
service rd
3
N
0          1 MILE
0          2 KILOMETERS

*Visitors encounter the spectacular Grand Falls on the fourth day of the featured MHT itinerary.*

limited because of dense forest and drift-wood accumulated along the shore. Take advantage of the few places—a small gravel beach, a campsite or two—where you can pause and enjoy the lakeside for lunch, a snack, or even a swim.

When you reach the junction with the Maine Hut Trail, turn left onto the Maine Hut Trail and follow it for 1.4 miles to the junction with the Shore Trail. At this point, you can choose to hike the final 2 miles via the Shore Trail (recommended) or the woodsy, inland Maine Hut Trail.

*Note:* In summer, the trail to Flagstaff Hut follows the Maine Hut Trail to the Hemlock Trail; in winter, the ski trail goes via Halfway Yurt. Both the summer and winter routes to Flagstaff Hut are clearly marked.

*Option:* Flagstaff Hut can also be reached in 2.2 miles from the Long Falls Dam Road Trailhead.

## DAY 4: FLAGSTAFF HUT TO GRAND FALLS HUT

**Distance:** 11.5 miles
**Elevation gain/loss:** 350 feet/480 feet
**Difficulty:** Easy
**Hut elevation:** 1049 feet
**Hut GPS:** 45.303°N, 70.207°W

The day begins with a 4.7-mile hike along the Maine Hut Trail to Bunting Landing, where you may opt to pick up a canoe or kayak (see "Paddling from Bunting Landing to Portage Point"). This trail is often wet and passes by buggy marshes, so bring insect repellent and perhaps a head net

# PADDLING FROM BUNTING LANDING TO PORTAGE POINT

Maine Huts and Trails (MHT) invites you to mix up your methods of locomotion on day 4. Instead of hiking the full distance (11.5 miles), you can opt to walk 4.7 miles, paddle 6 miles, and then walk the final 1.5 miles. Arrange a canoe or kayak rental from MHT in advance. As paddlers are required to return boats to the Bunting Landing pickup point, hiker-paddlers usually opt to reverse their route on day 5. If you prefer to hike out on your last day rather than paddle back, pay an additional fee to MHT to relocate the boat. MHT will advise on shuttle and car relocation options.

After the hike from Flagstaff Hut to Bunting Landing on day 4, pause for a summer swim before beginning to paddle, but beware of the surprisingly swift current. A 6-mile (two-to-three-hour) paddle down the Dead River brings you to an island; keep right to avoid the rapids. While passing the island, you will see a canoe dock at Portage Point on the right bank. If you are hiking on to Grand Falls Hut from here, stow your canoe and gear, and follow a short access trail to rejoin the clearly marked Maine Hut Trail.

in summer. From Flagstaff Hut, take the Birch Trail, which connects in 0.2 mile to the Maine Hut Trail, and turn left to follow the Maine Hut Trail north. The trail winds through Flagstaff Lake's eastern shoreline woods and lowlands.

At 2.6 miles from the Birch Trail intersection, the Maine Hut Trail crosses Gateway Drive twice; this is a paved access road to Long Falls Dam, with a gravel road spur to a small picnic area by the lake. Continue across Gateway Drive through spruce and hemlock forest for another 1.2 miles to where the trail crosses Long Falls Dam Road and briefly follows the gravel Dead River Road.

After crossing a bridge on Dead River Road over Black Brook, turn left to follow the Maine Hut Trail, which follows an old logging road through mature evergreen forests for 0.7 mile, at which point it crosses Dead River Road a second time. Look left along the service road to discover canoes stored at Bunting Landing on the Dead River (located at hand-carry site 8 on the MHT Trail Map, on the river right).

To continue the hike, follow the service road and the trail signs parallel to the Dead River on the river right for 5.5 miles to reach the Tom and Kate Chappell Footbridge spanning the Dead River. After crossing the bridge, you can continue straight along the wider ski trail (Maine Hut Trail) for 0.6 mile, or bear right onto the narrower Falls Trail for 0.3 mile, recommended because it passes spectacular Grand Falls. Where the two trails converge again, continue on the Maine Hut Trail for another 0.2 mile to another bridge, which crosses Spencer Stream. Continue uphill along the Maine Hut Trail for another 0.9 mile to Grand Falls Hut, or for the recommended route bear right after crossing Spencer Stream and follow the Fisherman Trail by the river, turning left after 0.9 mile to climb a short distance to the hut.

*Options:* Grand Falls Hut can also be reached in 7.8 miles from the Big Eddy/Grand Falls Trailhead, and in 1.2 miles in summer from the very remote Lower Enchanted Trailhead.

## DAY 5: GRAND FALLS HUT TO BUNTING LANDING TO CAR

**Distance:** 9 miles, depending on where your car or your ride pickup is located
**Elevation gain/loss:** 480 feet/350 feet
**Difficulty:** Easy

Retrace your steps to the Tom and Kate Chappell Footbridge. From there, follow the Maine Hut Trail south for 5.5 miles along the east side of the river to Bunting Landing, then continue south on the Maine Hut Trail to wherever you have left a car or arranged to be picked up. As of this writing, MHT is changing the recommended car park and shuttle pickup locations, so check with them about parking or arranging pickup.

*Options:* There are two additional summer options to consider for your final day. Hikers can opt for a quick exit by walking out 1.2 miles from Grand Falls Hut to the Lower Enchanted Trailhead (this may involve a substantial vehicle relocation fee; check with MHT). Alternatively, in season, water lovers can arrange with an outfitter (check with MHT for referrals) for a day in a canoe, kayak, or raft on the Dead River's whitewater toward the West Forks/Grand Falls Trailhead.

*Canoeing on the Dead River between Flagstaff Lake and Grand Falls Huts* (Photo by John Orcutt)

# APPALACHIAN MOUNTAIN CLUB HUTS

*Life is not measured by the number of breaths we take,*
*but by the number of moments that take our breath away.*

—Anonymous, inscribed on a plaque in an AMC hut

**Location:** Presidential Range, White Mountain National Forest, near Gorham, NH
**Distance:** Huts average 7 miles apart; full traverse 59.6 miles
**Elevation gain/loss:** 18,220 feet/18,130 feet
**Difficulty:** Moderate to difficult
**Terrain:** Mountain peaks with steep ascents and descents, rocky or boulder-strewn footpaths, exposed mountain ridges, and moderate wooded terrain
**Modes of travel:** Summer hiking; winter skiing and snowshoeing
**Season:** Summer (end of May to mid-September or mid-October); three huts are self-service in late fall, winter, and spring, and another three are self-service in May only
**Huts:** Eight huts (capacity 36 to 92), full service in season, by the bunk

---

**SEEKING A EUROPEAN-STYLE** hut-to-hut journey in the US? Yearn to hike the Appalachian Trail but with comfortable lodgings? Love connecting to the oldest hut system in America? The Appalachian Mountain Club (AMC) huts invite you to fulfill all these dreams and more. This system of eight full-service New Hampshire hostelries, punctuating almost 60 miles of trail through some of the most sublime landscapes in America, has roots in the nineteenth century when urban dwellers first sought out wilderness to restore physical and spiritual health (see "America's First Hut System").

The AMC huts are staffed by energetic young people known collectively as "croo," a deliberate and affectionate misspelling of *crew*. They offer meals, information, and good cheer, surrounding the mix of visitors with the spirit of hospitality. On any evening, you might find multigenerational family groups, next-generation hikers who wish to connect to their forebears through logbook entries, solo hikers who welcome evening socializing, friend groups, honeymooners, anniversary celebrants, and Appalachian Trail hikers taking a break from tent camping.

The Whites, the largest mountain expanse in New England, feature forty-three peaks exceeding 4000 feet and seven taller than 5000 feet, including Mount Washington (6289 feet). In addition, this rugged playground encompasses six wilderness areas, offers spectacular scenic ridge walks and viewpoints including Franconia Ridge and the Presidential Traverse, and is home to some of the most unpredictable weather in the country. On any one day, you might encounter weather conditions representing all four seasons! The traverse mostly follows the Appalachian Trail through some of its toughest and most beautiful stretches. Hut hikers confront long and steep rocky sections of trail built before the days of switchbacks, hike exposed ridges, summit boulder fields, and frequently scramble using hands and butt. They also enjoy smoother passages through deep woods, along streams, and across open mountainsides.

Huts, located about 7 miles apart, provide needed shelter when wind, fog, rain, or worse sweeps in. These large structures in the White Mountains are a small subset of the mostly rudimentary shelters numbering more than 250 that dot the Appalachian Trail. The summer full-service season coincides with optimal hiking weather. Hardy travelers can access three huts late in fall and can hike, ski, or snowshoe to these same huts in winter and spring when they are self-service and each site has only one caretaker on duty.

People—other hikers, your own companions, and members of the hut and trail croo—are the magic ingredient in the AMC huts. Croo, mostly college students exuding extraordinary energy, intelligence, and cooperative spirit, make this system unique. (See "The Croo: How Do They Do It?") Morning duty is the 6:30 wakeup for guests: a beautiful song delivered a cappella or a goofy ukulele duet. At mealtimes, the small staff bustles efficiently to serve multicourse, locally sourced meals prepared by one of its members. At breakfast, high-spirited amateur theatrics deliver essential information about Leave No Trace practices and blanket-folding methods and encourage guests to leave generous tips for croo. At dinner, croo members offer quirky introductions and invite questions. Perhaps the most impressive feat is physical and usually unseen: twice a week, croo members haul out waste and haul in fifty to one hundred pounds of supplies—all on simple packboards on their backs.

## HUTS AND AMENITIES

While each hut is unique, with its history recounted on placards and in notebooks, these structures have much in common. The White Mountains huts all feature a large gathering room with long tables and benches, coed bunk rooms (some in separate structures), gender-specific bathrooms with toilet stalls and cold running water, a kitchen and reception counter, a library (a special room or sometimes just a set of shelves), and a front porch. Bunk rooms are filled with beds stacked two or three high and stocked with three blankets and a pillow; each bunk offers a niche equipped with an LED light, shallow shelves, hooks, and an overhead net to organize gear.

In recent decades, the AMC has invested in green technology to reduce human impacts in these wild places and to model sustainable hut operations. Power comes from renewable sources, including solar panels, wind turbines (at six of the eight huts), and a small hydroelectric system at Zealand Falls. Waterless composting toilets, composting practices for food waste, stringent recycling, and adherence to Leave No

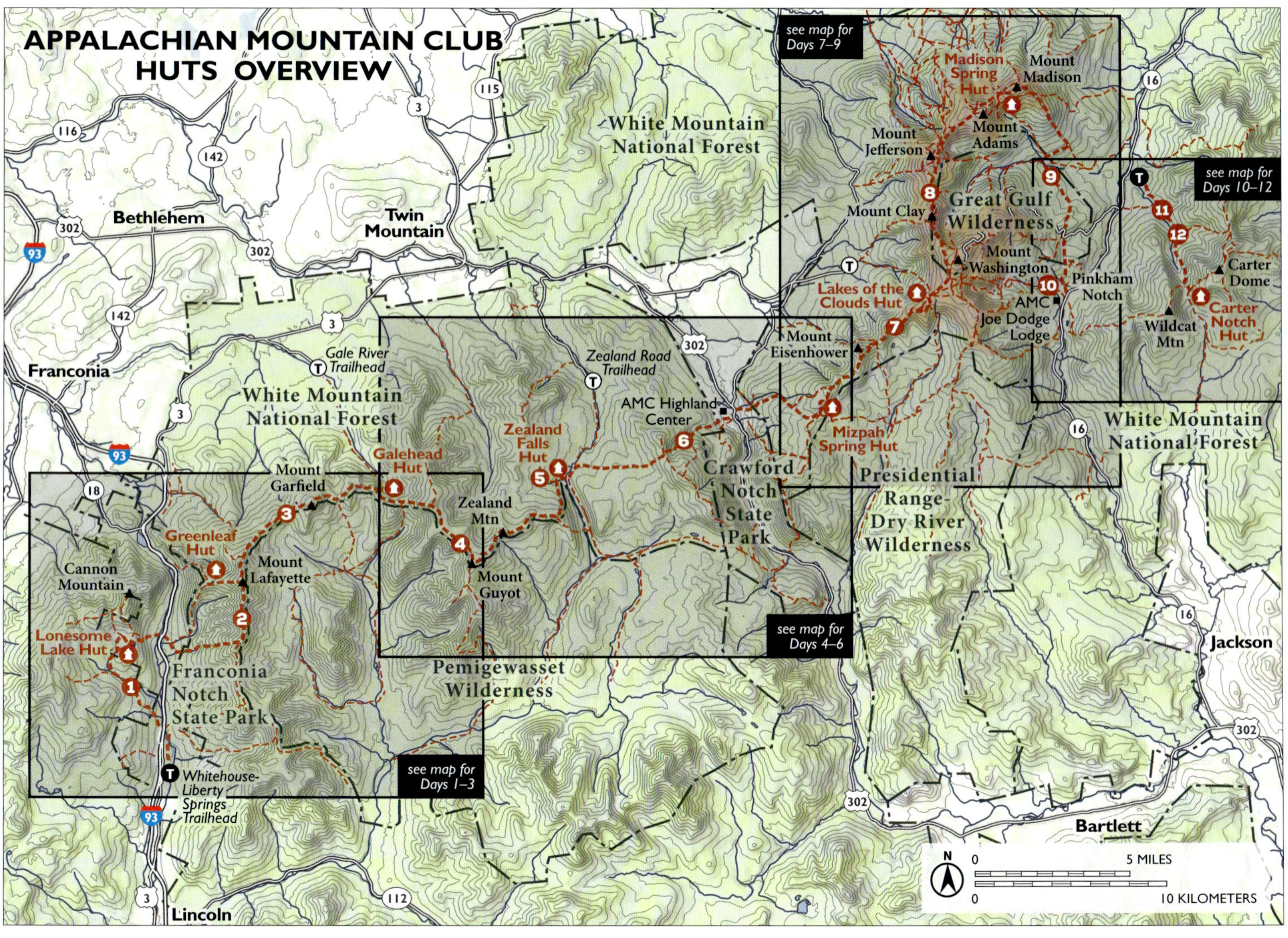
APPALACHIAN MOUNTAIN CLUB
HUTS  OVERVIEW
see map for Days 7–9
Madison Spring Hut
Mount Madison
Mount Jefferson
Mount Adams
16
White Mountain National Forest
115
3
116
142
Bethlehem
Twin Mountain
302
302
9
Great Gulf Wilderness
8
Mount Clay
11
12
see map for Days 10–12
T
Carter Dome
Mount Washington
10
Pinkham Notch
Carter Notch Hut
142
Lakes of the Clouds Hut
7
AMC Joe Dodge Lodge
Wildcat Mtn
Franconia
302
3
T
Gale River Trailhead
Zealand Road Trailhead
T
302
Mount Eisenhower
16
White Mountain National Forest
White Mountain National Forest
AMC Highland Center
6
Zealand Falls Hut
Mizpah Spring Hut
Presidential Range-Dry River Wilderness
93
Galehead Hut
5
18
Mount Garfield
Zealand Mtn
Crawford Notch State Park
3
Greenleaf Hut
Mount Lafayette
4
Mount Guyot
Cannon Mountain
2
see map for Days 4–6
Lonesome Lake Hut
Franconia Notch State Park
Pemigewasset Wilderness
1
Jackson
302
T
Whitehouse-Liberty Springs Trailhead
see map for Days 1–3
93
3
112
302
Bartlett
N
5 MILES
0
10 KILOMETERS
Lincoln

*Getting to know each other over dinner at Carter Notch Hut*

Trace principles all render these huts models for low-impact living.

During full-service season, the AMC huts offer two hearty multicourse meals served family style; breakfast is at 7:00 AM and dinner at 6:00 PM. Vegetarian, vegan, and other special diets can be accommodated with advance notice. Lunch is not provided; bring snacks or other provisions. Huts provide soup and baked goods for sale during the day.

In self-service seasons, guests carry in their own food and have access to the hut kitchen with stove, oven, and cookware for meal preparation. A caretaker, who keeps the woodstove fired up during chilly weather, is on duty from 7:00 AM to 10:00 AM and 4:00 PM to 10:00 PM daily.

## LONESOME LAKE HUT

This hut, an airy octagonal building with separate bunkhouses and bathroom, is a favorite with families. A short, steady uphill hike brings you to a shallow lake, inviting swimming and exploration of the special bog ecosystem. The hut sleeps forty-eight and is full service in summer, self-service in late fall, winter, and spring.

## GREENLEAF HUT

Situated on an open shelf below Mount Lafayette, this hut is visible from afar, encouraging hikers as they approach from Franconia Ridge. Multiple porches offer views back up the peak and across the small mountain tarn below and invite hikers to gather, chat, and reflect on nature's grandeur. The hut sleeps forty-eight and is full service in summer, self-service in May.

## GALEHEAD HUT

Measured by distance from the nearest trailhead, Galehead is the most remote hut, and after a recent renovation, it is the only one designed to ADA standards. With relatively

# SHORTER ITINERARIES

Most hikers do not undertake the full eight-hut traverse, choosing instead to stay at two to four huts over a few days. Two Appalachian Mountain Club (AMC) lodges, the Highland Center in Crawford Notch and Joe Dodge Lodge in Pinkham Notch, make for great overnights immediately before, during, or after trekking hut-to-hut.

There are multiple trailheads along the entire route taking off from I-93, US Highways 3 and 302, and State Route 16; you can begin a trek at either the east or west end or in the middle. Here are three options for shorter itineraries.

**North Presidential Traverse** (four days, three nights). Start at the Highland Center and hike to Mizpah Spring Hut. On day 2, trek to Lakes of the Clouds Hut for the night, then on to Madison Spring Hut (day 3 overnight); exit at Pinkham Notch.

**Franconia Ridge Trail** (two or three nights). Starting at Lafayette Place Campground, hike to Greenleaf Hut (via the Old Bridle Path or Falling Waters Trail), then to Galehead Hut (overnight), and head out via the Gale River Trail; there is an option to spend an additional night at Zealand Falls Hut and then hike out by way of the Zealand Trail.

**Lonesome Lake Hut to Greenleaf Hut** (three days, two nights). Begin at Lafayette Place Campground and hike to Lonesome Lake Hut to overnight. Retrace your steps the next day and follow the Falling Waters Trail, continuing along the Franconia Ridge Trail to Greenleaf Hut (overnight), then exit via the Old Bridle Path.

For more options and trailhead information, consult with AMC reservations staff and check out Steven D. Smith's *White Mountain Guide* (see Resources).

fewer visitors, this hut is described by its croo as "chill" and boasts the best sunset views. Galehead sleeps thirty-eight and is full service in summer, self-service in May.

## ZEALAND FALLS HUT

This cozy hut, situated right next to the multiple strands of Zealand Falls and a short hike up from Crawford Notch, attracts families with kids and the young at heart. It sleeps thirty-six and is full service in summer, self-service in late fall, winter, and spring.

## MIZPAH SPRING HUT

Design flourishes, including a designated upstairs library, a lofty common room, and special carpentry details, elevate this hut, the newest in the chain (completed in 1964). It sleeps sixty and is full service in summer, self-service in May.

## LAKES OF THE CLOUDS HUT

Named for two small alpine lakes and the high elevation, Lakes of the Clouds Hut is the largest and busiest (capacity for ninety-two people), down a steep cairn-marked trail from Mount Washington's summit. Each bunk room fits up to fifteen overnight guests in berths stacked three high under low ceilings. The hut is full service in summer.

## MADISON SPRING HUT

In a col between Mount Adams and Mount Madison, this high alpine hut offers welcome shelter to hikers tired from traversing major peaks in the Presidential Range. Visitors can touch the stone walls of the original hut in the bunk rooms, where elements of the past have been seamlessly incorporated into the new structure. The hut sleeps fifty-two and is full service in summer.

## CARTER NOTCH HUT

The oldest building in the AMC hut system, Carter Notch still occupies its original stone walls. Two bunkhouses with bathrooms are hidden upslope on this rocky, heavily wooded site, with a short walk to the impressive jumble of huge rocks known as the Ramparts and two mountain lakes. The hut sleeps forty and is full service in summer, self-service in late fall, winter, and spring.

## PLANNING AND PREPARATION

**Contact:** www.outdoors.org/lodging-camping/huts; (603) 466-2727

**Booking:** Call for availability and reservations

**Membership:** Not required; individual and family memberships available; members receive discounts on lodging and merchandise, as well as an annual magazine and access to local chapters

**Rates:** $$$; reduced rates for children ages three to seventeen

**Transportation:** Most hikers use both a personal vehicle and the AMC shuttle bus (available in summer; consult website and trailhead signboards for schedule) to get to and from the trailheads; local taxi services available

## MAPS

The best overall set of maps is the AMC's White Mountain Trail Map Set—Map 1: Presidential Range and Map 2: Franconia-Pemigewasset cover the traverse (1:42,240 scale). They are designed to be used with Steven D. Smith's *White Mountain Guide* (see Resources), but can be purchased and used separately. If you want to explore

*Trail maintenance volunteers and the hut croo often haul heavy loads.*

# THE CROO: HOW DO THEY DO IT?

What are the secrets to the unique and highly successful Appalachian Mountain Club (AMC) hut service model? Throughout the full-service season, up to 40,000 hikers overnight in the eight huts, occupying the 414 total bunks and consuming nearly 80,000 meals. Since the 1930s, seasonal crews of college students have delivered superb mountain hospitality. They prepare and serve two hearty meals per day, pack in heavy loads of perishables twice weekly, keep huts clean and safe, educate and inform visitors, assist with search and rescue, and more, all the while staying calm, helpful, and cheerful. Croos live and work together in close quarters off the grid, eleven days on and three days off. It's intense!

Operationally, the huts are well-oiled machines, running on time-tested procedures and steered by a couple of hut supervisors and eight seasonal hut masters. The croo members are smart, hardworking young adults who identify with the AMC mission and love the mountains.

But to really understand the magic of croo hospitality, you must look to culture and traditions. Croo culture engenders a deep sense of community. Close-knit teams generate the necessary energy, creativity, and resilience that makes this hut system go 'round. Bonding is encouraged through croo nights, when croo spend two nights together off the mountain; Sunday meetings to discuss how things are going; and group agreements crafted by each croo to shape their own live-work patterns. New croo understand from the outset that they are keepers of a long tradition of mountain hospitality.

The super-positive culture is reinforced by quirky traditions lovingly handed down over generations. Some croo favorites include blanket-folding demonstrations, which are humorous daily skits passed down like oral histories that include costumes and props; pronsing, which is when croo remove their aprons with a group cheer; truck notes, or quirky messages, pictures, love notes, invitations, and "mass mailings" passed from croo to croo during the twice-weekly packboard runs; and croo rocks, or private places away from guests, often large sitting rocks, to retreat, rest, and chat. The Old Hutcroo Association (OHA), an alumni association founded 1933 "to bring people together, people who share a lifelong bond," has a website dedicated to croo news, lore, and legends and sponsors fun social events and opportunities to revisit the huts.

These traditions, and the cultural cohesion they forge, help ensure high morale, excellent service, and memorable experiences for both workers and guests every summer in the White Mountains.

side trips or vary the routes, the map set and Smith's book are quite useful.

Hut to Hut on the Appalachian Trail in the White Mountains of New Hampshire (6th edition, Wilderness Map Co.) is a less expensive, less detailed (1:80,000 scale), but sufficient option—a solid topographic overview map for those who do not need detailed turn-by-turn directions.

USGS topo maps are not necessary for this traverse.

## PACKING TIPS

Bring a sleeping bag liner and earplugs (optional).

## OTHER TIPS

Pets are not allowed in huts. Pack out trash, food waste, and recyclables. An array of souvenirs and practical items including batteries, headlamps, hiking poles, clothing, and snacks can be purchased at the huts with cash or credit card.

## ITINERARY: EIGHT-HUT TRAVERSE

*59.6 miles, twelve days, eleven nights, including two rest days*

Directions for the eight-hut traverse, traveling south to north, follow the Appalachian Trail nearly all the way. The traverse can be done in the opposite direction as well. The addition of two rest days makes this traverse the longest in the guidebook. Rest days allow time and space to recover from the rigors of the route, and to explore the waterfalls, fishing streams, side trails, woodlands, and lookouts around the huts.

Most people will want to do sections of the full traverse rather than the whole route in one hike (see "Shorter Itineraries"). If you haven't hiked in New Hampshire's White Mountains before, these routes may take longer and feel harder than anticipated. Day-by-day directions include the trailhead nearest each destination hut to assist in alternative plans.

## DAY 1: WHITEHOUSE TRAILHEAD TO LONESOME LAKE HUT

**Distance:** 3.1 miles
**Elevation gain/loss:** 1340 feet/20 feet
**Difficulty:** Easy
**Hut elevation:** 2760 feet
**Hut GPS:** 44.1384°N, 71.7033°W
**Trailhead:** Whitehouse Trailhead (Liberty Springs Trailhead) 44.1004°N, 71.6820°W

### Getting There

From Concord, drive north on I-93 for about 67 miles. Take exit 34A to merge onto US Highway 3 north, toward the Flume Gorge. Hikers park 0.2 mile north of the Flume Visitor Center parking lot.

Start at the Whitehouse Trailhead (a.k.a. Liberty Springs Trailhead), located at the hikers' parking lot off US 3, just north of the Flume Visitor Center. Stage a car at the end of the traverse at Pinkham Notch or the Nineteen Mile Brook Trailhead, or get a shuttle ride to either Liberty Springs Campground or the Whitehouse Trailhead. A waiting vehicle eliminates the need to time your exit journey with the shuttle schedule.

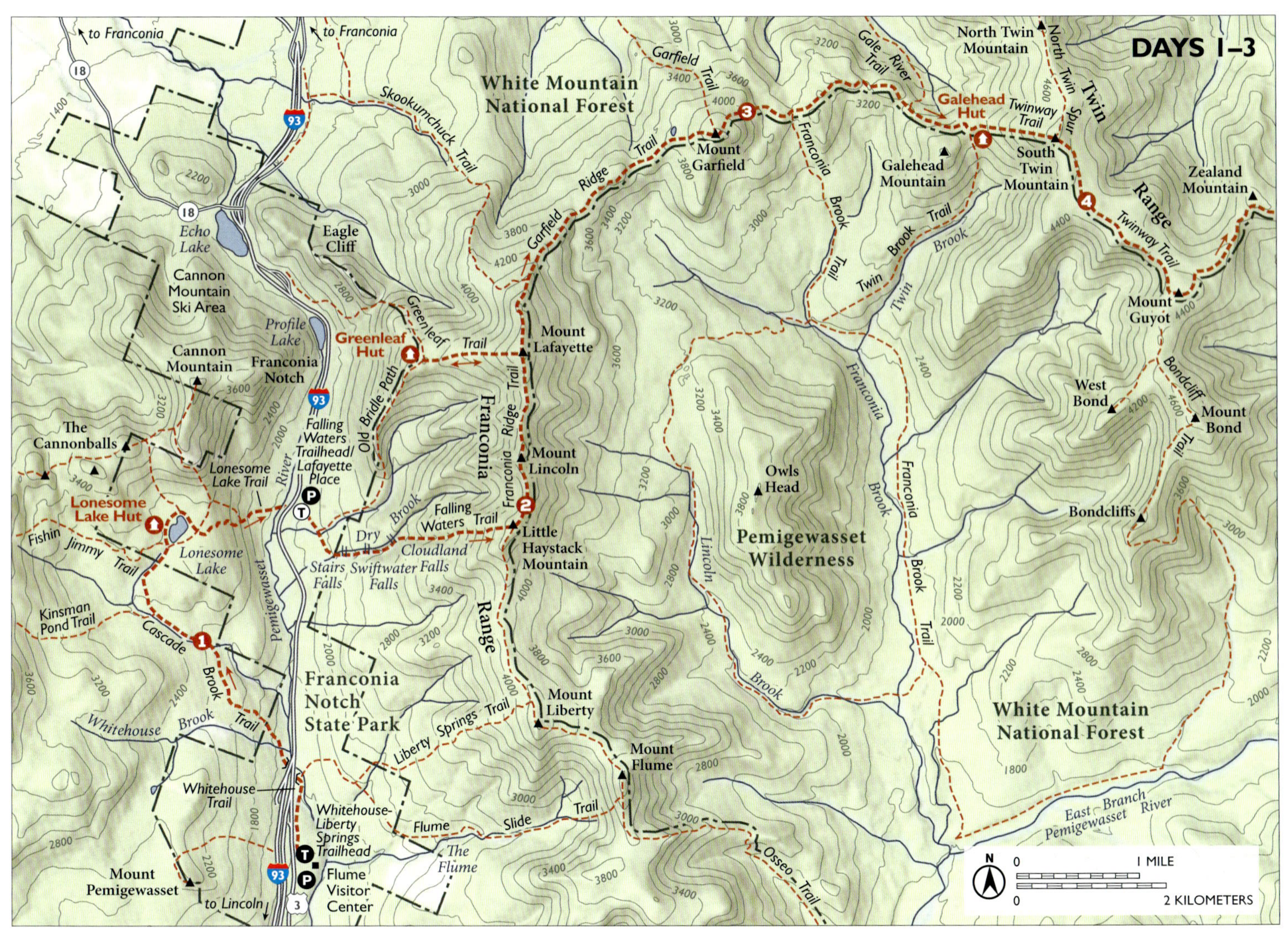
DAYS 1–3
to Franconia
to Franconia
White Mountain National Forest
Garfield Trail
Gale River Trail
North Twin Mountain
North Twin Spur
Galehead Hut
Twin
Twinway Trail
Mount Garfield
Galehead Mountain
South Twin Mountain
Range
Zealand Mountain
Skookumchuck Trail
Garfield Ridge Trail
Franconia Brook Trail
Twin Brook Trail
Twinway Trail
Mount Guyot
Echo Lake
Eagle Cliff
Greenleaf Trail
Mount Lafayette
West Bond
Bondcliff Trail
Mount Bond
Cannon Mountain Ski Area
Profile Lake
Greenleaf Hut
Franconia Ridge Trail
Cannon Mountain
Franconia Notch
Old Bridle Path
Franconia
Mount Lincoln
Owls Head
Bondcliffs
The Cannonballs
Falling Waters Trailhead/Lafayette Place
Brook
Franconia Brook Trail
Lonesome Lake Trail
Lonesome Lake Hut
Dry Brook
Falling Waters Trail
Little Haystack Mountain
Pemigewasset Wilderness
Fishin Jimmy Trail
Lonesome Lake
Cloudland Falls
Stairs Falls
Swiftwater Falls
Range
Lincoln Brook
Kinsman Pond Trail
Cascade Brook Trail
Pemigewasset River
Franconia Notch State Park
Mount Liberty
White Mountain National Forest
Whitehouse Brook
Liberty Springs Trail
Mount Flume
Whitehouse Trail
Whitehouse-Liberty Springs Trailhead
Flume Slide Trail
East Branch Pemigewasset River
Mount Pemigewasset
to Lincoln
The Flume
Flume Visitor Center
Osseo Trail
N
1 MILE
2 KILOMETERS

## On the Trail

Follow the Whitehouse Trail north, paralleling I-93 for 0.8 mile on a flat path; at 0.6 mile, merge with a paved bike path. Turn left (west) just before the bridge over the Pemigewasset River; the trail follows the river, passing under the two lanes of I-93 to the Cascade Brook Trail sign. Follow the Cascade Brook Trail (marked with white Appalachian Trail blazes plus blue blazes) steadily uphill in a northwesterly direction, paralleling and crossing the aptly named Cascade Brook several times. Brook crossings require rock hopping.

Continue on the Cascade Brook Trail past the junction for the Kinsman Pond Trail, up through hemlock and mixed hardwood forests. The last 0.8 mile rises steeply; boulders on the trail bed make for a challenging final ascent to Lonesome Lake Hut. Arriving at a small dam, notice the lake, a dock, and the hut above to the left in the trees.

*Option:* The shortest way to this hut is the 1.6-mile Lonesome Lake Trail from Lafayette Place Campground. This route is described below (in the opposite direction) as the first section of the Lonesome Lake Hut to Greenleaf Hut tramp.

## DAY 2: LONESOME LAKE HUT TO GREENLEAF HUT

    **Distance:** 7.5 miles

    **Elevation gain/loss:** 3850 feet/2080 feet

    **Difficulty:** Moderate to difficult

    **Hut elevation:** 4200 feet

    **Hut GPS:** 44.1600°N, 71.6606°W

Take the easy, well-marked Lonesome Lake Trail 1.6 miles (through three long switchbacks) to Lafayette Place Campground in Franconia Notch State Park. Follow the tunnel signs under I-93 to the Falling Waters Trailhead. The Falling Waters Trail, marked with blue blazes, parallels and crosses Dry Brook several times and passes scenic Stairs Falls, Swiftwater Falls, and Cloudland Falls as it gains more than 3000 feet in elevation in 3 miles, bringing you to the junction with the Franconia Ridge Trail at Little Haystack Mountain.

Turn left (north) at the junction with the Franconia Ridge Trail. Vast views on both sides of the ridge are a highlight, with Cannon Mountain to the west and the Pemigewasset Wilderness to the east. This walk progresses from Little Haystack Mountain (4760 feet) to Mount Lincoln (5089 feet) and on to Mount Lafayette (5260 feet), the highest peak in the south Presidential Range. From atop Mount Lafayette, look to the west to see the hut. Leave the Franconia Ridge Trail at the peak of Mount Lafayette, going west on the Greenleaf Trail, and descend a steep 1050 feet over 1.1 miles to get to Greenleaf Hut.

*Options:* For the shortest access to Greenleaf Hut, take the Old Bridle Path (2.9 miles) from the trailhead at the Lafayette Place parking lot (44.1415°N, 71.6819°W). Similarly, the Falling Waters Trail, which also starts at the Lafayette Place parking lot, is another option that skips the Lonesome Lake Trail leg. See above for a detailed description of this route, which is longer and steeper than the Old Bridle Path but rewards adventurers with spectacular views from along the Franconia Ridge Trail to the summit of Mount Lafayette.

# AMERICA'S FIRST HUT SYSTEM

The Boston-based Appalachian Mountain Club (AMC) was founded in 1876 by a group of urbanites seeking a deeper connection with nature. Instead of another learned society, the founders—mostly academics—opted to create a "vigorous, full-blooded, ardent club" (see Charles E. Fay's "The Appalachian Mountain Club" in Resources). This intellectually engaged and highly social organization has a clear geographic focus and conservation mission to "promote the protection, enjoyment, and understanding of the mountains, forest, waters and trails of the Appalachian region."

The White Mountains of New Hampshire—part of the Appalachian chain and relatively close to Boston—were already affected in the nineteenth century by heavy logging and early forays into mass tourism. Mount Washington, for example, had a cog railway by 1869 and a large hotel on top by 1873. Proximity to Boston and other urban centers and the clear need for protection made the White Mountains the logical target for the AMC's early work. Committed to both scientific and artistic goals, the AMC began commissioning maps and supporting scientific projects and publications. Improvements on the ground included building trails, shelters, and huts.

In 1888, the AMC built the first recreational mountain hut in America just as such structures were becoming popular in Europe. Located between Mount Adams and Mount Madison, Madison Spring Hut (which has since been rebuilt several times) initiated the first phase of the AMC's efforts to provide hikers and researchers with access to the steepest, rockiest, most remote stretches of the north Presidential Range. In 1901, in response to

## DAY 3: GREENLEAF HUT TO GALEHEAD HUT

**Distance:** 7.7 miles
**Elevation gain/loss:** 3140 feet/3570 feet
**Difficulty:** Difficult
**Hut elevation:** 3800 feet
**Hut GPS:** 44.1879°N, 71.5687°W

Retrace your steps from yesterday 1.1 miles up to the Mount Lafayette summit to join the Garfield Ridge Trail, walking north along the exposed ridge and passing the junction on the left for the Skookumchuck Trail at 0.8 mile.

Follow the Garfield Ridge Trail as it swings to the northeast, descending to a low point at 1.7 miles, then ascend a small knob and then up a larger hump onto a ledge; pause to look back for a view of Mount Lafayette. After a rough descent into a tangled col, the trail ascends Mount Garfield. Take the short side trail south 60 yards to the summit, and absorb the spectacular views from the

the deaths of two hikers in a violent storm near Mount Washington, the AMC built an emergency refuge on the flanks of this peak. The shelter was replaced in 1915 by the first Lakes of the Clouds Hut. Meanwhile, a small stone hut was sited at Carter Notch in 1914. Since expanded, this is the oldest remaining original mountain hut in the AMC system and in the US. By 1916, caretakers at these three huts were providing meals and lodging for a steady stream of hikers.

Joe Dodge, dynamic AMC hut master from 1928 to 1955, expanded the operation. Between 1929 and 1932, he oversaw the construction of Zealand Falls Hut, Greenleaf Hut, and Galehead Hut and integrated the Lonesome Lake Cabins (later replaced by Lonesome Lake Hut). The original AMC huts were also expanded or improved during Dodge's tenure. A charismatic, fiercely determined figure, Dodge took the huts to new levels of operational effectiveness. His unpublished 1935 "Hutmans' Handbook" articulates the policies, procedures, and training methods that help shape a fresh croo of college students into gracious hosts and effective caretakers.

The full system—the second largest in the US—was finally completed in 1964. Mizpah Spring Hut, sited between Zealand Falls to the west and Lakes of the Clouds to the east, was the final addition to a rustic hospitality chain stretching from Franconia Notch to Pinkham Notch. A recent proposal to add a ninth hut was withdrawn by the AMC due to concerns about human impacts on wildlands.

foundation of an old fire tower. This area is a good place for a lunch break.

Rejoin the Garfield Ridge Trail, and descend past the junction on the left with the Garfield Trail at 3.7 miles. The Garfield Ridge Trail continues to descend steeply through a tricky ledge section and passes the junction on the right with the Franconia Brook Trail at 4.4 miles. Continue on a series of arduous ups and downs along an eastern spur of Mount Garfield, descending steeply to pass the junction on the left with the Gale River Trail at 6 miles. The Garfield Ridge Trail sidles around the steep north slope of Galehead Mountain, reaching a junction with the Twinway Trail and the Frost Trail at 0.6 mile beyond the Gale River Trail junction. Follow the sign for Galehead Hut, which is about 40 yards south from this junction.

*Option:* Galehead Hut, the most remote of the AMC huts, can also be accessed by a 4.7-mile hike with 2250 feet of elevation gain up

DAYS 4–6
3
1600
1800
1600
2000
1800
2000
2200
Middle Sugarloaf
16
White Mountain National Forest
Hale Brook Trail
Zealand Rd
Mount Echo
to Twin Mountain
Mount Washington Hotel
302
Mount Clinton Rd
1800
2200
Mount Eisenhower
3400
3200
2800
Crawford Path
Mount Pierce
7
Mizpah Cutoff Trail
Gibbs Falls
3800
Mizpah Spring Hut
North Twin Trail
2000
2200
2400
P
P
T  Zealand Trailhead
2200
2000
AMC Highland Center
P
Saco Lake
Avalon Trail
Crawford Path
Webster Cliff Trail
2800
3000
Presidential Range– Dry River Wilderness
Mount Jackson
Mount Hale
Lend-A-Hand Trail
3600
3000
Zealand Trail
3200
Mount Tom
3800
6
Mount Avalon
Mount Willard
3800
Mount Webster
Webster Cliffs
North Branch Gale River
Gale River Trail
3800
3200
North Twin Mountain
North Twin Spur
Zealand Falls Hut
5
Zealand Falls
Avalon-Zealand Trail (A-Z Trail)
3600
Willey Range Trail
Mount Field
3600
Crawford Notch State Park
Crawford Notch
3000
3
Galehead Hut
Twinway Trail
1
South Twin Mountain
4
Twin Range
Zealand Mountain
3400
Twinway Trail
Zeacliff Outlook
V
Zeacliff Pond
Zeacliff Trail
Ethan Pond Trail
Whitehall Brook
Mount Willey
Ethan Pond
3000
Kedron Flume
1600
Galehead Mountain
Twin Brook Trail
4400
Mount Guyot
Bondcliff Trail
Whitehall Brook
2800
3200
Ethan Pond Trail
Webster Cliff Trailhead
Saco River
302
Pemigewasset Wilderness
2200
West Bond
Mount Bond
3600
3200
2800
2400
Thoreau Falls Trail
Thoreau Falls
Shoal Pond
3000
2200
White Mountain National Forest
3200
2200
2400
1800
2000
1400
1200
N
2 MILES
3 KILOMETERS
3000
3200
2000
to North Conway

from the Gale River Trailhead (44.2329°N, 71.6098°W).

## DAY 4: GALEHEAD HUT TO ZEALAND FALLS HUT

**Distance:** 7 miles
**Elevation gain/loss:** 1900 feet/3120 feet
**Difficulty:** Moderate
**Hut elevation:** 2700 feet
**Hut GPS:** 44.1949°N, 71.4971°W

From Galehead Hut, return via the Frost Trail to the junction of the Garfield Ridge Trail and the Twinway Trail, continuing east and steeply uphill on the Twinway Trail for 0.8 mile to South Twin Mountain. A more open and level stretch of the Twinway Trail continues southeast for about 2 miles, past a junction with the Bondcliff Trail at 2.8 miles. The Twinway Trail swings northeast, up Mount Guyot, and then down about 1.3 miles to Zealand Mountain at 4.1 miles. There are no views from this peak, so it's probably not worth taking the 0.1-mile side trail.

The Twinway Trail descends gradually along the ridge until reaching a steep descent aided by a ladder. Pass tiny Zeacliff Pond on the right, and ascend to the junction with the Zeacliff Trail at 5.7 miles. Shortly after the Zeacliff Trail junction, take the 75-yard loop path to Zeacliff Outlook, a great place to take a break and admire magnificent views that encompass the vastness from Crawford Notch over the Pemigewasset Wilderness to Franconia Ridge. Rejoin the Twinway Trail, and follow it through a birch forest, crossing two branches of Whitehall Brook to arrive at the junction with the Lend-A-Hand Trail on the left. Turn right and Zealand Falls Hut soon comes into view.

*Option:* Zealand Falls Hut can also be reached in 2.3 miles from the Zealand Trailhead (44.2232°N, 71.4785°W).

## DAY 5: REST DAY

Short day hikes to Zealand Falls (right near the hut) and Thoreau Falls (44.1693°N, 71.4726°W) are rewarding and not taxing. Directions are available at the hut.

## DAY 6: ZEALAND FALLS HUT TO MIZPAH SPRING HUT

**Distance:** 7.6 miles
**Elevation gain/loss:** 1880 feet/1300 feet
**Difficulty:** Moderate
**Hut elevation:** 3800 feet
**Hut GPS:** 44.2194°N, 71.3695°W

From Zealand Falls Hut, descend east on the rocky Twinway Trail through birch forest for 0.5 mile (if you haven't already, visit lovely Zealand Falls off to the right) to the well-marked Zealand Trail junction. Turn left (north) onto the Zealand Trail for 0.2 mile. Turn right (east) at the junction of the Zealand Trail with the yellow-blazed A-Z Trail (Avalon-Zealand Trail).

Follow the A-Z Trail for 2.7 miles on level ground skirting several ponds, then ascend to pass the junction with the Willey Range Trail. After another 80 yards, the trail passes the spur trail on the left to the peak of Mount Tom. Continue on the A-Z Trail for another mile, descending steadily along the south side of a gully formed by Crawford Brook, to join the Avalon Trail, which continues straight (east) downhill for another 1.2 miles to the AMC Highland Center. Coin-operated showers are available at the old train depot, with lunch and resupply options at the adjacent Highland Center.

From the Highland Center parking lot, climb the stairs to cross US 302, then continue up a set of stone stairs to the Crawford Connector, a short trail that connects to the blue-blazed Crawford Path after 0.2 mile. Ascend the Crawford Path through lovely deciduous woods. In 1.8 miles, turn right to follow the Mizpah Cutoff Trail for 0.7 mile to Mizpah Spring Hut.

*Option:* The shortest route to Mizpah Spring Hut starts at the AMC Highland Center (44.2194°N, 71.4120°W) and continues via the Crawford Path to the Mizpah Cutoff Trail, as described above.

## DAY 7: MIZPAH SPRING HUT TO LAKES OF THE CLOUDS HUT

    **Distance:** 4.7 miles
    **Elevation gain/loss:** 1800 feet/720 feet
    **Difficulty:** Moderate to difficult
    **Hut elevation:** 5012 feet
    **Hut GPS:** 44.2588°N, 71.3190°W

From Mizpah Spring Hut, go north on the Webster Cliff Trail for 0.8 mile to rejoin the Crawford Path in 0.1 mile, after reaching the summit of Mount Pierce (4312 feet). Enjoy good views down to the AMC Highland Center to the west, into the Presidential Range–Dry River Wilderness to the east, and off to the northern Presidential Range peaks to the north.

Follow the Crawford Path for 1.2 miles northeast from its junction with the Webster Cliff Trail to the junction with the Mount Eisenhower Loop Trail (option to bear left for 0.2 mile to bag the 4760-foot peak). Continue on Crawford Path for 0.5 mile to reach the Mount Eisenhower Loop Trail, where it rejoins the Crawford Path. Continue on the Crawford Path for 1.2 miles, passing the Mount Eisenhower Trail on the right, to the junction with the Mount Monroe Loop Trail. (The option to bear left to take the rough Mount Monroe Loop Trail over the two summits of Mount Monroe adds 350 feet of elevation.)

Be sure to stay on the trail along this particularly fragile alpine stretch of the ridge. The enormous white building with the bright red roof far below on the left (west) is the Mount Washington Hotel at Bretton Woods. Continue downhill on the Crawford Path, past the second Mount Monroe Loop Trail juncture, for 0.7 mile to Lakes of the Clouds Hut.

*Options:* Shorter routes to Lakes of the Clouds Hut include the sheltered Ammonoosuc Ravine Trail (3.1 miles), which starts from a parking lot trailhead on Cog Railway Base Road (44.2705°N, 71.3497°W; 1.1 miles east of the junction of Cog Railway Base Road with Mount Clinton Road and Jefferson Notch Road), and the Crawford Path down from the summit of Mount Washington (1.5 miles).

## DAY 8: LAKES OF THE CLOUDS HUT TO MADISON SPRING HUT

    **Distance:** 6.8 miles
    **Elevation gain/loss:** 1870 feet/2060 feet
    **Difficulty:** Moderate to difficult
    **Hut elevation:** 4825 feet
    **Hut GPS:** 44.3277°N, 71.2832°W

From Lakes of the Clouds Hut, continue northeast on the Crawford Path between the two alpine lakes for 0.1 mile, taking the

*Twinway Trail between Galehead and Zealand Falls Huts under gray skies*

left fork at the junction with the Tuckerman Crossover Trail and Camel Trail to continue on the Crawford Path. Climb steadily uphill for 0.7 mile and turn left onto the Westside Trail, sidling across the western flank of Mount Washington for a mile, crossing under the cog railway, to the junction with the Gulfside Trail at 1.7 miles. Follow the Gulfside Trail, marked by yellow blazes and large cairns, for 5 miles.

Pass the junctions on the right for the Mount Clay Loop Trail and the Sphinx Trail. Arrive at the south end of the Mount Jefferson Loop Trail about 1.9 miles after the junction of the Crawford Path and the Gulfside Trail. The option to take the Mount Jefferson Loop Trail up to the summit adds a 300-foot ascent but little extra time. At Edmands Col, you are 3.2 miles from Madison Spring Hut.

The Gulfside Trail ascends about 525 feet over the next 1.5 miles to Thunderstorm Junction. A large cairn marks Thunderstorm Junction between Mount Adams (5799 feet, on your right) and Mount Sam Adams (5585 feet, on your left). (You have an option to climb 310 feet to scale Mount Adams, then follow the cairn-marked Airline Trail north-northeast down the rocky cone of the mountain to reconnect with the Gulfside Trail.) Continue steadily northeast downhill on the Gulfside Trail through rocky terrain for 0.9 mile to Madison Spring Hut.

*Options:* Two trails, both about 3.8 miles in length and with 3550 feet of elevation gain, provide direct access to Madison Spring Hut from the Appalachia Trailhead off US 2. The Valley Way Trail is more sheltered; the Airline Trail, with its long, exposed stretches, is better for fair-weather days.

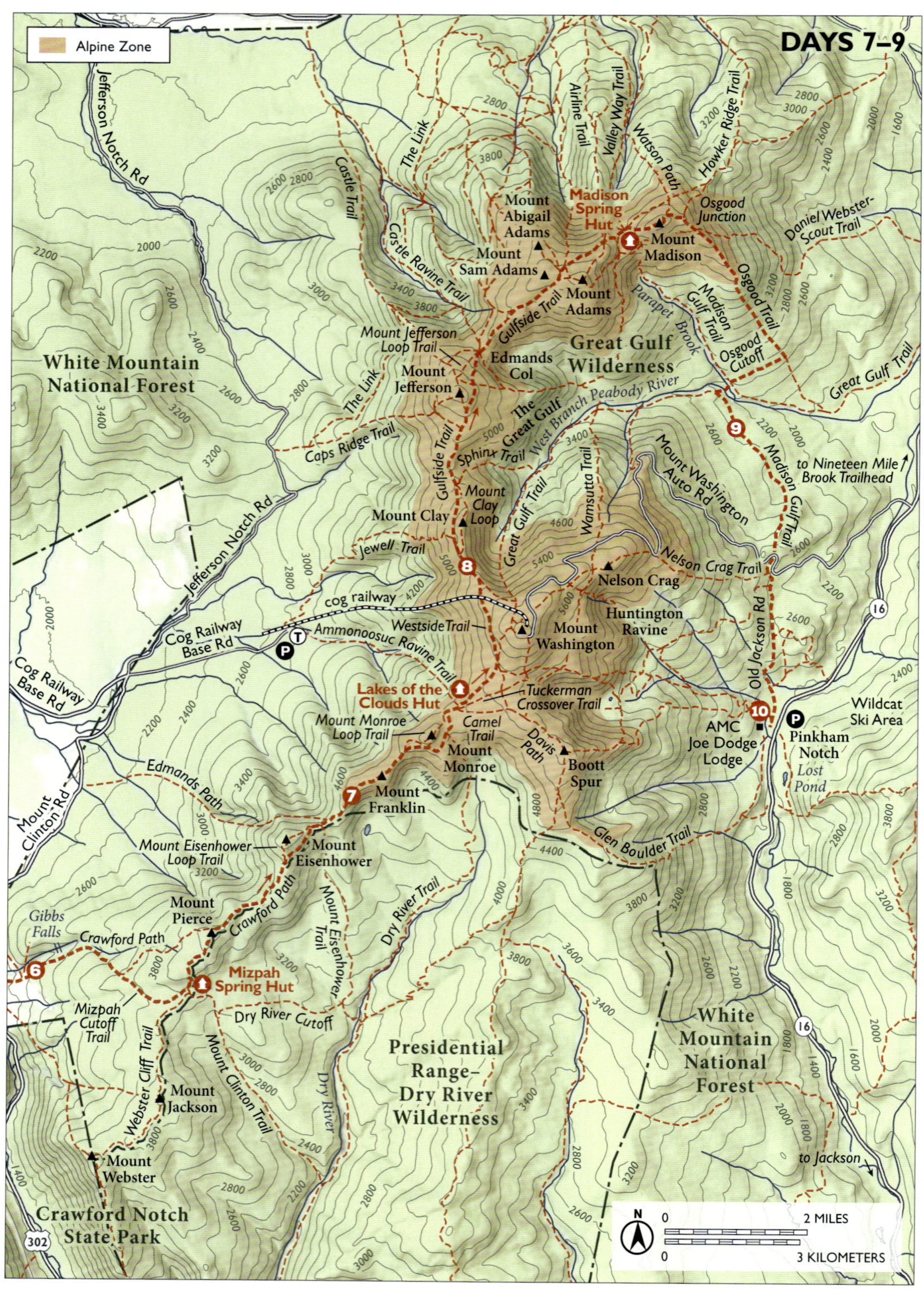
DAYS 7–9
Alpine Zone
Jefferson Notch Rd
White Mountain National Forest
Jefferson Notch Rd
Cog Railway Base Rd
Cog Railway Base Rd
Mount Clinton Rd
Castle Trail
Castle Ravine Trail
The Link
The Link
Caps Ridge Trail
Gulfside Trail
Mount Jefferson Loop Trail
Mount Jefferson
Mount Abigail Adams
Mount Sam Adams
Mount Adams
Edmands Col
Gulfside Trail
Madison Spring Hut
Mount Madison
Airline Trail
Valley Way Trail
Watson Path
Howker Ridge Trail
Osgood Junction
Daniel Webster-Scout Trail
Osgood Trail
Madison Gulf Trail
Parapet Brook
Osgood Cutoff
Great Gulf Trail
Great Gulf Wilderness
The Great Gulf
Sphinx Trail
West Branch Peabody River
Gulfside Trail
Mount Clay
Mount Clay Loop
Jewell Trail
Great Gulf Trail
Wamsutta Trail
Mount Washington Auto Rd
Madison Gulf Trail
to Nineteen Mile Brook Trailhead
cog railway
Cog Railway Base Rd
Ammonoosuc Ravine Trail
Westside Trail
Mount Washington
Nelson Crag
Nelson Crag Trail
Huntington Ravine
Old Jackson Rd
Lakes of the Clouds Hut
Mount Monroe Loop Trail
Mount Monroe
Camel Trail
Tuckerman Crossover Trail
Davis Path
Boott Spur
AMC Joe Dodge Lodge
Pinkham Notch
Lost Pond
Wildcat Ski Area
Edmands Path
Mount Franklin
Mount Eisenhower Loop Trail
Mount Eisenhower
Mount Pierce
Crawford Path
Mount Eisenhower Trail
Dry River Trail
Glen Boulder Trail
Gibbs Falls
Crawford Path
Mizpah Spring Hut
Dry River Cutoff
Mizpah Cutoff Trail
Webster Cliff Trail
Mount Clinton Trail
Mount Jackson
Dry River
Presidential Range– Dry River Wilderness
White Mountain National Forest
Mount Webster
Crawford Notch State Park
302
16
16
to Jackson
N
0        2 MILES
0        3 KILOMETERS
2800
3000
2800
2600
2400
2200
2000
1600
2200
2000
2400
2600
2800
3000
3200
3400
3800
5000
5200
5400
5600
4600
4400
4200
4000
3800
3600
3400
3200
3000
2800
2600
2400
2200
2000
1800
1400
1600

## DAY 9: MADISON SPRING HUT TO JOE DODGE LODGE

**Distance:** 7.6 miles
**Elevation gain/loss:** 540 feet/3350 feet
**Difficulty:** Difficult
**Lodge elevation:** 2032 feet
**Pinkham Notch GPS:** 44.2622°N, 71.2459°W

From Madison Spring Hut, ascend 0.6 mile to the Mount Madison summit (5366 feet). The rough trail, marked with large cairns, requires scrambling up and over the boulder-strewn mountaintop. At the summit, take care to continue east on the Osgood Trail (in foggy, windy weather, be careful not to take the Watson Path or the Howker Ridge Trail, which both veer north). At Osgood Junction, where both the Parapet Trail and the Daniel Webster-Scout Trail cross the Osgood Trail, continue to descend through more very rocky terrain in a southeasterly direction for another 2 miles to Osgood Cutoff. Turn right (west) at Osgood Cutoff, heading generally southwest for 0.6 mile to reach the Madison Gulf Trail. Along the way you will pass a junction on the left with the Great Gulf Trail, after which the two trails run together.

The two trails soon cross Parapet Brook, and then the Madison Gulf Trail comes in on the right (north) to join the Osgood Cutoff and the Great Gulf Trail. The three trails continue together for a very short ways, crossing the West Branch Peabody River to reach a T intersection. Here the Osgood Cutoff ends, and the Madison Gulf Trail turns left (south), while the Great Gulf Trail goes straight (west). Turn left at the T to follow the Madison Gulf Trail south for 2 miles downhill until it

*The AMC croo signs their packboards at the end of the season.*

crosses the paved Mount Washington Auto Road and connects with Old Jackson Road.

Continue on Old Jackson Road, a well-marked old bridleway, for 1.8 miles at a moderate descent to Pinkham Notch. Joe Dodge Lodge, on State Route 16 south of Gorham, is a good place to take a break—either overnight or for a short refreshment stop if you plan to push on to Carter Notch Hut in one long day.

## DAY 10: REST DAY

Enjoy the comforts of the Joe Dodge Lodge on this rest day. Take a shower, rest in a comfy bed or bunk, partake of leisurely meals in the dining room, and curl up with a good book in the living room or library. The lodge also offers free programs including guided day hikes and evening talks on astronomy and other topics. Keep in shape with a short hike to Square Ledge (0.8 mile one-way) or Lost Pond (1.7 miles one-way).

## DAY 11: PINKHAM NOTCH TO CARTER NOTCH HUT

**Distance:** 3.8 miles

**Elevation gain/loss:** 1900 feet/0 feet

**Difficulty:** Moderate

**Hut elevation:** 3288 feet

**Hut GPS:** 44.2593°N, 71.1953°W

**Trailhead:** Nineteen Mile Brook Trailhead 44.3019°N, 71.2211°W

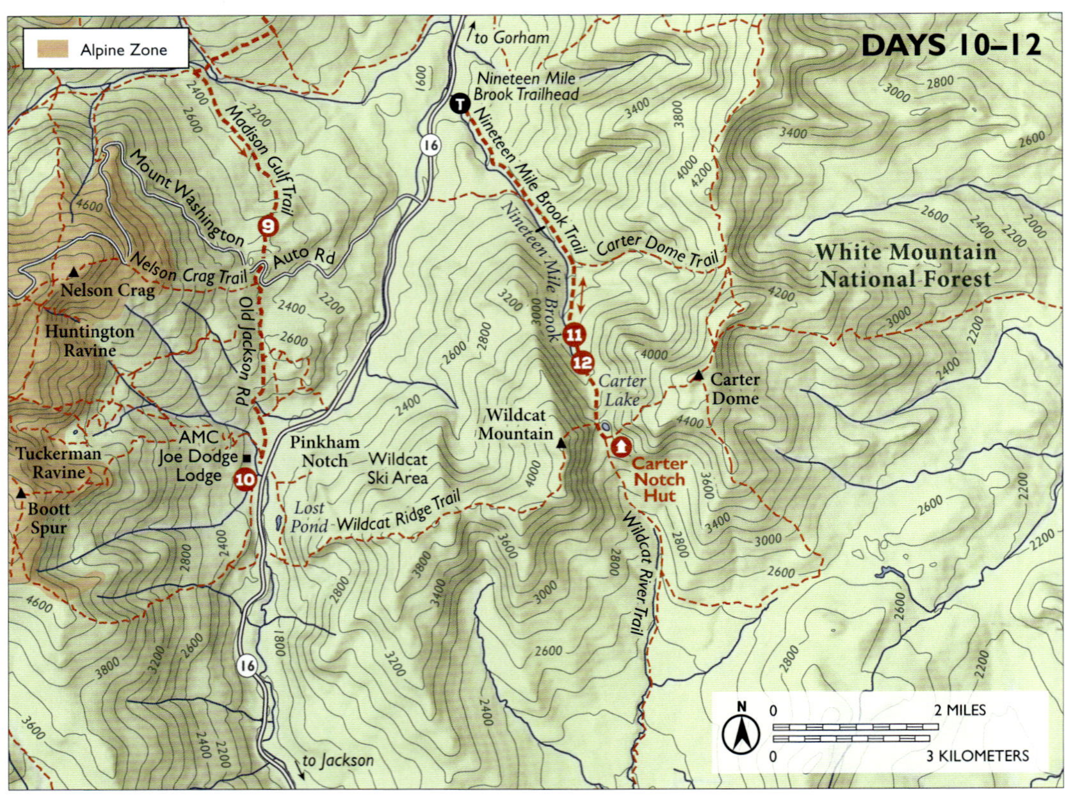

*Looking back on Lakes of the Clouds Hut from the slopes of Mount Washington*

## Getting There

From Pinkham Notch, head north on SR 16 on foot or by car for 3 miles. The Nineteen Mile Brook Trailhead (a stop on the AMC shuttle) is on the right, a mile past Mount Washington Auto Road.

## On the Trail

The Nineteen Mile Brook Trail, the easiest and shortest trail to Carter Notch Hut, ascends moderately along an old logging road beside the brook, crossing two tributaries and reaching a concrete dam at 1.2 miles. The trail gets rougher as it approaches the junction with the Carter Dome Trail at 1.9 miles. Continuing upward, the trail crosses the brook several times by footbridge, then continues to the junction with the Wildcat Ridge Trail at 3.6 miles. The Nineteen Mile Brook Trail drops steeply after this junction, passing Carter Lake and a second smaller lake before reaching Carter Notch Hut after 0.2 mile.

*Option:* You can ascend to Carter Notch Hut via the Wildcat Ridge Trail (which the Appalachian Trail follows), but this route is longer, steeper, and quite exposed. Smith's *White Mountain Guide* provides navigation details (see Resources).

## DAY 12: CARTER NOTCH HUT TO PINKHAM NOTCH

**Distance:** 3.8 miles
**Elevation gain/loss:** 0 feet/1900 feet
**Difficulty:** Moderate

Retrace your steps from the previous day, descending from Carter Notch Hut via the Nineteen Mile Brook Trail for 3.8 miles to the Nineteen Mile Brook Trailhead and parking lot.

# ADIRONDACK HAMLETS TO HUTS

*The lands of the state, now owned or hereafter acquired, constituting the forest preserve as now fixed by law, shall be forever kept as wild forest lands.*

—New York State constitution, Article XIV, establishing the Adirondack Park's "forever wild" provision

**Location:** Adirondack Park, northeastern New York; office in Saranac Lake, New York

**Distance:** Distance between lodgings depends on itinerary; featured itinerary 46.1 miles (23.4 miles hiking, 19.8 miles paddling, 2.9 miles portaging)

**Elevation gain/loss:** 4070 feet/4120 feet

**Difficulty:** Easy to difficult, depending on itinerary

**Terrain:** Low mountain peaks, valleys, deep forests, lakes, and rivers, with towns, hamlets, and private inholdings

**Modes of travel:** Summer hiking, paddling, and biking; winter skiing and snowshoeing

**Season:** Year-round

**Huts:** Existing lodgings in area communities

---

**THE NEWEST US HUT SYSTEM** has no huts! Adirondack Hamlets to Huts (AHH) offers a new hut-to-hut model, working with existing lodging businesses in local communities to shelter and support recreational travelers. The 6.1-million-acre Adirondack Park was established in the late nineteenth century—the first state forest preserve in the nation. Today, the park, roughly half private and half publicly owned, combines pristine wilderness and restored forests with private inholdings including 101 towns and hamlets, farms, timber operations, and resorts. Forty-five percent of the public lands is designated wilderness with mechanized transport prohibited, and 52 percent is preserved as wild forest (with bikes, snowmobiles, and other mechanized transport allowed).

AHH seeks to honor the distinctive natural and cultural history of the park, designing treks that incorporate the myriad trails, waterways, and local hostelries, which range from cabins to motels to Great Camps—rustic, elegant Gilded Age lodging compounds. The organization coordinates reservations and logistics, acting like a travel agent for trekkers. With the park's 3000 lakes and ponds and 30,000 miles of rivers and streams to pick from, AHH offers a variety of hiking and paddling treks, with some tours combining both with other methods of human-powered travel. After a full day on the water or on the trail, travelers may sleep at a rustic resort one night and at an elegant lodge the next, eat at area restaurants, indulge in trail lunches prepared by local eateries, or enjoy self-prepared meals.

*Blue Mountain Lake from the summit of Castle Rock Mountain* (Photo by John DiGiacomo)

Since the early nineteenth century, writers have exclaimed over the wild beauty of the Adirondack Park. Reverend John Todd observed in 1845: "The fact is new and seems strange to many that there should be in the northeastern part of New York a wilderness almost unbroken and unexplored, embracing a territory considerably larger than the whole state of Massachusetts; a territory exhibiting every variety of soil, from the bold mountain that lifts its head up far beyond the limit of vegetable life to the most beautiful meadow land on which the eye ever rested." The Adirondack Mountains are the park's centerpiece, with forty-three high peaks exceeding 4000 feet. The Adirondack Park—the size of Yellowstone, Glacier, Yosemite, and Everglades National Parks combined—is also home to the headwaters of the Hudson and St. Lawrence Rivers and Lake Champlain. Popular resort destinations include Lake George and Saranac Lake. Lake Placid, about 15 miles east of Saranac Lake, hosted the Winter Olympics in 1932 and 1980.

The dense forests of upstate New York drew not only nature pilgrims but also timber entrepreneurs and loggers. As early as the 1870s, cries of alarm rose in response to mass deforestation. New York was losing precious scenic resources, and erosion and flooding caused by logging were harming water quality downstate and threatening lucrative canal routes. In 1894, the "forever wild" section of the state constitution designated this area as a forest preserve, in which existing and "hereafter acquired" state lands were to be protected and "the timber thereon [never] be sold, removed or destroyed." This act of the New York legislature set the stage for the federal Wilderness Act of 1964. While camping in the Adirondacks in 1946, Howard Zahniser, a leader of the Wilderness Society, first articulated the idea that "we need some strong legislation which will be similar in effect on a national scale to what Article XIV, Section 1 is to the New York State Forest Preserve. We need to reclaim for the people, perhaps through their representatives in Congress, control over the wilderness regions of America." Less than twenty years later, the Wilderness Act—authored primarily by Zahniser—was passed into law by the US Congress.

The Adirondack Park embodies the conviction that humans and nature can live in harmony. New York State, seeking to boost the economy of this area, promotes the Adirondacks as an outdoor recreation destination and maintains a 2000-mile network of trails. The state is keen to draw visitors to the Adirondacks from around the world. Recognizing that AHH's "hut dreams" could help realize this goal, two different state agencies awarded planning grants to the organization. Using an exemplary planning process (see "Planning a Community-Based Hut System"), AHH engaged local communities, identified and prioritized potential routes, and developed a business model to stimulate economic development through nature-based tourism with a light imprint on the land.

According to its mission statement, AHH is a nonprofit that "creates, manages and promotes an internationally-acclaimed hamlet-to-hut system that fosters vibrant communities by advancing economic development, conservation and wellness." Every route begins and ends in a local community. Similar to village-to-village walking in the United Kingdom, AHH seeks to connect communities using existing trail networks and water routes. Local officials, landowners, and business owners are mostly very cooperative and enthusiastic about the concept's potential. So far, AHH relies on existing accommodations for initial routes and aspires to own and manage a few lodgings in select locations throughout the park.

AHH opened for business in 2020 after test runs in 2018 and 2019, offering three different routes ranging from two to four days, with plans to add more routes over time. The initial routes include one or two days of paddling on the Fulton Chain of Lakes, along with the option for one or two days of either hiking or biking. Treks can be customized by working with the owners, and longer adventures are planned.

Local restaurants provide breakfasts and dinners, and bag lunches can be purchased for on-trail picnics. Proposed places of lodging will provide kitchen facilities for trekkers who want to prepare their own meals. Gear shuttle and car relocation services are available, and you can choose either self-guided or guided treks. Tours require minimal specialized personal gear and accommodate a range of skill and fitness levels.

This system reflects the values and experience of its founders, Joe Dadey and Jack Drury (see "Founders' Story"). They aim to open backcountry experiences to a wide range of outdoor enthusiasts and recruit the next generation of support for environmental protection. A five-hour drive from New York City, the Adirondacks are accessible to a diverse population. AHH, according to its website, wants to "help bring new visitors to places that are often overlooked in favor of more well-traveled Adirondack destinations. So we spread the love. And the crowds."

## FOUNDERS' STORY

Joe Dadey and Jack Drury bring a well-matched skill set to creating a hut system. They have both lived and worked in the Adirondacks for years—as licensed guides and in outdoor leadership positions. Both are former college professors (Joe at Paul Smith's College and Jack at North Country Community College, both in New York state). Jack is a planner by nature and profession; he has operated an educational consulting firm and worked nationally and internationally. Joe is a doer; he has been a forest ranger, has led forty-day youth wilderness programs, and has conducted study-abroad programs focusing on sustainable and adventure tourism. Jack, with degrees in outdoor education, also attended three trainings with mentor Paul Petzoldt, founder of the National Outdoor Leadership School. Joe earned a master's degree in outdoor recreation and a PhD in environmental policy and communication. Both men love to connect people and communities with nature. Everything they do is a form of environmental education.

Joe and Jack hatched the idea of Adirondack Hamlets to Huts in 2015. Just back from a student trip to New Zealand, Joe was fired up about huts. Jack was a veteran of environmental campaigns, including an effort to prioritize and establish a series of community-based trails in light of a long-standing regional debate over whether a rail line should be ripped up to create a recreational trail. They decided to establish a hut system in the Adirondacks centered on economic development and community education. Together they have worked tirelessly to win hearts, minds, and grant funding in the region and have launched a hut-to-hut model that has great promise.

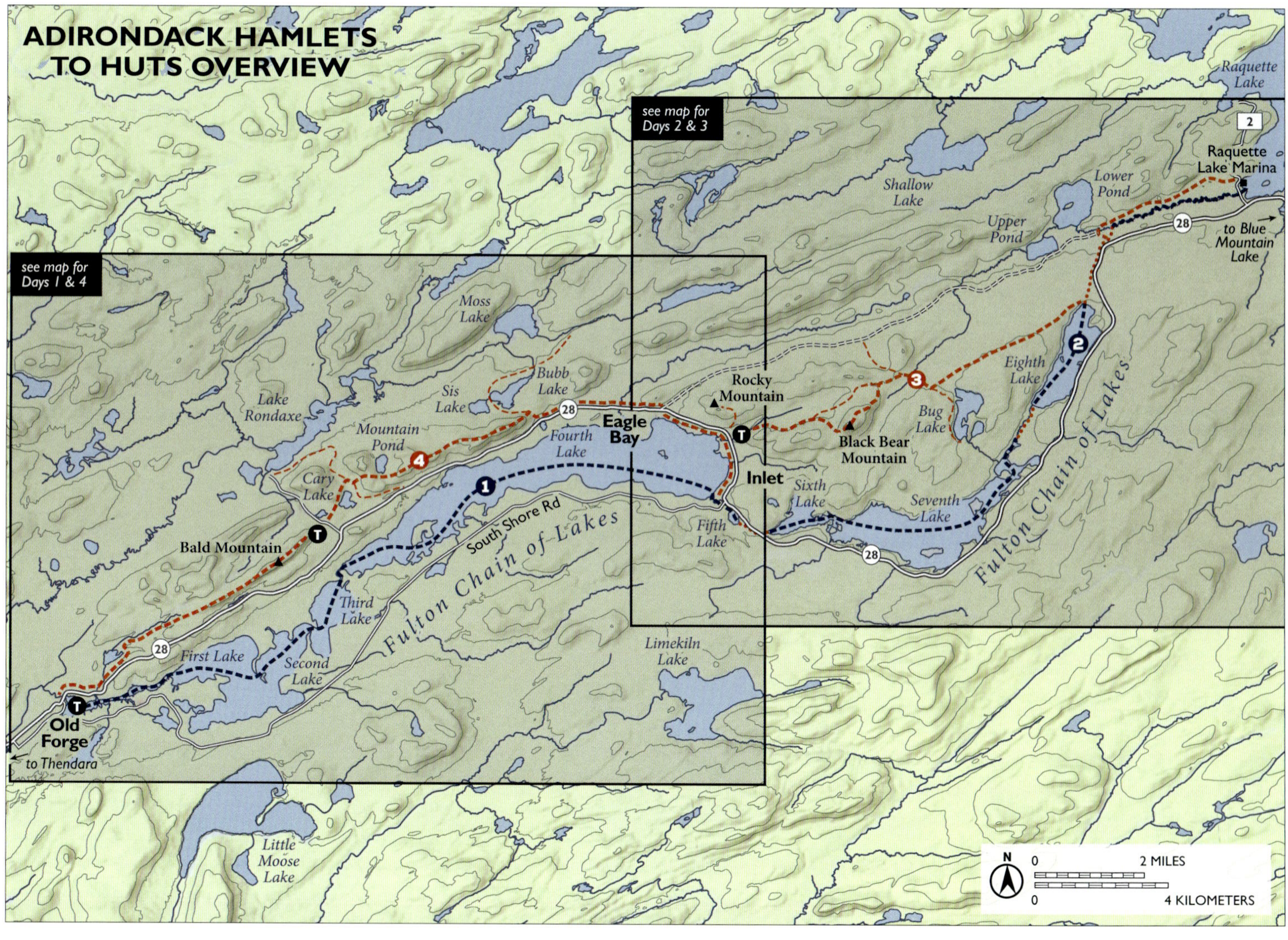
ADIRONDACK HAMLETS
TO HUTS OVERVIEW
Raquette Lake
2
see map for Days 2 & 3
Raquette Lake Marina
Shallow Lake
Lower Pond
Upper Pond
28
to Blue Mountain Lake
see map for Days 1 & 4
Eighth Lake
2
Moss Lake
Bubb Lake
Rocky Mountain
3
Bug Lake
Fulton Chain of Lakes
Sis Lake
Lake Rondaxe
28
Eagle Bay
Black Bear Mountain
Mountain Pond
4
Fourth Lake
T
Inlet
Seventh Lake
Cary Lake
1
Sixth Lake
T
South Shore Rd
Fifth Lake
Bald Mountain
Fulton Chain of Lakes
28
Third Lake
Fulton Chain of Lakes
28
First Lake
Second Lake
Limekiln Lake
T
Old Forge
to Thendara
Little Moose Lake
N
0    2 MILES
0    4 KILOMETERS

Trekkers stay in affiliated lodges, camps, cabins, hostels, and motels in communities along the route. Future huts and other lodging venues may need to be constructed to fill gaps in the overnight system, establish trail connections, and make routes operational. Some locations will have several lodging options, whereas others will have only one—specifics that will change over time. AHH, a work in progress, was opening as we wrote this chapter. Check the website or give them a call for the most up-to-date information on lodging options and available routes.

In some locations, you may select lodging with or without kitchen facilities, and you will receive a list of dining options and grocery stores in each hamlet along the route. Reservations include staying in a hamlet the night *before* departure; so, unlike other hut systems, trips are noted with more nights than days (e.g., four nights, three days).

## PLANNING AND PREPARATION

**Contact:** www.adkh2h.org; office (518) 354-5100; mobile (315) 657-1320; info@adkh2h.org

**Booking:** Reservations required; route options listed on the website; make reservations by phone; AHH is developing an online booking system that will allow trekkers to reserve accommodations; rent canoes, kayaks, or bikes; and make shuttle arrangements

**Membership:** In development at time of publication

**Rates:** $$$; AHH aims to provide a range of options that make the routes affordable to a wide demographic

*The hamlet of North Creek has welcoming eateries and shops.* (Photo by John DiGiacomo)

**Transportation:** The following circuit starts and ends in Old Forge, which can be reached by personal vehicle; the Adirondack Railroad operates in the park and stops in Thendara (1.6 miles from Old Forge)

## MAPS

Simple PDF maps downloadable from the AHH website may be supplemented in the future by customized maps of the routes that highlight the natural (e.g., swim spots, waterfalls, and vistas) and cultural (e.g., historic landmarks) features along the way. Meanwhile, the Old Forge Area Outdoor Adventure Map (Green Goat Maps) covers the circuit very well at 1:40,000 scale; the

Adirondack Paddler's Map South (Paddlesports Press) at 1:50,000 scale contains less detail. The traverse is covered in six 1:24,000 USGS quad topo maps, which provide more detail than necessary: Old Forge, Limekiln Lake, Mount Tom, Big Moose, Eagle Bay, and Raquette Lake.

### PACKING TIPS

Make meal decisions in advance (restaurant meals, packed lunches, and/or self-prepared meals); plan and pack accordingly. Bring two bags: a day pack for the trail and a duffel bag (recommended) for personal clothing and gear; this will be transported by AHH to each overnight destination. Pack only what you need, and avoid loose items and tie-ons. Waterproof bags or plastic trash bag liners are recommended for day packs. Be sure to pack in-town clothes and footwear. Include a bag for dirty laundry.

### OTHER TIPS

Blackfly season extends roughly from early May through mid- to late June. Book canoe and bike rentals in advance; AHH will help coordinate this. Consider renting wheels to pull the canoe for portages, and pay attention to instructions on how they work.

### ITINERARY: FULTON CHAIN LOOP

*Five nights, four days; 45.6 miles including 23.4 miles hiking, 19.3 miles paddling, 2.9 miles portaging*

The Fulton Chain of Lakes is a string of eight lakes created by damming the Moose River. Starting and ending in Old Forge, the route involves two days of scenic paddling on this classic waterway, ending at Raquette Lake, followed by two days of hiking (gravel biking option also available) back to Old Forge.

*Participants celebrate the first Adirondacks Hamlets to Huts trip. (Photo by John DiGiacomo)*

# PLANNING A COMMUNITY-BASED HUT SYSTEM

Using an innovative hut-to-hut model, Adirondack Hamlets to Huts (AHH) creates synergies by broadly engaging the citizens and economies of Adirondack hamlets with recreational use and conservation of the region's lands and waters. Two preliminary planning processes, with funding from the New York State Department of State and the New York State Department of Environmental Conservation, incorporated extensive community consultations with local officials, business owners, and citizens. At dozens of meetings, folks were invited to vet the concept; contribute ideas about sites, trails, and cultural attractions; and voice questions and concerns. Which features should be incorporated in AHH routes? Where might clients eat and sleep, and how might they engage with locals?

Founders Joe Dadey and Jack Drury then worked with interested citizens and state and local officials to identify and evaluate the fifty-nine potential trekking routes that emerged from the two state-funded projects. Spending weeks in the field, they mapped and described each potential route, cataloging natural features and cultural attractions. For each route, they identified implementation challenges, came up with a set of questions and observations, and applied a ranking system to rate the route's feasibility and desirability. The initial routes were selected after reviewing the results with state and local officials.

This community-based planning model positions the organization to work with folks throughout the region as new routes are added in coming years.

On the second day at Seventh Lake, there are great opportunities for swimming and picnicking, as well as a chance to visit Cathedral Pines, a grove of white pines over three hundred years old. Paddlers are advised to take care; these lakes are very popular with motorboats. The hiking route invites trekkers to ascend three peaks with great views: Black Bear Mountain (2448 feet), Rocky Mountain (2205 feet), and Bald Mountain (2350 feet). Directions to your lodgings and to restaurant and grocery stores in town are provided by AHH.

*Note:* The following route description was kindly provided by AHH cofounder Joe Dadey. Due to the pandemic, this is the only itinerary in the book we were unable to experience in person as part of our research, though Sam participated in the first AHH pilot trip on a similar route.

### NIGHT 1: STAY IN OLD FORGE

Travelers are encouraged to arrive early in the afternoon so they can explore the community and take care of any last-minute details.

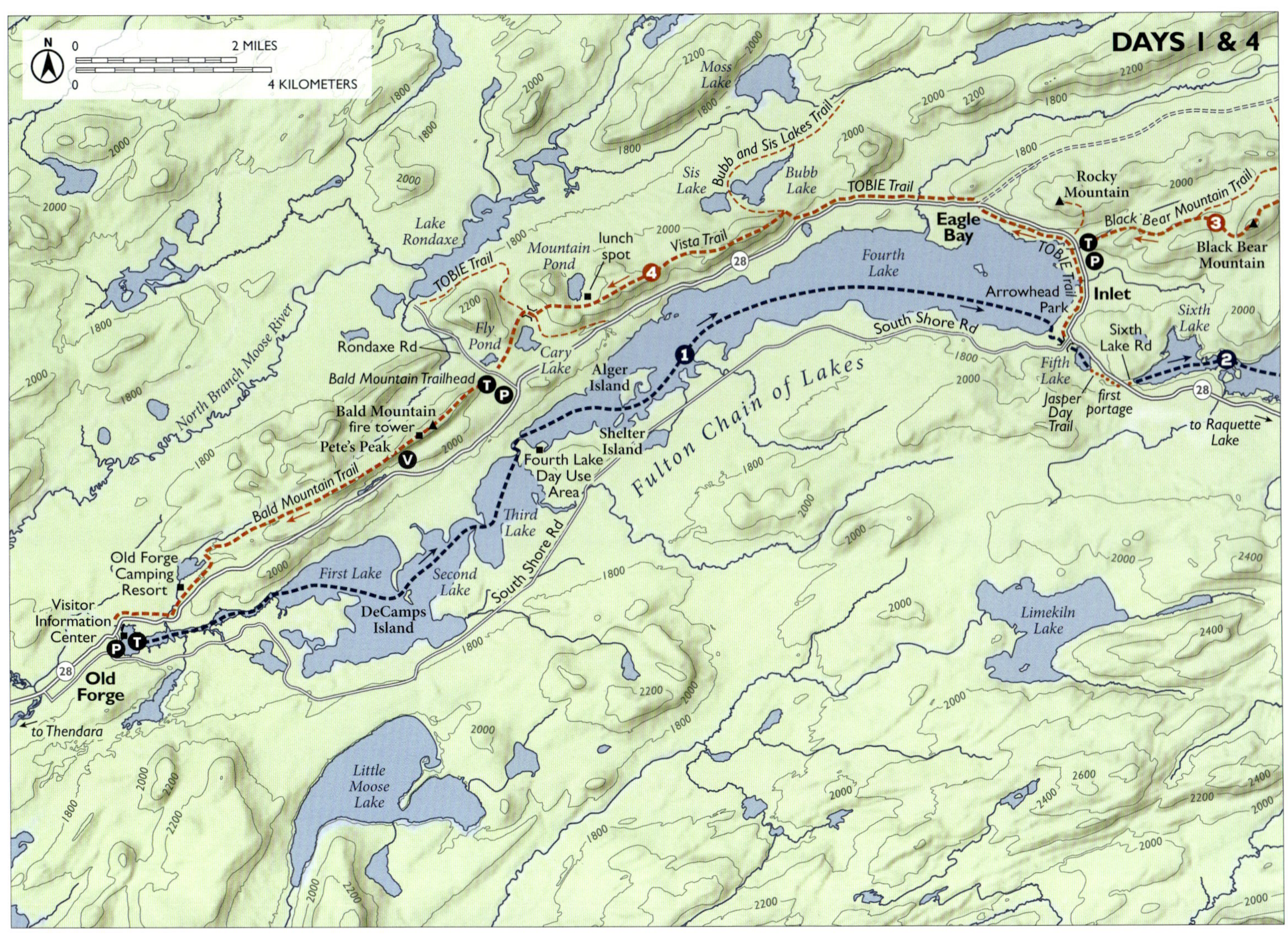

DAYS 1 & 4
N
2 MILES
4 KILOMETERS
Moss Lake
Bubb and Sis Lakes Trail
Sis Lake
Bubb Lake
TOBIE Trail
Rocky Mountain
Black Bear Mountain Trail
Black Bear Mountain
Lake Rondaxe
Mountain Pond
lunch spot
Vista Trail
Eagle Bay
TOBIE Trail
Fourth Lake
TOBIE Trail
Fly Pond
Cary Lake
Arrowhead Park
South Shore Rd
Inlet
Sixth Lake
Rondaxe Rd
Alger Island
Sixth Lake Rd
Fifth Lake
Bald Mountain Trailhead
Fulton Chain of Lakes
Jasper Day Trail
first portage
to Raquette Lake
North Branch Moose River
Bald Mountain fire tower
Pete's Peak
Shelter Island
Fourth Lake Day Use Area
Bald Mountain Trail
Third Lake
Old Forge Camping Resort
First Lake
Second Lake
DeCamps Island
South Shore Rd
South Shore Rd
Limekiln Lake
Visitor Information Center
Old Forge
to Thendara
Little Moose Lake

*Paddling Browns Tract near Raquette Lake (Photo by John DiGiacomo)*

## Getting There

From Albany, drive west on I-90 (tolls apply) toward Utica. Take exit 31 for State Route 12 north. Proceed on SR 12 to Alder Creek, where you continue north on SR 28 to Old Forge.

From Syracuse, drive east on I-90 (tolls apply). Take exit 33 toward Verona/Rome, and follow SR 365 to Barneveld. Proceed on SR 12 to Alder Creek, where you continue north on SR 28 to Old Forge.

### DAY I: PADDLE OLD FORGE TO INLET

**Distance:** 10.4 miles
**Elevation gain/loss:** None
**Difficulty:** Easy
**Trailhead:** 43.71161°N, 74.96901°W

Paddlers put in at the small dock to the left (north) of the Visitor Information Center (where there are restroom facilities) and to the right (south) of the dam and the covered walkway that crosses just below the dam. A large paddling map sign and trail register identify the entry point. Parking is available in the lot on the other side of the dam across from the put-in location.

Proceed down First, Second, and Third Lakes, then through a relatively narrow channel into expansive Fourth Lake. At DeCamps Island on Second Lake, trekkers can stretch their legs and swim. The Bald Mountain fire tower is visible from Second and Third Lakes to the left (north) atop the rocky and cliff-ridden ridge. At the end of the channel connecting Third and Fourth Lakes, the NYSDEC Fourth Lake Day Use Area (with restrooms) is a good place to stop for lunch.

On Fourth Lake, paddle south of Alger Island (state campground), passing Shelter Island on the right. The hamlet of Inlet lies

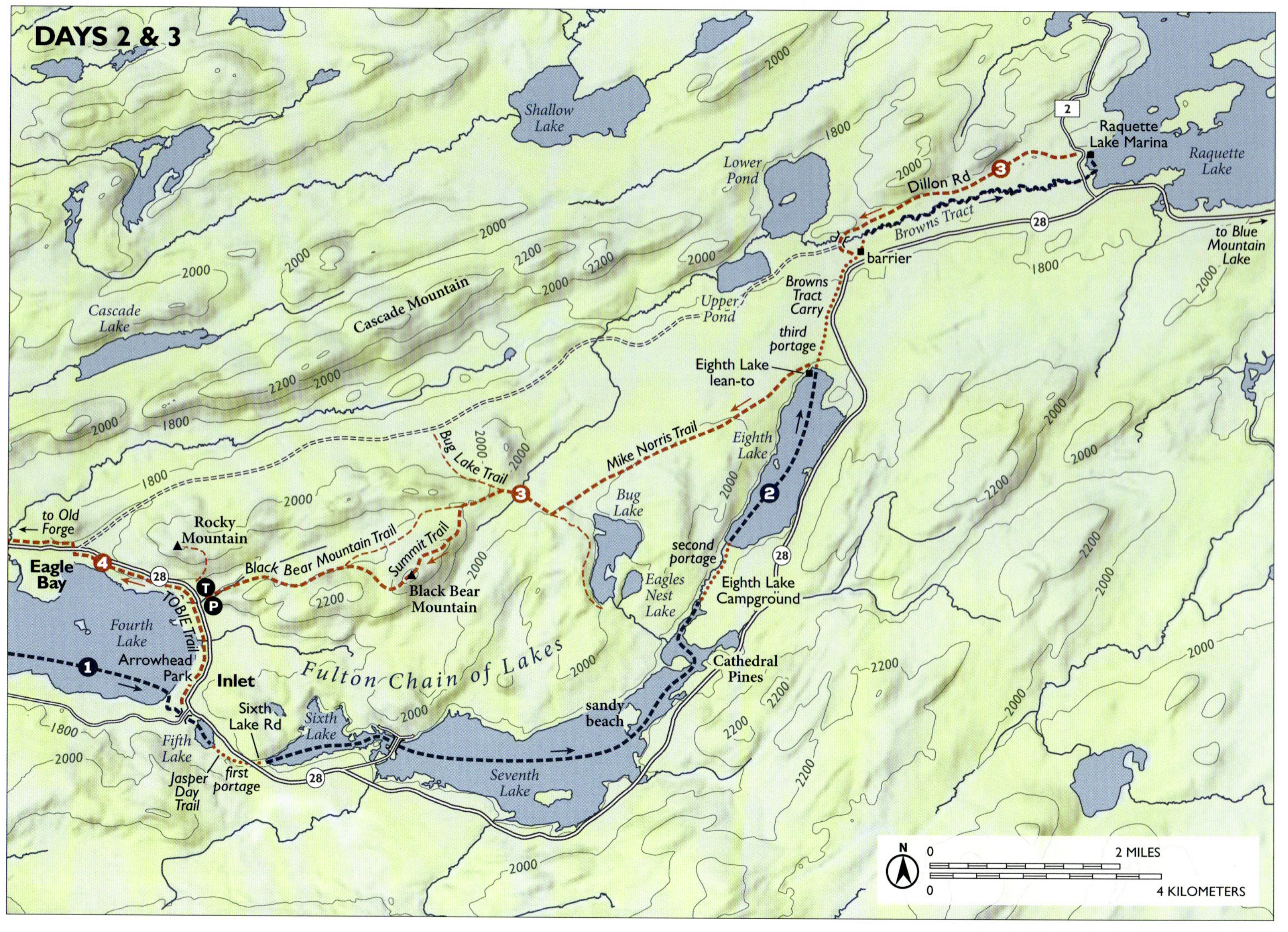
DAYS 2 & 3
Shallow Lake
Lower Pond
1800
2000
2
Raquette Lake Marina
Raquette Lake
Dillon Rd
3
Browns Tract
28
to Blue Mountain Lake
1800
barrier
Browns Tract Carry
Upper Pond
third portage
Eighth Lake lean-to
2000
Cascade Lake
Cascade Mountain
2000
2200
2200
2000
1800
Bug Lake Trail
2000
Mike Norris Trail
Eighth Lake
2000
3
Bug Lake
2
to Old Forge
Rocky Mountain
Black Bear Mountain Trail
Summit Trail
2000
2200
second portage
Eagles Nest Lake
28
Eighth Lake Campground
Eagle Bay
4
28
Black Bear Mountain
TOBIE Trail
T
P
Fourth Lake
1
Arrowhead Park
Inlet
Fulton Chain of Lakes
2000
Cathedral Pines
2200
2200
sandy beach
Sixth Lake Rd
Sixth Lake
1800
Fifth Lake
2000
Jasper Day Trail
first portage
28
Seventh Lake
2000
N
0
2 MILES
0
4 KILOMETERS

at the far northeast end of Fourth Lake. Before settling in for the night, consider ascending Rocky Mountain. Take the TOBIE Trail 1 mile north to access the trailhead for this 1.2-mile round-trip hike with great views. Alternatively, summit this peak at the end of day 3 or the beginning of day 4.

## DAY 2: PADDLE INLET TO RAQUETTE LAKE

**Distance:** 11.8 miles (8.9 miles paddling, plus three portages adding up to 2.9 miles)

**Elevation gain/loss:** 30 feet/80 feet on portages

**Difficulty:** Moderate to difficult (due to length of portages)

**Trailhead:** 43.75353°N, 74.79635°W

The passageway (inlet) to Fifth Lake lies southeast of Arrowhead Park and takes paddlers under the South Shore Road Bridge. The first portage begins at the far end of tiny Fifth Lake and is marked by several small docks. Do not proceed to the right down the very narrow waterway; instead, follow the first portage (0.6 mile total) briefly uphill on the signed Jasper Day Trail to SR 28, where you turn right (southeast) and proceed on a sidewalk along SR 28. Just past a gas station, cross SR 28 via a crosswalk. Bear left onto Sixth Lake Road to a grassy area just above the dam, where you put in at Sixth Lake. An unnamed island (43.7491°N, 74.7268°W) about two-thirds of the way down Seventh Lake has a great sandy beach on its western side and a sheltered cove on the other; both are great places for a break.

Just before the northeast terminus of Seventh Lake, across from the south end of Eighth Lake Campground, look for the water-based access to Cathedral Pines. Hop out of the canoe or kayak and hike about 200 yards to immerse yourselves in this splendid grove. After viewing the pines, canoe north a short distance to the sandy landing at the south end of Eighth Lake Campground.

The second portage at the southern end of Eighth Lake Campground goes through the campground (restrooms and a good swimming beach). After the 1-mile portage, paddle to the northwest end of Eighth Lake for the final portage (1.3 miles total). Before hauling your boat, note the beautiful sandy bottom below the lake's surface and consider pausing to swim. The portage, also known as Browns Tract Carry, roughly parallels SR 28, continuing straight past a barrier at 43.8027°N, 74.6915°W. Shortly after the barrier, the portage trail continues onto a boardwalk through a swamp to the put-in location at Browns Tract.

Canoe east on Browns Tract, a delightful waterway that meanders through a tamarack swamp where several beaver dams require special maneuvering. Paddlers pass under a roadway bridge as Browns Tract empties into Raquette Lake. Once back on open water, proceed to the left (north) and land at the Raquette Lake Marina.

## DAY 3: HIKE RAQUETTE LAKE TO INLET

**Distance:** 10.9 miles

**Elevation gain/loss:** 1860 feet/1840 feet

**Difficulty:** Moderate

**Trailhead:** East end of Dillon Road (43.81295°N, 74.65698°W)

Starting from the east end of Dillon Road, just across from the Raquette Lake Post

*Camp Huntington, originally Camp Pine Knot, is one of the famed Great Camps of the region.* (Photo by John DiGiacomo)

Office, continue north as the road quickly veers to the left (west) behind the community library. Proceed west on Dillon Road, a kind of boat storage graveyard, which turns into a path at 1.2 miles. Cross the Dillon Path Bridge at 2.2 miles (43.803611°N, 74.695079°W), and turn left after the bridge onto a short section of trail that heads southeast and connects at the barrier at 2.6 miles; this is the junction with the Browns Tract Carry, the previous day's third portage. Turn right at the barrier, to walk south along Browns Tract Carry toward Eighth Lake. Just before reaching the Eighth Lake lean-to (43.7898°N, 74.6986°W), veer right (southwest) at 3.6 miles to follow the pleasant woodland Mike Norris Trail, a snowmobile trail in winter.

At 6.1 miles, the Mike Norris Trail reaches a **T** junction with the Bug Lake Trail. Turn right (northwest) to follow the Bug Lake Trail about 0.5 mile to the junction on the left with the Black Bear Mountain Trail. Turn left (southwest), following the Black Bear Mountain Trail to a split in the trail at 7.2 miles, where you can either bear right (west) on the Black Bear Mountain Trail or bear left to drop southwest on the Summit Trail. We recommend ascending Black Bear Mountain on the Summit Trail, which rejoins the alternate peak-avoiding trail at 9.2 miles. The Summit Trail leads to a series of open ledges before the top of Black Bear Mountain, marked by stretches of open rock facing southeast and great 180-degree views.

Continue up and over the mountain and walk 2 miles to the junction with SR 28. Cross the highway to reach the sidewalk on the opposite side of SR 28, which is also the TOBIE Trail. Turn left (south) and follow the sidewalk on the TOBIE Trail along SR 28 for about 1 mile into the hamlet of Inlet.

## DAY 4: HIKE INLET TO OLD FORGE

**Distance:** 13 miles
**Elevation gain/loss:** 2180 feet/2200 feet
**Difficulty:** Moderate to difficult, due only to mileage
**Trailhead:** 43.75353°N, 74.79635°W

Head north out of Inlet on the same sidewalk along the TOBIE Trail that you walked in on the previous day. At about 1 mile, you come to the parking lot where you encounter the Rocky Mountain Trailhead. Consider summiting this peak, if you haven't already, even though it will add 1.2 miles to your hiking day. At the trailhead and parking lot, re-cross SR 28 to return to the sidewalk and follow the TOBIE Trail west into Eagle Bay, where the trail crosses SR 28 at a crosswalk. There is an unmanned information center here with restrooms. At 3.7 miles, take a right (west-northwest), leaving the TOBIE Trail to briefly (for 0.2 mile) follow the Bubb and Sis Lakes Trail before turning left (west-southwest) upon reaching the junction with the Vista Trail, which is also marked on some maps as the Scenic Mountain Trail.

Follow the Vista Trail west along a ridge that parallels SR 28, which is below to the left. Keep an eye out to the right (northeast)

for a view of Bubb, Sis, and Moss Lakes. The trail drops down the ridge on its approach to Mountain Pond; there is a spur trail on the right at 6.5 miles to a rocky outcropping on the edge of Mountain Pond, a great spot for lunch. Continue your descent on the Vista Trail until its brief junction with the TOBIE Trail at 7.3 miles. Turn right on the TOBIE Trail, cross a bridge (at 43.7540°N, 74.8950°W), and then quickly turn left, continuing to follow the Vista Trail along the west side of tranquil Cary Lake.

The trail comes within sight of Fly Pond on the right before crossing Rondaxe Road at 8.1 miles, where you will find the Bald Mountain Trailhead and parking lot (43.7456°N, 74.8997°W). From here, follow the Bald Mountain Trail to the fire tower at its summit, enjoying fabulous views overlooking Second, Third, and Fourth Lakes below. Proceed past the fire tower down the mountain's western ridge, pausing at Pete's Peak viewpoint at 9.6 miles. Follow the trail, a snowmobile trail in winter, down the ridge, turning sharply left (south) before reaching the Old Forge Camping Resort.

Continue through the Old Forge Camping Resort and veer left before crossing Beaver Brook to arrive at SR 28. Turn right (west) on SR 28, staying on the sidewalk, and follow signs to Old Forge, less than a mile away.

## NIGHT 5: STAY IN OLD FORGE

Check out the old-fashioned, extensively stocked hardware store before departing.

# PORCUPINE MOUNTAINS WILDERNESS STATE PARK

*In the late 1960s Senator [Joseph] Mack and the Gogebic and Ontonagon boards of supervisors fully intended to break up the park and mine, log, and build road through here. A large amount of people got up in arms about that and managed to save the park. Then the environmentalists got goofy and decided every man-made thing had to be destroyed to call this a wilderness area. This meant another fight for they and the commercial interests that wanted the cabins destroyed! So you see, what you enjoy and appreciate now has been fought for.*

*—J. Vann Hulla, Oct. 1979, Section 17 Cabin logbook*

**Location:** Porcupine Mountains Wilderness State Park, near Silver City, Michigan

**Distance:** Cabins 4 to 6 miles apart; featured itinerary 22.7 miles

**Elevation gain/loss:** 2400 feet/2400 feet

**Difficulty:** Easy to moderate

**Terrain:** Low mountains cloaked in old-growth hemlock-hardwood forest along Lake Superior

**Modes of travel:** Hike

**Seasons:** Park open year-round; backcountry cabins open mid-May through November

**Huts:** 15 backcountry cabins (capacity 2–8); 17 cabins total in park, 4 yurts, plus tiny house on wheels; self-service; exclusive use

---

**MICHIGAN'S PORCUPINE MOUNTAINS WILDERNESS STATE PARK** (PMWSP), little known outside the region, is a jewel among the nation's state parks. With 21 cabins and yurts and multiple family-friendly, hut-to-hut traverse options, the "Porkies" offers one of the oldest, largest, and most accessible hut systems in the US. This nearly 60,000-acre park—the largest of Michigan's state parks—is set along the spectacular shoreline of Lake Superior, the largest freshwater body in the world. With nearly two-thirds preserved as wilderness, this expansive remnant of

OPPOSITE:  *Several waterfalls punctuate the Little Carp River.*

old-growth hemlock-hardwood forest boasts nearly 100 miles of hiking trails and 23 miles of groomed cross-country ski trails, which offer deep woods, ridgeline views, lakes, streams and waterfalls, and abundant wildlife. The park also attracts backpackers, downhill skiers, paddlers, swimmers, hunters, anglers, and car campers.

The mountains get their name from the native Ojibwe, who recognized a crouching porcupine in the silhouette of this low-lying range. The forest cloak has been characterized by the Michigan Natural Features Inventory as "the largest and best tract of virgin Northern Hardwoods in North America," including hemlock and sugar maple, American basswood, yellow birch, white pine, and northern white cedar. The scenic Presque Isle, Big Carp, and Upper Carp Rivers—with seemingly countless waterfalls—run through the park, which is also home to the popular Lake of the Clouds and other jewel-like lakes. Naturalists have identified at least fourteen different ecological communities in this pristine setting. Visitors imbibe the wonder of vibrantly healthy wilderness inhabited by a vast number and astonishing density of species of plants, fungi, mammals, birds, insects, and reptiles. Learn more from *The Last Porcupine Mountains Companion*, an insightful guidebook by retired ranger Michael Rafferty and retired park interpreter Robert Sprague.

The beauty of the Porkies was almost destroyed by loggers, copper miners, and others seeking to extract abundant natural resources. In 1925, the first superintendent of Michigan State Parks floated the initial, but unsuccessful, proposal to create a state park. In 1935, the US Congress failed to act on a bill to acquire a large parcel for the nation. Finally, in 1940, the Save the Porcupine Mountains Association launched a campaign to protect this beloved retreat. Created by local businessman Ray Dick, his son Bud, and family friends Walter Speaker and Edwin Johnson, this group realized that if logging continued at its current pace, their beloved forest would be gone within five years. Around the campfire at Dick's cabin near Presque Isle, they hatched a plan to save the Porkies.

Journalist and conservationist Ben East, who reported on the birth of this movement, helped rally fellow conservationists, including nationwide organizations, to the cause. The group enlisted established authors to sing the praises of this little-known, threatened landscape. Ecologist Aldo Leopold was perhaps the most influential conservation writer to join the cause. In an article in *American Outdoors* titled "The Last Stand," he argued for preserving this remnant of old-growth forest as a sort of forest museum and living reminder of what has been lost. "[The Porcupine forest] is a symbol. It portrays a chapter in national history which we should not be allowed to forget. When we abolish the last sample of The Great Uncut, we are, in a sense, burning books." After five years of dedicated campaigning by the association, the Michigan legislature protected the area as a state park.

Despite this status, commercial interests continued to exert pressure to allow more logging and other development, including building roads in the old forest. Finally, in 1972, a plan to designate a large parcel as state wilderness was adopted, and 40,808 acres were rededicated under Michigan's Wilderness and Natural Areas Act as a Wilderness State Park. The park is now a wilderness reserve of old-growth forest ringed by mostly reforested park land that offers amenities including campgrounds, a visitors center, a small downhill ski area, and year-round cabins and yurts.

When land receives a wilderness designation, the managing agency usually makes efforts to restore the area to an untrammeled state so that human structures and activities do not disturb ecosystems. In the mid-70s, fearing that the Michigan Department of Natural Resources would dismantle the cabins in the newly defined wilderness, longtime park users lobbied to preserve them. Joseph Van Hulla, from a nearby Wisconsin town, developed a novel and effective advocacy strategy. In addition to spearheading a letter-writing campaign to state officials, he left powerful messages in the cabin logbooks, encouraging other users to join the effort. By the late '70s, the master plan for the park was amended to define the existing cabins as "non-conforming uses" in the wilderness and allow them to remain.

Thirty years earlier, Leopold had articulated this vision: "I would like to see the Porcupine region preserved as an act of national contrition.... To this end it had best be kept roadless, axeless, and hotel-less, and open only to ski or foot travel." Since the 1970s, the wilderness section of the park has remained roadless, and its ancient trees continue to thrive. There is no hotel, but there are cabins. The Porkies offer hardy hikers a unique combination of pristine wilderness and comfortable rustic huts for overnight shelter. Would Leopold approve? We think so.

## HUTS AND AMENITIES

The park's rental cabins combine once-private structures adapted for public use, former ranger outposts, and log and stick-style (wood frame construction) cabins purpose-built for visitors beginning in the late 1940s. The twelve original backcountry cabins were in or near what is now wilderness. Over the years, five cabins and four yurts have been added, most accessible via a short drive or short walk or ski in. While a few of these newer cabins are large and boast more amenities, like the backcountry cabins, they lack electricity and cookstoves. The Porkies cabins are popular with hunters and anglers and attract many repeat visitors mostly from Michigan, Ohio, and Wisconsin.

We highlight the fifteen rustic backcountry cabins accessible only by foot and easily connected to form a multiday traverse (all shown on the park map below to help you plan your traverse). While not initially conceived as a hut-to-hut system, these cabins link readily to support trips of two to five or more days. On average, the cabins are

*Lake of the Clouds Cabin blends in well with the surrounding forest.*

spaced about 4 to 6 miles apart and 1 to 3 miles from trailhead parking, making this system a great option for families with children and people new to hut-to-hut travel. Four of the cabins are on the North Country Trail and six are on the Lake Superior Trail.

The cabins are self-service, supplied with basic cooking and eating utensils; unlike for other self-service huts described in the book, overnight visitors must bring their own cookstoves and fuel. Each hut has bunk beds with mattresses, a woodstove for heating, fire extinguishers, counterspace for food preparation, and a common area with picnic table, benches, and chairs. Some cabins have outhouses close by, while others require a steep uphill hike. Collect drinking water from nearby lakes, rivers, or streams, and be sure to filter it. The rustic cabins do not have electricity; in addition to headlamps, we recommend bringing a lantern or other light source to illuminate the interior. The windows have screens. Each cabin has an outdoor fire ring with log seating.

Cabins are supplied with a bow saw (with extra blades), work gloves, and an axe for cutting up down and dead trees into firewood. Leaving firewood for the next group is an important part of the cabin ethos (see "Firewood: Paying It Forward"). Plan to spend an hour or two a day on this pleasant chore.

## WILDERNESS CABINS

Visitors can choose from eleven cabins within the park wilderness boundary.

### MIRROR LAKE CABINS

The first ones built specifically for park visitors (from 1946 through 1947), these log cabins, with two, four, and eight bunks, are a few hundred yards apart along Mirror Lake. They're great places to stay for swimming, fishing (splake and brook trout), and paddling. Each cabin has a canoe or rowboat.

### BIG CARP RIVER CABINS

Four miles in, the three cabins near where the Big Carp River empties into Lake Superior are the most remote from a trailhead. Lake Superior (four bunks) was purchased by the Michigan DNR from Save the Porkies leaders Ray Dick and Walter Speaker. Dick also owned Big Carp 6, which probably dates from the 1930s; the park booster and his wife retained rights to use the cabin long after it was integrated into the park lodging system. Big Carp Cabin 4, built 1948, is perched on the riverbank beside the trail. The busy Carpville cabins make a great base for exploring the lakeshore and river, with a series of waterfalls and swimming holes unfolding upstream.

### SECTION 17 AND GREENSTONE FALLS CABINS

There are four-bunk cabins, both stick-style, on opposite sides of the Little Carp River.

Section 17, a repurposed ranger cabin, is very private and accessed via a footbridge. These cabins are only 1.3 miles from a trailhead.

### LITTLE CARP CABIN

Situated high above where the Little Carp River flows into Lake Superior, this four-bunk cabin is 2.7 miles from a trailhead and 1.5 miles from the Big Carp River cabins.

### LAKE OF THE CLOUDS CABIN

One of the most popular, this four-bunk cabin is less than a mile from the Lake of the Clouds overlook, the most visited spot in the park, with access to stunning views along the Escarpment Trail. Use the cabin rowboat to fish (bass are catch and release only) or to gather water from a spring across the lake (tastes better than lake water).

### LILY POND CABIN

This sweet four-bunk cabin faces the pond and looks east toward several low hills, the worn remnants of this once mighty mountain range. The cabin comes with a rowboat and canoe, good for catching brook trout or simply enjoying the pond. It is 2.5 miles from the Little Carp River trailhead.

## OTHER BACKCOUNTRY CABINS

While they are not inside the wilderness boundary, it is possible to link these four cabins via a traverse.

### CROSSCUT CABIN

This "little cabin that could" has served over the years as a permit booth, ski warming hut, and now cozy two-person cabin near the wilderness boundary. It is open to cross-country skiers in winter, and firewood is provided.

### SPEAKERS CABIN

Built in 1978 near the site of a cabin owned by early park supporter Walter Speaker, this four-bunker is a great place to enjoy the many moods of mighty Lake Superior. It is 1 or 2 miles from trailheads.

### COTTEN CABIN

Not far from Speakers, this spacious cabin where Tiebel Creek flows into Lake Superior sleeps eight and has covered front and back porches and a small screened picnic house. Cotten was recently converted to public use, which may result in a higher rental fee.

### BUCKSHOT CABIN

On the shore of Lake Superior, and 2.5 miles from the Mirror Lake trailhead, this 1948 four-bunk cabin was the first one built in stick style.

## PLANNING AND PREPARATION

**Contact:** 906-885-5275; www2.dnr.state.mi.us; search for park in alphabetical list

**Membership:** No discount for members of Friends of the Porkies

**Rates:** $

### BOOKING

For reservations, call 800-44-PARKS or visit http://midnrreservations.com. Cabins and yurts can be booked up to six months in advance and fill up quickly. To book a series of cabins for a multiday traverse, we recommend talking to a reservation agent on the phone.

A reservation is not a backcountry permit; visitors must check in with the visitor center staff for permits, cabin keys, and a parking pass before setting out on the trail. Each visitor must also have a Michigan Recreation Passport.

### TRANSPORTATION

A private vehicle is necessary to get to the Porkies.

### MAPS

The park brochure map is sufficient for navigating a traverse, and the map featured in this book offers a great overview of the park and its cabins. But if you would like a more detailed map, you have two options. The Porcupine Mountains Wilderness State Park Trail Map (1:24,000) produced by Michigan Trailmaps.com is two-sided, waterproof, and features topographic (contour) lines. The Porcupine Mountains Wilderness State Park map, on the other hand, is a single-sided, waterproof, smaller-scale (1:64,000) topographic map sold at the park visitor center. For more exhaustive detail, there are also six USGS topo maps at 1:24,000 scale that cover the park.

### PACKING TIPS

Bring a small cookstove, stove fuel, a water filtration system, and toilet paper. The cabin interiors can feel dark; bring headlamps, candles, and/or a lantern to brighten your stay. Fire starters are also helpful. Gaiters and waterproof boots come in handy during muddy seasons.

# FIREWOOD: PAYING IT FORWARD

Gathering firewood is more than a chore. This humble task, necessary to keep a cabin cozy, is also a way to connect with your fellow hut enthusiasts and a gratifying opportunity to spend time amid ancient trees. When you first open the cabin door, note the collection of logs and kindling. The woodpile is a gift from the visitors who came before you! Leaving an ample supply for the next visitors is an important aspect of Porkies cabin culture. Spend a few hours in this ancient rite to pay it forward as the previous visitors have done for you.

The hunt for firewood is full of challenges and pleasures. Think of the cabin's saw and axe as tools for slowing down and engaging with your surroundings. Since people have been gathering wood in the area for years, you may need to range quite far from the cabin. As you search, closely observe the mature trees, seedlings, and saplings emerging under their canopy. Evaluate likely logs; is it old and rotten, young and green?  Dry or wet?

Once you find a good source of down and dead wood, figure out how to proceed. What is your proficiency with the axe and saw?  Be safe! Observe the tension in the branches as they repose on the forest floor. Where and how will you make the cut safely? Find a long, steady stroke with the bow saw; sink into a rhythm. Try counting the rings on the branches you cut, and inhale the scent of the sap and sawdust.

Figure out how to haul the wood back to the cabin, while disturbing the forest as little as possible. You may choose to haul logs back and then cut and split them near the fire pit. Enjoy the feel and sound of cleanly split wood, and beware of tricky knots. Carry the wood into the cabin and stack it neatly. Take satisfaction in a job well done. At the end of your stay, leave a nice stack for the next group, and sweep the floor and steps to make them feel extra welcome.

## OTHER TIPS

You must purchase a Michigan Recreation Passport for the period of your stay. Bring a utility tool to change saw blades if necessary. This is bear country; take proper safety precautions with food. These mature woods yield wonders to people who slow down; we recommend you stay awhile and spend more than one night at each cabin. Consider wood gathering and water hauling as opportunities to get acquainted with the terrain.

Before the trip, read Aldo Leopold's "The Last Stand," his rallying cry to preserve the Porkies. Years later, it was published in a collection titled *The River of the Mother of God and Other Essays.* Michael Rafferty and Robert Sprague's guidebook, *The Last Porcupine Mountains Companion,* is the most thorough resource for this park.

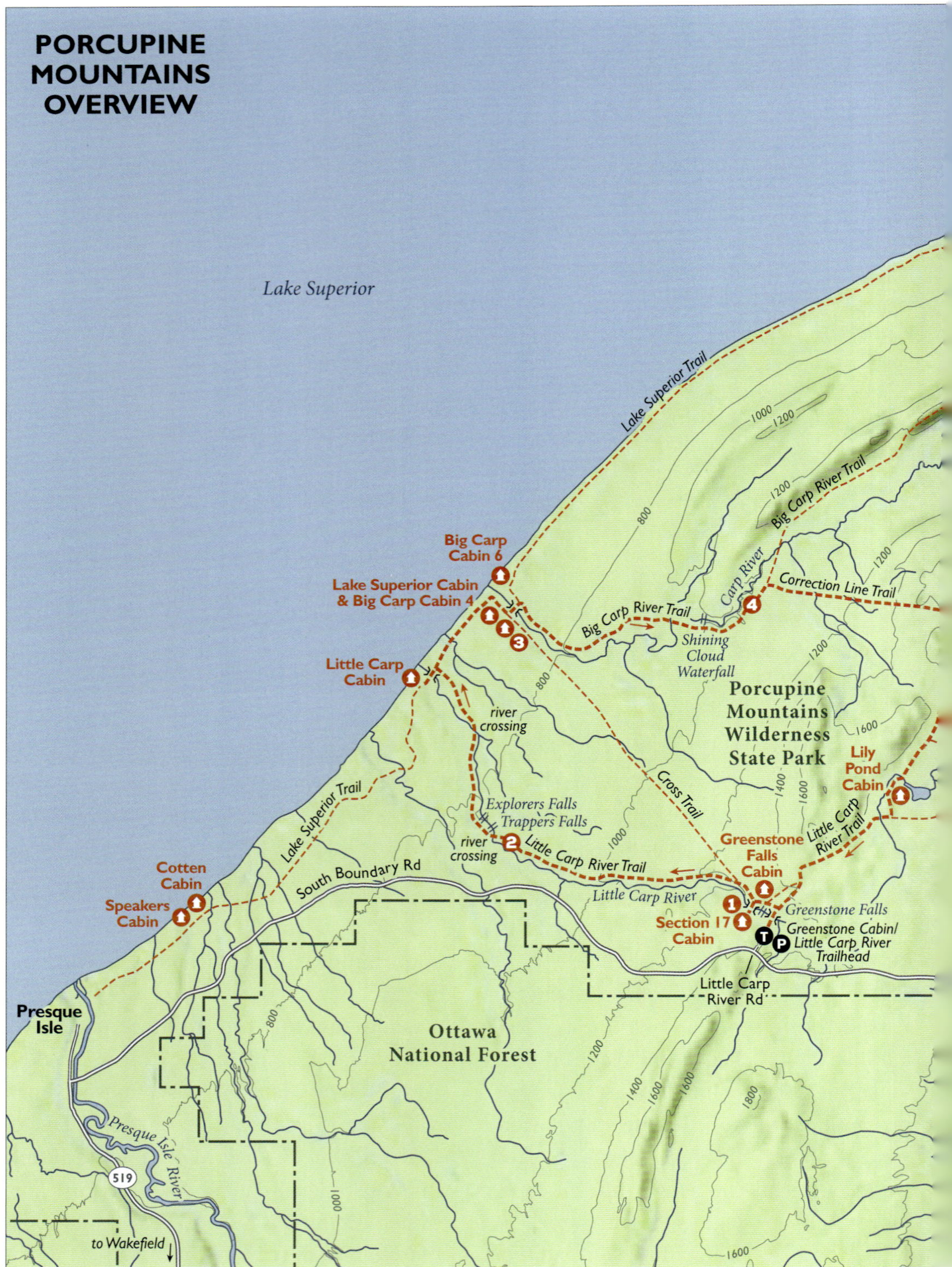
PORCUPINE MOUNTAINS OVERVIEW
Lake Superior
Lake Superior Trail
1000
1200
800
Big Carp River Trail
1200
1200
Carp River
Big Carp Cabin 6
Lake Superior Cabin & Big Carp Cabin 4
3
Big Carp River Trail
4
Correction Line Trail
Little Carp Cabin
Shining Cloud Waterfall
1200
Porcupine Mountains Wilderness State Park
river crossing
800
1600
Lily Pond Cabin
Lake Superior Trail
Explorers Falls
Trappers Falls
river crossing
2
1000
Little Carp River Trail
Cross Trail
1400
1600
Little Carp River Trail
Cotten Cabin
South Boundary Rd
Greenstone Falls Cabin
Speakers Cabin
Little Carp River
1
Greenstone Falls
Section 17 Cabin
Greenstone Cabin/ Little Carp River Trailhead
T
P
Presque Isle
Little Carp River Rd
800
Ottawa National Forest
1200
1400
1600
1600
1800
Presque Isle River
519
1000
to Wakefield
1600

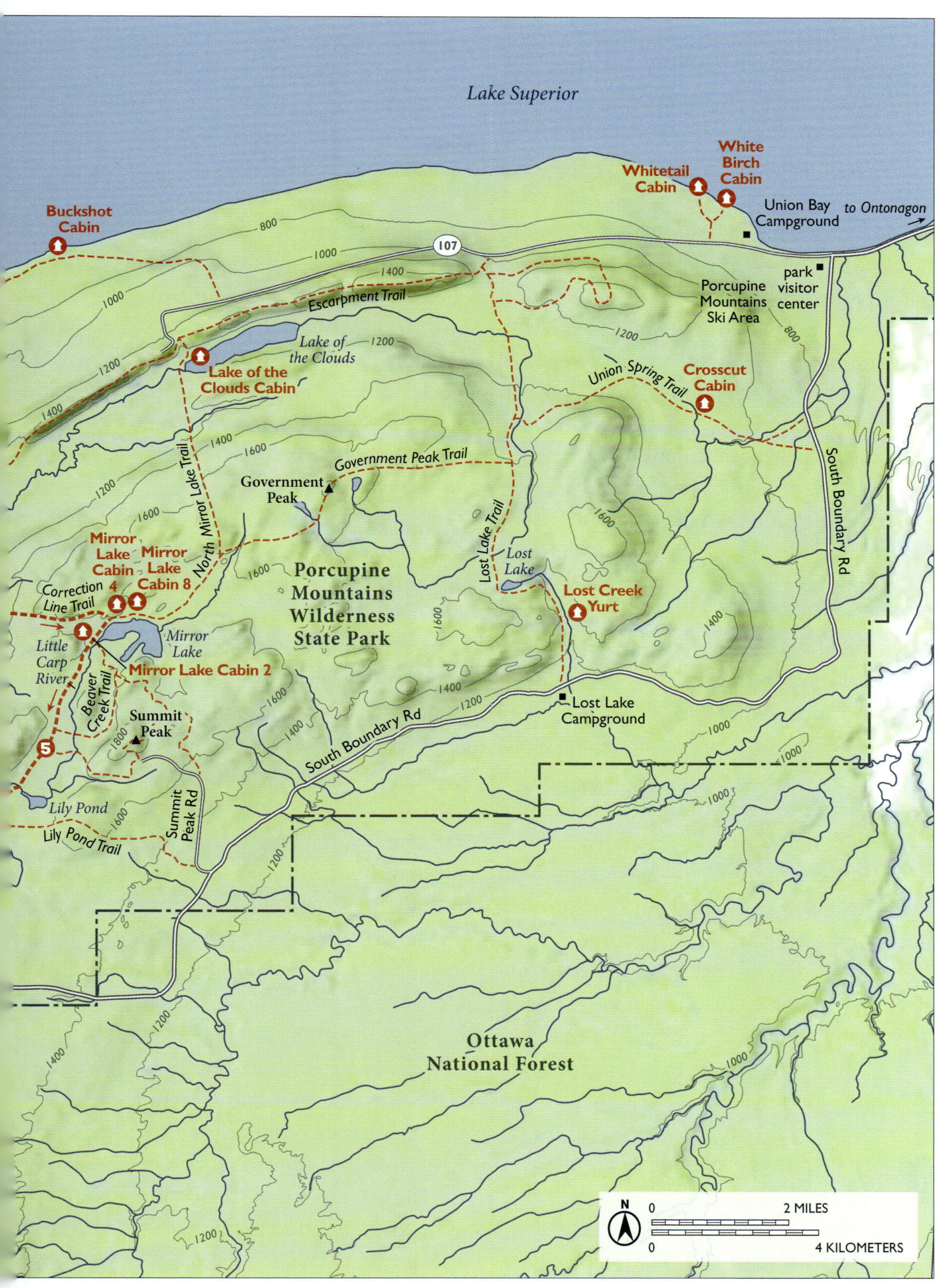

Lake Superior
Buckshot Cabin
Whitetail Cabin
White Birch Cabin
Union Bay Campground
to Ontonagon
107
800
1000
1400
Escarpment Trail
park visitor center
Porcupine Mountains Ski Area
1200
800
1000
1200
Lake of the Clouds
Lake of the Clouds Cabin
1400
1600
Government Peak Trail
Union Spring Trail
Crosscut Cabin
Government Peak
North Mirror Lake Trail
1200
1600
Lost Lake Trail
1600
Lost Lake
Mirror Lake Cabin 4
Mirror Lake Cabin 8
Correction Line Trail
Lost Creek Yurt
1400
South Boundary Rd
Little Carp River
Mirror Lake
Mirror Lake Cabin 2
Beaver Creek Trail
1600
1400
1200
Lost Lake Campground
1000
5
Summit Peak
1800
South Boundary Rd
1400
1000
Lily Pond
Summit Peak Rd
1600
Lily Pond Trail
1200
Porcupine Mountains Wilderness State Park
Ottawa National Forest
1000
1400
1200
N
0          2 MILES
0          4 KILOMETERS

## ITINERARY: BIG AND LITTLE CARP RIVERS THREE-CABIN TRAVERSE

*22.7 miles; five days, four nights*

This 23-mile route follows two of the park's most scenic trails—the Little Carp River Trail and the Big Carp River Trail—and provides a taste of the sometimes-tempestuous Lake Superior Trail. The trails, frequently marked with blue dots and diamonds, are easy to follow, and junctions are consistently marked with clear signage. But many, especially the Correction Line, can be muddy.

Our route and cabin selection, partly determined by availability, took us into the heart of the wilderness. We stayed in the Section 17, Big Carp 4, and Mirror Lake 4 cabins; these three are all near at least one other cabin, allowing you to modify your itinerary, depending on availability and group size. The itinerary incorporates a rest day, a two-night stay at either the mouth of the Big Carp River or on Mirror Lake. That extra day allows you to experience these special places more deeply. Spend daylight hours exploring waterfalls and swimming holes on the Big Carp River, or running from waves and skipping rocks on Lake Superior. If you're enjoying a rest day at Mirror Lake, explore the nearby awe-inspiring hemlock groves, and go swimming, fishing, or boating on this pristine lake.

### DAY 1: TRAILHEAD TO SECTION 17 CABIN

**Distance:** 1.3 miles

**Elevation gain/loss:** 130 feet/370 feet

**Difficulty:** Easy
**Hut elevation:** 1150 feet
**Cabin GPS:** 46.7243°N, 89.8348°W
**Trailhead:** Greenstone Cabin Trailhead (46.7163°N, 89.8283°W)

### Getting There

From Duluth, Minnesota, take US Highway 2 east around the south side of Lake Superior. Upon entering Michigan, continue to Wakefield, and then follow US 28 east to Bergland for 20 miles. Then head north 18 miles on State Route 64 to Silver City. At the lake, turn left. The park entrance is 3 miles west on SR 107.

From Madison, Wisconsin, take Interstate 39 north to begin this approximately 300-mile-drive. After about 150 miles, take one of several routes north to Bergland, Michigan. Pick up SR 64N and continue 18 miles to Silver City, then turn left (west) and travel 3 miles to the park on SR 107. Turn left onto South Boundary Road, and look for the driveway to the visitor center in less than 100 yards.

### On the Trail

From the park visitor center, return to South Boundary Road, then turn right (west), and drive 15 miles. At the Little Carp River Trailhead sign, turn right onto the Little Carp River Road, which leads less than half a mile to a parking lot with a restroom.

When you're ready to begin your trek, leave the parking lot, turn right (northeast) through a gate, and follow the Little Carp River Road 0.4 mile to the footbridge across the Little Carp River. Turn left (northwest) at the next junction to follow the Little Carp River Trail. At 0.75 mile, pass the junction

*Keeping the woodpile stocked is a constant but enjoyable task in huts.*

with the Lily Pond and South Mirror Lake Trail, and continue along the Little Carp River Trail to a viewpoint featuring Greenstone Falls at 1 mile. At 1.15 miles, pass Greenstone Falls Cabin on the right, and continue a very short distance; turn left at the sign for the Section 17 Cabin. Cross the river at 1.25 miles and scramble up the bank to arrive at the cabin.

## DAY 2: SECTION 17 CABIN TO BIG CARP CABIN 4

**Distance:** 7.6 miles
**Elevation gain/loss:** 440 feet/980 feet
**Difficulty:** Easy
**Hut elevation:** 600 feet
**Cabin GPS:** 46.7668°N, 89.8848°W

Cross the river on the footbridge and rejoin the Little Carp River Trail. Keep left (west-northwest) at 0.4 mile, passing the junction with the Cross Trail. Stay on the Little Carp River Trail, high above the river through deep hemlock, maple, and yellow birch for the next 1.5 miles before dropping toward the river at about 2.2 miles.

Reach the first of two river crossings at 3.4 miles; keep an eye out for beaver dams. A bit farther on are Trappers Falls and Explorers Falls, both good places to stop. At the next crossing, at 4.8 miles, the best option is a line of stones that runs between the blue-blazed trees on each bank.

At 6.1 miles, take a quick side trip left, across a bridge, and then up a long set of stairs to check out Little Carp Cabin. If you opt for this detour, retrace your steps. Then continue west on the last 0.2 mile of Little Carp River Trail, through a large maple grove with lakeshore campsites.

Reaching the signed junction, turn right (northeast) to walk 1.1 miles along the rugged lakeshore on the Lake Superior Trail. At the mouth of the Big Carp River, you reach a junction. Facing upriver or southeast, you can see the Lake Superior Cabin down a path to your right and the Big Carp 6 Cabin across the river on the left (there was once a bridge here). Straight ahead (southeast) follow the Lake Superior and Big Carp River Trails about 100 yards to Big Carp Cabin 4.

## DAY 3: REST DAY

Enjoy a rest day at Big Carp River 4 by exploring the stream, gazing out across Lake Superior, restocking the firewood, reading a book, or doing whatever relaxes you.

## DAY 4: BIG CARP 4 CABIN TO MIRROR LAKE CABIN 4

**Distance:** 7.9 miles
**Elevation gain/loss:** 1370 feet/420 feet
**Difficulty:** Easy to moderate
**Hut elevation:** 1550 feet
**Cabin GPS:** 46.7645°N, 89.7753°W

If you continued to Mirror Lake on Day 3, enjoy a rest day at the lake. If your rest day was spent at Big Carp River, continue the trek to Mirror Lake today. Just outside the cabin, follow the Big Carp River Trail upstream to cross the footbridge at 0.15 mile. Turn left and walk downstream briefly, then follow the trail as it jogs right (northwest) and uphill to a signed trail junction at

0.3 mile. Do not follow the Lake Superior Trail straight (northwest); instead make a U-turn to follow the Big Carp River Trail (southwest) upstream. Passing waterfalls and pools, the trail continues mostly along the high bank until you reach a river crossing at 3.2 miles. Look downstream for two parallel downed trees that you can walk across. At the signed trail junction at 4.5 miles, leave the Big Carp River Trail to turn right (east) onto the Correction Line Trail to Mirror Lake.

At 6.5 miles, the trail ascends into a maple grove and begins to level out, with fine stands of hemlock trees on the hillsides on the left (north). The trail remains level for the next mile, with low cliffs visible to the north. A steep descent through towering hemlocks brings you to Mirror Lake. Turn left (east) to find the cabin close by on the north shore of the lake.

## DAY 5: MIRROR LAKE TO TRAILHEAD

**Distance:** 5.9 miles
**Elevation gain/loss:** 470 feet/640 feet
**Difficulty:** Easy

Mirror Lake, the source of the Little Carp River, also marks the beginning of the trail bearing the same name. Exit the cabin and go right, following the trail southwest along the shore and into the woods along the west side of the Little Carp River. At a junction with the Beaver Creek Trail at 1.75 miles, continue straight (southwest) for another 2.5 miles to Lily Pond. A bench on the footbridge across the pond outlet (note the beaver dam) is a good place to stop to rest and enjoy a snack.

At the end of the footbridge, turn right (west) to pass Lily Pond Cabin. The trail dips south and reaches a signed junction with the Lily Pond Trail at 3 miles. Turn right (west) at this junction to continue on the Little Carp River Trail. Cross the river at 3.3 miles, and continue to a signed junction (46.7239°N, 89.8231°W).

From here turn left to follow the Little Carp River Trail to Little Carp River Road. Continue straight across the footbridge over the Little Carp River and follow the road back to the gate and parking lot where you began on Day 1.

## OTHER ITINERARIES

Create your own adventure. If the Porkies are calling to you, make plans with a flexible frame of mind. The park is relatively small and well stocked with wilderness cabins connected by a web of trails. Limited reservation options may end up shaping your itinerary, but almost any combination of cabins can be the basis of a great hut-to-hut adventure.

Look for loops that start and end from the same trailhead. For a nice route for families with kids or for people who don't like carrying stuff long distances, start at Little Carp River Road, and stay at either Section 17 or Greenstone Falls and then at Lily Pond. From this trailhead, you can also launch a long, ambitious loop, starting with Section 17, Greenstone Falls, or Lily Pond. You then move on to any of the Mirror Lake cabins, onward to Lake of the Clouds or Buckshot on Superior, along the shore to the collection of cabins at the mouth of the Big Carp River, and then eventually back to the parking lot at Little Carp River Road.

The Lake of the Clouds trailhead is the starting point for a great loop hike. Descend to the Lake of the Clouds Cabin, spend the night, or continue on toward Mirror Lake, another overnight option. Continue around to Greenstone Falls or Section 17 Cabins. Head back by way of the Big Carp cabins, and then return to the trailhead via Big Carp River Trail or by way of the Lake Superior Trail to Buckshot Cabin and then to the trailhead.

Consider traveling out and back to a single cabin for a few days. Speakers Cabin or the larger Cotten are both a short walk in from trailheads on the west side of the park. Buckshot, poised on the shore of Lake Superior, is accessible from near the Lake of the Clouds Scenic Area. If you have two vehicles or are comfortable with hitchhiking to reclaim your car, plan a route that begins and ends at different trailheads.

Cabin logbooks hold records of proven past itineraries. We were delighted to read that some visitors spent a couple of nights in one cabin and then moved less than a quarter mile to another across the river (Greenstone Falls, then Section 17). Handwritten entries testify that many Porkies visitors seek the special thrill of quiet immersion—staying in place—more than the rewards of maximizing miles traveled.

# BOUNDARY COUNTRY TREKKING

*It was far too cold to travel slowly. We pushed hard on our sticks, and the skis hissed over the powder-dry snow. We were the only ones abroad, the only ones foolish enough to be outside when we did not have to be. Still, fresh deer tracks crossed the lake, and on the portage into Cedar there were signs of rabbits, weasels, and mice.*

—Sigurd F. Olson, *The Singing Wilderness*

**Location:** Boundary Waters Canoe Area Wilderness, Superior National Forest, northwest of Grand Marais, Minnesota
**Distance:** Yurts 12 miles apart; full traverse 21 miles
**Elevation gain/loss:** 1030 feet/1130 feet
**Difficulty:** Novice to intermediate (due to distance on day 2)
**Terrain:** Boreal forest, lakes, creeks, and meadows; nearly level terrain
**Modes of travel:** Winter skiing, snowshoeing, and fat-tire biking
**Season:** Mid-January through April
**Huts:** Two yurts (capacity 7), self-service, exclusive use

---

**THE FORESTS AND LAKES** of northern Minnesota beckon not only paddlers in summer but also Nordic skiers in winter. Indeed, winter may be the best time to experience the deep quiet and remoteness of this wilderness territory stretched along the Canadian border. Boundary Country Trekking (BCT) offers a yurt-to-yurt ski traverse along the 16.8-mile Banadad Trail in the Boundary Waters Canoe Area Wilderness (BWCAW), a vast preserve of lakes and woods cherished by generations of vacationers from the Upper Midwest. Established in 1964 and designated a roadless wilderness in 1978, this reserve made up of more than 1 million acres encompasses more than 1000 lakes and rivers and more than 1500 miles of canoe routes. In the winter, hardy visitors not only have the place to themselves but can also enjoy the BWCAW without the famously abundant biting summer bugs! The forest is thick with balsam fir, spruce, and birch trees. In addition to spotting moose tracks, you might glimpse plump spruce grouse and hear wolves howling at night.

The Banadad Trail opened in the early 1980s along historical logging roads dating back to the 1920s. BWCAW legislation allows trails to be groomed by snowmobile in this wilderness, even though all other maintenance must rely on hand tools only. The Banadad Trail is maintained by volunteers, members of the Banadad Trail Association, a ski touring club, and a Twin Cities school ski team. A small network of snowshoe and ski trails laces the woods at the east end of the Banadad Trail, which also connects to a 125-mile Northwoods network of Nordic ski trails, some associated with area resorts.

The yurt-to-yurt package incorporates all you need and a little more. Guests check in at the Poplar Creek Guesthouse B&B to get oriented, fill out a free BWCAW permit, and hand over meal provisions (packed in a cooler) and personal overnight supplies to the BCT staff. Skiers are then shuttled to the beginning of the trail—you can start from either the east or west end—with one member of the party carrying a Garmin inReach so the BCT folks can track your progress. It is a treat to approach the yurt at the end of the day and find the hut host waiting to greet you, provide orientation, and then bid you goodnight! The host has not only delivered provisions to your overnight home but also fired up the woodstove. In the morning, leave your stuff behind; it will be reliably delivered to the next yurt or to the guesthouse.

## HUTS AND AMENITIES

The same impulse behind backcountry yurts in the West gave rise to the first BCT yurt in the Midwest. Proprietors Barbara and Ted Young responded immediately to a 1983 article in *Cross Country Skier* magazine about Kirk Bachman's yurts in Jackson, Wyoming. By 1984, using an old-fashioned treadle sewing machine, they had constructed their own yurt starting with a kit from Bachman.

## CROFT YURT

This shelter is located just outside the wilderness boundary, about 8 miles from the west end of the Banadad Trail. A comfortable retreat, Croft Yurt is illuminated by the central oculus by day and by a hanging propane lantern at night. The interior feels spacious, with a large dining table and chairs in the center and bunk beds arranged along the sides. Don't worry about the bitter Minnesota cold: the very warm sleeping bags come with thick fleece liners. The kitchen area holds all the basic implements and utensils for meal preparation. A woodstove keeps the space warm. Drinking water is available from five-gallon plastic dispensers.

## TALL PINES YURT

A newer canvas-and-wood structure, Tall Pines Yurt is located on Hooker Lake at the east end of the Banadad Trail near the Poplar Creek Guesthouse B&B. Ringed with windows, this yurt otherwise features the same amenities as Croft Yurt. Outside, stoke up the wood-fired sauna to warm your bones and ease tired muscles before sleep.

## PLANNING AND PREPARATION

**Contact:** www.boundarycountry.com/yurt-ski.html; (218) 388-4487; bct@boundarycountry.com

**Booking:** Call or email to inquire about availability and make a reservation

**Membership:** An associate membership in the Banadad Trail Association is included in the booking fee

**Rates:** $$$

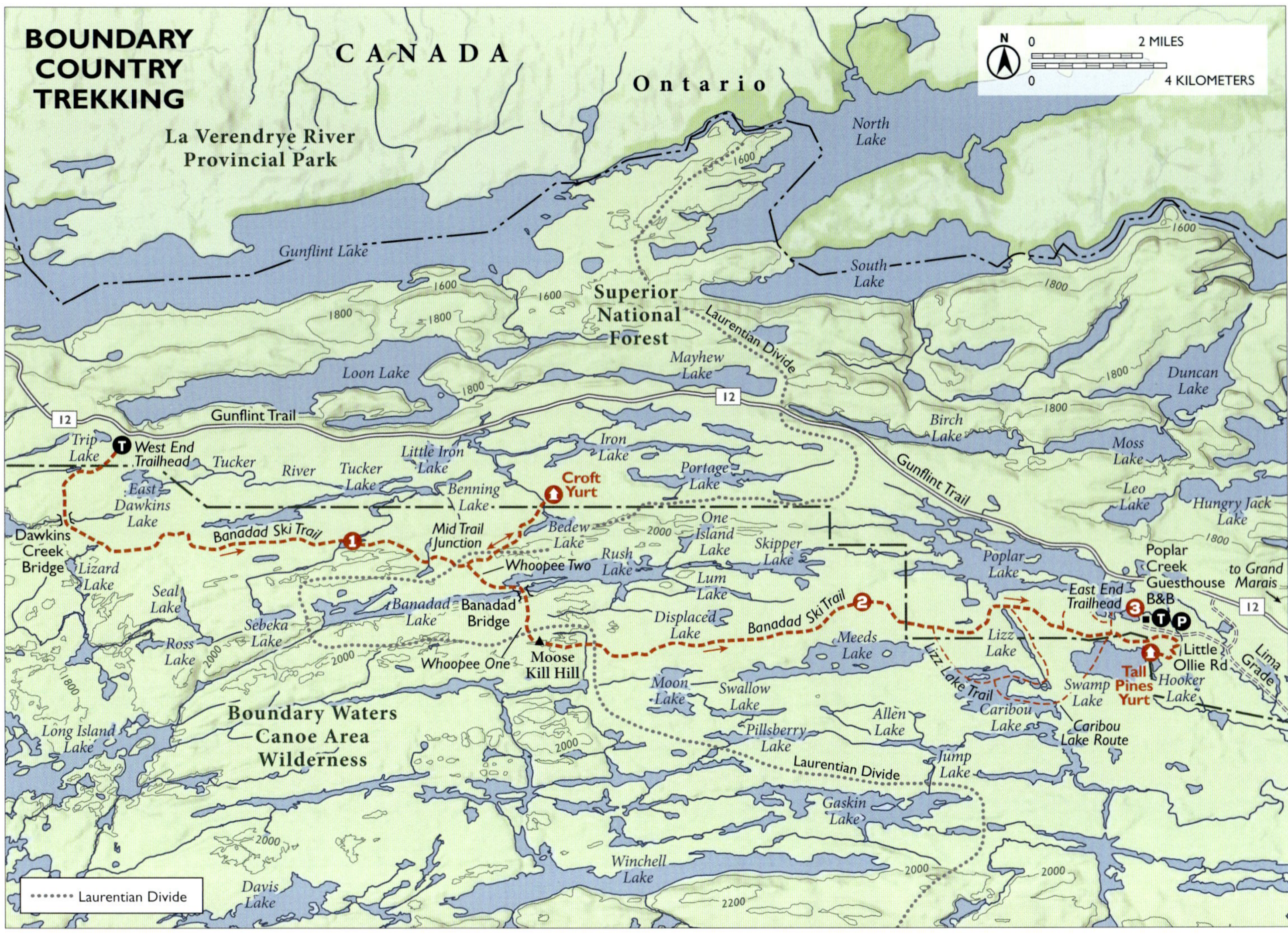
BOUNDARY COUNTRY TREKKING
N
0   2 MILES
0   4 KILOMETERS
CANADA
Ontario
La Verendrye River Provincial Park
North Lake
South Lake
1600
1800
Duncan Lake
Moss Lake
Leo Lake
Hungry Jack Lake
Birch Lake
Gunflint Lake
1600
1800
Superior National Forest
Laurentian Divide
Mayhew Lake
12
Gunflint Trail
Gunflint Trail
Loon Lake
1800
12
Trip Lake
West End Trailhead
Tucker River
Tucker Lake
Little Iron Lake
Iron Lake
Portage Lake
Croft Yurt
Benning Lake
East Dawkins Lake
Dawkins Creek Bridge
Lizard Lake
Banadad Ski Trail
1
Mid Trail Junction
Bedew Lake
One Island Lake
Skipper Lake
2000
Whoopee Two
Rush Lake
Lum Lake
Poplar Lake
East End Trailhead
Poplar Creek Guesthouse B&B
to Grand Marais
12
Seal Lake
Sebeka Lake
Ross Lake
2000
Banadad Lake
Banadad Bridge
Displaced Lake
Banadad Ski Trail
2
Meeds Lake
Lizz Lake
3
T P
Lima Grade
Whoopee One
Moose Kill Hill
Lizz Lake Trail
Little Ollie Rd
Tall Pines Yurt
Hooker Lake
Swamp Pines Lake
Caribou Lake
Caribou Lake Route
1800
Long Island Lake
Boundary Waters Canoe Area Wilderness
2000
Moon Lake
Swallow Lake
Pillsberry Lake
Allen Lake
Jump Lake
Laurentian Divide
Gaskin Lake
Winchell Lake
2000
2200
Davis Lake
2000
Laurentian Divide

**Transportation:** Park at the Poplar Creek Guesthouse B&B; shuttle service to the trailhead is included in the pricing

## MAPS

The Banadad Ski Trail map provided by BCT is very good and includes points of interest along the trail. A GPX file of this map can be downloaded from www.banadad .org/trail-info. The National Geographic Boundary Waters East Map 752 covers the trail at a much larger scale; while this map is not necessary for navigation, it provides a useful overview of the route.

## PACKING TIPS

In case of extreme cold (below 0 degrees Fahrenheit), be prepared with extra layers, very warm mittens, insulated ski boots, a balaclava, and a thermos of hot tea. Bring food to prepare in the yurt in a cooler; observe wilderness regulations prohibiting glass containers. Classic cross-country skis are recommended.

## OTHER TIPS

A sleeping bag and liner are provided. Skiers are required to purchase a Great Minnesota Ski Pass (by phone, in person, or at www.dnr.state.mn.us/licenses/skipass/index .html) and to secure a free BWCA day permit (provided by BCT at registration). Start both days of the traverse before noon to ensure arrival at the yurt in daylight. The price includes delivery of gear and food to both yurts. Last-minute supplies (groceries, beverages) can be purchased at the Trail Center at Poplar Lake. The US Forest Service's *Boundary Waters Canoe Area*

*Wilderness Trip Planning Guide* includes a helpful section about winter travel, with an emphasis on the need for "a high degree of preparation, planning, skill, and self-reliance" (see Resources).

## ITINERARY: BANADAD TRAIL

*20.8 miles, three days, two nights*

Mostly in designated wilderness, this traverse follows the Banadad Trail, with short excursions off the main trail to get to the yurts. Even though largely unmarked, the

*On the trail between Tall Pines Yurt and Poplar Creek Guesthouse*

*The host at Tall Pines Yurt welcomes weary travelers.*

trail is groomed and surprisingly easy to follow. The skiing is easy, but the distances and cold temperatures make this itinerary somewhat challenging. The traverse works in either direction; we chose to ski west to east, with the shorter leg on the first day and a long ski and a sauna at Tall Pines Yurt on the second day.

The track is flanked by thick forest much of the time, with occasional openings at meadows and frozen beaver ponds. You cross the Laurentian Divide several times; from this ridge, waters flow north to Hudson Bay and the Arctic Ocean and south to Lake Superior and the Atlantic. The Laurentian Divide adds a few hills—and speedy downhill runs—to the traverse, which is otherwise mostly flat.

### DAY 1: WEST END TRAILHEAD TO CROFT YURT

**Distance:** 8.3 miles
**Elevation gain/loss:** 520 feet/570 feet
**Difficulty:** Novice
**Hut elevation:** 1936 feet
**Hut GPS:** 48.0558°N, 90.6288°W
**Trailhead:** Poplar Creek Guesthouse B&B, 48.0366°N, 90.4734°W

### Getting There

From Grand Marais, head north on Gunflint Trail (County Road 12) for 28 miles. Turn left on Lima Grade. After 0.8 mile, turn right on Little Ollie Road, and then right onto Poplar Creek Drive. The B&B shuttle will take you west to the starting point.

### On the Trail

The single-track groomed ski trail heads southwest from the trailhead into the woods. After 1.5 miles, the trail crosses the Dawkins Creek Bridge and turns gradually east. At 6.7 miles, the first encounter with the Laurentian Divide begins with a mild 50-foot climb over 0.2 mile, followed by a similar descent over the next 0.2 mile.

At 7.2 miles, you reach the Mid Trail Junction; turn left (northeast) onto a spur trail to Croft Yurt. The mile to the yurt is mostly downhill and includes an exhilarating (or terrifying, depending on your skiing prowess) 0.2-mile descent of 75 feet about a half mile from the yurt. On the right, a sign indicates a right turn to the yurt, visible less than 50 yards from the trail.

## DAY 2: CROFT YURT TO TALL PINES YURT

**Distance:** 11.4 miles
**Elevation gain/loss:** 520 feet/560 feet
**Difficulty:** Intermediate
**Hut elevation:** 1860 feet
**Hut GPS:** 48.0295°N, 90.4681°W

Return to the spur trail and turn left, heading southwest for 1.1 miles back to the Mid Trail Junction. At the signed junction, turn left (south-southeast), descending the hill known as Whoopee Two. Cross the Banadad Bridge, between Banadad Lake and Rush Lake, at 1.8 miles. The trail turns south, ascending Whoopee One for about 0.75 mile to a ridge at 2.25 miles, then descends Moose Kill Hill and turns east.

At about 6.5 miles, the trail breaks out of the woods into a frozen wetland, then plunges back into the forest tunnel. It passes two turnoffs on the right for the Lizz Lake Trail at 7.7 and 8.7 miles and a turnoff on the left for the Tim Knopp Trail at 9.6 miles, then crosses the Caribou Lake Route at 10 miles. At 10.7 miles, just before reaching Little Ollie Road, turn right off the Banadad Trail onto the signed trail to the yurt. Ski the final 0.7 mile to Tall Pines Yurt, sited just above Hooker Lake.

## DAY 3: TALL PINES YURT TO POPLAR CREEK GUESTHOUSE

**Distance:** 1.1 miles
**Elevation gain/loss:** 0 feet/10 feet
**Difficulty:** Novice

Return to the junction with the Banadad Trail, then turn left; watch for the sign indicating a right turn onto a spur trail to the Poplar Creek Guesthouse B&B, and your waiting car.

# NEVER SUMMER NORDIC

*Each day is a journey, the journey itself a destination.*
　　　　　—Matsuo Bashō, *The Narrow Road to the Deep North*

**Location:** State Forest State Park near Walden, Colorado
**Distance:** Huts 4 to 5 miles apart; featured itinerary 11.7 miles
**Elevation gain/loss:** 1500 feet/1760 feet
**Difficulty:** Novice; added difficulty in winter due to inconsistent trail markings
**Terrain:** Slopes of Medicine Bow Mountains, rolling terrain through open hillsides and meadows, forest, and streambeds
**Modes of travel:** Winter skiing and snowshoeing; spring, summer, and fall hiking and biking
**Season:** Year-round
**Huts:** Ten huts (eight yurts, two cabins, capacity 5 to 9), self-service, exclusive use

---

**COLORADO IS RICH IN HUT-TO-HUT** systems. Never Summer Nordic (NSN), even though close to Rocky Mountain National Park, is among the most remote. NSN's eight yurts and two cabins are both backcountry destinations in their own right—launching pads for vigorous hikes to alpine lakes and peaks in summer, and bowl and ridge skiing in winter. A few of the yurts, close to the road, are particularly well sited for families. The original three yurts are located 4 to 5 miles apart and make for a great multiday traverse. Started as a winter ski and snowshoe destination, NSN now operates year-round, with more than 80 miles of trails in the system. While winter is the busiest season overall, July is the system's busiest month.

State Forest State Park is a lesser-known Colorado mountain playground in the Medicine Bow Mountains. Just below Cameron Pass (10,276 feet), this 71,000-acre park is encircled to the east by three federal wilderness areas: Rawah, Neota, and Never Summer. North Park, a huge grassland valley just west of the NSN huts, was labeled "paradise to all grazing animals" by explorer John C. Frémont. White settlers

OPPOSITE:  *Departing Ruby Jewel Yurt in fresh snow*

arriving in the nineteenth century expelled the Native inhabitants and exterminated the large mammal populations in a few decades. Today, the original large mammals —except bison—are again thriving. Indeed, nearby Walden is celebrated as the moose-viewing capital of the state; the State Forest State Park visitor center is named after this majestic beast. The Arapaho National Wildlife Refuge, just south of Walden, sustains not only moose, elk, and antelope but also profuse wildfowl and other birdlife.

Established in 1970, State Forest State Park offers prime recreational territory while also operating under a mandate to generate revenue in support of public education. NSN concession fees join a revenue stream that also draws from timber sales.

Like many hut systems in the West, NSN was founded in the 1980s. Rodney Ley, an outdoor recreation professional, opened the first three yurts in the winter of 1986–87. Because yurts come in kit form and are relatively easy to construct, Ley managed to acquire permits, construct the decks, and open the yurts for business all within about six months. Although Ley envisioned the original three in terms of a yurt-to-yurt traverse, he quickly saw that visitors preferred the huts as base camps for exploration and play; this continues today. The next owners, stepping up in 1992, added three more yurts and two cabins. The Graves family, which has owned the system since 2002, continues to expand strategically. In addition to placing two more backcountry yurts, they have opened several larger, very comfortable frontcountry structures near the business headquarters. Since the recent renewal of their state park concession, plans are afoot to address deferred maintenance and to possibly add up to ten more yurts within the next twenty years.

## HUTS AND AMENITIES

The NSN hut system offers five 16-foot yurts (capacity five), three 20-foot yurts (capacity nine), plus two cabins (capacity six to eight). NSN yurts are circular coated-canvas structures illuminated by a small top dome and side windows. All the necessities for cooking, sleeping, and keeping warm are provided inside. When the cozy, but dim interiors become claustrophobic, venture outside and take in the view from the front deck. The decks not only expand living space in warm weather but also provide shelter underneath for firewood and the propane tank.

Inside, the yurts are pretty basic and offer compact living. There are bunk beds with double-wide bottom bunks, plus a few extra mattresses. For meal preparation, you find two-burner propane stoves, cookware, and eating utensils, with plastic dishpans nearby for cleanup. A sturdy table (sometimes a fold-up) provides a surface for eating, sorting, journaling, and playing cabin games. Heat radiates from the woodstove, which must be fed constantly. A tall, vertical shelf unit organizes firewood by size, with newspaper and tiny kindling at the top and the big, long-burning logs at the bottom.

The water supply comes from snowmelt in winter; small signs indicate the best collection spot outside each yurt. In summer, consult the NSN staff and website for best sources; these include nearby streams and a potable water station on County Road 41 near the reservoir. Always treat or boil drinking water obtained from a natural source.

### GRASS CREEK YURT

Close to the road and accessible across gently sloping and flat terrain, this yurt is a great destination for families or first-time backcountry yurt adventurers. The location near the North Michigan Reservoir makes this a convenient choice for fishers in both winter and summer.

### RUBY JEWEL YURT

Ruby Jewel Yurt, located halfway to Jewel Lake from the trailhead, provides access to alpine high country on the slopes of Clark Peak (12,960 feet). Nestled in a dense lodgepole pine and spruce forest, this yurt can also be a great place to hunker down and enjoy the woods. Ruby Jewel is only 100 yards from the larger Clark Peak Yurt (capacity nine); large groups can rent both and spend quality time together in this beautiful backcountry area.

### NORTH FORK CANADIAN YURT

From the deck of this yurt situated on the brow of a hill, enjoy expansive views of the Medicine Bow Mountains and keep a lookout for moose in the meadow below. This yurt serves as a base for hiking or skiing journeys to Kelly Lake (5 miles) and Clear Lake (6 miles).

## PLANNING AND PREPARATION

**Contact:** www.neversummernordic.com; (970) 723-4070; yurts@neversummernordic.com

**Booking:** Check availability and make reservations via website; two-night minimum when booking online; for hut-to-hut itineraries of one night per hut, contact NSN manager; book up to one year in advance; no refunds

**Membership:** None

**Rates:** $

**Transportation:** Personal vehicle required; no public transportation to State Forest State Park

### GETTING THERE

Most of the yurts are sited along County Road 41, which splits off from State Route 14 about 25 miles east of Walden and 78 miles west of Fort Collins. County Road 41, although remote, is plowed frequently.

### MAPS

For people going from trailhead to yurt only, NSN maps are sufficient. However, those skiing or hiking yurt-to-yurt will find these maps not detailed enough. A freehand sketch map, posted on the website and supplied to customers, provides an overview of the system. Use this for planning, not for navigation on trail. The most detailed map, essential for the traverse described in this guidebook, is the 1:38,000 scale Mountain Jay Media Rawah Wilderness map, sold at NSN headquarters. Note, however, that it does not include all the trail names.

The Moose Visitor Center on SR 14 in Gould stocks two moderately useful trail maps: The State Forest State Park Complete Trail Guide maps briefly describes the

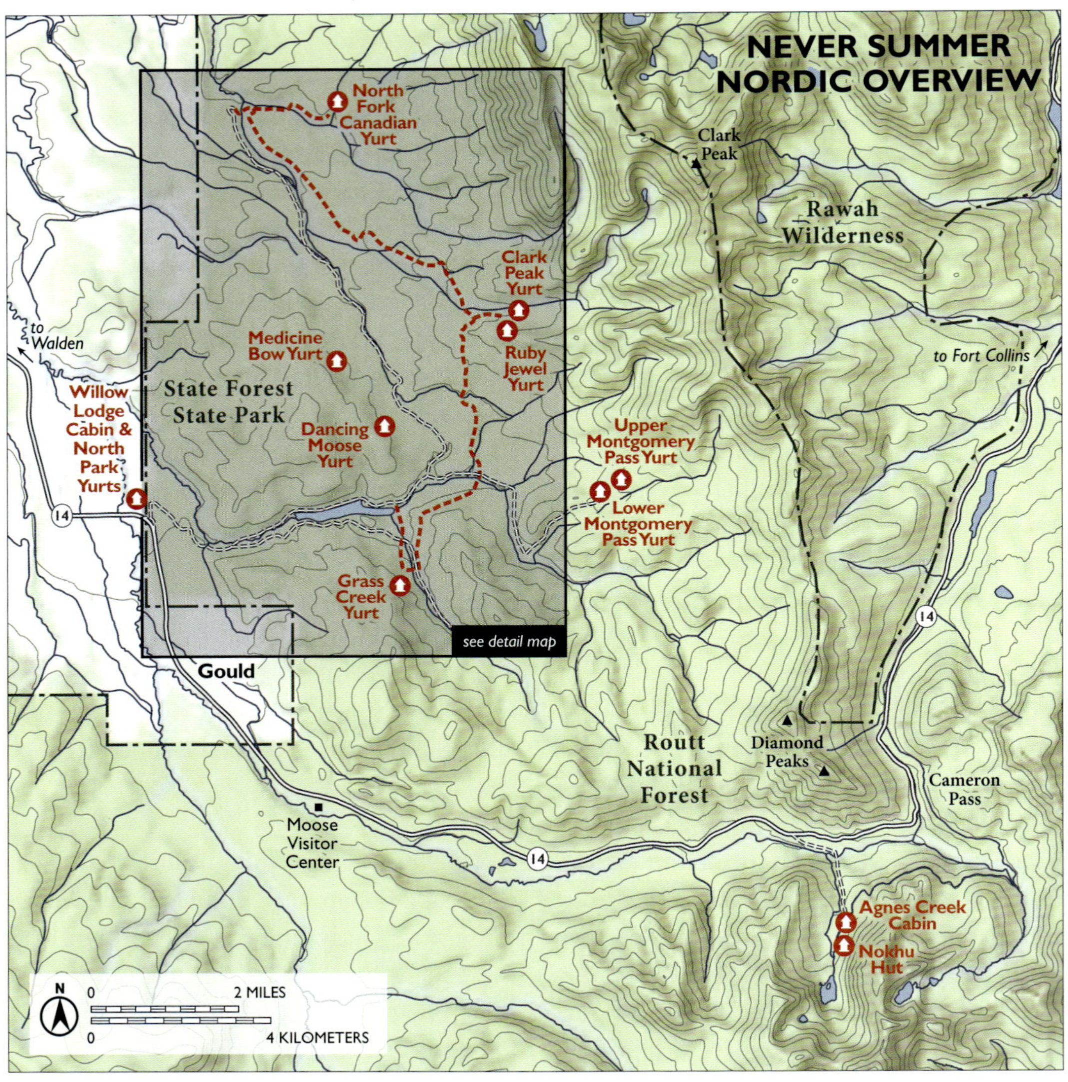


recreational trails in the park, with most huts indicated though not named. The State Forest State Park Trail Map brochure also shows the park's trails and most of the huts (also unnamed).

## PACKING TIPS

Metal-edged touring skis are recommended. Skins recommended only if venturing onto surrounding slopes for downhill turns.

## OTHER TIPS

Rent skis in Fort Collins or Steamboat Springs (there's no rental outlet in the immediate area). Engage NSN to relocate your car to the Closure Trailhead for a small fee, or use two cars for the traverse, parking one at the first trailhead at Grass Creek and the other at the Closure Trailhead. Purchase a State Park Pass (either a daily pass for each day of your trip or an annual pass) and display it in each parked vehicle. Passes can be purchased online, through local merchants including NSN, and at the Moose Visitor Center.

NSN offers gear haul for a fee and also rents sleds for visitors to haul in their own gear. There is the option to stay overnight in large, higher-amenity yurts at NSN headquarters before or after the traverse. Pets are not allowed in or near huts in winter but are allowed in summer.

## ITINERARY: THREE-YURT TRAVERSE

*11.7 miles, four days, three nights*

Skirting the western slopes of the Medicine Bow Mountains below Clark Peak, this short, enjoyable traverse anchors NSN's system and works in any season. While NSN yurts and cabins are situated amid extensive networks of hiking, equestrian, and snowmobile trails, markers are inconsistent and often invisible in deep snow. State Forest State Park trails are marked only at major junctions with brown signs naming destinations. Small hut signs with directional arrows point the way to specific huts. Trails are also indicated by orange poles and trail marker posts. Routes from trailheads to yurts are marked with blue diamonds emblazoned with yurt symbols; yurt-to-yurt routes visible on printed maps are not consistently signed, and deep snowpack can obscure signage.

A State Forest State Park ten-year strategic plan may relocate or eliminate one or more trails described in this guide, while trail maintenance by local volunteer groups is currently in flux. To ensure the best possible experience, review your route with staff at the State Forest State Park Moose Visitor Center and with NSN staff for the latest information. Keep your maps and compass handy, and be prepared to backtrack occasionally to keep on route.

In winter, the trails to NSN yurts are not groomed. Sections of trail overlap with snowmobile routes, usually groomed by volunteers. Many of these trails follow logging roads, so they are relatively easy to identify in winter. If you are lucky, you may find that other skiers have broken trail before you.

*Special signs point the way to the huts.*

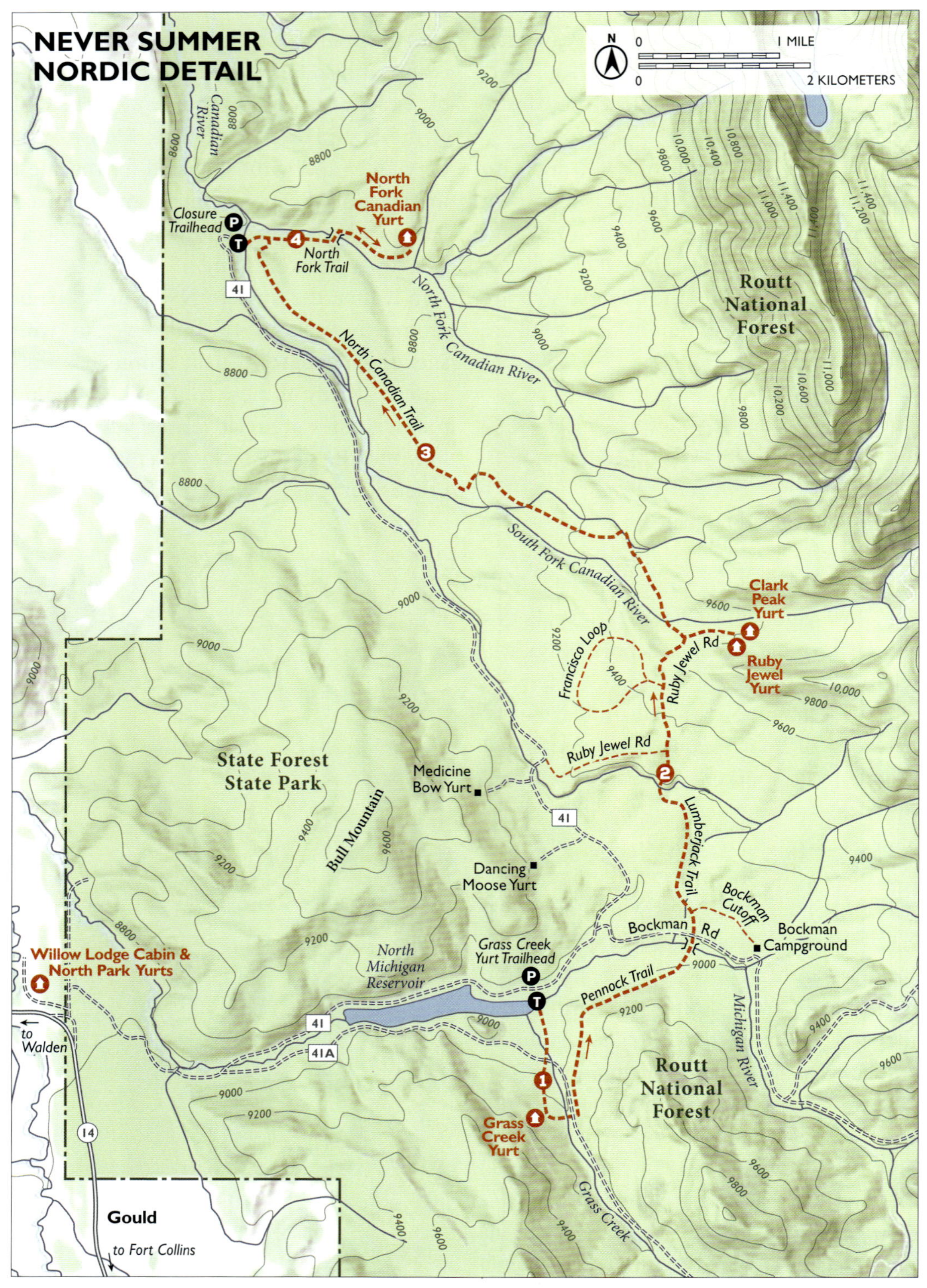
NEVER SUMMER
NORDIC DETAIL
N
0 1 MILE
0 2 KILOMETERS
Canadian River
8600
8600
9200
9000
8800
9200
9000
9800
10,000
10,400
10,800
11,000
11,200
11,400
11,400
11,000
10,600
10,200
9800
9600
Routt
National
Forest
Closure
Trailhead
P
T
41
4
North Fork Trail
North
Fork
Canadian
Yurt
8800
8800
8800
North Canadian Trail
North Fork Canadian River
9000
9200
9200
3
South Fork Canadian River
9000
9200
9000
Francisco Loop
9200
9400
9600
Clark
Peak
Yurt
Ruby Jewel Rd
Ruby
Jewel
Yurt
10,000
9800
9600
Ruby Jewel Rd
2
State Forest
State Park
Medicine
Bow Yurt
41
Lumberjack Trail
9400
9200
9400
9600
Bull Mountain
Dancing
Moose Yurt
Bockman
Cutoff
Bockman Rd
Bockman
Campground
9000
Willow Lodge Cabin &
North Park Yurts
8800
9200
North
Michigan
Reservoir
Grass Creek
Yurt Trailhead
P
T
Pennock Trail
9200
9000
Michigan River
9400
9600
to
Walden
41
41A
9000
9000
1
9200
Routt
National
Forest
9600
9800
14
9000
9200
Grass Creek Yurt
Grass Creek
9400
9600
9800
Gould
to Fort Collins
9400

*A sunny below zero day at the North Fork Canadian Hut*

## DAY 1: TRAILHEAD TO GRASS CREEK YURT

**Distance:** 0.8 mile

**Elevation gain/loss:** 40 feet/130 feet

**Difficulty:** Novice

**Hut elevation:** 9100 feet

**Hut GPS:** 40.5459°N, 105.9882°W

**Trailhead:** Grass Creek Yurt Trailhead (40.5557°N, 105.9899°W)

### Getting There

From Fort Collins, follow SR 14 west for about 78 miles. After descending from Cameron Pass, pass State Forest State Park's Moose Visitor Center in Gould. After mile marker 54, turn right on CR 41; the NSN headquarters, a house with offices and a small retail space, will be on the left. Enter the park, following CR 41 for 2 miles along the north side of North Michigan Reservoir. The trailhead will be on the left, just after the reservoir and state park cabins.

### On the Trail

From the parking area, cross to the south side of CR 41 and then follow the blue-diamond-marked trail south. Descend to cross a road (CR 41A), and then gently ascend to Grass Creek Yurt.

## DAY 2: GRASS CREEK YURT TO RUBY JEWEL YURT

**Distance:** 4.1 miles

**Elevation gain/loss:** 960 feet/370 feet

**Difficulty:** Novice

**Hut elevation:** 9600 feet

**Hut GPS:** 40.5828°N, 105.9637°W

From Grass Creek Yurt, bear north-northeast to quickly join Grass Creek Road, paralleling Grass Creek. Follow it to the junction with CR 41A, where a sign indicates the beginning of the Pennock Trail. Follow the intermittently marked Pennock Trail to its end in 1.1 miles, briefly skirting a recent timber cut, then turn east alongside the meadow formed by the North Fork Michigan River as it approaches the reservoir. Cross the river by bridge to where the Pennock Trail ends at Bockman Road.

Take the Lumberjack Trail north, uphill, following signs to Ruby Jewel Yurt. Pass by the Bockman Cutoff and continue on the Lumberjack Trail north-northwest for 1.3 miles to its junction with Ruby Jewel Road. The Lumberjack Trail, primarily for snowmobiles, is not well marked. Keep a sharp eye out for the occasional orange trail marker poles sticking out of the snow. The trail first ascends gently through open and wooded hillsides, and then climbs more steeply to approach Ruby Jewel Road.

At the junction, turn right and head north-northeast on Ruby Jewel Road, passing the cutoff to Francisco Loop, and climb steeply over an exposed hillside before descending to pass the junction with the North Canadian Trail. Turn right (east) to continue on Ruby Jewel Road for 0.5 mile through a corridor of tall evergreens over gently rolling terrain. Look out for the sign pointing right, then turn to find Ruby Jewel Yurt. The yurt is about 75 yards off the trail on a rise. Clark Peak Yurt is nearby.

## DAY 3: RUBY JEWEL YURT TO NORTH FORK CANADIAN YURT

**Distance:** 5.4 miles
**Elevation gain/loss:** 260 feet/1130 feet
**Difficulty:** Novice
**Hut elevation:** 8800 feet
**Hut GPS:** 40.6131°N, 106.0031°W

Return 75 yards to Ruby Jewel Road, following it west 0.5 mile to the junction with the North Canadian Trail. Turn right (northwest) to follow the North Canadian Trail 4 miles to the junction with the North Fork Trail, near the confluence of the North Fork and the South Fork Canadian River.

At the junction, turn right (east) to follow the North Fork Trail, marked with NSN blue diamond trail signs, about a mile to the yurt. The trail begins on the south side of the North Fork of the Canadian River, then crosses a bridge over the river and ascends a broad meadow on the north bank. Enjoy great views of the mountains in all directions as you approach the yurt perched on the hill above in a sweeping curve.

## DAY 4: NORTH FORK CANADIAN YURT TO CLOSURE TRAILHEAD

**Distance:** 1.4 miles
**Elevation gain/loss:** 250 feet/150 feet
**Difficulty:** Novice
**Trailhead GPS:** Closure Trailhead (40.6143°N, 106.0223°W)

Leaving the yurt, reverse your incoming route by circling back around and down the hill to head west, following the NSN blue diamonds until you reach the junction of the North Fork Trail and the North Canadian Trail. Look back for great views of the Medicine Bow Mountains defining North Park's northern boundary. You can also glimpse the distant Park Range to the far west. *Note:* When skiing west back from the yurt, you see the *backs* of these blue diamond signs, which are posted to guide people *from* the Closure Trailhead *to* the yurt.

Ski past the junction with the North Canadian Trail, continuing west on the well-marked North Fork Trail to cross the South Fork of the Canadian River. The trail briefly follows a tributary, then swings west-northwest to ascend to the Closure Trailhead and parking area. Find your vehicle and drive south on CR 41 for 8.5 miles to return to the starting location near the park entrance and NSN headquarters.

# TENTH MOUNTAIN DIVISION HUT SYSTEM

*What does skiing give to the mountaineer? What but wings to his slow-plodding feet? Hickory wings on which he can escape the bounds of method and precision that define the practice slopes on which he learned the mechanics. Wings which free him to travel, through the winter, across the snowfields that gather, cloudlike, on distant mountains.*

—David Brower, *Manual of Ski Mountaineering*

**Location:** Rocky Mountains and White River, Arapaho, and San Isabel National Forests near Aspen, Vail, Leadville, and Breckenridge, Colorado

**Distance:** Huts 6 to 10 miles apart; 13.3 miles in Itinerary 1; 25.4 miles in Itinerary 2

**Elevation gain/loss:** Itinerary 1: 2380 feet/2390 feet; Itinerary 2: 4710 feet/6380 feet

**Difficulty:** Some novice trails, most intermediate to advanced

**Terrain:** High alpine terrain, forest trails, and logging roads (some shared with snowmobiles), meadows, streambeds, and alpine ridgelines

**Modes of travel:** Winter skiing and snowshoeing; summer hiking and biking

**Season:** Winter (Thanksgiving to the end of April); some huts open year-round, others winter and/or summer only

**Huts:** Thirty-four huts, inns, and cabins (capacity 3 to 20), self-service, exclusive use, and by the bunk

---

**CENTRAL COLORADO, PACKED WITH SOME** of the Rocky Mountains' highest peaks, is arguably the premier downhill ski destination in the United States. The area—defined by Aspen, Vail, Leadville, and Breckenridge—is also a vast retreat for backcountry skiers seeking comfortable overnight quarters away from glitzy resorts.

The largest backcountry ski hut system, dedicated to human-powered access, education, and preservation, is actually a cooperative organization with a common information and reservation system. This umbrella organization—formally known as the Tenth Mountain Division Hut System (TMDHS)—includes the Tenth Mountain Division Hut Association (fourteen huts), the Summit Huts Association (five huts), the Alfred A. Braun and Friends Huts (eight huts), and the Grand Huts Association (one hut). This unique system of huts also encompasses several privately owned huts, inns, and cabins: the Continental Divide Cabin, the Point Breeze Cabin, the Polar Star Inn, the Seipel Hut, the Shrine Mountain Inn (three separate cabins), and Vance's Cabin. Some of these offer a higher level of amenities including private quarters and showers and may be booked for exclusive use. Each distinctive set of huts is connected to the others not only by the reservation system but also by a trail web totaling more than 350 miles.

The Tenth Mountain Division Hut Association (TMDHA), the system's core, honors a special World War II unit that trained in the region and advanced ski technology by testing and honing outerwear, skis, and boots in a frigid wilderness setting (see "The Tenth Mountain Division of the US Army and Its Legacy"). The TMDHA was incorporated as a nonprofit in 1980. In order to launch this hut and trail system in prime recreational territory, the organization had to raise money and convince the US Forest Service (USFS) to allow permanent structures on public land. Fundraising prowess and deep political and deal-making experience got the job done. After the permit to build the first hut was rejected, Fritz Benedict (see "Founder's Story") and Robert McNamara, former US secretary of defense, convinced USFS administrators of their good intentions by providing a $250,000 bond to be used to raze the proposed huts and restore the lands if these structures were to be deemed useless or harmful. The first two huts opened in 1982 and were a great success. The bond was returned, and new huts were added almost yearly through the 1980s, with further additions to the system in the 1990s and in 2003.

The TMDHA created a nonprofit management template for funding, building, and maintaining backcountry huts in Colorado's high Rockies. Following their lead, other organizations that support and develop huts sprang up in the region. The Summit Huts Association, Alfred A. Braun Hut System, and Grand Huts Association all emerged in the late 1980s and 1990s; these nonprofits, united under the TMDHA booking system, operate huts with specific regional identities. Summit Huts, founded in 1989, manages five huts in Summit County near Breckenridge; the newer huts—conceived as family-friendly destinations more than hut-to-hut way stations—provide amenities such as indoor toilets and saunas. South of Aspen, the Braun huts, operated by the US Ski Association since the 1950s, were acquired in 1997 by a nonprofit that initiated extensive renovations and formed an alliance with the group supporting Friends Hut, established in 1984 in honor of a group of friends who died in a plane crash. The Grand Huts Association—with a single hut to date—is a geographical outlier; their Broome Hut, in Grand County, is more than 50 miles northeast by road from any other hut.

The spectacularly sited huts in this combined system—wood and stone or all wooden—recall sizable structures in the Swiss, French, and Italian Alps. Like their European counterparts, these overnight dwellings can be profoundly social. The communal gathering spaces promote easy camaraderie, and the shared sleeping quarters are refuges of quiet fellowship. Unlike the European huts, however, these are smaller and are self-service; visitors haul and prepare their own food, stoke the fire, chop

*Shrine Mountain Inn comprises three large privately owned cabins (Walter's, Chuck's, and Jay's), each with separate upstairs and downstairs accommodations. Walter's Cabin looks welcoming blanketed in fresh snow.*

wood, shovel the passages to the privy, and clean up after themselves. While the huts were designed for backcountry skiers, most are open to other nonmotorized uses including snowshoeing, and in the summer, some welcome visitors who hike, bike, ride horses, or join in a llama trekking group!

The TMDHS huts draw all sorts of adventurers to Colorado's high mountains. While people come from far and wide, 80 percent of hut users are from Colorado. You encounter ambitious athletes who challenge body and soul to travel long distances at lofty elevations in freezing temperatures and uncertain weather conditions. And you meet family groups with adolescent or grown children celebrating togetherness through shared physical exertion in convivial, remote hut settings.

The system, designed for multi-hut traverses, is now used primarily by those seeking a base camp, staying several days at a single hut and devoting daylight hours to exploring, making downhill turns, or cocooning with companions in comfort. We saw all sorts of ski equipment on the access trails. Close-in hut users often sport narrow classic skis; snowshoes are also common in early winter. Telemark skis, revived in the 1970s and popular into the early 2000s, are now largely replaced by alpine touring skis, which promote fast downhill runs after long uphill trudges with the help of skins.

# THE TENTH MOUNTAIN DIVISION OF THE US ARMY AND ITS LEGACY

The Tenth Mountain Division Hut Association honors the men of the Tenth Mountain Division of the US Army, who trained during World War II at Camp Hale in central Colorado. This isolated training center near Leadville, Colorado, established in 1942, focused on the special challenges of winter combat. Trained by skilled skiers recruited from elite East Coast colleges and the Upper Midwest, with its heritage of Nordic skiing, soldiers learned to ski and survive in this extreme mountain environment and developed lifelong friendships.

Visit the Colorado Snowsports Museum in Vail to enjoy documentary film footage of young men "finding their feet" on skis under arduous conditions. The Tenth's signal achievement in the war was breaking the German defensive line in Italy's Apennine Mountains. Despite suffering heavy casualties during the winter of 1944–45, the Americans managed the seemingly impossible task of penetrating the entrenched German position at the top of Riva Ridge in February 1945, allowing Allied forces to push farther into Europe.

While the victory at Riva Ridge brought international acclaim to this elite army division, another lasting legacy of these mountain soldiers is the United States ski industry. After the war, Tenth Mountain Division veterans founded twelve major resorts, including Aspen, Vail, Breckenridge, and Copper Mountain, not far from Camp Hale. Tenth Mountain Division veterans also came home to manage another seventeen resorts and to direct thirty-three ski schools. Fritz Benedict, a Tenth Mountain Division veteran trained as an architect, played pivotal roles not only in the launching the downhill ski industry but also in establishing the Tenth Mountain Division huts and trails system.

Founded in 1980, with the first two huts opening two years later, this hut system pays homage to the brave soldiers who trained at Camp Hale. Names of individual huts also resonate with the memorial impulse; several are named after Tenth Mountain Division veterans: Uncle Bud's Hut, built in 1989, is named after Bud Winter, and Skinner Hut, built in 1990, is named after William Wood Skinner. Former secretary of defense Robert McNamara and his wife, Margy, funded the first two huts, which bear their names; the two Benedict Huts, built in 1997 and known as Fritz and Fabi, were named after Fritz Benedict and his wife.

Beyond the hut system that bears its name, Tenth Mountain Division veterans also shaped other influential US outdoor organizations. David Brower became the first full-time executive director of the Sierra Club, transforming a regional body into a national conservation advocacy association. Paul Petzoldt founded the National Outdoor Leadership School, a nonprofit global wilderness school based in Lander, Wyoming.

TMDHA staff can help select the huts and routes best suited to your skills and visions of a good time. While a few of the huts can be accessed with relative ease from the trailhead, this hut system is recommended for intermediate to advanced skiers with backcountry experience. As lowlanders, we contracted with a guide service to ensure maximum safety and comfort on the four-day intermediate to advanced traverse featured below (see Itinerary 2). The two featured itineraries barely scratch the surface of the remarkable number of options. Want to sample more huts and trails in the Tenth Mountain Division Hut System? Among the easiest to reach are Vance's Cabin, 3.1 miles from the Tennessee Pass Trailhead, and Broome Hut, 1 mile from another trailhead. The Summit Huts offer many possibilities including cozy Francie's Cabin, less than 2 miles from the trailhead, and the brand-new Sisters Cabin. The best huts for kids include Broome Hut, Continental Divide Cabin, Shrine Mountain Inn, Uncle Bud's Hut, and Sangree M. Froelicher Hut.

Before or after your hut-to-hut adventure, avoid the glitz and expense of Vail or Aspen and visit the town of Leadville, which offers a friendly hostel and bed-and-breakfasts, a local history museum, and a great community swimming pool. Downhill ski at the modest Ski Cooper, or check out the Tennessee Pass Nordic Center, with 16 miles of groomed trails. These folks also run the Tennessee Pass Cookhouse, a ski-in yurt offering luxury dining.

*A memorial to the soldiers of the Tenth Mountain Division at Tennessee Pass*

## HUTS AND AMENITIES

The TMDHS huts are mostly one- or two-story structures with peaked roofs and prominent entryways built from logs or wood framing and stone. Quite a few huts are perched above timberline at elevations higher than 11,000 feet; others are nestled on wooded slopes; all offer great views. Enter through the mudroom to divest boots and outerwear, then continue into the spacious interior, divided into kitchen and dining/seating areas. The centrally situated wood-burning stove dispels chills and dries damp gear after a day outside. Ample firewood is available.

# FOUNDER'S STORY

*I think of the huts as a way to get back to the simplicity that skiing was all about. It was so simple, so easy, and inexpensive.*
—Fritz Benedict, founder of the Tenth Mountain Division Hut Association

Frederic "Fritz" A. Benedict (1914–95) was a man of his times, channeling ideas and developments in the larger culture into infrastructure for downhill and backcountry skiing. And he was more than simply a man of his times. Uniquely positioned by his training as an architect and planner, and his experience as a skier and member of the US Army's Tenth Mountain Division, Benedict deserves credit for the shape, scope, and vision of the largest hut system in the US.

Benedict explored connections between recreation and landscape as a young man. His 1938 landscape architecture master's thesis, "Hiking Trails in the Lower Wisconsin River Valley," proposed a 150-mile loop trail punctuated with overnight shelters. Benedict later moved to Taliesin, architect Frank Lloyd Wright's Wisconsin home and studio, where he served as head gardener and studied architecture with the master. An expert skier, Benedict was drafted into the Tenth Mountain Division, training at Camp Hale near Leadville, Colorado. While a combat soldier in Europe, he probably observed European ski centers.

After the war, Benedict moved to Aspen where he joined other Tenth Mountain Division veterans to launch the American downhill ski industry in Colorado. Trained as a planner, he was responsible for the master plans of Aspen, Vail, and Snowmass. The first chairman of Aspen's Planning and Zoning Commission and a member of the Pitkin County Planning Commission, Benedict lent his expertise to the increasingly vexing issues attendant upon the rapid growth of the ski industry. As an architect, he followed the modernist credo "form follows function"; his buildings, utilizing local materials, were designed to fit harmoniously with their natural settings.

Special spaces are designed to facilitate meal preparation and sleeping. Cooking zones vary from cozy to spacious. Overnight guests share spaces fitted with countertops, propane cooktops, dry sinks, and open shelving well stocked with dishes and pots. Beds are distributed downstairs and up—in bunk rooms and in sleeping spaces with single or double beds. A few huts offer one or two private rooms with a double bed. Detached outhouses are the norm; be prepared to shovel the path to these facilities after a long day on the trail. The Benedict Huts privy—with two glass walls for

At age sixty-six, Benedict surveyed the industry he had helped create. As skiing in America went from a recreational activity to a luxury lifestyle pursuit, something essential had gotten lost: the simple joy of skiing in the majestic Colorado mountains. In 1980, Benedict joined a group of ski friends to develop,

*Fritz Benedict, founder of the Tenth Mountain Division Hut system*

according to the association's mission statement, "a mountain hut system that promotes understanding and appreciation of the natural environment while developing individual self-reliance." He leveraged influential friendships accrued over decades to fund the non-profit organization; his planning experience was a crucial asset to the fledgling organization as it drew up plans and negotiated access and permits. Benedict designed the first two huts in the Tenth Mountain Division Hut Association (TMDHA) system himself; Margy's Hut and McNamara Hut set a standard for solid construction, functional design, the graceful flow of interior spaces, and harmonious siting within rugged mountain terrain.

The TMDHA inspired the founding of other backcountry hut systems in the 1980s and 1990s, setting the highest standards for huts, professional operations, and finances. Because this nonprofit is well funded by enthusiastic and affluent supporters, hut stays are modestly priced. Amid the glamorous madness of the American ski industry, Benedict and his friends managed to create an antidote—a no-frills system of backcountry lodgings that promote nature immersion and self-reliance, and recapture "the simplicity that skiing was all about."

optimum views—is particularly memorable. While winter users rely on snowmelt for water, summer recreationists may need to carry drinking water some distance and follow purification procedures. Described here are only the huts included in the featured itineraries.

### CONTINENTAL DIVIDE CABIN

Built in 2007, this privately owned cabin and its neighbor, Point Breeze Cabin built in 2011, each sleep eight. Nicely appointed with handcrafted furniture, the cabin offers comfortable seating including rocking chairs around the woodstove and places to

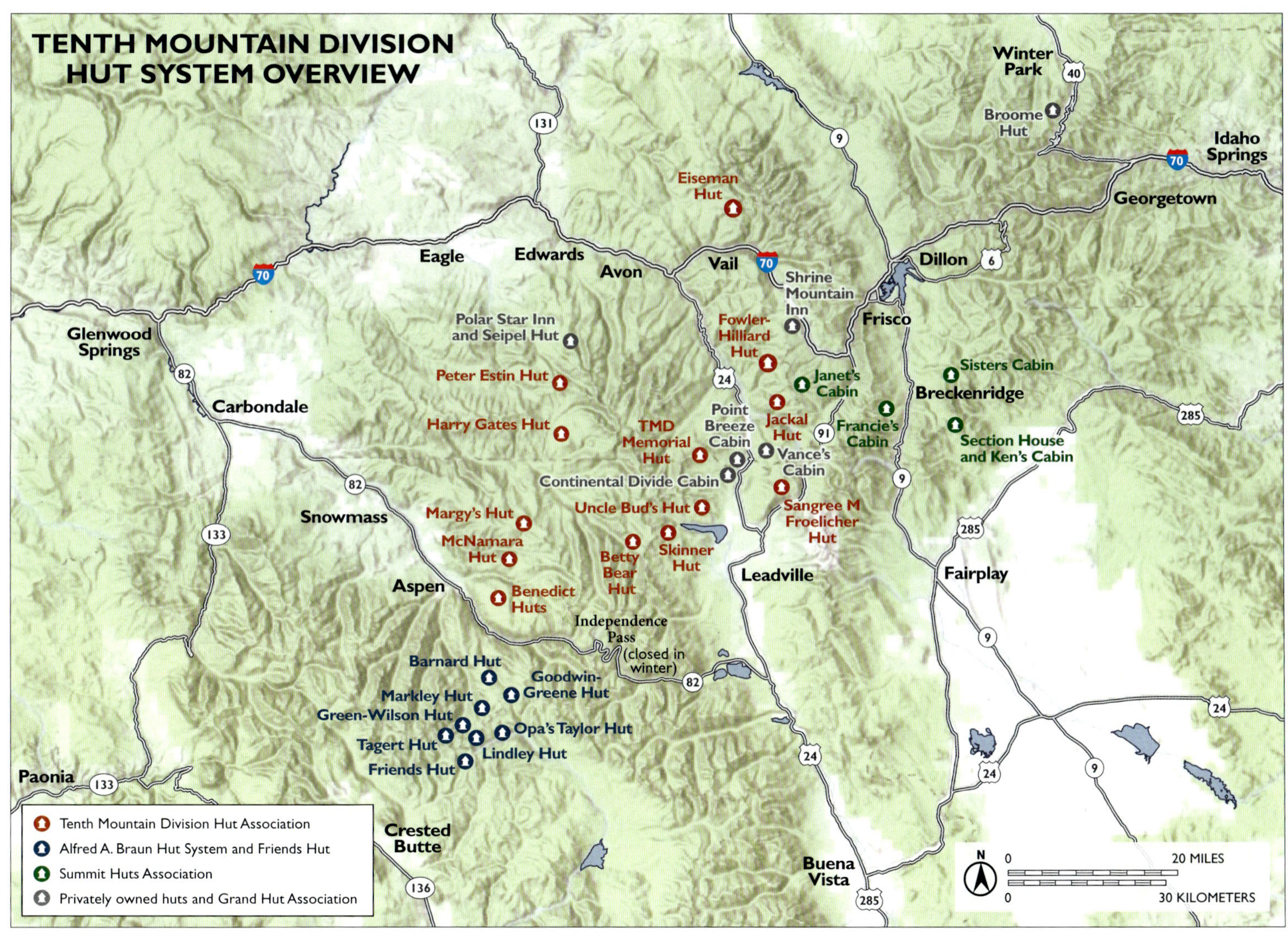
TENTH MOUNTAIN DIVISION
HUT SYSTEM OVERVIEW
Winter Park
Broome Hut
Idaho Springs
Georgetown
Eiseman Hut
Eagle
Edwards
Avon
Vail
Shrine Mountain Inn
Dillon
Frisco
Polar Star Inn and Seipel Hut
Fowler-Hilliard Hut
Janet's Cabin
Sisters Cabin
Breckenridge
Glenwood Springs
Peter Estin Hut
Jackal Hut
Francie's Cabin
Carbondale
Harry Gates Hut
Point Breeze Cabin
TMD Memorial Hut
Vance's Cabin
Section House and Ken's Cabin
Continental Divide Cabin
Snowmass
Margy's Hut
Uncle Bud's Hut
Sangree M Froelicher Hut
McNamara Hut
Betty Bear Hut
Skinner Hut
Leadville
Fairplay
Aspen
Benedict Huts
Independence Pass (closed in winter)
Barnard Hut
Goodwin-Greene Hut
Markley Hut
Green-Wilson Hut
Opa's Taylor Hut
Tagert Hut
Lindley Hut
Friends Hut
Paonia
Crested Butte
Buena Vista
Tenth Mountain Division Hut Association
Alfred A. Braun Hut System and Friends Hut
Summit Huts Association
Privately owned huts and Grand Hut Association
N
0   20 MILES
0   30 KILOMETERS

play games and otherwise while away dark evenings. Equipped with propane burners, the kitchen is fully stocked with cooking utensils; there is a propane barbecue on the porch. Food storage options include a solar-operated refrigeration chest for summer use. Access to firewood and to the outhouse is by covered breezeway. Outside, tour the property developed by owner Lee Rimel and visit the tepee and the shepherd's wagon.

## TENTH MOUNTAIN DIVISION MEMORIAL HUT

Built in honor of the nation's ski troops, this hut embodies TMDHA standards in design and amenities. The solidly constructed two-story log building welcomes visitors with a wide front porch outside and plenty of seating inside. Upstairs there are bunks for sixteen. The hut, heated by two wood-stoves, offers a fully equipped kitchen with gas cooking burners. Situated at 11,370 feet elevation near the Continental Divide just below Homestake Peak, this hut commands outstanding views. Water is from snowmelt, and lights are solar powered.

## SHRINE MOUNTAIN INN

This delightful cluster includes three privately held cabins: Jay's (sleeps twelve), Chuck's (two separate units, each sleeping six), and Walter's (two separate units, each sleeping six) feature folksy, artistic touches and comforts beyond the norm. Enjoy indoor flush toilets, hot showers, towels, and beds with pillows and pillowcases (bring your own sleeping bag). There is a sauna for extra pleasure. Commodious porches offer views of Shrine Mountain and the Gore Range.

## FOWLER-HILLIARD HUT

Similar in design and amenities to the Tenth Mountain Division Memorial Hut, this hut, which sleeps sixteen, is named for two people killed in a climbing accident. Perched below Resolution Mountain, it affords 360-degree views of the terrain where the Tenth Mountain Division troops once trained. Enjoy great skiing near the hut and on the west slopes of Resolution Mountain.

## JACKAL HUT

One of the highest (11,660 feet) of the TMDHA huts, Jackal Hut gets its name from the contraction of Jack Schuss and Al Zesiger, two major donors. Sleeping sixteen, the hut features amenities and a design similar to Fowler-Hilliard Hut and the Tenth Mountain Division Memorial Hut. To the west is the jagged Mount of the Holy Cross, around which the TMDHA system revolves, with the spectacular Collegiate Peaks splayed out on the western horizon.

## PLANNING AND PREPARATION

**Website:** www.huts.org; (970) 925-5775

**Booking:** Members can book nearly a year ahead via the lottery and early reservations period. Beginning in June, reservations are open to all for the following winter season. Summer reservations can be made after November 1 of the previous year. Braun and Friends Huts are not booked through the lottery.

**Membership:** Not required. Members of the Tenth Mountain Division Hut Association, Summit Huts Association, and Grand Huts Association are eligible to participate in the early booking process, which includes a reservations

*Intimate Ken's Cabin, restored in partnership with the USFS and Summit Huts Association, is one of the oldest in the Breckenridge area.*

lottery and an early call-in and online reservations period.

**Rates:** $ to $$; rates vary across the organizations; see website for pricing

**Transportation:** There is public transportation to the major alpine ski resorts (check websites); visitors to the few huts linked to these resorts can manage without a personal vehicle; otherwise, no public transportation to most trailheads

### MAPS

The TMDHA provides a printed brochure with a map that is very helpful for trip planning. For on-trail navigation, purchase (through the TMDHA online store: www.hutstore.org/10th_Mountain_Hut _Maps_s/4.htm) eight different 1:24,000 scale USGS topo maps covering the entire winter-use trail system and two summer-use trail maps. Downloadable and printable PDF versions of these maps are also available on the website. A 36-by-36-inch color wall map depicting the whole hut system is also for sale. User-sourced GPX files for any of the trails and for some hut-to-hut routes can be downloaded from the website.

### PACKING TIPS

Bring a sleeping bag, pillowcase, ski goggles, and other safety gear. Skis with metal edges and climbing skins are recommended. Skiers in this system favor alpine touring or telemark ski equipment.

## OTHER TIPS

Consult "Tips for Getting a Lottery Trip" on the website to maximize your chances of getting a winter reservation and call the TMDHA booking staff for advice. Dogs are not allowed in the huts.

Do not go alone. Practice prudent backcountry and winter mountain travel techniques. On the website, see the FAQ for a link to emergency contact information for the relevant sheriffs' offices. While only a few of the TMDHA huts are in marked avalanche territory, routes between huts cross, or pass next to, avalanche-prone terrain. Even though this book avoids avalanche-prone itineraries, we join with the TMDHA to recommend that at least one member of the party be trained in evaluating avalanche and snow stability hazards, and in wilderness first aid. Members of the party should carry emergency overnight shelter equipment including a tarp or bivvy, sleeping pad, shovel, and probe.

## ITINERARY 1: TENNESSEE PASS TO MEMORIAL HUT

*13.3 miles, three days, two nights*

An easy introduction to the hut-to-hut experience, this itinerary begins with a short first day followed by a moderate day appropriate for novice skiers ready to stretch their skills on an intermediate route. This itinerary incorporates overnight stays in a private, exclusive-use lodge and in a shared hut operated by the TMDHA. Because you are paying for the entire Continental Divide Cabin, which sleeps eight, this option is best suited to a larger group.

The winter trail to the hut follows the Colorado Trail/Continental Divide Trail for the first half. The trail is well marked with blue diamonds, but users should be alert to intersecting ski trails in the area. There are several routes to the hut; the directions below accord with the Continental Divide East West/Betty Bean digital map on the TMDHA website. Note that the winter ski trail varies somewhat from the summer hiking trail. Skins are not necessary.

## DAY 1: TENNESSEE PASS TO CONTINENTAL DIVIDE CABIN

**Distance:** 0.8 mile
**Elevation gain/loss:** 170 feet/90 feet
**Difficulty:** Novice
**Hut elevation:** 10,500 feet
**Hut GPS:** 39.3577°N, 106.3220°W
**Trailhead:** Tennessee Pass Trailhead 39.3624°N, 106.3119°W

### Getting There

From the north, take exit 171 off I-70 toward Minturn, then follow US Highway 24 for 24 miles to the well-signed Tennessee Pass Trailhead just opposite the turnoff to Ski Cooper. The large parking lot, with a toilet, is on the west side of the highway.

From the south, reach the junction of US 24 and State Route 91 north of Leadville, then follow US 24 north for 8.7 miles to the Tennessee Pass Trailhead on the left.

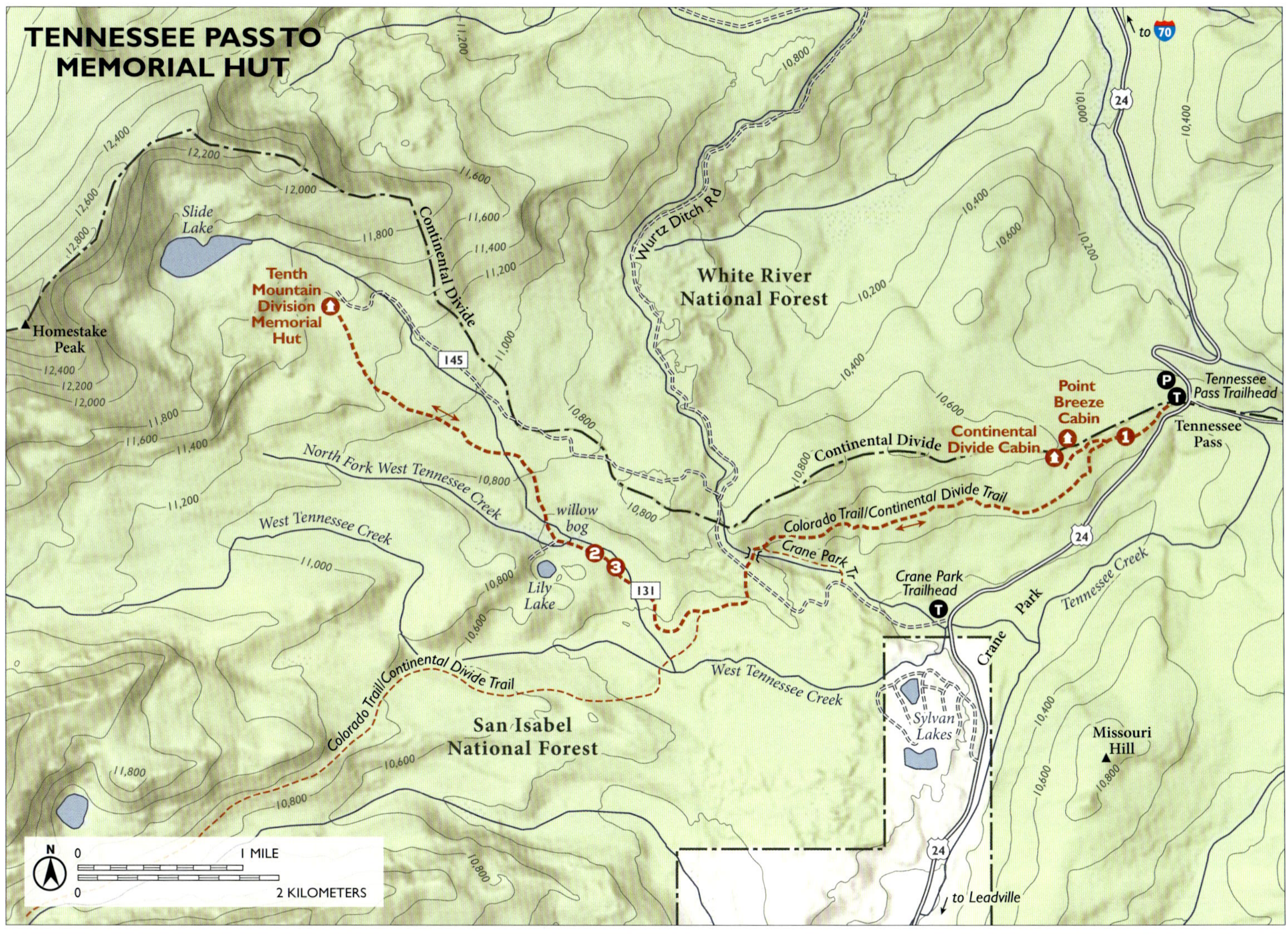

TENNESSEE PASS TO MEMORIAL HUT
to 70
Slide Lake
Homestake Peak
Tenth Mountain Division Memorial Hut
Continental Divide
Wurtz Ditch Rd
White River National Forest
Point Breeze Cabin
Continental Divide Cabin
Tennessee Pass Trailhead
Tennessee Pass
P
T
145
Continental Divide
Continental Divide
Colorado Trail/Continental Divide Trail
North Fork West Tennessee Creek
West Tennessee Creek
willow bog
2
3
131
Lily Lake
Crane Park Tr
Crane Park Trailhead
T
Crane Park
Tennessee Creek
24
Colorado Trail/Continental Divide Trail
San Isabel National Forest
West Tennessee Creek
Sylvan Lakes
Missouri Hill
to Leadville
24
10,400
10,000
10,200
10,600
10,800
10,200
10,400
10,600
10,800
11,000
11,200
11,400
11,600
11,800
12,000
12,200
12,400
12,600
12,800
N
0   1 MILE
0   2 KILOMETERS

## On the Trail

Two trails depart from the parking lot. Find the route nearest to US 24 (not the trail near the outhouse), and head southwest. Follow the gently ascending Continental Divide Trail (CDT) for 0.5 mile, until you see a sign for a spur trail to the cabins. Take a right and head to the Point Breeze and Continental Divide Cabins.

### DAY 2: CONTINENTAL DIVIDE CABIN TO TENTH MOUNTAIN DIVISION MEMORIAL HUT

**Distance:** 6 miles
**Elevation gain/loss:** 1490 feet/630 feet
**Difficulty:** Intermediate
**Hut elevation:** 11,370 feet
**Hut GPS:** 39.3689°N, 106.3868°W

Retrace yesterday's spur trail back (northeast) 0.3 mile to the junction, then turn right and follow the CDT southwest. At 2.3 miles, you arrive at a well-marked intersection at a bridge (39.3549°N, 106.2976°W). Do not take the sharp left onto the Crane Park Trail; instead, bear gently left (southeast), staying on the CDT. At 2.5 miles, the CDT intersects with Wurtz Ditch Road. Cross the road, and continue along the CDT until the intersection at 2.9 miles with Forest Road 131 (39.349°N, 106.3587°W).

At this point, leave the CDT, which veers left (southwest). Follow FR 131 northwest toward the north end of Lily Lake. Continue for 0.7 mile to reach the dense willow bog north of Lily Lake (39.3522°N, 106.3675°W), depart FR 131, and take the marked trail to the hut (north) at 4 miles. (This part of the route, with intersecting trails and the willow bog, can be confusing; use a map, compass,

and GPS to stay on course.) The trail passes through a boggy area, then climbs along the right side of a large clearing. You may want to put on climbing skins for the final 1.5-mile ascent northwest to north-northwest to the hut.

### DAY 3: TENTH MOUNTAIN DIVISION MEMORIAL HUT TO TENNESSEE PASS

**Distance:** 6.5 miles
**Elevation gain/loss:** 720 feet/1670 feet
**Difficulty:** Intermediate

Reverse the route of the past two days, continuing past the turnoff to the Continental Divide Cabin and back to the Tennessee Pass Trailhead and parking lot.

*Private facilities under the Tenth Mountain Division umbrella, like Walter's Cabin, offer more amenities and special touches than the association huts.*

## ITINERARY 2: HAUTE ROUTE

### *26.3 miles, four days, three nights*

This itinerary is for more adventurous and skilled skiers, traveling over terrain rated mostly intermediate through advanced; the route presents some navigation challenges. The first day is short and relatively easy. The next two days are long and hard—best to get an early start! Day 3, with a grueling ascent to Jackal Hut, may tax the abilities of some intermediate skiers and those not fully acclimatized. Consider instead making this a two-night trip, descending on day 3 from Fowler-Hilliard to the Pando Trailhead or Camp Hale Trailhead (see "Two-Night Option").

The traverse requires two cars, one at Vail Pass where you begin and the other at the Pando Trailhead. (Alternatively, you can exit at the Camp Hale Trailhead, which is about a mile south of Pando.) Or you may be lucky enough to have a friend in the area who will drop you off at Vail Pass and pick you up a few days later. The TMDHA website lists shuttle and custom ride service vendors, an expensive option. If you engage a guide service, transportation support is included in the package.

Navigation can be challenging on this route; blue diamond markers are sparse to nonexistent for long stretches. Fresh snow requires breaking trail. We highly recommend using an altimeter with the GPS digital maps to find your way across unmarked sections of the route.

### DAY 1: VAIL PASS TO SHRINE MOUNTAIN INN

**Distance:** 2.7 miles

**Elevation gain/loss:** 790 feet/180 feet
**Difficulty:** Novice
**Hut elevation:** 11,209 feet
**Hut GPS:** 39.4926°N, 106.2912°W
**Trailhead:** Vail Pass Trailhead 39.5460°N, 106.2415°W

### Getting There

Take exit 190 off I-70 for Vail Pass. Find the overnight parking lot immediately upon exiting, and park in the area designated for the Tenth Mountain Division Huts. There is a toilet at the rest area located a short distance from the trailhead.

### On the Trail

Today's route climbs gently up the right (northwest) side of West Tenmile Creek. From the trailhead, follow the multiuse Shrine Pass Road southwest for less than 100 yards before bearing left to take the nonmotorized ski trail that parallels the road. The trail is well marked with blue diamonds and blue poles in exposed areas. Look for ptarmigans, squirrels, and other wildlife. After 2.3 miles, turn left (southwest) through a gate, following the wooded trail for 0.4 mile to Shrine Mountain Inn.

### DAY 2: SHRINE MOUNTAIN INN TO FOWLER-HILLIARD HUT

**Distance:** 7.1 miles
**Elevation gain/loss:** 1530 feet/1220 feet
**Difficulty:** Intermediate
**Hut elevation:** 11,660 feet
**Hut GPS:** 39.4926°N, 106.2912°W

The terrain on the west side of Wingle Ridge is exposed to west winds, so check

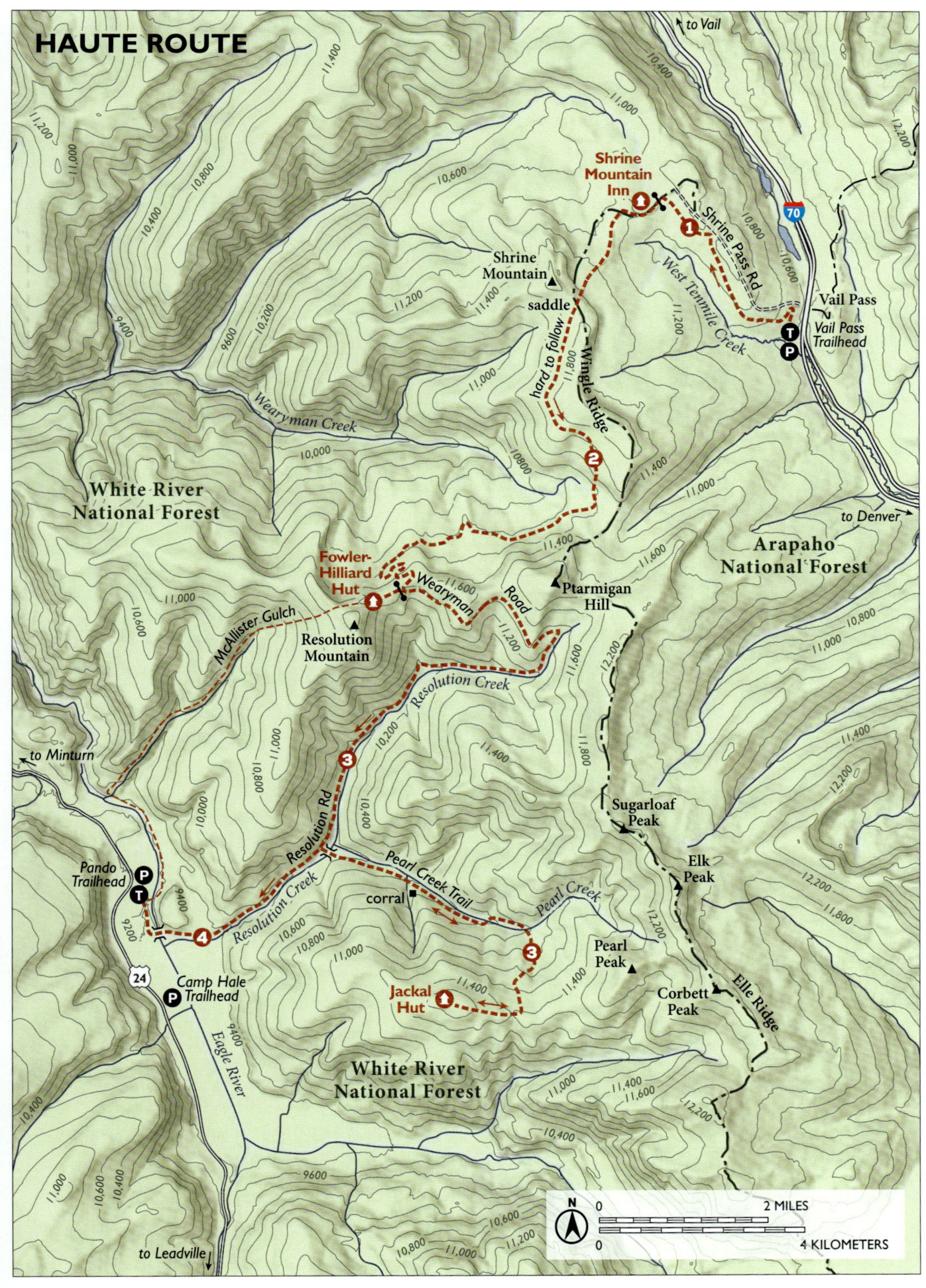
HAUTE ROUTE
to Vail
Shrine Mountain Inn
70
Shrine Pass Rd
Shrine Mountain
West Tenmile Creek
saddle
hard to follow
Vail Pass
Vail Pass Trailhead
Wingle Ridge
Wearyman Creek
White River National Forest
to Denver
Arapaho National Forest
Fowler-Hilliard Hut
Wearyman
Road
Ptarmigan Hill
McAllister Gulch
Resolution Mountain
Resolution Creek
to Minturn
Resolution Rd
Resolution Creek
Sugarloaf Peak
Elk Peak
Pando Trailhead
Pearl Creek Trail
corral
Pearl Creek
Pearl Peak
Elle Ridge
Camp Hale Trailhead
24
Jackal Hut
Corbett Peak
Eagle River
White River National Forest
to Leadville
N
0        2 MILES
0        4 KILOMETERS

## TWO-NIGHT OPTION

On day 3, skip Jackal Hut and instead descend 8.5 miles directly to the trailhead. Follow the directions for day 3 until you arrive at the confluence of Resolution and Pearl Creeks. Then consult the directions for day 4 for this final stretch, which continues down Resolution Road for another 1.5 miles to the flats at Eagle River, and bears right to the Pando Trailhead. Alternatively, a more popular exit from Fowler-Hilliard Hut is to take McAllister Gulch down to the Pando Trailhead. While this route is faster, shorter, and encounters fewer snowmobiles, it is more difficult.

the weather in advance. Depart the Shrine Mountain Inn on the trail marked Shrine Mountain, climbing south-southwest on the blue diamond–marked trail. Toward the end of this 1.3-mile ascent, the trail climbs steeply to Shrine Mountain Saddle (at 11,732 feet; 39.5318°N, 106.2558°W), located on the left (south) of the prominent red-rock peak of Shrine Mountain. Stop for a brief rest. Descend southward, using an altimeter to follow a contour of about 11,700 feet just above the tree line on a south-southwest bearing. This exposed section of the route along the west side of Wingle Ridge is barely marked.

At 2.6 miles, the trail turns south-southeast at 39.5152°N, 106.2580°W and continues through occasional groves of spruce. At 3.5 miles, before the end of Wingle Ridge, turn west-southwest at 39.514°N, 106.2592°W and cross an open snowfield. Continue southwest, then veer south through some woods and into a small meadow to cross the head of Wearyman Creek (39.5067°N, 106.2530°W). The trail

turns sharply right (west) and soon merges with a wide forest road.

About 2.5 miles after crossing the head of Wearyman Creek and 5.9 miles from Shrine Mountain Inn, the road begins to ascend up four long switchbacks. Watch for the gate to the right at 11,467 feet (39.4949°N, 106.2854°W) at 6.8 miles. Go through the gate and ascend, then descend gently southwest for the last 0.25 mile to the hut.

### DAY 3: FOWLER-HILLIARD HUT TO JACKAL HUT

**Distance:** 10 miles
**Elevation gain/loss:** 2210 feet/2350 feet
**Difficulty:** Intermediate to advanced
**Hut elevation:** 11,660 feet
**Hut GPS:** 39.4382°N, 106.2774°W

From the hut, retrace the trail back to the gate. Turn right (east) and follow Wearyman Road slightly downhill as it zigzags on a contour of about 11,400 feet for 2 miles. As you curve around the Ptarmigan Hill slopes, notice two communication structures perched above. Due south of Ptarmigan

Hill (39.4887°N, 106.2588°W; 11,371 feet), take a sharp right (south-southwest) turn onto Resolution Road. Follow the orange diamonds on Resolution Road (be alert for snowmobiles), descending gently south-southwest, then west and eventually southwest, paralleling Resolution Creek for 3.6 miles until you reach the confluence of Resolution and Pearl Creeks at 6 miles from Fowler-Hilliard Hut.

Turn left onto FR 715 (39.4602°N, 106.2995°W; 9,701 feet), and cross Resolution Creek by bridge. After about 50 yards, look to the left (west) for blue diamonds marking the beginning of the Pearl Creek Trail. This is a good place to stop for a break, put on skins, and study the map. The final 4-mile ascent to Jackal Hut involves 2000 feet of elevation gain and requires careful navigation with maps and an altimeter: there are almost no blue diamond markers. Leave FR 715 and follow the Pearl Creek Trail east-southeast up the creek drainage for 2 miles.

At about 0.9 mile (10,052 feet elevation) from where you left FR 715, turn left across an unnamed creek; note the makeshift corral on the right. The trail crosses to the north side of Pearl Creek at 7.7 miles from Fowler-Hilliard Hut, at 10,300 feet, for less than 0.5 mile (to 10,584 feet), then crosses back to the south side of the creek. At this point, Pearl Creek Junction (39.4489°N, 106.2642°W; 10,580 feet, 8.25 miles from Fowler-Hilliard Hut), the trail turns sharply south and climbs steeply up a ridge for 1.2 miles to a saddle at 11,400 feet, 9.2 miles for the day. Turn sharply right (west), ascending gently along a ridge to the hut in 0.8

mile. Exult in fabulous views of the Collegiate range to the south before you drop down the final few hundred yards to the hut.

## DAY 4: JACKAL HUT TO PANDO TRAILHEAD

**Distance:** 6.5 miles
**Elevation gain/loss:** 180 feet/2630 feet
**Difficulty:** Intermediate
**Trailhead GPS:** Pando Trailhead, 39.4547°N, 106.3328°W

Reverse the day 3 route and descend to the bottom of the Pearl Creek Trail. After skiing the ridge from the hut, look out for a rare arrow on a blue diamond, affixed to a large spruce tree, indicating that you should bear right (north) at 39.4436°N, 106.2647°W to remain on the trail. When you reach Pearl Creek Junction (39.4489°N, 106.2642°W; 10,580 feet), cross the creek and follow the trail west-northwest to the junction with Resolution Road.

If you haven't already, remove your skins and get ready for the final 1.5-mile descent on Resolution Road (southwest) to the Eagle River flats. Take the left fork (south), crossing Resolution Creek at 5.4 miles, then quickly bear right on Hospital Road, following Resolution Creek to its confluence with the Eagle River at 5.9 miles. Turn right (northwest) here to follow Resolution Mountain Road for about a half mile; turn left to reach the Pando Trailhead just off US 24.

*Note:* A more popular route from Jackal to the Pando Trailhead is via Ranch Creek Road; while shorter and faster, it is more difficult and not recommended due to avalanche terrain.

# SOUTHWEST NORDIC CENTER

*You are one with your skis and nature. This is something that develops not only the body, but the soul, and it has a deeper meaning for a people than most of us perceive.*

*—Fridtjof Nansen, Norwegian explorer*

**Location:** Rio Grande National Forest near Conejos, Colorado, and Chama, New Mexico
**Distance:** Yurts 2.8 to 6 miles apart; featured itinerary 17.3 miles
**Elevation gain/loss:** 2670 feet/2510 feet
**Difficulty:** Intermediate; trails strenuous but not difficult, wayfinding skills required
**Terrain:** High mountain backcountry terrain with some steep ups and downs; evergreen forest, meadows, and clearings laced with forest roads
**Modes of travel:** Winter skiing and snowshoeing
**Season:** Winter (exact dates depend on snowpack)
**Huts:** Four yurts (capacity 6), self-service, exclusive use

---

**THIS RUSTIC HUT SYSTEM, FEATURING** impeccably maintained, custom-made yurts, occupies great backcountry skiing terrain on the Colorado–New Mexico border far from any large town. While the yurts are in Colorado, viewpoints along the trail and from the huts open to the Chama River valley south in New Mexico. The owner does zero marketing, instead relying on word of mouth. Repeat visitors come not only for the alpine scenery, reliable snowpack, and homey yurts but also for touring and bowl skiing around each yurt, and for ridgeline and mesa-top vistas. Designed for hardy backcountry skiers, the Southwest Nordic Center (SWNC) hut system provides everything you need but also requires a good measure of common sense and self-reliance, and solid navigation skills.

Established in the late 1980s, the SWNC is the child of Doug MacLennan, an outdoor recreation professional based in Taos, New Mexico. Doug does it all! He built the huts (in collaboration with a skilled carpenter), including sewing the canvas skins that cover them. This hands-on owner-operator is in the backcountry three days a week during winter, lavishing attention on these canvas-and-wood structures. He also chops and stocks wood for fuel, marks trails, hauls supplies, and handles reservations. A longtime telemark skier, he often breaks trail by headlamp while servicing the huts, and enjoys a few downhill turns along the way.

MacLennan originally envisioned a string of yurts along a traverse, with huts placed every four miles between Cumbres Pass and the Wolf Creek Ski Area near Pagosa

Springs, Colorado. But as he added yurts, he noticed that users preferred to ski into a single hut rather than make the traverse. Even though fewer than 20 percent of visitors do the traverse, MacLennan sings the praises of the multiday hut-to-hut sojourn and recommends at least two nights in each yurt, allowing visitors to explore the area and try out the stellar skiing opportunities.

The SWNC huts are located in the southern San Juan Mountains between Pagosa Springs and Alamosa in Colorado and Taos. The yurt-to-yurt trails, near the Rio Grande River headwaters, are close to the Continental Divide Trail and just south of the South San Juan Wilderness. Visitors often spot fox, elk, mule deer, ravens, owls, hawks, and other birdlife. Sometimes black bear and wildcats cross your path. The forests, dominated by Engelmann spruce, are looking ragged due to the spruce budworm infestation. Timber is actively harvested in this part of the Rio Grande National Forest.

## HUTS AND AMENITIES

All four Rio Grande National Forest huts are 16-foot-diameter yurts comprising a single room with a tidy kitchen area equipped with plenty of pots, pans, and cooking utensils and a three-burner propane cookstove. There is a picnic table for eating, reading, and playing games; two propane lanterns light the space. Each yurt is heated by a woodstove. The firewood station on the deck has ample fuel and a great wood-splitting setup. Water is by snowmelt. Special touches include colorful rugs (folded on arrival) to spread on cold floors, and a detachable toilet seat; warmed by the woodstove, the seat feels great when installed in the frigid outhouse! These cozy, exclusive-use yurts sleep up to six people on sheet-covered foam mattresses with pillows; besides the bunk beds, there are two additional mattresses for possible overflow. The clothesline with clothespins near the stove is handy for drying clothes. *Hygge!*

*Tracks in the snow on the way to Neff Mountain Yurt*

### NEFF MOUNTAIN YURT

Located on the northeastern flank of Neff Mountain, this popular yurt is easy to get to from the Neff Mountain Trailhead. Enjoy forested glades, and the mountain bowl with great ski runs near the yurt. You can ski up and around Neff Mountain to enjoy views south across the valley.

### TRUJILLO MEADOWS YURT

Perched on the west side of a sweet meadow, the yurt faces east toward Trujillo Meadows and beyond into the South San Juan Wilderness. The nontechnical terrain invites gentle downhill turns that are well suited for Nordic touring.

### FLAT MOUNTAIN YURT

Tucked into the trees at the edge of a meadow, Flat Mountain Yurt is near a treeless ridge separating the upper Wolf Creek drainage and the Chama River basin. From the yurt, ski up to the ridge for views of the Chama River valley and fabulous sunsets. The adventurous skier might venture west toward the Continental Divide or descend nearly 3000 feet to the Chama River basin.

### GROUSE CREEK YURT

This stand-alone yurt has its own trailhead (a 4-mile ski in) and is located below the ridge that runs north from Jarosa Peak (11,766 feet). It offers distant views of bold Blanca Peak (14,351 feet) across the San Luis Valley in the Sangre de Cristo Mountains.

### PLANNING AND PREPARATION

**Contact:**   www.southwestnordiccenter.com; (575) 758-4761; yurt@newmex.com

*Colorful rugs, hung up between visitors, comfort cold feet on winter nights.*

# HUT TRIPS INSPIRE CREATIVITY

While life's waymarks are elusive, we become more practiced at finding them. This poem inscribed in the Flat Mountain Yurt logbook by visitors Mario and Stephanie captures the spirit of navigating these trails.

### Ode to the Little Blue Diamond

Little blue diamond,
You elusive wooden piece.
In the beginning you hid yourself,
Making us meander & zig zag.
Laughing at us say "here? no, here?".
Smiling to your little red partner.
But as the path left the road,
You became our motivation.
Waist deep in snow,
You were such a beautiful constellation.
Tangled with skis pointing in every direction,
There we saw you, & your timing perfection.
You and your friends, the dead car and cabin,
Erased the tired, the doubts, the second thoughts we were having.
We take you with us,
A metaphor for life's mountains.
Because as Rihanna would say,
Shine bright like a diamond.

**Booking:** Check availability and make reservations via website or by phone; the online booking system supports reservations for up to two yurts; call to book three or more yurts
**Membership:** None
**Rates:** $
**Transportation:** Driving directions to trailheads available on website; no public transportation to trailheads

**MAPS**

The SWNC website provides PDF maps for driving routes to the Trujillo Meadows and Neff Mountain Trailheads, an overview of the Cumbres Pass yurt system, and a trail map with routes from trailheads to each of the yurts. These PDF trail maps are adequate for navigation if you know the terrain, but they do not pinpoint hut locations. We recommend that first-time users purchase the USGS 1:24,000 quadrangle topo map for Cumbres (2001) or download a map of the terrain on Gaia, Avenza Maps, or another GPS app. Pinpoint in advance the precise hut locations on the print or digital maps.

## PACKING TIPS

Metal-edged backcountry skis and skins are recommended. Telemark or alpine touring gear is recommended for those intending to enjoy some downhill turns.

## OTHER TIPS

Dogs are not allowed in the huts.

## ITINERARY: THREE-YURT TRAVERSE

*17.3 miles, four days, three nights*

This three-hut traverse is a great way to experience most of the SWNC trails, and three of the four yurts. Consider spending an extra night at one of the yurts to allow time for bowl and ridge skiing. This area, laced with forest roads, is very popular not only with human-powered travelers but also with snowmobilers. Trails are not groomed; you may find that the trail has been broken by snowmobiles or other skiers. A large map posted at the Trujillo Meadows Trailhead indicates territories strictly for skiers and for snowmobilers, as well as shared zones.

The SWNC system is accessed by two trailheads between Cumbres Pass (10,022 feet) and La Manga Pass (10,230 feet): the Neff Mountain Trailhead (located at mile 7.7 from the New Mexico border on Colorado State Route 17, near a little cabin settlement called Rendezvous) and the Trujillo Meadows Trailhead (located at mile 4.25, on SR 17 near Cumbres Pass). This particular itinerary requires two cars: leave one at the Trujillo Meadows Trailhead, where the traverse ends, and another at the Neff Mountain Trailhead to begin. Alternatively, you can use only one car if you devise a circular route that begins and ends at the same trailhead. Both trailheads offer overnight parking.

The names for the forest roads that serve as trails are taken from the USGS 1:24,000 quadrangle topo map for Cumbres. Signs marking the forest roads, often snow covered and sometimes nonexistent, are difficult to find. It is therefore best to study the USGS map in advance to familiarize yourself with the roads in relation to the route descriptions.

The SWNC trails are marked with a combination of blue- or yellow-painted diamonds and streamers tied to trees. Blue diamonds and a combination of blue and orange streamers generally mark travel from a trailhead to a yurt; yellow diamonds and a combination of blue and yellow streamers generally mark yurt-to-yurt travel. Both can be difficult to spot. Pay attention! The yurts are clearly indicated on topo maps but out of sight from the trail. Mark precise hut locations on your map in advance, and pay close attention to trail junctions and turn-offs. Due to the challenges around spotting some trail markers, GPS coordinates of key turns and junctions are included below. Navigation is pretty straightforward with practice, a marked map, and use of GPS.

*Neff Mountain Yurt insulated by a deep snowpack*

## DAY 1: TRAILHEAD TO NEFF MOUNTAIN YURT

**Distance:** 2.8 miles

**Elevation gain/loss:** 780 feet/210 feet

**Difficulty:** Novice

**Hut elevation:** 10,400 feet

**Hut GPS:** 37.0387°N, 106.4259°W

**Trailhead:** Neff Mountain Trailhead (37.0385°N, 106.4111°W)

### Getting There

From Alamosa, Colorado, head south on US Highway 285 for 28 miles, then south on SR 17 for 36 miles toward Cumbres Pass. The Trujillo Meadows trailhead is 0.2 mile before the pass at the junction with Forest Road 118. Leave one car here, then backtrack 3.4 miles on SR 17 to the Neff Mountain Trailhead.

### On the Trail

From the Neff Mountain Trailhead parking lot, cross SR 17 from east to west to find the trail. Marked with blue diamonds, the trail heads north-northwest along the fairly level course of FR 116. At 0.6 mile, the trail curves west and continues to a fork/junction at 1.9 miles. This is where FR 116 continues right (west). At this fork, leave FR 116 and bear left to get to the yurt. Begin to climb southwest up an old logging road. Soon the trail takes a hairpin curve to proceed east and then southeast. Proceed up a wooded slope to pass through a gate (or over the gate if it is covered with snow) at 2.3 miles.

Leave the woods for an open meadow at about 2.6 miles; to your right (south) is a skiable slope coming off Neff Mountain. Neff Mountain Yurt is about 250 yards directly

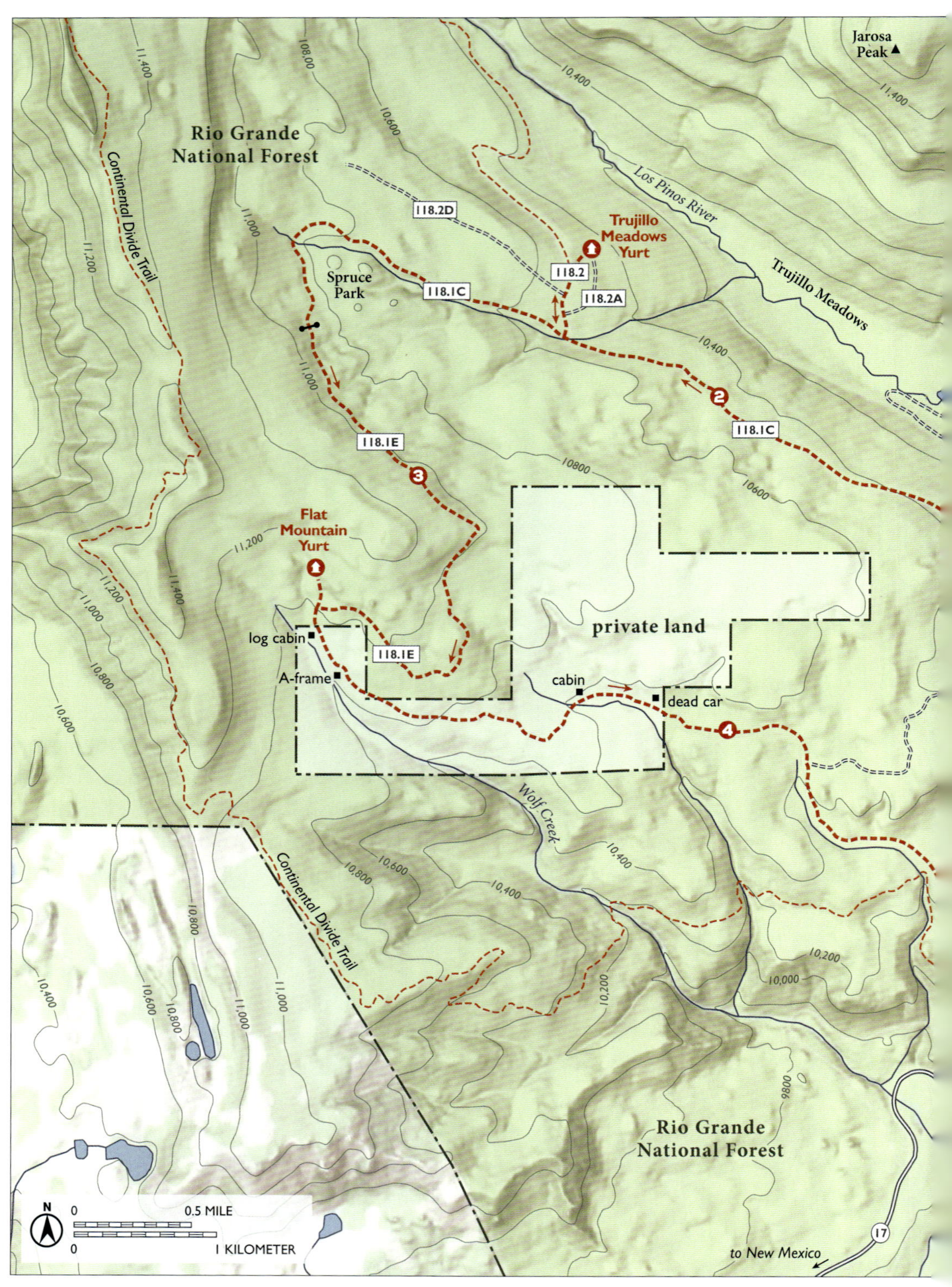

Jarosa Peak ▲
Rio Grande National Forest
Continental Divide Trail
11,400
108.00
10,400
Los Pinos River
10,600
11,000
11,200
118.2D
Trujillo Meadows Yurt
118.2
118.1C
Spruce Park
118.2A
Trujillo Meadows
10,400
11,000
2
118.1C
10,600
118.1E
3
10,800
private land
Flat Mountain Yurt
11,200
11,400
10,800
log cabin
118.1E
11,200
11,000
A-frame
cabin
dead car
4
10,600
Wolf Creek
Continental Divide Trail
10,800
10,600
10,400
10,400
10,200
10,000
9800
Rio Grande National Forest
N
0        0.5 MILE
0                1 KILOMETER
17
to New Mexico

# SOUTHWEST NORDIC CENTER OVERVIEW

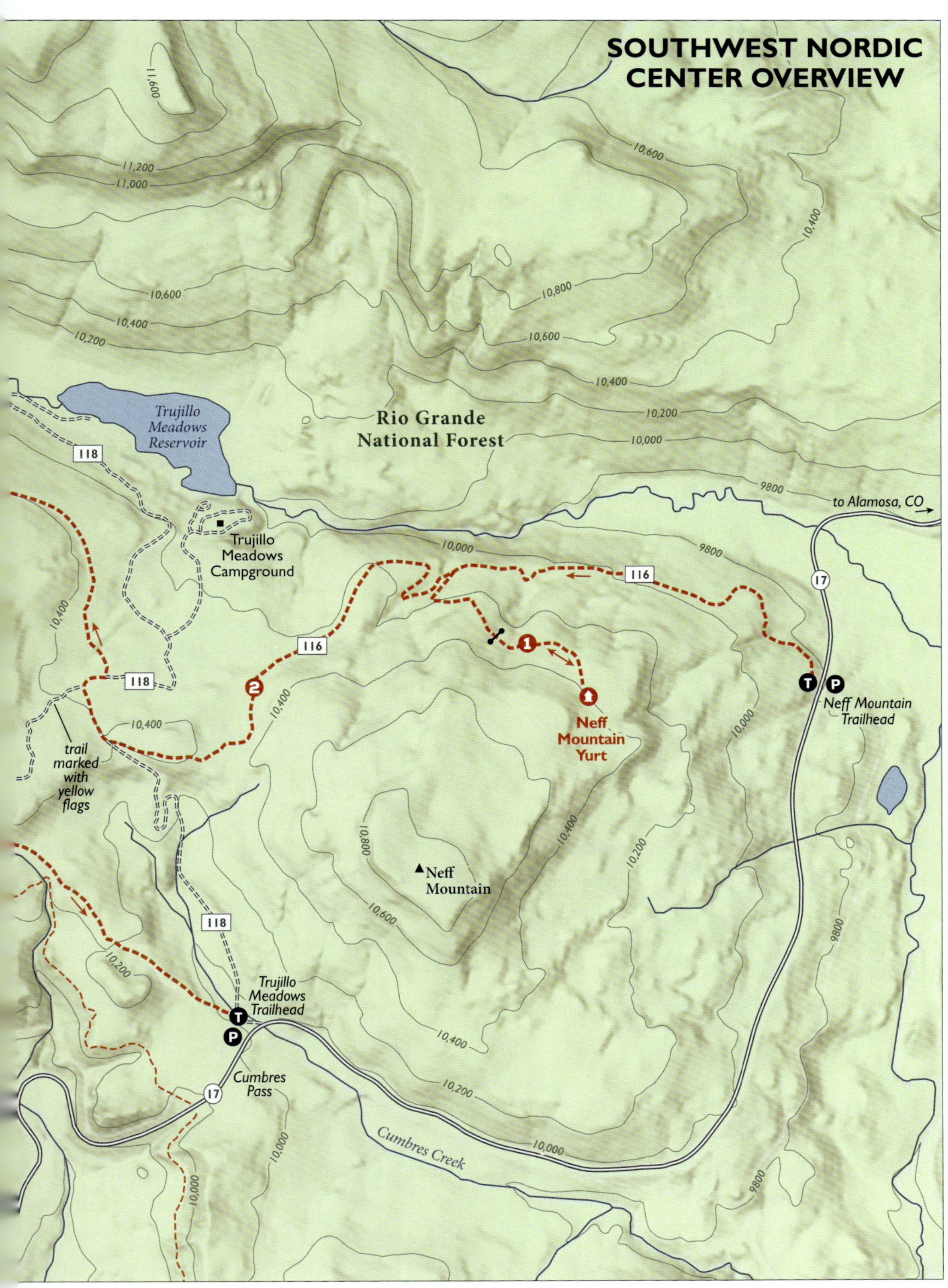

in front of you (south) but remains out of sight. Follow the blue diamonds, streamers, or blazes and continue south by a clump of trees to the yurt at 2.8 miles.

### DAY 2: NEFF MOUNTAIN YURT TO TRUJILLO MEADOWS YURT

**Distance:** 6 miles
**Elevation gain/loss:** 740 feet/660 feet
**Difficulty:** Novice
**Hut elevation:** 10,482 feet
**Hut GPS:** 37.0599°N, 106.4810°W

Ski 0.9 mile from Neff Mountain Yurt back to FR 116 and turn left, following the yellow markers for about 2.1 miles until you reach the junction with FR 118 (37.0357°N, 106.4550°W) at 3 miles from Neff Mountain Yurt. The trail junction is a good place to stop for lunch or a snack. Turn right onto FR 118. After another 0.2 mile (3.2 cumulative miles for the day), you will see both blue and yellow markers; the yellow markers turn left, leading to the Flat Mountain Yurt Trail. Do not turn here.

Continue on FR 118 for another 0.1 mile to the left-hand turnoff onto FR 118.1C (37.0389°N, 106.4557°W). Take great care to look for this turn and follow the blue markers onto FR 118.1C, continuing for about 2 miles from this junction. Upon reaching 5.7 cumulative miles from Neff Mountain Yurt, follow the blue markers and turn right onto FR 118.2 (37.0557°N, 106.4818°W).

Within 0.2 mile, you will see turnoffs for FR 118.2A on your right and for FR 118.2D on your left. Pass these turnoffs and continue on FR 118.2, looking for a turnoff down to the right; this turnoff is marked with two sets of blue and orange streamers on the right and also with a blue diamond (37.0592°N, 106.4815°W). Turn right at this junction, and ski a short distance down through the spruce trees to find the yurt perched on the west side of a sweet little clearing overlooking Trujillo Meadows.

### DAY 3: TRUJILLO MEADOWS YURT TO FLAT MOUNTAIN YURT

**Distance:** 4.5 miles
**Elevation gain/loss:** 1060 feet/470 feet
**Difficulty:** Intermediate
**Hut elevation:** 11,066 feet
**Hut GPS:** 37.0434°N, 106.4974°W

Retrace yesterday's route 0.35 mile back to the junction with FR 118.1C (37.0557°N, 106.4818°W). Turn right (northwest) to follow FR 118.1C, marked by yellow diamonds and blue and orange streamers. Reach Spruce Park, a broad meadow, at 1.4 miles. Here the trail turns sharply to the left in a broad U-turn, then turns southeast. This is where FR 118.1C changes to FR 118.1E. When making this turn, hug the tree line to the right and keep eyes peeled for blue streamers that will lead you up the forest road (FR 118.1E) to the right and past a gate (if it's not buried). Ascend gently on FR 118.1E, noting great views to your left (northeast) before the trail turns sharply right (southwest) at 3.2 miles. FR 118.1E descends southwest for about 0.7 mile before curving west briefly, and then turning to ascend toward the northwest.

At 4.4 miles, ski down a gentle slope into a meadow facing a ridge to the south; below is a log cabin with a green roof. Begin to look for a right turn (north) to the yurt, tucked into the trees at the meadow's north

*The sometimes-elusive blue diamond trail marker*

edge and not easily visible from the forest road (the road has changed names on maps from FR 118.1C to FR 118.IE by this point). The right turn (37.033°N, 106.5029°W) is at the top of small hill, marked with a yellow diamond, and leads uphill about 0.1 mile to the yurt.

## DAY 4: FLAT MOUNTAIN YURT TO TRUJILLO MEADOWS TRAILHEAD

**Distance:** 4 miles

**Elevation gain/loss:** 100 feet/1180 feet

**Difficulty:** Intermediate

**Trailhead GPS:** Trujillo Meadows Trailhead, 37.0217°N, 106.4467°W

Begin by retracing yesterday's route 0.1 mile back to the junction with FR 118.IE. Turn right on FR 118.IE and ski down a small hill about 30 yards, looking for a left turn marked by three unpainted wooden diamonds on a small scrubby tree. When you turn left, you will be skiing straight (south) on a forest road that quickly enters private land. Following the blue and orange streamers, ski below the green-roofed log cabin on your right, then continue slightly uphill; this stretch of forest road is bounded by iron pipes, and an iron fence veers southeast. Continue past an elevated A-frame structure on the right at 0.5 mile.

At 1.2 miles, watch for trail markers where the road jogs left (northeast) and enters a long meadow. Follow this trail as it passes by a cabin under a ridge on your left (north) and then veers right (southeast), reaching the "dead car" landmark (a rusty old hulk of a car) in a fenced meadow at 1.7 miles (37.0373°N, 106.4764°W). Continue east across another meadow; follow the orange and blue streamers into the woods until you reach a junction where several trails meet at 2.3 miles (37.0348°N, 106.4669°W).

At this junction, follow blue markers and turn right on a forest road leading south and then southeast through the woods. At 2.9 miles, the clearly marked trail crosses a meadow and enters the woods again. For the next mile, the trail descends southeast across a lovely open slope, bringing you to the Trujillo Meadows Trailhead at 4 miles.

# SAN JUAN HUTS

*Seek not the paths of the ancients,*
*Seek what they sought.*

—Matsuo Bashō, *Words by a Brushwood Gate*

**Location:** Grand Mesa, Uncompahgre, San Juan, Gunnison, and Manti–La Sal National Forests, with bike routes extending into Moab, Utah; office based in Ridgway, Colorado
**Distance:** Itinerary 1 (hiking and/or skiing): Huts 4 to 8 miles apart, full traverse 29.5 miles; Itinerary 2 (biking): Huts 27 to 37 miles apart, traverse 146 miles total
**Elevation gain/loss:** Itinerary 1: 4130 feet/6490 feet; Itinerary 2: 9680 feet/13,890 feet
**Difficulty:** Moderate hiking; intermediate skiing; beginner to expert biking
**Terrain:** Hike or ski from Telluride to Ouray: mountain forests and meadows, well-graded trails; bike from Telluride to Gateway: steep mountain terrain, open tableland, high desert canyonlands, dirt and gravel roads, single-track alternative routes on most sections
**Modes of travel:** Spring, summer, and fall hiking and biking; winter and spring skiing
**Season:** Early May to end of November for hiking; late November to early June for skiing; June to end of September for biking
**Huts:** Sixteen huts (capacity 8) by the bunk; self-service on the hike/ski route, self-service+ on the bike route

---

**SOUTHWEST COLORADO, BOASTING THE TOWERING** San Juan Mountains, wild rivers, and picturesque old mining towns, attracts outdoor enthusiasts every season of the year. The San Juan Huts (SJH), a multimodal system, matches hut-studded routes with options for hikers, skiers, and bikers. Established in the late 1980s, SJH now comprises sixteen huts, the largest number owned and operated by a single private US hut system. Owners Joe Ryan and daughter Kelly draw on more than thirty years' experience to offer "adventures without the weight" to fit, independent folks seeking immersive experiences in this region (see "Founders' Story").

The SJH jumped into hut-to-hut ski operations during the late 1980s and soon added a hiking season. And about a decade later, Joe Ryan responded to the rise of mountain biking by developing the first hut-to-hut biking system in the US. Rugged cyclists share with skiers the dream of traveling on their own power all day, overnighting in a cozy hut, and then rising to do it all again. SJH is still the only system to offer hut-to-hut routes specifically designed for bikers. They offer multiple attractive hut-to-hut journeys varying by season and means of transport. For hikers and skiers, there is the 30-mile Sneffels Traverse from Last Dollar Pass above Telluride to the old mining and spa town of Ouray. Biking adventures—over dirt and gravel

*San Juan Huts mountain bikers pass through Colorado ranchland atop high mesas.*

road with optional single-track sections—include a five-day ride from Telluride to Gateway (146 miles) and longer journeys from either Telluride or Durango to Moab, Utah (both 215 miles). The Tour of the Canyons from Grand Junction to Moab covers 165 miles on mostly paved roads over three days.

Hikers and skiers enjoy classic Rocky Mountain high country on the Sneffels Traverse. The trail wends through shady conifers and groves of fluttering aspens, with open views across meadows to spectacular peaks and ridges. In late summer, watch out for the distinctive orange-frilled chanterelle mushrooms; we added these plump fungi to every dish on the menu! After the final night, the hiker can look forward to a restorative soak in Ouray Hot Springs or two private hot springs. The town-owned facility features three pools filled with odorless mineral water ranging from 88 to 108 degrees Fahrenheit.

Bikers begin in the mighty mountains, then stretch their legs across mesa-top rangelands dotted with livestock, abandoned homesteads, and occasional trophy homes, and pedal through stands of ponderosa pine and poplar in the Uncompahgre National Forest. Brace yourself for the dizzying descent into the Paradox Valley and the tiny hamlet of Gateway, where red canyon walls rise from the Dolores River lowlands. The Telluride-to-Gateway route loses nearly 14,000 feet in elevation. The longer routes to Moab incorporate an additional heart-pumping two-day push up 3500 feet and down another 4000 feet.

## FOUNDERS' STORY

Joe and Kelly Ryan, a father-daughter team, operate the largest hut system in the US. Joe, a fiercely determined, gregarious man, created the business, in the 1980s. His mission was to provide people an affordable backcountry journey to enjoy nature, learn outdoor skills, and experience healing benefits. Over several decades, he figured out how to navigate the necessary partnerships, identify likely users, and generate enough income to support a family. His daughter, Kelly, grew up in the family business. After college, she embraced many modes of adventure travel around the world and worked as a climbing guide in Alaska. Back in Colorado, Joe, who had expanded the business to include mountain bikers, was getting burned out and told Kelly that he might have to close the business to which she replied, "Hang on, Dad, I'll be there!" And since 2010, the pair have run the San Juan Huts (SJH) together.

Joe Ryan, whose parents were drawn to Colorado in search of a cure for his asthma as a child, ultimately made this recreational playground home. After years of travel and work as a guide in the outdoor industry, in the early 1980s he settled in the southwest corner of Colorado to work toward a hut system inspired by the Alpine Club of Canada (ACC) huts. But unlike the nonprofit ACC and the neighboring nonprofit Tenth Mountain Division Hut System, with its access to influential patrons with deep pockets, Joe's enterprise—a small family business—embodied a distinctly American approach rooted in rugged individualism. He spent several years exploring the San Juan Mountains to find the right traverse

Hike or bike? For a taste of each, we highlight one hike and one bike trek. Both options share the experience of remarkably simple but comfortable backcountry huts.

### HUTS AND AMENITIES

The San Juan huts, tucked into wooded locations, are basic but comfortable 16-by-16-foot wood-frame structures clad in trademark green metal. With a capacity of eight, these can be overnight homes to a single group, or gather together individuals and small groups for shared overnight experiences. Elevated outhouses with composting toilets are located nearby. Inside the huts, you find bunks with mattresses arranged along two walls. The kitchen area at the far end is equipped with cookware and utensils, a propane stove, lanterns, and large water containers. The woodstove is centrally positioned to keep the place cozy. Crazy Creek chairs and sleeping bags are provided; bring a sleep sheet, sleeping bag liner, or your own sleeping bag.

and locations for ski huts. Joe devised a simple, rugged hut design, which became the template for all sixteen huts in place today. A major challenge was working with federal land agencies. Initially, the US Forest Service (USFS) required the huts to be temporary structures. Eventually, as trust built between the Ryans and local agency staff, the huts were left in place—and became available for hikers in summer. Kelly has brought the business into the twenty-first century, developing a robust website and savvy marketing plan. Joe applauds his daughter: "Kelly's energy has been huge! Nobody works as hard as Kelly, organizing things, working on the web, humping loads to the huts, and whatever needs to be done."

*Joe Ryan and his daughter, Kelly, run the San Juan Huts together.*

Together the Ryans have managed to maintain business continuity over two generations. SJH exemplifies the prevalent business model for huts in the US: the privately owned and operated enterprise that constantly evolves in response to the market and to recreational trends. This operation offers a glimpse of one key strand of the future of US hut systems.

Hikers and skiers in the San Juans pack in their own meal provisions—be they freeze-dried meal packets or the ingredients for gourmet backpacker repasts. You can request that the SJH folks deliver provisions (for a fee) to the Blue Lakes Hut, midway through the traverse, in keeping with this system's "lighten the load" ethos. Cyclists, on the other hand, are prodigiously provisioned at every hut along the way. Abundant supplies of canned and dry goods, snacks, fresh produce, cheese, eggs, and bacon will satisfy every appetite and dietary preference. A special SJH cookbook offers recipes inspiring best use of the foodstuffs. Bike huts are restocked every three to five days with food, water, soda, beer (extra charge), and other supplies as needed.

## PLANNING AND PREPARATION

**Contact:** www.sanjuanhuts.com; (970) 626-3033; info@sanjuanhuts.com

**Booking:** Check website for availability; reservations must be made by phone; , each group designates a leader, who will compile the roster

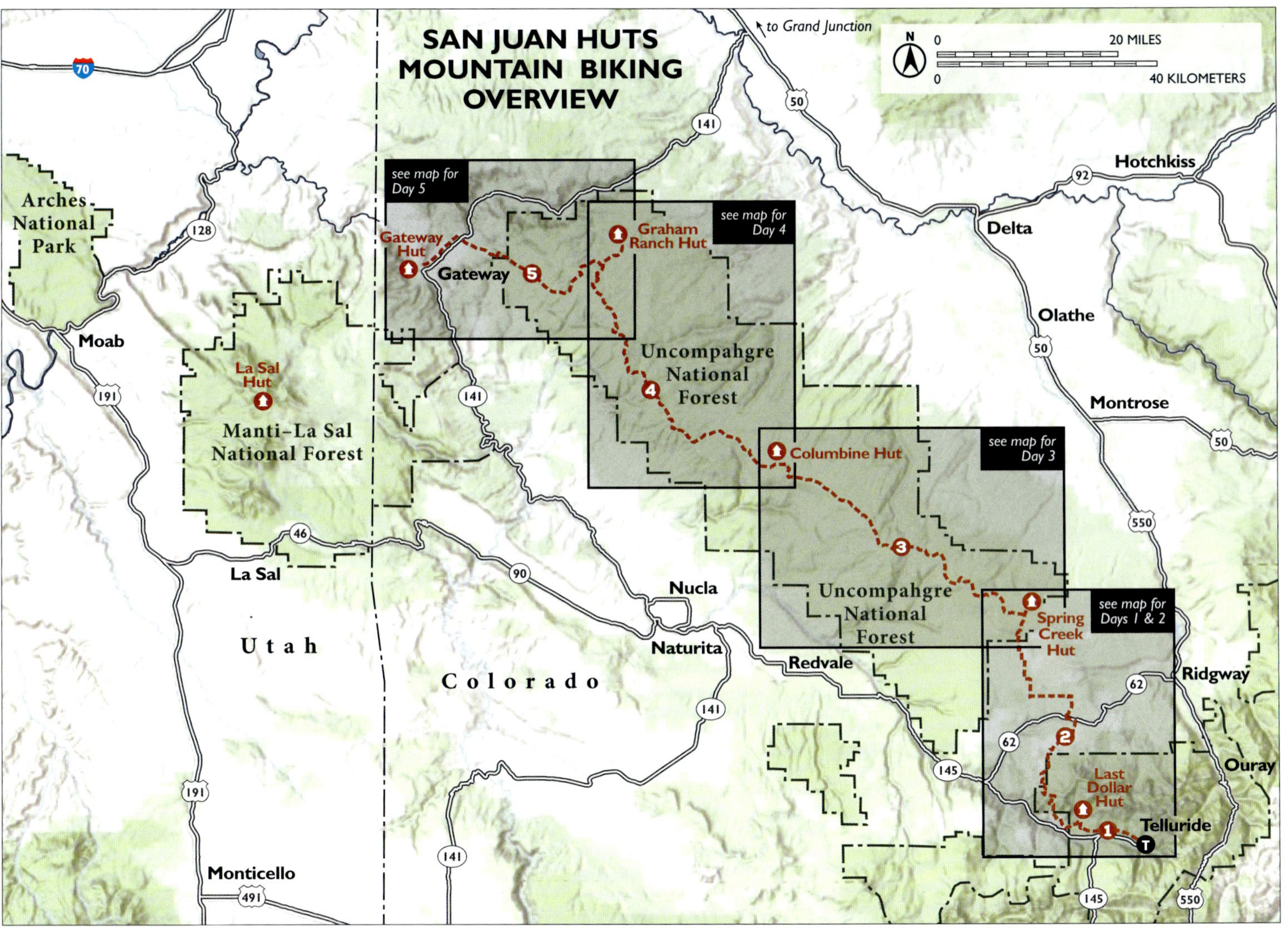

SAN JUAN HUTS
MOUNTAIN BIKING
OVERVIEW
to Grand Junction
N
0
0
20 MILES
40 KILOMETERS
70
Arches National Park
Moab
191
128
La Sal Hut
Manti–La Sal National Forest
46
La Sal
191
Monticello
491
Utah
Colorado
141
141
141
90
141
see map for Day 5
Gateway Hut
Gateway
5
Graham Ranch Hut
see map for Day 4
4
Uncompahgre National Forest
Columbine Hut
see map for Day 3
3
Uncompahgre National Forest
Nucla
Naturita
Redvale
Spring Creek Hut
see map for Days 1 & 2
62
62
145
2
Last Dollar Hut
1
Telluride
T
Ridgway
Ouray
145
550
550
550
Hotchkiss
92
Delta
Olathe
50
Montrose
50
50

and forward the liability waiver link to each participant to sign and return; patrons receive—by mail or directly from Ridgway headquarters— hut keys, printed maps, GPX map files to download, and detailed written route descriptions

**Membership:** None

**Rates:** $; option to book the entire hut to accommodate a group or for greater privacy

**Transportation:** Organize your own trailhead transportation with two cars, leaving one at the end of the route and the other at the launch point; shuttle service can be arranged from Telluride, Durango, Grand Junction, Montrose, Moab, and Gateway (see www.sanjuan huts.com/travel-resources)

## MAPS

SJH provides PDFs of topographical maps on its website for the hike/ski trail and mails detailed topo maps for cycling routes to clients.

## PACKING TIPS

Bring a sleeping bag liner or sleep sheet. If you will be skiing, metal-edged touring skis and skins are recommended.

## OTHER TIPS

Acclimate to high elevation by arriving in the area a few days early. Cell phone service is very spotty. SJH advises that digital devices distract from the core experience of their trips, which is to get away from the push and pull of everyday life! Hikers and skiers on the Sneffels Traverse are responsible for fetching and treating water from nearby streams, springs, or snowpack with a pump or gravity filter and iodine or a UV light. Hiking and skiing guests are requested to resupply huts with water for the next visitors. Download one of the three detailed planning guides, or "bibles," for hikers, skiers, and bikers in advance of making final plans (see www.san juanhuts.com/documents).

## ITINERARY 1: SNEFFELS TRAVERSE

*29.5 miles, five days, four nights*

Start this journey high above Telluride at Last Dollar Pass (10,676 feet) to traverse the north side of the Sneffels Range, maintaining an average elevation of 9500 feet. Enjoy the broad, well-marked track through alpine meadows, aspen groves, and coniferous forests, and take in the spectacular views.

For security reasons at owner's request, exact hut locations are not included in this book. Detailed directions to the huts and to water sources at the huts are provided only to paying customers by SJH. The trails are marked with blue diamonds, with tree blazes and pink or orange flags here and there. Some ski trailheads are different from hiking trailheads; check with SJH.

### DAY 1: LAST DOLLAR PASS TO NORTH POLE HUT

> **Distance:** 8.3 miles
> **Elevation gain/loss:** 260 feet/970 feet
> **Difficulty:** Intermediate
> **Hut elevation:** 9960 feet
> **Trailhead:** Last Dollar Pass Trailhead 38.0051°N, 107.9507°W

**Getting There**

From Telluride, take State Route 145 west for 3.4 miles, turning right on Airport Road.

SNEFFELS TRAVERSE
Willow Creek
Middle Fork Leopard Creek
East Fork Leopard Creek
Stough Draw
Dallas Creek
9000
9400
9600
9200
9800
9000
9600
10,000
North Pole Hut
West Fork
Box Factory Park
Dallas Trail 200
Cocan Flats
9400
8800
9200
9600
Dallas Trail 200
North Pole Peak
West Fork
Vance Creek
10,000
Hayden Peak
11,600
10,000
12,200
Mount Sneffels Wilderness
Blue Lakes Trail
Alder Creek Trail 510
log trapper's cabin
9400
10,400
11,200
11,800
12,000
13,000
12,600
12,400
Wolcott Mountain
11,600
12,200
13,200
13,000
10,000
Last Dollar Pass Trailhead
P T
10,800
11,000
11,400
10,200
Ruffner Mountain
Mears Peak
12,200
12,600
11,600
12,000
12,800
13,400
11,800
11,200
Whipple Mountain
10,600
10,000
10,200
10,400
10,800
11,000
11,200
11,600
12,000
Campbell Peak
13,000
13,200
Dallas Peak
Last Dollar Rd
10,400
10,600
10,000
10,200
10,400
11,600
11,200
11,400
10,400
10,600
Uncompahgre National Forest
9600
Last Dollar Rd
9400
8800
145
9000
Telluride Regional Airport
Airport Rd
9000
9400
8800
145
San Miguel River
San Miguel River
9400
8200
9000
9800
10,200
9200
9000
9200
10,000
145
to Cortez
Telluride Ski Resort

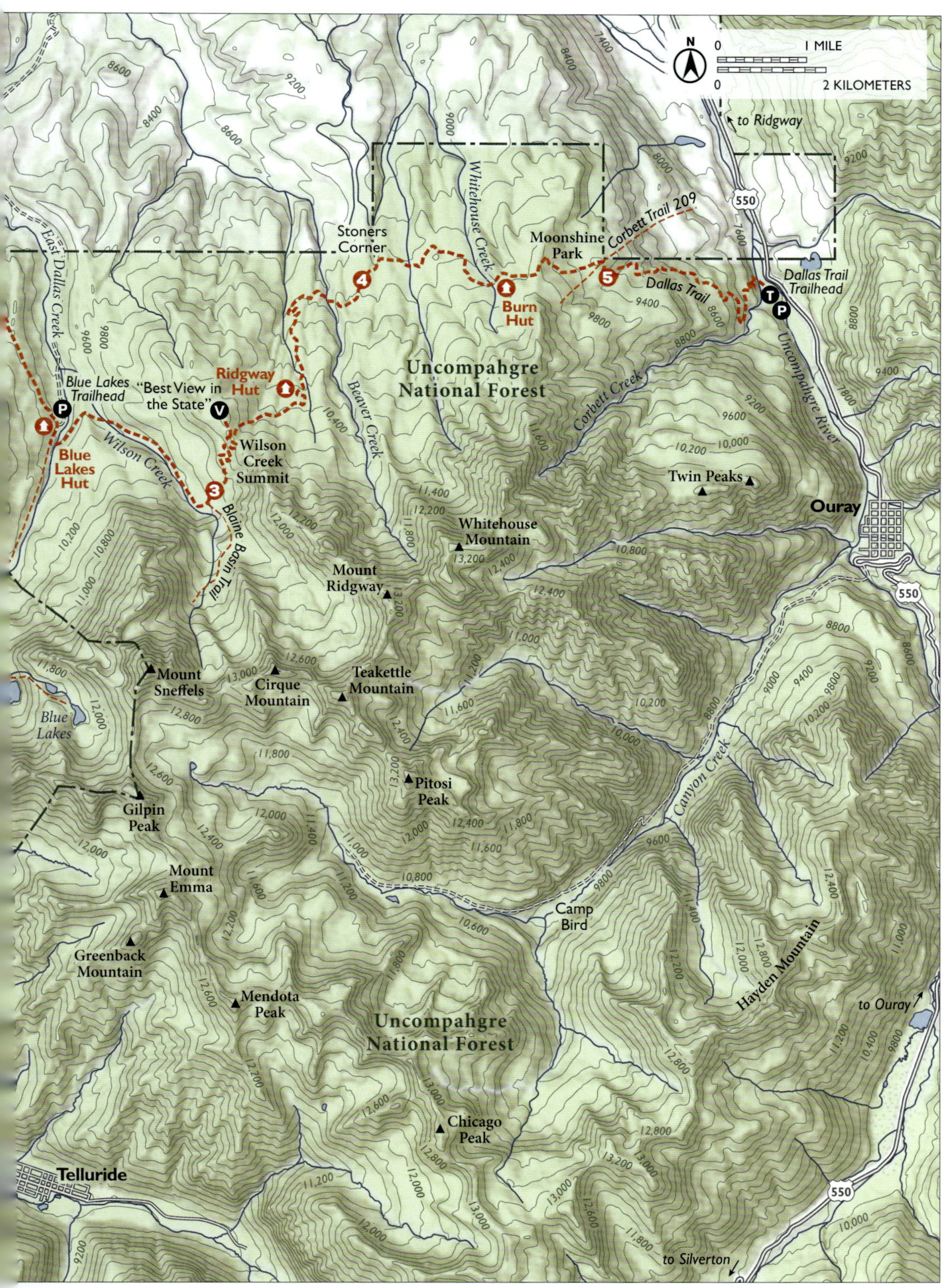
N
0    1 MILE
0    2 KILOMETERS
to Ridgway
550
8600
8400
9200
8600
9800
9600
9800
8000
9200
7400
8400
9000
8000
7600
9200
9400
Whitehouse Creek
Stoners Corner
Moonshine Park
Corbett Trail 209
4
Burn Hut
5
Dallas Trail
Dallas Trail Trailhead
T
P
Uncompahgre National Forest
Corbett Creek
Uncompahgre River
9400
8800
8600
9800
9400
9600
9200
10,200
10,000
1,800
9400
Twin Peaks
Ouray
550
East Dallas Creek
Blue Lakes Trailhead
"Best View in the State"
Ridgway Hut
V
Wilson Creek Summit
Blue Lakes Hut
P
3
Wilson Creek
Blaine Basin Trail
Beaver Creek
10,400
11,400
12,200
11,800
11,600
Whitehouse Mountain
13,200
12,400
Mount Ridgway
13,200
12,400
11,000
10,800
10,800
10,200
10,000
Canyon Creek
9600
10,200
10,200
9000
9400
9800
9200
8800
8600
8800
9400
10,200
10,800
11,000
11,800
9600
9800
9200
Blue Lakes
11,800
12,000
12,600
12,800
Mount Sneffels
13,000
Cirque Mountain
12,600
Teakettle Mountain
11,600
11,600
12,400
Pitosi Peak
12,000
13,200
2,400
3,200
Gilpin Peak
12,600
12,000
12,400
11,600
12,000
11,000
11,200
11,400
10,800
10,600
Camp Bird
Mount Emma
12,200
Greenback Mountain
12,600
Mendota Peak
12,200
Uncompahgre National Forest
Hayden Mountain
12,800
12,200
12,800
11,200
12,400
11,000
10,400
9800
to Ouray
12,600
13,000
13,000
12,800
Chicago Peak
13,200
13,000
12,600
11,800
Telluride
9200
11,200
12,000
12,000
10,000
550
to Silverton

*Approaching North Pole Hut at the edge of a meadow on the Sneffels Traverse*

Just before the airport, bear right onto Last Dollar Road and ascend steeply for about 9 miles to the trailhead.

**On the Trail**

The first day in the traverse is the longest and loses almost 1000 feet in elevation. Alder Creek Trail 510 begins on the north side of Last Dollar Road, 200 feet northeast of Last Dollar Pass. Head northwest on the Alder Creek Trail 510. After a series of switchbacks, the trail turns right (east) at 0.6 mile and continues northeast, crossing into the Mount Sneffels Wilderness. Upon reaching a roofless, log trapper's cabin in the southwest corner of a large clearing at 2.9 miles, the trail exits the northeast corner of this clearing and begins to head north, with Hayden Peak and North Pole Peak looming on the right (east).

After 4.2 miles, the Alder Creek Trail turns into the Dallas Trail 200. The trail heads east after crossing Willow Creek and, just after crossing the Middle Fork Leopard Creek at 7.5 miles, passes out of the Mount Sneffels Wilderness. Continuing east, follow the trail up a forested ridge and down the other side to a small clearing with aspen and spruce on the perimeter.

Look for a large tree with a blue diamond marking the Dallas Trail, and turn left, heading north to leave the Dallas Trail and follow a short path to the hut. This is an easy spot to miss. If you reach the East Fork Leopard Creek, you have walked about five minutes too far. North Pole Hut is located on the edge of a meadow, west of beaver ponds below the north face of Hayden Peak (12,987 feet), with great views of North Pole Peak (12,208 feet).

### DAY 2: NORTH POLE HUT TO BLUE LAKES HUT

**Distance:** 7.4 miles
**Elevation gain/loss:** 1160 feet/1700 feet
**Difficulty:** Intermediate
**Hut elevation:** 9430 feet

Begin by returning south through the meadows and then turning left (east) at the junction with the Dallas Trail. After a clearing, the trail crosses the East Fork Leopard Creek at 0.3 mile, and soon an old logging road joins the trail and then departs it. Keep on the trail by following the diamonds, blazes, and flags. Note the views of Cimarron Ridge briefly to the northeast from a hilltop at 1.4 miles. Drop down to cross a shallow stream (Stough Draw), and soon turn left along a gentle ridgeline heading northeast as the trail briefly follows a logging road before turning right (east) to cross the West Fork Dallas Creek.

After the trail goes through a gate in a wire fence and enters the meadow at Box Factory Park, turn left (slightly north, then west) on a dirt road (you are still on the Dallas Trail) to cross a second West Fork Dallas Creek. Soon, at 3.3 miles, the Dallas Trail joins County Road 9 for a short distance up a slight hill, then leaves the road with a turn to the right (east). Continue on the Dallas Trail to pass through an old wooden gate in a forested area at 4.2 miles, then on to cross Vance Creek at 5.4 miles.

At 5.7 miles (38.0528°N, 107.8242°W), the trail parallels a wire fence with a gate. Don't go through the gate; instead, stay on the Dallas Trail, which ascends to the right and passes between two hills. Follow the trail left (east) into Cocan Flats at 6.2 miles and turn southeast to follow an old logging road for about a mile, then bear right, following a road uphill a short distance to the hut.

## DAY 3: BLUE LAKES HUT TO RIDGWAY HUT

**Distance:** 5 miles
**Elevation gain/loss:** 1640 feet/1090 feet
**Difficulty:** Intermediate
**Hut elevation:** 10,200 feet

Return to the base of the hill and turn right (east) on the logging road to continue on the Dallas Trail. At 0.3 mile, turn right into the parking area for the Blue Lakes Trailhead and stay on the Dallas Trail, which is also called the Wilson Creek Trail 203 at this point. Cross East Dallas Creek, then continue to cross Wilson Creek. The Dallas Trail parallels Wilson Creek southeast for the next mile, then crosses over it and soon turns north-northeast, at a junction with the Blaine Basin Trail at 2.7 miles.

Ascend north-northeast for a mile; this very steep (900 feet of elevation gain) climb brings you to the Wilson Creek Summit, a small saddle at 11,000 feet. Look for the side trail on the left to an overlook with stunning views of Mount Sneffels (some call this one of the best views in the state). Return to the Dallas Trail and follow it northeast for 1.3 miles to Ridgway Hut, sheltered in the trees.

## DAY 4: RIDGWAY HUT TO BURN HUT

**Distance:** 4.2 miles
**Elevation gain/loss:** 730 feet/70 feet
**Difficulty:** Easy
**Hut elevation:** 9940 feet

Leave Ridgway Hut by following the Dallas Trail east of the hut, heading briefly downhill to cross a small stream, then turn left (north) to cross Beaver Creek at 1.6 miles. Continue east and then north to Stoners Corner (38.0574°N, 107.7525°W). At Stoners Corner, get on the road and go right (south) for approximately 20 feet, then turn left (east) and cross a small creek. Follow the trail markers heading east to cross another creek at 2.8 miles; the trail follows a road northeast for 0.3 mile. At 3.3 miles (38.0589°N, 107.7452°W), the trail departs from the road, heading southeast, paralleling the road for about 0.3 mile before turning right (south) and rejoining it. Turn left (southeast) onto the road; cross Whitehouse Creek at 4.1 miles. The hut is about 100 yards farther.

### DAY 5: BURN HUT TO OURAY

**Distance:** 4.6 miles
**Elevation gain/loss:** 340 feet/2660 feet
**Difficulty:** Easy

Return to the road and turn right (northeast), soon coming to Moonshine Park, a large, steep meadow, at less than 0.1 mile. Note the US Forest Service sign at the top of the meadow; continue east on the Dallas Trail, passing an intersection with the Corbett Trail 209 at 2.1 miles. Follow the Dallas Trail east-southeast. A series of switchbacks takes you through red sandstone cliffs, then down to the Dallas Trail Trailhead on US Highway 550. Ouray is south, and Ridgway is north.

In Ouray, 1.8 miles from the trailhead, treat yourselves to a soak in the hot springs.

## ITINERARY 2: MOUNTAIN BIKE TELLURIDE TO GATEWAY

*142.7 miles; five days, four nights*

Start with a very steep uphill, then—after your first night—settle into moderate up and down terrain with some very long downhill stretches. This route follows gravel and dirt roads. SJH provides registered riders with fourteen pages of turn-by-turn route descriptions and accompanying maps for each day. Precise directions to the huts are provided only to clients; hut locations on the maps in this book are purposefully left vague.

SJH maps out nineteen single-track alternatives for sections of the basic route, for those seeking extra challenges. To determine the suitability of specific alternative routes for your skill level, consult SJH materials and staff to make informed choices. Note that off-road, backcountry trails are not always easy to follow; you must be comfortable with the possibility of losing your way occasionally before recovering the route.

Ideal for beginners, this itinerary sticks to gravel and dirt secondary roads, except for one single-track alternative on day 5.

### DAY 1: TELLURIDE TO LAST DOLLAR HUT

**Distance:** 13.1 miles
**Elevation gain/loss:** 2860 feet/510 feet
**Difficulty:** Difficult
**Hut elevation:** 10,925 feet
**Trailhead:** Telluride Middle/High School 37.9411°N, 107.8209°W

**Getting There**

Ride your bike from the San Miguel County Courthouse in the center of Telluride and proceed west on West Colorado Avenue for 0.8 mile to the roundabout in front of the Telluride Middle/High School. There is no free overnight parking in Telluride, so you'll need to find a place in advance to park if you bring a car.

**On the Trail**

Starting at the roundabout in front of Telluride Middle/High School, follow the paved

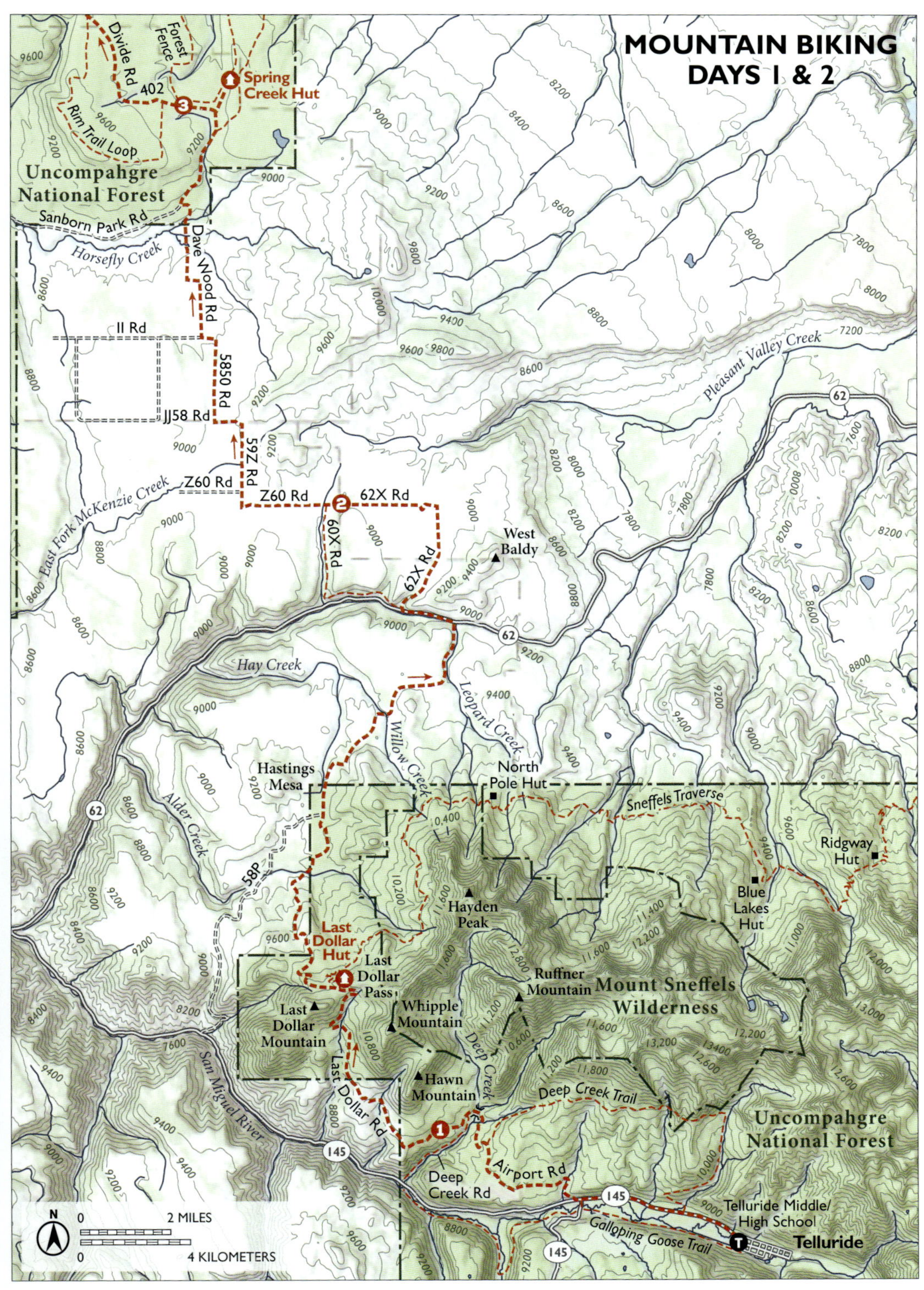
MOUNTAIN BIKING
DAYS 1 & 2
Spring Creek Hut
Divide Rd
Forest Fence
402
Rim Trail Loop
Uncompahgre National Forest
Sanborn Park Rd
Horsefly Creek
Dave Wood Rd
II Rd
5850 Rd
JJ58 Rd
59Z Rd
Z60 Rd
Z60 Rd
62X Rd
60X Rd
62X Rd
West Baldy
East Fork McKenzie Creek
Hay Creek
62
62
Pleasant Valley Creek
Leopard Creek
Willow Creek
Hastings Mesa
North Pole Hut
Sneffels Traverse
Ridgway Hut
Blue Lakes Hut
Alder Creek
62
58P
Hayden Peak
Ruffner Mountain
Mount Sneffels Wilderness
Last Dollar Hut
Last Dollar Pass
Last Dollar Mountain
Whipple Mountain
Deep Creek
Hawn Mountain
Last Dollar Rd
San Miguel River
145
Deep Creek Rd
Airport Rd
Deep Creek Trail
Uncompahgre National Forest
145
Galloping Goose Trail
Telluride Middle/High School
Telluride
145
N
0        2 MILES
0        4 KILOMETERS

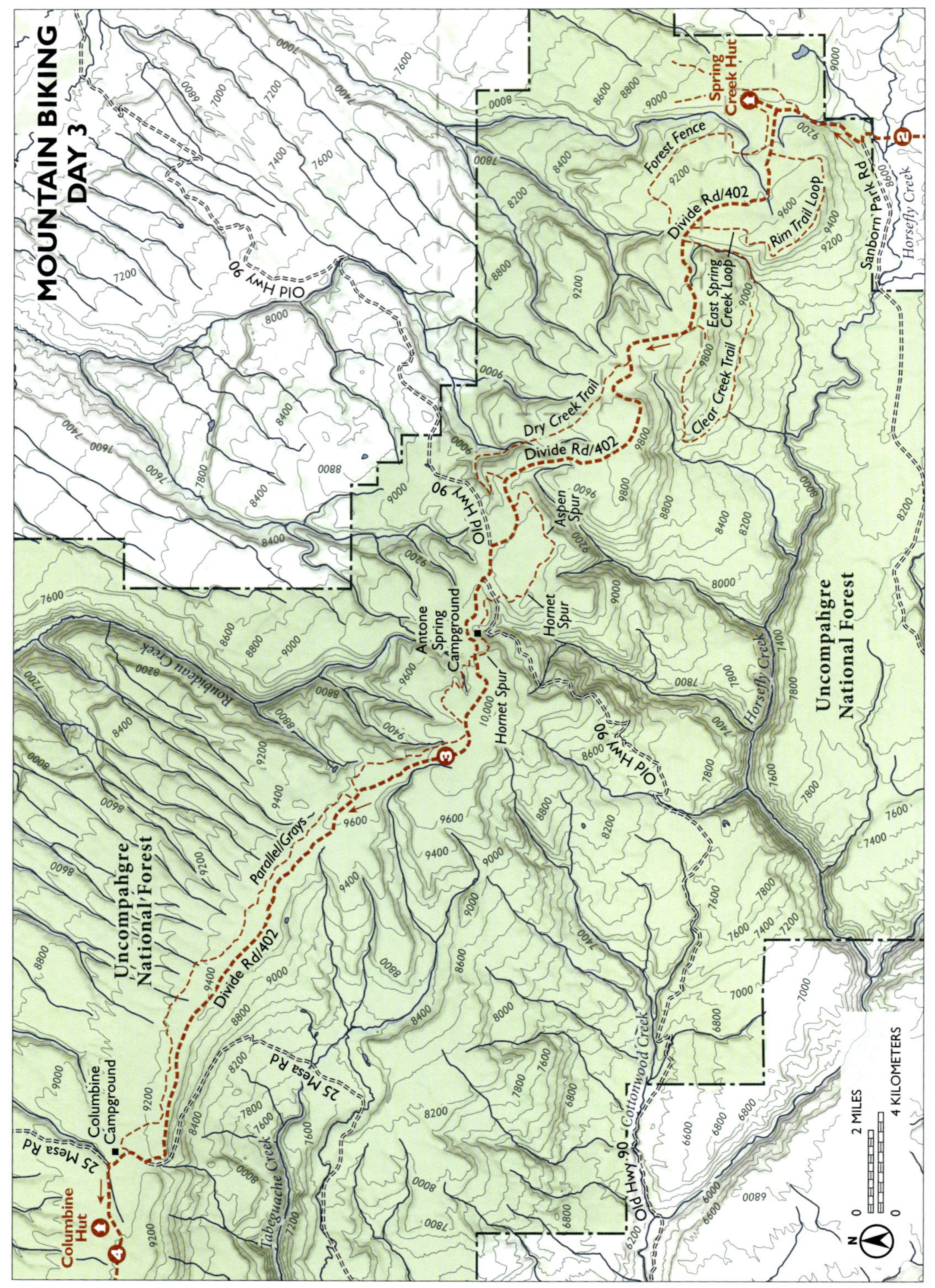
MOUNTAIN BIKING
DAY 3
Spring Creek Hut
Forest Fence
Divide Rd/402
Rim Trail Loop
Sanborn Park Rd
Horsefly Creek
East Spring Creek Loop
Clear Creek Trail
Dry Creek Trail
Divide Rd/402
Old Hwy 90
Aspen Spur
Hornet Spur
Antone Spring Campground
Hornet Spur
Old Hwy 90
Uncompahgre National Forest
Horsefly Creek
10,000
Parallel/Grays
Roubideau Creek
Uncompahgre National Forest
Divide Rd/402
25 Mesa Rd
Tabeguache Creek
Columbine Campground
25 Mesa Rd
Columbine Hut
Old Hwy 90
Cottonwood Creek
Uncompahgre National Forest
2 MILES
4 KILOMETERS
N
0
0

bike trail on the north side of SR 145 for about 3 miles before turning right onto Airport Road. At the top of Airport Road, turn right onto dirt Last Dollar Road and follow for the next 8.3 miles to Last Dollar Pass. The ride up to the pass (10,980 feet) gains about 2000 feet in elevation in the last 5 miles!

Having arrived at the pass, the final quarter mile to the hut gains 300 more feet, making the distance almost impossible to pedal. Push your bikes the final stretch to arrive at the hut, and take in the views: Dolores Peak, Wilson Peak, El Diente Peak, Mount Wilson, Lizard Head, and Sunshine Peak to the east; Whipple Mountain nearby to the south; the Abajo Mountains (part of the Bears Ears National Monument) to the southwest; and your destination, Utah's La Sal Mountains, to the west.

## DAY 2: LAST DOLLAR HUT TO SPRING CREEK HUT

**Distance:** 27 miles

**Elevation gain/loss:** 1380 feet/3100 feet

**Difficulty:** Moderate

**Hut elevation:** 9170 feet

Walk your bike down a steep path on the north side of the hut to Last Dollar Road. Descend the steep downhill over dirt and then gravel roads to get off the mountain and into ranchlands that have served as film sets for the John Wayne version of *True Grit* and the iconic Marlboro cigarette TV commercials.

At 10.5 miles, turn left (west) onto paved SR 62 for a quick downhill jaunt that brings you after 1.1 miles to 62X Road, a gravel road, at which point you turn right (north). Follow 62X as it climbs steadily onto an open mesa with vast cattle- and sheep-grazing lands dotted with abandoned old homesteads and mansions just outside the Telluride orbit. Follow the zigs and zags of 62X as it takes on different names along the way (see SJH directions for turn-by-turn details), until you reach the junction with 11 Road at mile 21.

Turn left (west) to follow 11 Road for 0.2 mile, then turn right (north) at Dave Wood Road. Follow Dave Wood Road for 2 miles, at which point you descend into a broad valley and pass under high tension wires, reaching the intersection of Dave Wood Road and Sanborn Park Road at mile 24.1. Go right (north-northeast) at the intersection, continuing on Dave Wood Road until its intersection with Divide Road at 25.8 miles, at which point you turn left (north) onto Divide Road/402, following the sign to Columbine Pass.

Turn right (north-northeast) after only 0.2 mile at a sign reading "Spring Creek Rim 536."

## DAY 3: SPRING CREEK HUT TO COLUMBINE HUT

**Distance:** 34 miles

**Elevation gain/loss:** 1960 feet/1960 feet

**Difficulty:** Moderate

**Hut elevation:** 9170 feet

Retrace the route from yesterday on Spring Creek Rim 536, then turn right (west) on Divide Road/402. The first 10.2 miles climb gently uphill until reaching the third San Juan Overlook (each overlook offers a different perspective on the San Juan Mountains). From here, there is a roughly 2-mile downhill, followed by steady uphill with a few flats for another 4 miles, where you

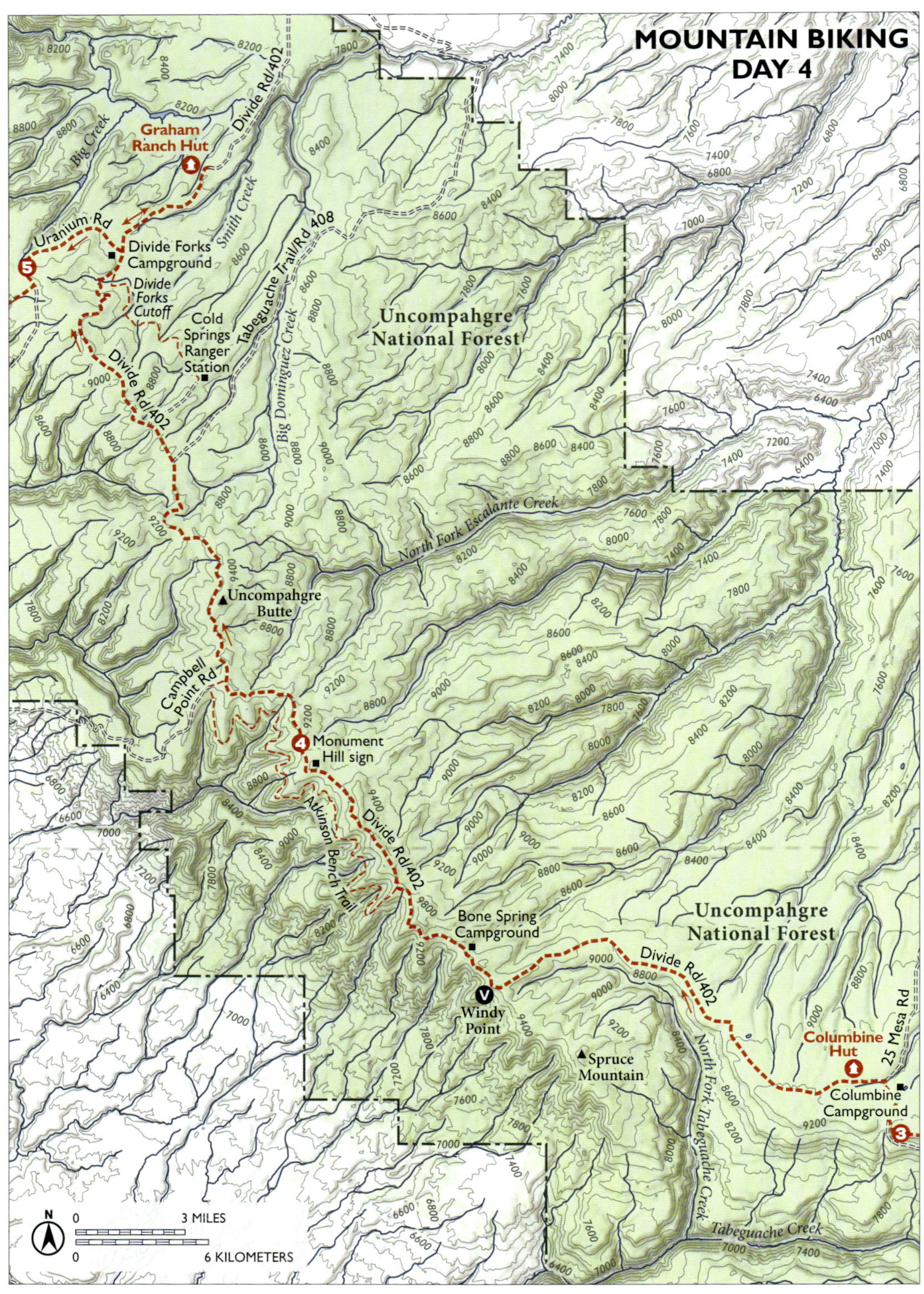

MOUNTAIN BIKING
DAY 4
Graham Ranch Hut
1
Big Creek
8200
8400
8200
8800
8800
Divide Rd/402
Uranium Rd
5
Divide Forks Campground
Smith Creek
Divide Forks Cutoff
Cold Springs Ranger Station
Divide Rd/402
Tabeguache Trail/Rd 408
Big Dominguez Creek
Uncompahgre National Forest
North Fork Escalante Creek
9000
9200
9400
Uncompahgre Butte
8800
Campbell Point Rd
4
Monument Hill sign
Atkinson Bench Trail
Divide Rd/402
Bone Spring Campground
Windy Point
V
Spruce Mountain
Uncompahgre National Forest
Divide Rd/402
North Fork Tabeguache Creek
Columbine Hut
25 Mesa Rd
Columbine Campground
3
Tabeguache Creek
N
0          3 MILES
0          6 KILOMETERS

reach the intersection with Old Highway 90 at 16.1 miles. Continue at this junction on Divide Road/402 by bearing left at the intersection. The next 3.5 miles climb steadily, with some flat sections, until you reach Antone Spring Campground on the left at mile 18.6.

From here, the road descends steadily for about 14 miles, passing Columbine Campground and reaching a T intersection, where you turn left (toward Windy Point) on Divide Road/402 for 1.4 miles before reaching the turnoff to Columbine Hut, which sits on two trailers so it can be moved in case a wildfire threatens the site. The hut occupies a pleasant wooded area; in the evening, seek out the nearby sitting rock for some quiet contemplation.

## DAY 4: COLUMBINE HUT TO GRAHAM RANCH HUT

**Distance:** 36.4 miles
**Elevation gain/loss:** 1510 feet/2410 feet
**Difficulty:** Moderate
**Hut elevation:** 8258 feet

Retrace the trail from the hut to Divide Road/402 and continue right (west) toward Windy Point for 9.3 miles. As you continue

*Pedaling the single-track Ute Creek Trail between Telluride and Gateway*

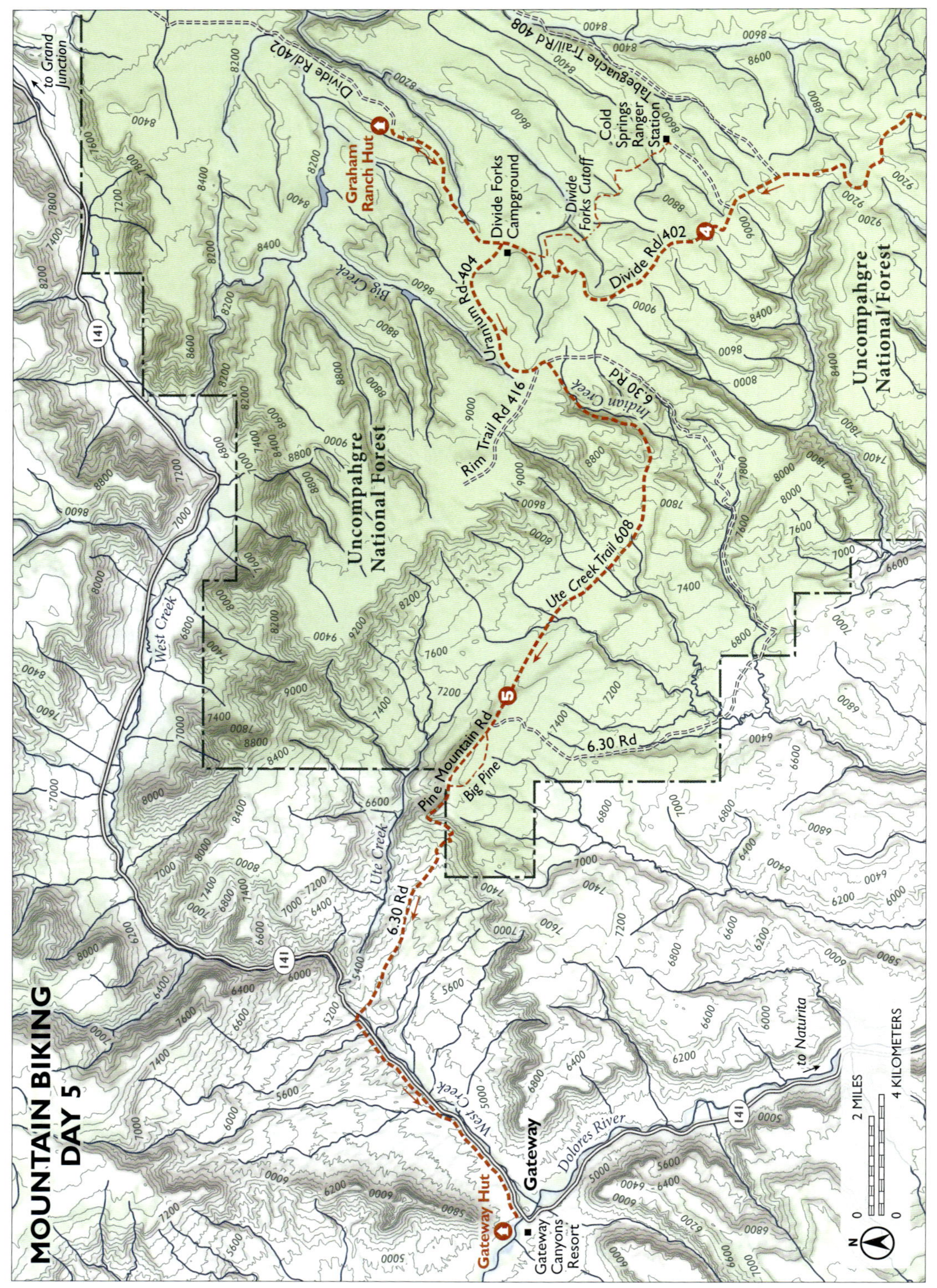

MOUNTAIN BIKING
DAY 5
to Grand Junction
Divide Rd/402
Tabeguache Trail/Rd 408
Graham Ranch Hut
Cold Springs Ranger Station
Divide Forks Campground
Divide Forks Cutoff
Divide Rd 402
Uranium Rd 404
6.30 Rd
Indian Creek
Rim Trail Rd 416
Uncompahgre National Forest
Uncompahgre National Forest
Big Creek
Ute Creek Trail 608
West Creek
Pine Mountain Rd
Big Pine
6.30 Rd
6.30 Rd
Ute Creek
West Creek
Gateway Hut
Gateway
Gateway Canyons Resort
Dolores River
to Naturita
141
141
141
141
N
2 MILES
4 KILOMETERS

west beyond Windy Point, enjoy views of the La Sal Mountains in the distance. Continue on Divide Road/402 west and then northwest through mesa country for a total of 36.4 miles. Along the way you will pass signs for Monument Hill, Campbell Point Road, Uncompahgre Butte, Tabeguache Trail/Road 408, Divide Forks Campground, and other turnoffs before reaching Graham Ranch Hut.

## DAY 5: GRAHAM RANCH HUT TO GATEWAY HUT

    **Distance:** 32.2 miles
    **Elevation gain/loss:** 2250 feet/5890 feet
    **Difficulty:** Moderate
    **Hut elevation:** 4632 feet

Begin the day by backtracking gently uphill on Divide Road/402 for the first 3.4 miles. When you reach the Divide Forks/Uranium Road intersection, turn right (northwest) onto the Uranium Road/404 Road. After passing the Rim Trail Road 416 on the right (at 6.3 miles), look for the sign at 6.7 miles marking the Ute Creek Trail 608, an 8-mile single-track alternative to the standard route.

It is the only alternative route described in this itinerary. We chose it for its great natural beauty and the presence of some wonderful "flowy" stretches. The first mile or so is very rocky and technical, as are a number of subsequent sections. We ended up walking about one-third of the trail, including the first section; it was simply too difficult for us to cycle comfortably. On the other hand, about half of the trail is "flowy"— not so much in the "terrain-induced roller coaster experience, with little pedaling or braking necessary" sense of the term (the International Mountain Bicycling Association definition), though there is definitely some of that, but more in the sense of being a fairly smooth, easy, relaxing ride that provides relief from picking one's way among endless boulders, roots, and rocks.

The Ute Creek Trail rejoins the standard route at mile 20.6. By this point, Uranium Road has turned into Pine Mountain Road. Pine Mountain Road continues west mostly on level, wooded terrain before turning into 6.30 Road (6³⁄₁₀), a long, beautiful, steep downhill to Gateway. This dizzying gravel road, cut into the mountainside, plunges into rugged red-rock canyons toward West Creek and SR 141. The last few miles of steep 6.30 Road are surfaced with fine sand, which can turn to mud in rainy weather. At the **T** intersection with SR 141, turn left (southwest) and follow the paved highway for 4.3 miles through Gateway to the hut, located near the confluence of West Creek and the Dolores River.

If you seek luxury after the rugged ride, skip the hut and check into the full-service Gateway Canyons Resort and visit the spa, lounge in the pool, and enjoy a restaurant meal. Or overnight in Gateway Hut and then indulge yourself at the resort.

*Note:* The full Telluride-to-Moab route (215 miles) adds two days after Gateway. Day 6 begins with the passage through John Brown Canyon, which features sculptural red-rock formations, before a daunting 3500-foot climb. After a night at La Sal Hut, day 7 finishes with an awesome 4000-foot descent into Moab canyon country.

## AMERICAN PRAIRIE RESERVE

*The circle of ecological compassion we feel is enlarged by
direct experience of the living world, and shrunken by its lack.*
—Robin Wall Kimmerer, *Braiding Sweetgrass*

**Location:** North-central Montana near Winifred
**Distance:** Huts 5 to 7 miles apart; featured itinerary 19.7 miles
**Elevation gain/loss:** 2250 feet/2310 feet
**Difficulty:** Easy
**Terrain:** Rugged prairie along the Judith and Missouri Rivers, ranging from flat grasslands and sagebrush steppes to forested coulees
**Modes of travel:** Hiking, biking, and paddling
**Season:** One hut open year-round, two huts open spring through fall; dates depend on weather
**Huts:** Three huts (capacity 9), self-service, exclusive use, no water on-site

---

**ON MONTANA'S NORTHERN PLAINS,** American Prairie Reserve (APR) aims to create the largest nature reserve in the continental US, and huts play a key role in this visionary project. Facing the challenge of raising public awareness about this remote prairie ecosystem, APR plans to operate a system of ten huts. At the time of writing, three were complete and open to visitors. APR knows that intimate local engagement is crucial to raising awareness and nurturing passions to protect and conserve. More than recreational shelters, APR huts are designed as infrastructure to educate visitors about conservation and as public access portals to a rugged and threatened American landscape. This organization is open to new ideas and public feedback. Staff are experimenting with design, locations, and programming for the huts. Stay in an APR yurt or cabin and contribute your ideas on how to support this organization's long-range vision.

OPPOSITE: *Vistas of the Pasayten Wilderness from Cedar Creek Trail in the Methow Valley*

This large-landscape conservation project operates in a creative public-private partnership to protect one of the largest and most remote tracts of prairie remaining in the US. The prairie is the fastest-disappearing biome on the planet; it once covered one-third of the US, but now only fragments remain. Founded in 2001, APR acquires privately owned "infill" properties to stitch together existing public lands for habitat restoration, wildlife conservation, and public access. Since 2004, the non-profit has acquired and leased grazing rights to more than 420,000 acres, extending wildlife protection beyond the boundaries of huge federal reserves including the US Fish and Wildlife Service's Charles M. Russell National Wildlife Refuge (916,000 acres) and the Bureau of Land Management's Upper Missouri River Breaks National Monument (375,000 acres). The long-term goal is to encompass a continuous expanse of about 3 million acres, which scientists indicate is large enough to sustain a resilient prairie ecosystem. By comparison, Yellowstone National Park is about 2.2 million acres.

As habitat is gradually restored, the mammals who roamed the upper plains when explorers Meriwether Lewis and William Clark crossed them in 1805 and 1806 will flourish. In an area now largely given over to cattle ranching, APR has taken steps to restore the bison, which was nearly annihilated in the nineteenth century. A herd of several hundred now roams a parcel in the eastern section of the reserve; you can overnight among the bison and enjoy dark skies at APR's Buffalo Camp.

The huts, located in the western section of the reserve with plans to expand east, are the second system in the US not in the mountains. In contrast with the arresting beauty of mountain peaks and forests, the prairie reveals its wonders gradually. APR visitors are invited to slow down and explore. On these semiarid mixed grasslands, a kind of "American Serengeti," you encounter expansive prairie dog colonies, sagebrush steppes, forested coulees writhing upward from riverbanks to high plateaus, and plants ranging from the yucca and prickly pear of the desert to the pine trees and wild roses of higher elevations. Enjoy stands of mature cottonwoods on the Judith River, living testimony to the riverine habitat before it was altered by dams and overgrazing. Mule deer, white-tailed deer, and pronghorn antelope are plentiful; elk and bighorn sheep also inhabit the prairie, as do many smaller mammals, 20 species of reptiles and amphibians, and 230 species of birds, including the sage and sharp-tailed grouse and bald eagles.

The Missouri River, meandering through the Missouri Breaks (a.k.a. "badlands" in the Dakotas), defines this terrain. It has "broken" the soft and hard layers where striated high banks are punctuated by fantastic earthen shapes. When the Corps of Discovery encountered this stretch of the mighty river in 1805, they bemoaned its forbidding, desertlike aspect but also marveled at the never-ending scenes of geological enchantment.

*Admiring Council Island near where the Judith River joins the Missouri* (Photo by Rachel Regan)

APR huts, initially two yurts and one frame building, are exceptionally spacious and well appointed. Used primarily as drive-up base camps for multiday explorations of the prairie and rivers, they make great habitations for hikers, birders, hunters, and anglers. Large enough to accommodate an extended family or several friends' groups, the yurts are also perfect sites to celebrate special occasions.

To travel hut-to-hut, APR challenges users to create their own adventure, in both wayfinding and modes of travel. Instead of following a designated trail, you are encouraged to set off cross-country with a GPS device and find your own way. It's good to know that prairie flora, inured to trampling by massive bison herds, is not threatened when visitors trek off trail. Mike Kautz, APR's director of public access and recreation, encourages visitors to mix up modalities, to cross the landscape on foot, on bike, on horseback, by canoe, or by some combination thereof. Lewis and Clark, after all, paddled, walked, and rode horseback on their historic journey up the Missouri River to the Pacific Ocean. As APR creates more huts in other sections of the vast 125-mile-wide reserve, more opportunities for human-powered, hut-to-hut travel will emerge.

The most adventurous hut-to-hut travelers will relish the challenges of a multiday APR journey. Keep in mind that at present this system has no potable water at the hut sites. Visitors must haul water to the huts by car in advance of their hike or bike journey or carry water in their packs. At more than one gallon a day per person, this liquid load becomes quite a burden for trekkers relying exclusively on their own muscle power. You might consider making the trip on horseback—although relying on a beast of burden puts your trip beyond the scope of this guide. APR is working on improving the water supply options over the next couple decades. The roads also present challenges, depending on the season and weather conditions. Visitors should pay heed to weather and consult with APR staff about accessing the reserve when wet conditions are forecast.

## HUTS AND AMENITIES

Craighead and Founders Huts are clusters of three interconnected yurts: two 30-foot huts for living and sleeping and a third small yurt for the waterless toilet and dressing area. These gracious hostelries beckon visitors with roomy living spaces equipped with a gas range, kitchen counters, cabinets with cooking and eating implements, comfortable chairs, two large tables with chairs and benches, and a small library themed to each setting. Sleeping quarters for nine are distributed into rooms accommodating two or three, with nice touches including bunk-side reading lights. Outdoor solar panels power a chest-style refrigerator, indoor lights, and one charging station for small digital devices. In addition to propane heaters, these huts are equipped with air-conditioning units—an important amenity in the blistering summer months.

The Lewis and Clark Hut, opened two years after the yurts, is the first cabin-style structure. The design acknowledges the area's traditional ranch architecture in style and materials but adds some modern touches. Each hut is sponsored by donors who not only fund construction but also provide operating endowments.

Huts are sited for optimum enjoyment of the setting. Craighead is nestled in a majestic cottonwood gallery and surrounded by active ranchland. Founders sits below the brow of an upland plateau in sight of rugged woodland, with the tortured Missouri Breaks visible just over the rise. Lewis and Clark Hut overlooks the mighty Missouri. Guests will feel compelled to spend time outside. Find a chair, then sink into the prairie sights and sounds or gather with your group around the fire pit at night. Don't forget to look up to the stars twinkling in the ultra-dark sky of a region far from cities and light pollution.

### FOUNDERS HUT

Perched above the Missouri River valley and sited between a grassy upland plateau and a forested coulee, seasonal Founders Hut offers views of numerous central Montana mountain ranges. Climb over the rise to the northwest from the yurt and drink in the distant spectacle of the Missouri Breaks—badlands carved by the mighty brown river. This remote hut is open and accessible by road from April to October 19 and by nonmotorized access from October 20 to November 3; the hut is closed from November 3 to April.

# A LIVING LABORATORY ON THE PRAIRIE

The American Prairie Reserve (APR), defining itself as a living laboratory, supports vigorous research agendas with multiple partners. In 1999, the Nature Conservancy published *Ecoregional Planning in the Northern Great Plains Steppe*, pinpointing the most viable areas of the Northern Great Plains for long-term prairie conservation projects focused on biodiversity. The World Wildlife Fund (WWF) then initiated research in the area and recommended that an independent nonprofit be created to realize the goal of creating a huge bio-reserve of at least three million acres. In 2001, the Prairie Foundation—renamed American Prairie Reserve in 2004—came into being. For its first decade, APR partnered with the WWF in conducting inventories and wildlife migration studies, monitoring and protecting prairie dogs, researching the reintroduction of bison, and restoring streams and riparian areas.

Today APR continues to partner with the WWF, and with the Smithsonian Institution and Clemson University. APR also joins National Geographic's Last Wild Places initiative, capturing best practices and amplifying the scale of conservation efforts. Through this partnership, National Geographic supports two Fellows in residence at the Enrico Education and Science Center, which opened in 2015 on the eastern side of the reserve.

Education and research are vital components of APR's mission. APR teaches through site-specific signage near huts and campgrounds, through citizen science endeavors, and through volunteer projects. Each hut is associated with a theme, expounded through interior interpretive plaques and reflected in each hut library. Watch as APR develops new ways—perhaps also with portable huts—to orchestrate educational experiences in the vast prairie landscape.

## CRAIGHEAD HUT

Close to the PN Ranch complex, seasonal Craighead Hut is a welcoming gateway accommodation for visitors to the reserve. The yurt occupies a grassy site encircled by towering cottonwoods that thrive on this stretch of the Judith River. The cottonwood grove, or gallery, a feature of free-flowing riverine landscapes, is now rare in the Northern Great Plains. From early April until late October, the hut can be reached by four-wheel-drive vehicles. From late October through March, the hut is accessible only by foot, bike, horseback, or skis.

## LEWIS AND CLARK HUT

From a hillside above the Missouri River, the year-round Lewis and Clark Hut gives majestic views upriver to the confluence with the Judith and across to

*Founders Hut after a late September snowstorm*

Council Island, the site of several important nineteenth-century treaty gatherings. The first APR cabin-style hut features both a welcoming front porch and an expansive back porch oriented toward the river. Paddlers can leave their boat below for the night and enjoy a short hike uphill to the hut.

## PLANNING AND PREPARATION

**Contact:** www.americanprairie.org/where-to-stay; (877) 273-1123; mail@americanprairie.org
**Booking:** Check availability and make reservations via website
**Membership:** Not required; members receive a 20 percent discount
**Rates:** $
**Transportation:** Four-wheel-drive vehicles recommended; approach from Lewistown to the south or Malta to the north; the Amtrak station in Glasgow, west of Malta, has rental vehicles available

### MAPS

Download APR maps from the website; request a paper map (less detailed than the digital files) by phone or email. The PN map, in both digital and paper form, is the one with the most detail, including the locations of the huts. Using the free Avenza Maps app, download the PN map to your phone for navigation purposes.

### PACKING TIPS

Bring a sleeping bag and pillow, garbage bag, binoculars, and a hand lens or magnifying glass to enhance observations.

### OTHER TIPS

APR is very remote. There is no cell service. Bring your own potable water and be prepared to deliver water to the huts on your own. One gallon per person per day of drinking water is recommended.

Nonpotable water (high mineral content) for cleaning and other uses is available from a spigot at PN Ranch; fill a five-gallon jug, and then transport it and your drinking water to your hut. Bring firewood for the outdoor fire pit. Watch out for rattlesnakes in summer, and for prairie dog holes.

Check road and weather conditions and the live webcam of PN Ranch at www .americanprairie.org/road-and-weather -conditions. Under "gumbo" conditions after rain or snow, the clay soil turns to a thick, slippery mud, making roads impassable even to four-wheel-drive vehicles. A reliable four-wheel- or all-wheel-drive vehicle with at least eight inches of clearance and a full-size spare tire is recommended. It's best to enter the preserve with a full tank of gas.

Catered trips can be arranged with Lewis and Clark Trail Adventures (www.trail adventures.com) for groups of six or more. Consult APR for local sources to rent bikes, horses, or canoes.

## ITINERARY: THREE-HUT RAMBLE

*19.7 miles, seven days, six nights*

This leisurely traverse promotes APR's goal of immersion in a unique prairie landscape. Alternating travel with exploration days, this itinerary incorporates two nights at each hut. Of course, if you do not have time for a seven-day, six-night sojourn, feel free to shorten the trip. Stay one night at each hut, or settle into a single hut for several days and nights. Consider designing a multimodal traverse, mixing hiking, biking, paddling, or some combination of all three. Create your own journey.

With this itinerary, you travel hut-to-hut on easy-to-follow dirt roads (some disused and overgrown), except on day 2 when the road is partly erased through erosion. On exploration days, leave the trail and strike out cross-country, navigating by eye and GPS.

### DAY 1: APR STAFF BUILDINGS TO FOUNDERS HUT

**Distance:** 7 miles

**Elevation gain/loss:** 1360 feet/610 feet

**Difficulty:** Easy

**Hut elevation:** 3257 feet

**Hut GPS:** 47.6858°N, 109.7201°W

**Trailhead:** APR Staff Buildings parking area 47.6768°N, 109.6489°W

### Getting There

From Lewistown, drive north on US Highway 191 for 39 miles to Winifred. In Winifred, head east on Main Street, which turns into Seventh Avenue North at the edge of town. Turn left onto the Truck Bypass/Judith River Road. At about 0.6 mile, turn right, follow PN Bridge Road for 9.3 miles, then stay left to continue on PN Bridge Road/State Route 236.

Continue for about 34 miles, turning left (south) on the dirt road to PN Ranch before SR 236 crosses the Missouri River. The ranch access road parallels the Judith River. Pass a few ranch buildings before arriving at the APR Staff Buildings with a small parking area. Find a spigot with nonpotable well water; the trailer lobby has a landline phone for use in emergencies.

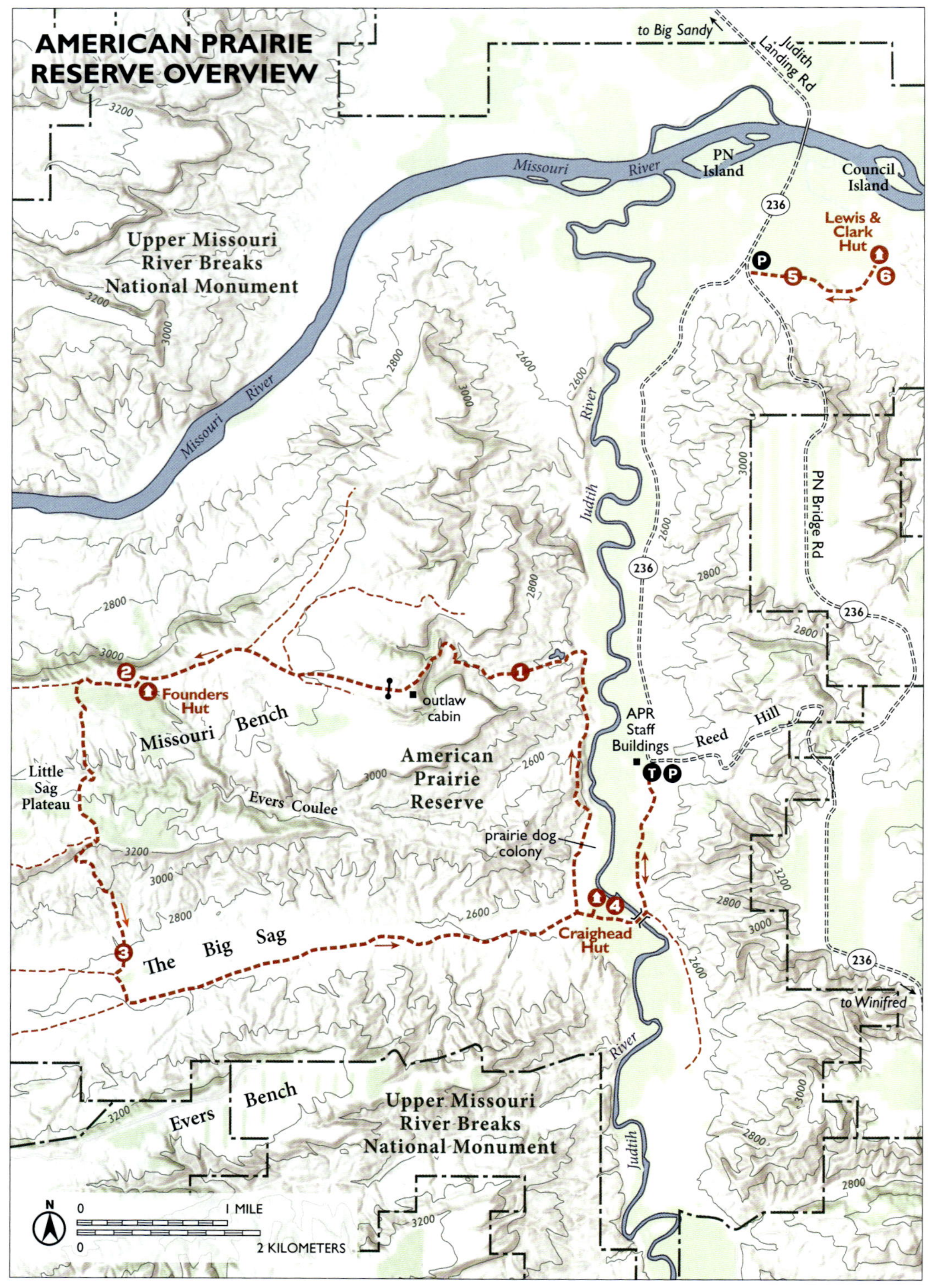
AMERICAN PRAIRIE
RESERVE OVERVIEW
to Big Sandy
Judith Landing Rd
Missouri River
PN Island
Council Island
236
Lewis & Clark Hut
P
5
6
Upper Missouri River Breaks National Monument
3200
3200
3000
2800
2600
2600
Missouri River
Judith River
3000
2800
2600
PN Bridge Rd
236
236
2800
3000
2
Founders Hut
outlaw cabin
1
Missouri Bench
American Prairie Reserve
APR Staff Buildings
Reed Hill
Little Sag Plateau
Evers Coulee
3000
2600
T P
3200
3000
2800
prairie dog colony
3200
3000
2800
2600
3
The Big Sag
Craighead Hut
4
2600
236
to Winifred
3000
2800
River
Evers Bench
Upper Missouri River Breaks National Monument
3200
Judith
2800
N
0          1 MILE
0          2 KILOMETERS

## On the Trail

Walk south, upriver, for 1 mile; turn right (west) to cross the bridge over the Judith River. Pass the driveway to Craighead Hut and continue walking along the road, away from the river. At 0.2 mile past the Craighead driveway, turn right (north), passing through a wide gap in the barbed wire fence flanked by brown trail markers. Follow the faint trail, a disused two-track road. Pass through a prairie dog colony, skirting the base of rugged hills on the left (west). After a livestock watering tank at 0.9 mile, the road begins to ascend northwest. Come to a trail marker and admire the Judith River flowing below.

At this point the trail wends along unstable bluffs prone to slow-moving landslides. For the next 0.2 mile, the trail disappears as the banks crack and slump toward the Judith below. Don't worry about wayfinding; stay above the cracks and keep heading northwest above the river. Catch sight of the APR Staff Buildings and parking lot where you began.

Continue north as the old two-track road reemerges; the barbed wire fence toward the river prevents cattle from ravaging the young cottonwoods on the banks. After 2.2 miles, the old road turns left (west) and begins to gradually ascend. Pass an old iron pump and a disused culvert, then follow the road left and up a grassy gulch. Pause at 3.2 miles to enjoy a pond, ringed with cattails. This water hole, created for cattle, is now used primarily by wild animals and birds. The road switchbacks gently upward to a steep bank and then curves onto the top of a plateau, where the edge is punctuated by gnarled pines. Look

back toward the Judith River and the Missouri Breaks. Stop for lunch or a drink at the ruins of an outlaw cabin.

The road continues westward high on the grassy Missouri Bench for 2.1 miles before reaching Founders Hut. When you encounter the barbed wire gate, take care to leave it as you found it, either open or closed.

### DAY 2: STAY AT FOUNDERS HUT

Spend the day exploring this rugged terrain. Scramble up the rise about 100 yards northwest of the hut and discover the rugged beauty of the Missouri Breaks. APR provides an interpretive sign here. Enjoy wandering west toward more prairie dog colonies and a scenic overlook of Arrow Creek (called Slaughter Creek by Lewis and Clark due to the large number of buffalo bones). To the east, explore the timbered draws (shaded in summer) that lead down from the Little Sag Plateau. Go by foot and bushwhack. Or if you are biking, there are about 15 miles of two-track mountain bike trails in this area.

### DAY 3: FOUNDERS HUT TO CRAIGHEAD HUT

**Distance:** 5.2 miles
**Elevation gain/loss:** 520 feet/1250 feet
**Difficulty:** Easy
**Hut elevation:** 2510 feet
**Hut GPS:** 47.6645°N, 109.6553°W

Take the road west from Founders Hut, turning left (south) at 0.5 mile to journey across the Little Sag Plateau. The road turns left (east) at 3.7 miles and follows the Big Sag. Turn left into the Craighead Hut driveway at 5.2 miles.

### DAY 4: STAY AT CRAIGHEAD HUT

Spend the day poking around the cottonwood gallery, exploring the banks of the Judith River (walking, fishing, swimming by the bridge, or paddling), observing the prairie dogs, and bushwhacking up the rugged coulees.

### DAY 5: CRAIGHEAD HUT TO LEWIS AND CLARK HUT

**Distance:** 6.5 miles
**Elevation gain/loss:** 370 feet/450 feet
**Difficulty:** Easy
**Hut elevation:** 2431 feet
**Hut GPS:** 47.7274°N, 109.6152°W

*A bedroom in Friends Hut* (Photo by Reid Morth)

Head east and cross the bridge, then walk north 1 mile back to the APR Staff Buildings, where you left your car on day 1. Elect someone to drive to the parking area near Lewis and Clark Hut while the remaining party hikes 4 miles north on SR 236 and then northeast on the road along the river. Turn right and at the gate signed for Lewis and Clark Hut; walk the final mile.

### DAY 6: STAY AT LEWIS AND CLARK HUT

Explore the confluence of the Judith and Missouri Rivers and paddle to Council Island, site of the 1846 Blackfeet–Flathead Council and the 1855 Isaac Stevens "Lame Bull" Treaty. A short way upstream is the spectacular White Cliffs section of the Missouri River. This area, now sparsely populated, is rich in history. Within 5 miles of the hut are a Corps of Discovery campsite (May 28, 1805); the Fort Chardon Trading Post (1844–45), the third fur trading post along the Upper Missouri; and Camp Cooke (1866–70), the first military outpost in Montana. There is also an important paleontological site nearby, where in 1855 Ferdinand Hayden discovered fossilized dinosaur bones, the first in the Western Hemisphere.

### DAY 7: DEPART FROM LEWIS AND CLARK HUT

If you parked your vehicle in the parking area near Lewis and Clark Hut, walk 1 mile to the hut parking lot. If you left your vehicle at the APR Staff Buildings, you will have an additional 4-mile hike on SR 236 along the river back to it.

# SUN VALLEY MOUNTAIN HUTS

*You'd have to come from a test tube and think like a machine to not engrave all of this in your head so you would never lose it.*

—Ernest Hemingway, looking across the Sawtooth Mountains

*Fortunate too is the man who has come to know the gods of the countryside.*

—Virgil, *Georgics*, book 2, line 493

**Location:** Sawtooth National Forest and National Recreation Area near Ketchum, Idaho
**Distance:** Huts 1.5 to 6 miles apart; featured itinerary 14.8 miles
**Elevation gain/loss:** 1880 feet/1880 feet
**Difficulty:** Novice to intermediate
**Terrain:** High mountain terrain with steep slopes, rolling meadows, forests, and streams
**Modes of travel:** Winter skiing and snowshoeing; summer hiking and biking
**Season:** Winter; two huts open in summer
**Huts:** Six huts (capacity 14–20, yurts, wall tents); self-service, exclusive use, and by the bunk

---

**BLESSED WITH CONSISTENT, DEEP POWDER** snow in winter and steeped in both geological, cultural, and recreational history, the greater Sun Valley area is home to Sun Valley Mountain Huts (SVMH), the first private backcountry hut-to-hut ski system in the US. Spread across the expansive Sawtooth Mountains region, these huts attract hard-core backcountry powder skiers and also trail-loving Nordic skiers. The system's huts extend beyond basic shelter; the large, distinctively decorated hostelries—small complexes of yurts, wall tents, and outdoor bathing facilities—are great spaces for backcountry group gatherings. This company (formerly Sun Valley Trekking) not only pioneered backcountry yurts but also perfected the design of the rectangular wall tent for comfortable overnights in the wilderness.

SVMH initially catered primarily to skiers. Most regulars are intermediate to advanced; the huts serve as base camps for bowl skiing and winter mountaineering. But several of the six huts, boasting short approaches with little elevation gain, also work well for family and friend groups and for Nordic skiers and snowshoers. To ensure safety and to properly initiate new users into the routines of hut life, SVMH requires that first-time users pay for a hut rental guide or hut host who leads the way to the hut; orients the group to hut layout and procedures; points out the trails, downhill runs, and other features; and then departs. SVMH offers additional service options; visitors can hire a trip guide or get a snowmobile rope tow up to the huts. Clients can engage a porter to carry in supplies or employ a snowmobile to bring in even more stuff! Two huts are open to hikers and bikers in summer; the biking is amazing!

Sited in central Idaho's geologically rich mountain playground, these backcountry encampments are spread across three mountain ranges: the granite spires of the Sawtooth Mountains in the north near Redfish Lake, the Smoky Mountains just south of Galena Pass, and the Pioneers in the southeast. With seven federal designations, this part of Idaho has more wilderness areas than anywhere else in the Lower 48. The Salmon River, with headwaters near Galena Pass, is packed with rainbow, cutthroat, and bull trout in its upper reaches. Wildlife abounds in this region; deer, elk, moose, and antelope range freely, along with bear, pine martens, and populations of plump spruce grouse. Although sightings are rare, elusive mountain lions, wolverines, and wolves also live here. The region is truly a "thin space" where the veil hiding the spirits of the countryside suddenly lifts to reveal mysterious powers of place, or *genius loci*.

## HUTS AND AMENITIES

SVMH offers rustic yet comfortable backcountry housing well suited to medium-sized or larger groups. The wall tents are crafted with local materials, including hand-milled pine boards. Both tents and yurts are enlivened by decorations invoking distant cultures—painted temples in Nepal and polychrome textiles in Mongolian yurts. Twinkly lights add interior cheer, and fluttering prayer flags greet visitors outside.

Most of the huts consist of two joined structures—some combination of yurts and wall tents. Floor plans of each hut are featured on the SVMH website. Woodstoves and an ample fuel supply keep these spaces warm. Kitchens come equipped with multiburner propane cookstoves, cookware, and dishes; a large table; and solar-powered lanterns to illuminate the space. Beds are equipped with covered mattresses. Special touches address visitors' comfort: the outhouses feature cushy Styrofoam seats, and indoor seating incorporates built-in backrests, a much-appreciated rarity in huts! Outdoors, each complex encompasses a sauna or hot tub, up to two outhouses, well-stocked woodsheds, picnic tables, and a charcoal or gas grill. In winter, water is from snowmelt, and in summer, from nearby streams or supplied by the hut owners. To ensure clean water in winter, dogs are banned from the huts, and a designated "pee tree" is located far away from the snowmelt area.

### FISHHOOK HUT

Near Redfish Lake and bordering on the Sawtooth Wilderness, this backcountry complex looks out on some of the highest mountains in the range, including Thompson Peak, Heyburn Mountain, Williams Peak, and Horstmann Peak. Approach this hut—a tent-yurt combination with capacity for fourteen—by an easy wooded trail, and find yourself at home in the oldest ski yurt in the US. Built in 1975 and later moved to

*The Boulder Yurts are near miles of groomed ski tracks and great for families with young children.*

the present location, this updated yurt continues to welcome visitors to the threshold of wilderness. Enjoy the unique wood-fired hot tub for an evening soak under the stars after a day of ski touring in the vicinity. Combine Fishhook Hut with Bench Hut for a two-hut traverse (see itinerary).

## BENCH HUT

Located above Redfish Lake and rebuilt in 2012, Bench Hut is a long wall tent featuring natural light, cozy common spaces, and an outdoor wood-burning sauna. Visitors can choose between challenging backcountry bowl skiing on the Heyburn massif and elsewhere and gentler ski touring or snowshoeing around the series of alpine lakes above the hut. This hut, with capacity for twenty users, can be linked with Fishhook Yurt and Williams Peak Hut (see Bonus Hut Opportunities) for a multinight ski traverse.

## BOULDER YURTS

Only 1.5 miles from the road, Boulder Yurts (7120 feet) in the Smoky Mountains are a favorite destination for families and mixed groups who seek opportunities for rustic togetherness and a perfect setting for sledding, ski touring, snowshoeing, and more. The two yurts accommodate nineteen people and are connected by a breezeway. The extensive Harriman Trail, which offers 18 miles of groomed tracks, is nearby.

## COYOTE YURTS

High in the Smoky Mountains at 8700 feet elevation, this remote set of connected yurts is ideal for intermediate and advanced skiers and snowboarders with avalanche training. The two Pacific Yurts, with capacity for nineteen, open to spectacular views of the craggy Boulder Mountains and the pyramidal Pioneers. Don't miss the custom-made swing

# A BRIEF HISTORY OF SUN VALLEY MOUNTAIN HUTS

In 1970, Joe Leonard envisioned "the first backcountry ski enterprise in the nation . . . to share the beauty of the winter mountains." Over the next decade, the vision became a reality through Leonard Expeditions, which offered multiday backpacking and horse-packing trips in the Sawtooth Mountains and developed a system of seasonal wilderness accommodations. In 1975, Leonard and one of his guides, Kirk Bachman, built the first yurt in the US for backcountry use. Paired with more traditional wall tents, Leonard's yurt encampments grew into a hut system that set the pattern for commercial hut-to-hut operations to support backcountry skiing in the US.

In 1982, Leonard sold his enterprise to Bob Jonas, a legendary ski local who has backpacked and skied the vast snow country of the region since his youth. Jonas believed wholeheartedly in the aesthetic and spiritual value of impermanent handmade canvas and local wood structures. Likening them to the covered wagons of the pioneers, he loved the way his tents and yurts brought clients closer to nature. Jonas took on the never-ending tasks of maintaining the huts and the guiding business. He cut, split, and hauled up to fifteen cords of wood annually for firewood. Every year, the huts and all their contents had to be dismantled, removed, and then hauled back in, reconstructed, and refurnished as per the US Forest Service (USFS) permit.

Jonas renamed the company Sun Valley Trekking to indicate his focus on skiing and backpacking. He moved the shelters closer to Sun Valley and to some higher locations closer to the best powder runs. As he added more sites, Jonas was able to serve a broader cross-section of skiers, offering treks ranging from gentle overnight tours to advanced

set positioned to launch you down the slope! Combine this yurt with Tornak Hut, located about 3.5 miles away. Coyote Yurts are a great base camp for hiking, mountain biking, and dining under the stars in summer.

### TORNAK HUT

Not far from Coyote Yurts, Tornak (8400 feet) is a capacious wall tent set high in the Smoky Mountains. With capacity for fourteen people, this hut, best suited for intermediate and advanced skiers, can be accessed entirely by human power or some combination of muscle and snowmobile power. Used by Sun Valley Adaptive Sports, this hut is handicapped accessible with a snowmobile assist; the interior is barrier-free.

trips into technical ski terrain. Along the way, he opened a very popular ski-in fine-dining yurt—perhaps the first in the nation.

Sun Valley Trekking came into its third set of owners in 2000. Joe and Francie St. Onge, seeking a place to settle and a business to run, happily took on their friend Bob Jonas's enterprise and his commitment to rusticity and adventure. Their goal is to "provide everything you need and nothing you don't….We believe in simplicity and comfort and wildness. Our purpose is to inspire the human spirit through adventure and exploration." The St. Onges have guided in mountains all over the world and are consummate hosts. Through the years, they have rebuilt or replaced all the huts and expanded into new territories. At long last, the USFS granted permission to leave the huts up year-round. Even while expanding the business to encompass hiking and biking, Joe and Francie are also keen to use the huts as community resource spaces and educational infrastructure. They host college classes and for twenty years have offered an intensive internship program. These huts have made the mystique of the mountains accessible to locals and visitors alike, which has led to strong support from and pride in this network.

Sun Valley Trekking has always straddled the guiding and hospitality sectors. But as the business prospered, the St. Onges realized that they could not do it all. So, in 2019, they sold the guiding business to Zach Crist of Sun Valley Guides and rechristened their operation Sun Valley Mountain Huts. Sun Valley Guides and Sun Valley Mountain Huts are fashioning a dynamic partnership to expand hut-to-hut and guided ski options in this enchanted part of the Intermountain West.

## PIONEER YURT

This 24-foot yurt is off by itself southeast of Ketchum in the Pioneer Mountains and has capacity for sixteen people. This lodging, at 8700 feet, offers comfort to skiers primed to ascend and then descend a broad swath of peaks, bowls, and meadows. Set in avalanche country, this yurt is not for novices! Summer visitors will encounter hikers en route to Hyndman Peak (12,008 feet), the highest in the Pioneers, and Peruvian shepherds and their flocks during grazing season.

### PLANNING AND PREPARATION

**Contact:** www.svtrek.com/huts; (208) 788-1966; info@svtrek.com

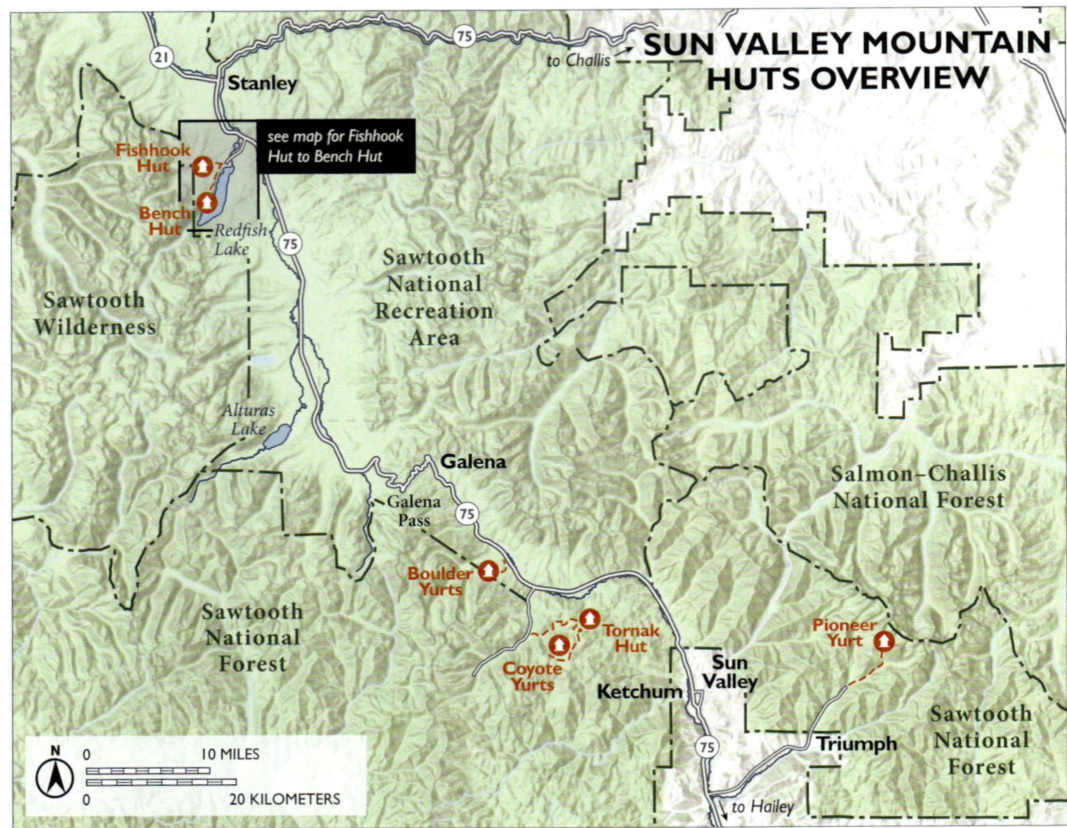


**Booking:** Check availability and make reservations via website or by phone; reservations can be made up to two years in advance

**Membership:** None

**Rates:** $$; rates depend on season; weekend rates apply; see website for details

**Transportation:** No public transportation to Redfish Trailhead; see website for shuttle options

## MAPS

The downloadable topo maps available on the SVMH website are quite good and best printed on 11-by-17-inch paper. The Sawtooth & White Cloud Mountains Trail Map (1:63,360) by Adventure Maps is helpful for a broad overview but not essential for navigation. The USGS 7.5-minute quadrangle maps provide more detail than necessary for navigation to and from the huts.

## PACKING TIPS

Bring your own sleeping bag and full cold-weather gear, including gaiters. (See equipment list on the SVMH website.) Backcountry skis with metal edges and skins are recommended. Alpine touring gear is recommended for turns on the mountain slopes.

## OTHER TIPS

While the huts are not in avalanche terrain, trekking through surrounding territory often requires avalanche preparedness. Guided and catered trips, porter services (gear haul), and snowmobile towing and support are available upon request. First-time visitors are required to hire a guide in winter; a guide is optional in summer.

In winter, dogs are not allowed at the huts. Dogs are allowed at Pioneer Yurt and Coyote Yurts in summer.

## ITINERARY: FISHHOOK HUT TO BENCH HUT

*14.8 miles, three days, two nights*

This easy-to-moderate traverse in the Redfish Lake area just south of Stanley, Idaho, gets you deep into the Sawtooth Mountains to sample SVMH's unique accommodations and amenities, including a wood-fired hot tub at Fishhook Hut. The paths are easy to recognize until you are close to the huts. Mileage and elevation gain and loss are moderate, so you will arrive at the huts with energy to spare.

For security reasons, at the hut owner's request, GPS coordinates and exact directions to the huts are not included. The navigation details and maps get you within a mile of the huts; final directions will be provided by your hut guide.

### DAY 1: STATE ROUTE 75 TO FISHHOOK HUT

**Distance:** 4.4 miles
**Elevation gain/loss:** 520 feet/170 feet
**Difficulty:** Novice
**Hut elevation:** 6800 feet

*Tornak Hut, a large wall tent, has decorations evocative of Tibet and other high mountain cultures.*

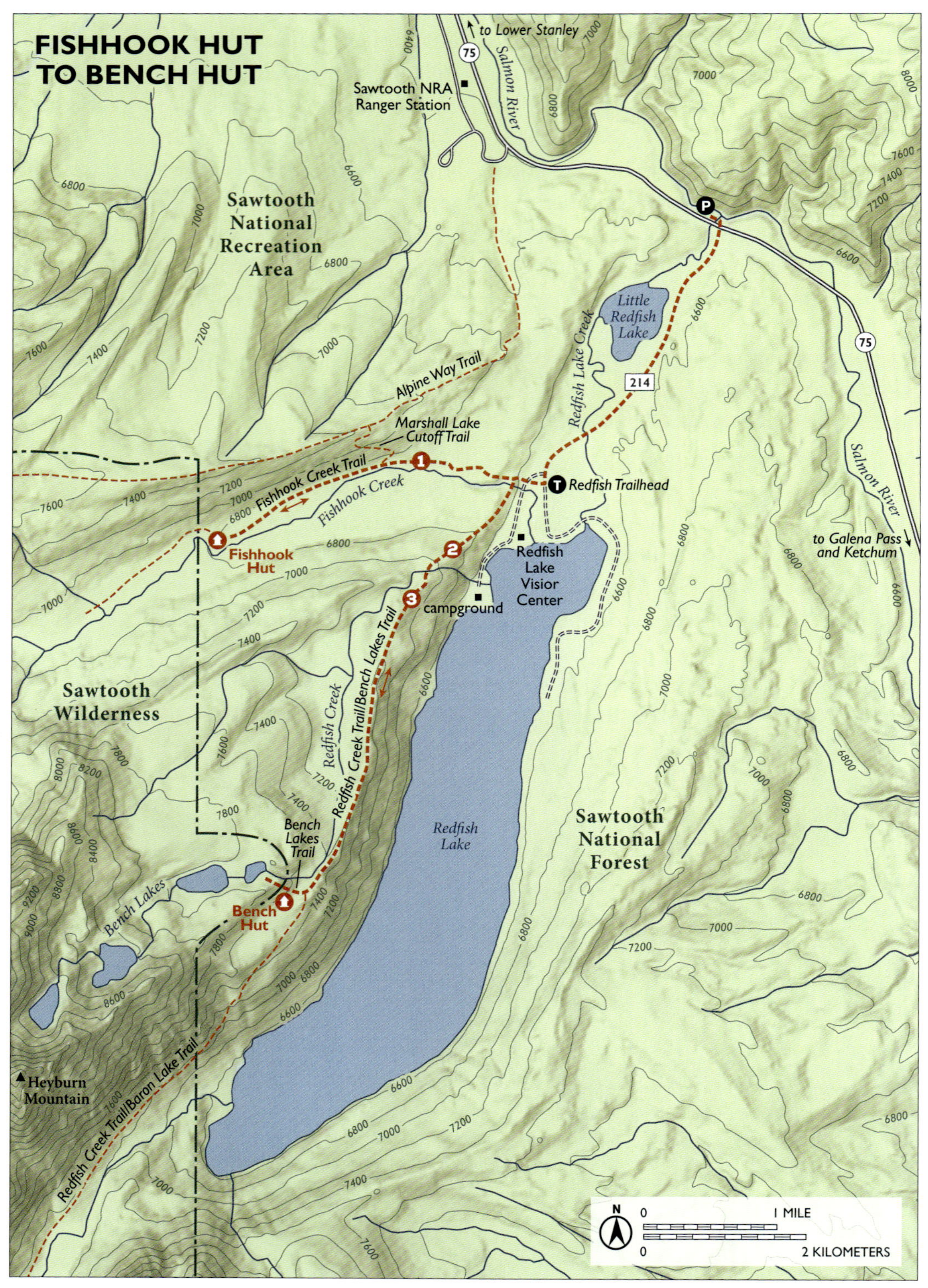


FISHHOOK HUT
TO BENCH HUT
to Lower Stanley
75
Sawtooth NRA
Ranger Station
Salmon River
Sawtooth
National
Recreation
Area
P
Little
Redfish
Lake
75
214
Redfish Lake Creek
Salmon River
Alpine Way Trail
Marshall Lake
Cutoff Trail
1
Fishhook Creek Trail
Fishhook Creek
T  Redfish Trailhead
to Galena Pass
and Ketchum
Fishhook
Hut
2
Redfish
Lake
Visior
Center
3  campground
Redfish Creek
Redfish Creek Trail/Bench Lakes Trail
Sawtooth
Wilderness
Sawtooth
National
Forest
Bench
Lakes
Trail
Bench Lakes
Redfish
Lake
Bench
Hut
Heyburn
Mountain
Redfish Creek Trail/Baron Lake Trail
N
0                    1 MILE
0                    2 KILOMETERS

**Trailhead:** SR 75 parking area 44.1687°N, 114.9009°W

## Getting There

Drive north on SR 75 from Ketchum, passing through Galena Pass, to reach Redfish Lake in 75 miles. About 0.1 mile past the turnoff to the Redfish Lake Visitor Center and Campground (heading north), pull over and park at a parking area on the east side of SR 75.

## On the Trail

From the parking area, walk or ski back to the Redfish Lake Visitor Center and Campground turnoff and turn onto the unplowed Redfish Lake access road. Ski 2 miles on the level road to the Redfish Trailhead, where both the Fishhook Creek Trail and the Redfish Creek Trail (Bench Lakes Trail) begin and run together for 0.25 mile.

At 2.25 miles, you will continue west on the Fishhook Creek Trail, passing the left-hand junction with the Redfish Creek Trail (Bench Lakes Trail). Continue west with Fishhook Creek on your left, passing on the right at 3 miles the Marshall Lake Cutoff Trail. Gently ascend on the Fishhook Creek Trail until you reach the sign for the wilderness boundary at 4 miles. Follow the directions to the hut provided by your guide.

## DAY 2: FISHHOOK HUT TO BENCH HUT

> **Distance:** 5.2 miles
> **Elevation gain/loss:** 1130 feet/430 feet
> **Difficulty:** Intermediate
> **Hut elevation:** 7400 feet

Reverse the route from yesterday, descending gently 1.75 miles east-northeast, and then southeast, on the Fishhook Creek Trail, turning right (southwest) onto the Redfish Creek Trail/Bench Lakes Trail, which is, confusingly, also signed as the Baron Lake Trail. Ascend along the high ridge of the glacial moraine that forms the west side of Redfish Lake. Enjoy stunning views of the lake and beyond to the White Cloud Peaks.

At 4.6 miles, turn right (west) at the signed junction, and follow the Bench Lakes

*A bright sign marks the designated pee tree.*

# HUT GUIDES, ESCORTS, AND CERTIFICATION

Just getting to a backcountry hut or yurt can seem daunting; once there, the many tasks confronting the first-time user may appear confusing. A paid or appointed guide or escort, or a system of advance training and certification, can help travelers overcome these obstacles, ensuring safety of the travelers and also safeguarding private property.

A guide is included in the hut fee for first-time users at Sun Valley Mountain Huts in Idaho and at some of Wallowa Alpine Huts' units (called a "first-day escort") in Oregon. The staff person meets the party in the morning and skis to the hut, leading the way. At the hut, the guide gives an orientation to the layout and systems, and also to opportunities in the surrounding terrain. After the guide departs, the party settles into the joys of hut life. Utah State University's Outdoor Program hires students as yurt hosts who meet with groups on campus to provide an orientation before they set off for the yurt.

Some outfits adopt a training and certification model. The Utah Nordic Alliance holds periodic training sessions on yurt routines and safety procedures; successful completion of the course, and resulting certification, is required to rent their yurt. The Boulder Group of the Colorado Mountain Club conducts training sessions focused not only on where things are in their two backcountry cabins but also on a range of outdoor skills including preparing firewood, starting fires in the woodstove, water purification techniques, and more. User groups must include at least one person who has completed the training.

Trail to the wilderness boundary and a trail registry. Follow the directions to the hut provided by your guide.

### DAY 3: BENCH HUT TO STATE ROUTE 75

**Distance:** 5.2 miles

**Elevation gain/loss:** 230 feet/1280 feet

**Difficulty:** Novice to intermediate

Reverse the route from yesterday, returning to the Bench Lakes Trail and the trail registry. Follow the Bench Lakes Trail east for a short way until it meets the Redfish Creek Trail/Baron Lake Trail.

Turn left (north-northeast) onto the Redfish Creek Trail and descend along the ridge, while enjoying stunning views. When you reach the junction with the Fishhook Creek Trail, continue straight past the Redfish Trailhead and back along the unplowed Redfish Lake access road to SR 75 and your car.

# RENDEZVOUS HUTS

*Every winter I'm asked the question: Why are you so happy? The first time it startled me; I had to think. But the answer came quickly. One reason I feel so good is I get to ski cross-country, every day, all winter.*

—Sally Portman, *Ski Touring Methow Style*

**Location:** Okanogan-Wenatchee National Forest near Winthrop, Washington

**Distance:** Huts 1 to 6 miles apart; featured itinerary 21.3 miles

**Elevation gain/loss:** 3070 feet/2950 feet

**Difficulty:** Novice to intermediate

**Terrain:** Gently rolling with some steep ascents and descents and long, straight stretches on forest roads; trails groomed in winter for both classic and skate skiers

**Modes of travel:** Winter skiing, fat biking (limited), and snowshoeing (limited); spring, summer, and fall hiking and biking

**Season:** Year-round

**Huts:** Five huts (capacity 8 to 10), self-service, exclusive use

---

**THE METHOW VALLEY IS TUCKED** away on the eastern slopes of the North Cascades. Relatively distant from major urban centers—Spokane is a roughly three-and-a-half-hour drive away, Seattle five to six hours in winter—this territory attracts numerous outdoor enthusiasts in winter and summer. The Methow Trails, encompassing more than 125 miles of groomed cross-country ski routes, are a major draw in winter. The five Rendezvous Huts, situated outside the town of Winthrop, provide unique opportunities to extend a single day's ski on well-groomed trails into an overnight or multiday experience. This is a great place to enjoy the deep quiet of the snow-kissed evergreen forest, sweeping views of the North Cascades, and abundant fresh, dry powder—and to revel in cold-weather activity, settling into a rhythmic kick and glide on classic skis or the more vigorous thrust and thrust of skate skis. A Rendezvous Huts trip can be empowering for a fledgling Nordic skier, as elevation changes are moderate and navigation easy on wide trails utilizing forest roads.

North of Lake Chelan and east of North Cascades National Park, the Methow River carves a sweet 70-mile valley stretching from the towns of Methow, Carlton, and Twisp to Winthrop and Mazama. With Winthrop taking the lead and reinventing itself in the early 1970s as a western-themed vacation destination, this valley is now home to thriving small-scale outdoor tourism and alternative agricultural enterprises. The Methow Trails—both actual trails and a nonprofit organization—embody the communitarian values and healthy outdoor culture of this special region. The trails, said to be North America's largest cross-country ski system, were inaugurated in the 1970s by a group of forward-looking local residents (see "Methow Trails: A Labor of Love"). The Rendezvous Huts developed in tandem with the trail system. Beginning in the early 1980s with a few temporary structures, the hut system evolved through a series of local owners. Ben and Virginia Nelson, originally from Alaska, are the fourth proprietors. Since buying the business in 2013, Ben—a man who likes to build and renovate—has added porches and other finishing touches to the huts.

Connected by a groomed trail system, the Rendezvous Huts attract classic and skate skiers. However, you also encounter skiers in telemark and even alpine touring gear; mountain slopes rising near several huts invite the dedicated backcountry ski enthusiast to try some downhill turns. There are also limited opportunities for winter fat biking (to Grizzly Hut) and snowshoeing (to Heifer Hut). This is a dog-friendly system; canine companions are allowed on more than 30 miles of trails and welcome in three of the five the huts. The current owners have expanded the Rendezvous Huts season beyond winter; hikers are now welcome in summer months, as are mountain bikers and fat-tire bikers.

## HUTS AND AMENITIES

The wood-framed huts, each roughly 250 square feet, are cozy and well appointed. The main floors are divided between kitchen and dining table on one side, and woodstove plus bunks on the other. Stairs lead up to a sleeping loft, furnished with several double-bed-sized mattresses and illuminated by windows during daylight hours. Kitchens are amply stocked with pots and pans, dishes, silverware, and several types of coffeemakers. The huts do not have sinks; water comes from snowmelt in winter or is delivered in five-gallon jugs. Stationary propane lanterns light up the interior; some huts also have solar-powered light fixtures.

Overnight guests make these rustic huts comfortable and convivial. Each hut sleeps 8 to 10 people. Most users opt to take advantage of the freight haul service; for a fee, hut staff will deliver water, as well as gear, foodstuffs, and beverages, by snowmobile trailer to the hut. Each hut is stocked with an extensive library of puzzles, playing cards, and board games to pass evening hours.

Huts are rented for exclusive use, making them attractive overnight gathering places for large family or friend groups. Many groups make a Rendezvous Hut visit an annual tradition; up to 80 percent are repeat visitors. This hut system, fully booked almost every winter, draws visitors primarily from the greater Northwest, especially from the Seattle region, although these overnight shelters are also very popular with the locals.

The Rendezvous Huts are open to day-trippers. Make the final uphill ascent

*The Rendezvous Hut is central to the Methow Trails, a network groomed for both skate and classic skis.*

to these little houses, pause on the porch for views, or venture inside to heat a cup of soup or tea. Remember that the huts are private property; look for the donation box for day users and contribute freely.

## HEIFER HUT

Heifer Hut, built in 1985 and remodeled in 2001, is the most removed from the other huts in this system. Set in the woods, with skiable slopes behind, it makes for a cozy and quiet retreat. Dogs are allowed.

## RENDEZVOUS HUT

Rendezvous Hut, just off the pass of the same name, is at the heart of this system. Along with nearby Gardner Hut, it is a popular day trip destination. Built in 1985 and remodeled in 2002, Rendezvous Hut offers great views up the valley. Dogs are allowed.

## GARDNER HUT

Built in 1998 and remodeled in 2007, Gardner Hut (4016 feet) is in the midst of the trail matrix. Large groups sometimes rent

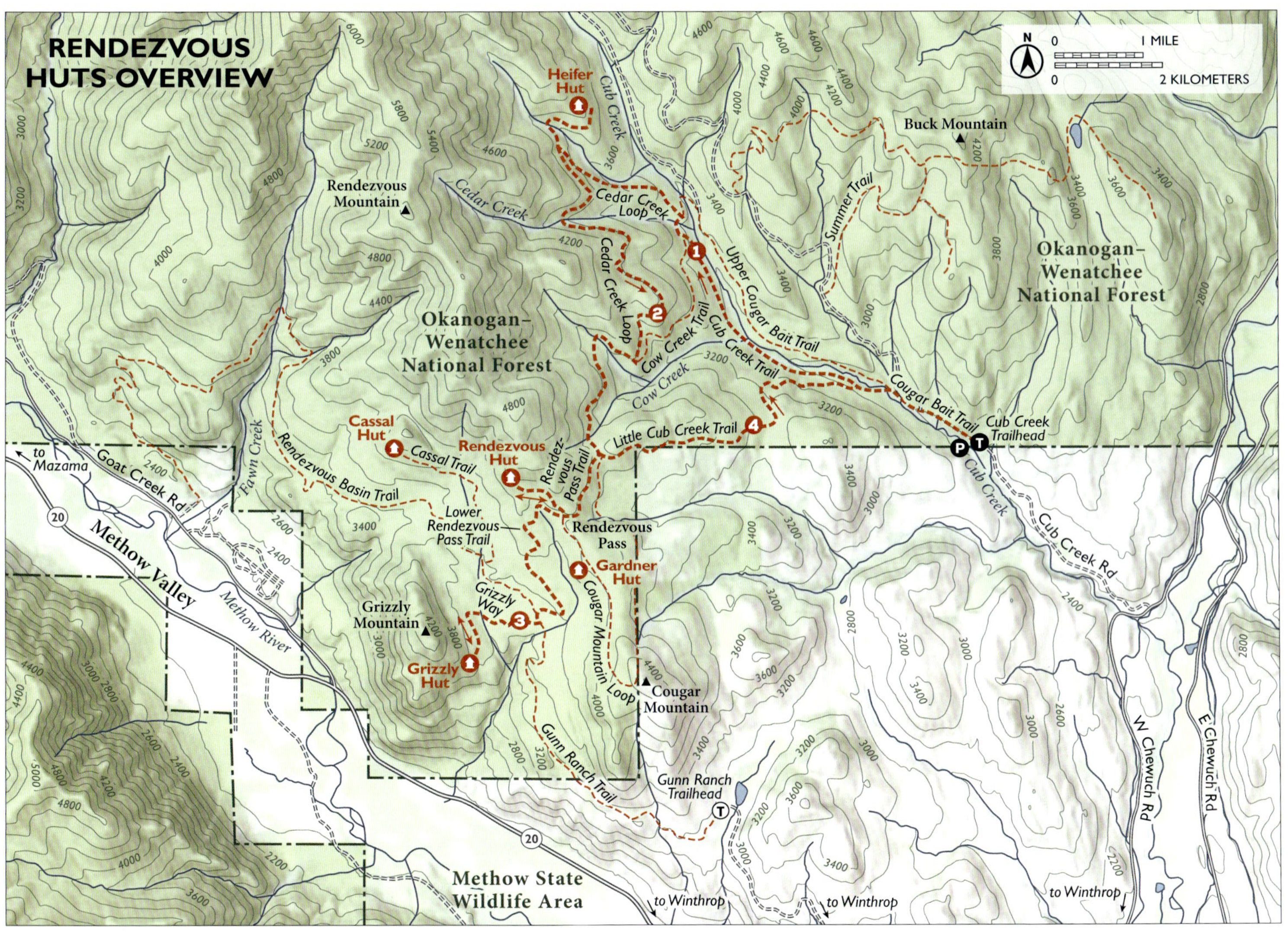
RENDEZVOUS HUTS OVERVIEW
N
0
1 MILE
0
2 KILOMETERS
Heifer Hut
Cub Creek
Buck Mountain
4200
6000
5800
5200
5400
4600
4600
4600
4000
4200
4800
Summer Trail
3400
3000
2800
3800
3400
3600
3400
3600
Okanogan–Wenatchee National Forest
3000
Rendezvous Mountain
Cedar Creek
Cedar Creek Loop
Cedar Creek Loop
1
Upper Cougar Bait Trail
Cub Creek Trail
4800
4000
4800
4400
3800
4200
2
Cow Creek Trail
Cub Creek Trail
3200
3400
Okanogan–Wenatchee National Forest
Cow Creek
3200
Cougar Bait Trail
Cub Creek Trailhead
P
T
Cassal Hut
Rendezvous Hut
Little Cub Creek Trail
4
3200
3400
Cub Creek
Cub Creek Rd
to Mazama
Goat Creek Rd
Fawn Creek
Cassal Trail
Rendezvous Basin Trail
Rendez-vous Pass Trail
3000
3400
3200
2800
2400
2400
2600
3400
Lower Rendezvous Pass Trail
Rendezvous Pass
Gardner Hut
3200
3000
2400
20
Methow Valley
Methow River
Grizzly Way
Grizzly Mountain
3
Cougar Mountain Loop
4200
3000
3800
Grizzly Hut
Cougar Mountain
4400
3600
3200
3000
3400
3600
3000
2600
2800
2800
3000
2400
W Chewuch Rd
E Chewuch Rd
2200
4400
4000
5000
4800
4200
2600
2800
3000
2400
2200
Gunn Ranch Trail
Gunn Ranch Trailhead
T
3000
3600
3400
20
3600
Methow State Wildlife Area
to Winthrop
to Winthrop
to Winthrop

*The latest addition to the Methow Trails, Grizzly Hut has sweeping views.*

both Gardner Hut and nearby Rendezvous Hut, transferring from one to the other for meals and merrymaking. No dogs in winter.

### GRIZZLY HUT

The newest hut, built in 2007, Grizzly Hut offers great views and nice interior details, including hooks for hanging everything. Dogs are allowed.

### CASSAL HUT

Cassal Hut (4069 feet), the most remote hut when accessed from the Cub Creek Trailhead, was built in 1996 and updated in 2009. Dogs are not allowed in winter.

## PLANNING AND PREPARATION

**Contact:** www.rendezvoushuts.com; (509) 996-2148 for reservations; (509) 996-8100 or (800) 257-2452 for gear haul and general questions; info@rendezvoushuts.com

**Booking:** Check availability and make reservations via website or by phone; huts are often reserved up to a year in advance

**Membership:** None

**Rates:** $; hut rental fees are about 30 percent lower outside the winter season; must also purchase a trail pass

**Transportation:** Personal vehicle required; North Cascades Scenic Highway/State Route 20 is closed in winter, so use I-90 or US Highway 2 from Seattle

## MAPS

The Methow Trails website (www.methowtrails.org/winter-maps) provides a good map (without contour lines) of the huts and trails of the Rendezvous area. Print out the PDF, or pick up a larger paper

# METHOW TRAILS: A LABOR OF LOVE

With fabulous ski terrain, consistent dry snow, and a great winter climate, Winthrop, Washington, almost became home to a big downhill ski resort in 1974 and again in 1984, as developers eyed profits from an attendant real estate boom. Instead, locals dedicated themselves to alternative visions. As activist Maggie Coon commented, "Instead of looking at grandiose projects to solve the economic woes of the valley, let's look at what's special in the Methow and build on that." The completion of the North Cascades Scenic Highway and the establishment of North Cascades National Park made Winthrop a destination for hikers and campers. Nordic skiing quickly grew in popularity, and more recently mountain biking has really taken off.

Three cross-country ski centers sprang up in the upper Methow Valley: Sun Mountain Lodge, the Mazama Trails/North Cascades Basecamp, and the Rendezvous Huts. Valley residents rallied to develop a groomed trail system on the valley floor under the auspices of the nonprofit Methow Valley Family Sports Club (founded in 1977 and later renamed the Methow Valley Ski Touring Association and eventually the Methow Valley Sport Trails Association, or MVSTA). Don Portman, who started the cross-country ski program at Sun Mountain Lodge, originated the idea of connecting three ski center trail networks with Winthrop's community trails to form one big system extending throughout the valley and surrounding slopes.

Creating this trail system took several decades and involved creative work by individuals, organizations, and local and state governments. Jay Lucas, the association's first executive

copy from one of many establishments in Winthrop. Green Trails offers topos of the Doe Mountain Quadrangle and Mazama Quadrangle at 1:69,500 scale, sold in Winthrop gear shops. Green Trails also produces one plastic map, No. 51SX, that covers the network.

## PACKING TIPS

Bring a sleeping bag (and pillow if desired). Classic or skate skis are recommended.

## OTHER TIPS

You must purchase a multiday Methow Trails Pass (see www.methowtrails.org /tickets-and-passes) to cover the duration of your trip. Snowshoeing is allowed only from the Cub Creek Trailhead to Heifer Hut (via the Upper Cougar Bait Trail). Fat-tire bikes are permitted from the Gunn Ranch Trailhead to Grizzly Hut. Gear haul option available for a fee (under $100). For car relocation or trailhead pickup and

director, figured out how to run MVSTA as a successful nonprofit enterprise. The Haub family, owners of Sun Mountain Lodge, helped secure crucial bank loans for the fledgling MVSTA. Several dedicated community members worked for years to secure permissions and permits from 180 different landowners, including the US Forest Service (USFS), to guarantee access and protect the natural state of the trail corridor. The monetary value of these permissions was crucial in leveraging matching funds from granting agencies. The MVSTA worked with city, county, and USFS officials to develop a recreation plan for the surrounding Okanogan County. This plan laid the groundwork for state grants, county assistance, changes in the county zoning codes incentivizing landowners to grant trail permissions, and eligibility for a portion of the county hotel-motel tax. Today the trail itself is a county park.

Methow Trails (the name was streamlined in 2014) is now a major economic engine in the region. In a 2015 economic impact study, Methow Trails reported nearly $6.7 million in direct expenditures by trail users, and with expenditures averaging $1,793 per trip. Seventy-four percent of the business community deem themselves highly or somewhat dependent on trail visitors, and 51 percent see trail enthusiasts as an increasing share of area visitors. But Methow Trails is more than an economic development vehicle. It is a labor of love created and sustained by valley residents. Altogether, Methow Trails reflects and promotes the values of a community at home in a beautiful, natural location, with aspirations to share and preserve this special environment.

drop-off options, consult with the Rendezvous Huts owners.

## ITINERARY: CUB CREEK CIRCUIT

*21.3 miles, four days, three nights*

The huts are bunched together along the Rendezvous Trails section of the Methow Trails. Our recommended itinerary can be easily modified; consult the Methow Trails map and the hut owners. Consider visiting an additional hut or two for a lunch or snack break. Or, instead of skiing hut-to-hut, book one hut for two to three nights and enjoy cocooning and daily ski tours.

Groomed daily for both skate and classic skiing, the Methow Trails bring the civilized pleasures of skiing on well-defined tracked routes to the backcountry hut experience. Trail sections are classified as beginner (green circles), intermediate (blue squares),

*Enjoying a lunch break with top-notch views at Rendezvous Hut*

and advanced (black diamonds), with most designated intermediate. However, we found the routes to be pretty easy within the larger context of backcountry hut-to-hut skiing. Even the advanced sections are only classified as such because classic Nordic skis can be difficult to control on long, steep descents, and traction can be challenging on the ascents.

Consult the Methow Trails Winter Trails map before setting out, and bring it along. Map signs marked with "You Are Here" arrows are posted at every intersection. Note the Methow Trails maps give distances in kilometers, while this book measures in miles.

## DAY 1: CUB CREEK TRAILHEAD TO HEIFER HUT

**Distance:** 5.1 miles
**Elevation gain/loss:** 1500 feet/170 feet
**Difficulty:** Novice to intermediate
**Hut elevation:** 4049 feet
**Hut GPS:** 48.6105°N, 120.2838°W
**Trailhead:** Cub Creek Trailhead
(48.5711°N, 120.2156°W)

### Getting There

Drive west out of downtown Winthrop on SR 20 for 0.25 mile and turn right onto West Chewuch Road. Follow West Chewuch Road for 6 miles and turn left onto Cub

Creek Road, following it for about 2 miles to the end at the Cub Creek Trailhead, which has overnight parking and outhouses.

### On the Trail

From the Cub Creek Trailhead, follow the Cougar Bait Trail northwest for 0.9 mile, bearing left at an intersection onto the Cub Creek Trail. Follow the gentle Cub Creek Trail through lovely ponderosa pine, fir, and cedar forests for 2.2 miles (passing the turnoff to the Little Cub Creek Trail) to where it ends at Cow Creek Trail. Turn right to reach the turnoff for the Cedar Creek Loop in 0.2 mile.

Turn left (northwest) and climb steeply up the Cedar Creek Loop for 1.2 miles before turning right (north); continue 0.6 mile to Heifer Hut. The final few hundred yards to the hut are steep, but take heart: you are almost there!

### DAY 2: HEIFER HUT TO RENDEZVOUS HUT

**Distance:** 5.9 miles
**Elevation gain/loss:** 770 feet/620 feet
**Difficulty:** Novice
**Hut elevation:** 4066 feet
**Hut GPS:** 48.5658°N, 120.2944°W

An easy, mostly downhill day begins by returning 0.6 mile to the junction with the Cedar Creek Loop and continuing straight (i.e., not turning left onto the section of the Cedar Creek Loop that you came up the day before) for 2.6 miles to the intersection with the Cow Creek Trail. You'll pass under the shadow of Rendezvous Mountain to the right (west).

Turn right (northwest) to follow the Cow Creek Trail as it ascends gently for 1.4 miles to pass the junction with the Little Cub Creek Trail. Continuing straight (now on the Rendezvous Pass Trail) for another 0.7 mile, reach Rendezvous Pass at a major trail intersection. From this intersection, continue straight (now on the Lower Rendezvous Pass Trail) for 100 feet, then turn right to follow the signed trail for 0.6 mile to Rendezvous Hut.

### DAY 3: RENDEZVOUS HUT TO GRIZZLY HUT

**Distance:** 3.2 miles
**Elevation gain/loss:** 100 feet/620 feet
**Difficulty:** Novice
**Hut elevation:** 3509 feet
**Hut GPS:** 48.5476°N, 120.2992°W

This short day begins with a 0.6-mile return to the junction with the Lower Rendezvous Pass Trail, where you turn sharply right onto the Lower Rendezvous Pass Trail and descend gently for 1.5 miles; turn left at the junction onto the Gunn Ranch Trail and continue 0.1 mile to the junction with Grizzly Way. Turn right (west) and follow Grizzly Way for 1 mile to Grizzly Hut, on the east slope of Grizzly Mountain.

For a longer ski, overnight at Cassal Hut instead of Grizzly Hut. Follow the directions above to the Rendezvous Basin Trail. Instead of turning right onto Grizzly Way, continue straight for 1 mile, then turn right on the Cassal Trail, following it for 2.5 miles to Cassal Hut.

For an optional side trip to Gardner Hut after skiing down from Rendezvous Hut, do not turn sharply right onto Lower Rendezvous Pass Trail. Instead proceed straight for less than half a mile to visit Gardner Hut.

Pause and refresh. Return by the same route to the junction and continue to Grizzly Hut.

### DAY 4: GRIZZLY HUT TO CUB CREEK TRAILHEAD

    **Distance:** 7.1 miles
    **Elevation gain/loss:** 700 feet/1490 feet
    **Difficulty:** Intermediate to advanced

Retrace your route back to Rendezvous Pass, turning left from Grizzly Way onto the Gunn Ranch Trail and then right onto the Lower Rendezvous Pass Trail. Follow this to the intersection with the Little Cub Creek Trail, turning right (east) onto the Little Cub Creek Trail (black diamond), descending steeply at times, for about 3 miles to join the Cub Creek Trail. (To avoid this black diamond trail, continue north on the gentle Cow Creek Trail for about 3 miles to its junction with the Cub Creek Trail, where you turn right (southeast) to reach the Cougar Bait Trail and the trailhead for an added 1.5 miles.)

Head east for 0.25 mile to the intersection with the Cougar Bait Trail. Turn right (southeast) and follow the Cougar Bait Trail for 0.8 mile to the Cub Creek Trailhead.

To transform the featured itinerary from a circuit to a traverse, begin day 4 by exiting via Grizzly Way to meet the Gunn Ranch Trail; turn right and continue 3 miles downhill to the Gunn Ranch Trailhead (2900 feet). The ski from Grizzly Hut to the Gunn Ranch Trailhead is 4.25 miles. This option requires two cars, a car relocation, or drop-off and pickup at the trailheads.

*Visitors use the woodstove at Heifer Hut for many purposes during their stay: to melt snow to drink, heat water for tea and coffee, and dry their boots.*

# MOUNT TAHOMA TRAILS

*Of all the fire mountains which, like beacons, once blazed along the Pacific Coast, Mount Rainier is the noblest.*

—John Muir, *Our National Parks*

**Location:** Elbe Hills State Forest, Tahoma State Forest, and Nisqually Land Trust lands near Ashford, Washington

**Distance:** South District huts 3 to 6 miles apart; North District hut 4.3 miles from trailhead; full traverse 25 miles, with driving between South and North Districts

**Elevation gain/loss:** 5100 feet/5080 feet

**Difficulty:** Novice to intermediate

**Terrain:** Forested terrain with steep slopes, some gradual inclines, and level stretches on logging roads

**Modes of travel:** Winter skiing and snowshoeing; summer hiking and biking

**Season:** Three huts open year-round; one hut open in winter only

**Huts:** Four huts (capacity 6 to 14), self-service, by the bunk

---

**MOUNT TAHOMA, THE PUYALLUP TRIBE'S** name for Mount Rainier, has a towering presence when visible from Seattle on clear days. About two hours southwest of the city, the Mount Tahoma Trails Association (MTTA) brings visitors face-to-face with the second-highest peak in the continental United States. The four huts, accessed by wide trails, provide shelter for groups and individuals who seek face time with the glaciated mountain and views of the other volcanic peaks in the Cascades. Charging very little for each overnight stay and maintaining no-fee trails, the MTTA makes it easy to enjoy the mighty mountain from state and private lands contiguous with the national park. The MTTA huts are shared, so be prepared for camaraderie.

Founded by dedicated volunteers in the early 1990s (see "Operating an All-Volunteer Hut System"), this hut and trail system bears the imprint of community support and regional partnerships. The MTTA is supported by user fees and donations from local businesses and through an annual gala, which is both a fundraiser and a reservations lottery; many prime weekend overnight slots are allocated during this Seattle-based event each year. The MTTA relies on a unique partnership between the Washington State Department of Natural Resources (DNR), a land trust, and a timber company. Many private hut systems located on federal lands must engage in ongoing, sometimes tricky, negotiations with the US Forest Service or other agencies. By contrast, Washington State has been a cooperative partner since the beginning of the MTTA.

Bob Brown, now a retired DNR district ranger, served not only as a visionary founding board member and active volunteer in this organization but also as a liaison between the MTTA and the DNR. These particular state forests are a recreational playground as well as a resource sustainably managed to benefit education in Washington. Remember this when you encounter stacks of stripped logs along the route or pass through woodland patches denuded of trees.

The MTTA huts are convenient to the Puget Sound area; the trail system is a less crowded alternative in summer to Mount Rainier National Park. The terrain is steep; while the huts are less than 5 miles from parking areas and about 3 miles apart, the journey requires good conditioning and, in winter, decent technique for skiers.

*Mount Rainier, or Tahoma, beckons on the approach from Ashford.*

## HUTS AND AMENITIES

The MTTA offers four spacious, well-appointed huts accessible by trails groomed for skiing in the winter. Three huts are located in the South District, and a fourth—open only in the winter—sits some miles away in the MTTA's North District. Designed and built by community members donating their time, each distinctive hut exhibits quirky details and homey comforts.

The Mount Tahoma hostelries defy notions of modest scale and rudimentary amenities conjured by the term *hut*. The MTTA huts are roomier and better appointed than most hut systems. Special features include continuous, thermostat-controlled propane heat and a stock of hut slippers and rubber boots. Rest easy on winter nights without worrying about stoking the woodstove! Gracious living spaces are stocked with couches (some doubling as foldout beds), dining tables and chairs, and solar-powered lighting. Each hut has separate quarters for the hut manager and ski patrol members.

# MULTIUSE TRAIL ETIQUETTE

The Mount Tahoma Trails Association (MTTA) trails, established and maintained by a band of avid skiers, now also attract users with snowshoes and hiking boots. Trails are groomed at least weekly in the winter. The compacted snow trails, perfect for speedy, safe back-country skiing, are wide enough to accommodate gentle turns downslope. While this trail network was created by and for skiers, more than half its users now travel it in snowshoes, which work well in this area characterized by steep slopes and periods of heavy, slick snowpack. And the new lightweight, high-tech snowshoes are easy to just strap on and go, unlike skis, which require skill-building and experience.

Trail signs introduce the basic rules of multiuse trail etiquette: "Share the trail!" Non-skiers are further instructed to stay off the groomed center and travel single file on the far side. But despite directives to keep to the side, many snowshoers opt to walk straight up the middle, creating obstacles for the speedy downhill skier and endangering them-selves. Others keep to the side but walk two by two—which pushes one walker onto the groomed track and into harm's way. Greater safety hazards are created by walkers, many with microspikes strapped to their boots. These winter hikers leave deep footprints (post-holes) and other surface deformations that freeze in place, damaging the skiers' safe, smooth path.

Regardless of equipment, everyone should be ready to follow the few simple instruc-tions emblazoned on the signs. Walkers, stay to the side. Skiers, watch out for snowshoers and hikers, even as you enjoy a speedy downhill run. And remember the golden rule: look out for others as you would have them look out for you.

## HIGH HUT

High Hut, perched on a ridge facing Mount Rainier, provides sweeping 360-degree views of the Olympics and the Seattle-Tacoma metro area to the west and Mount St. Helens and other Cascade peaks to the south and east. The first in the MTTA sys-tem, this cozy hut boasts a large dining table and comfortable seating options. Up to eight guests can sleep in the living space and in the upstairs loft on sleeping pads.

## BRUNI'S SNOW BOWL HUT

Three-story Bruni's Snow Bowl Hut is a mountain chalet with a spacious living room, an expansive kitchen, and a large upstairs bunk room with bunk beds and sleeping pads for fourteen people. This exposed hut also features an expansive sundeck great for soaking in the views. High winds can cre-ate quite a soundtrack at night. Be sure to follow the fluttering prayer flags downslope and visit the gazebo, a charming six-sided

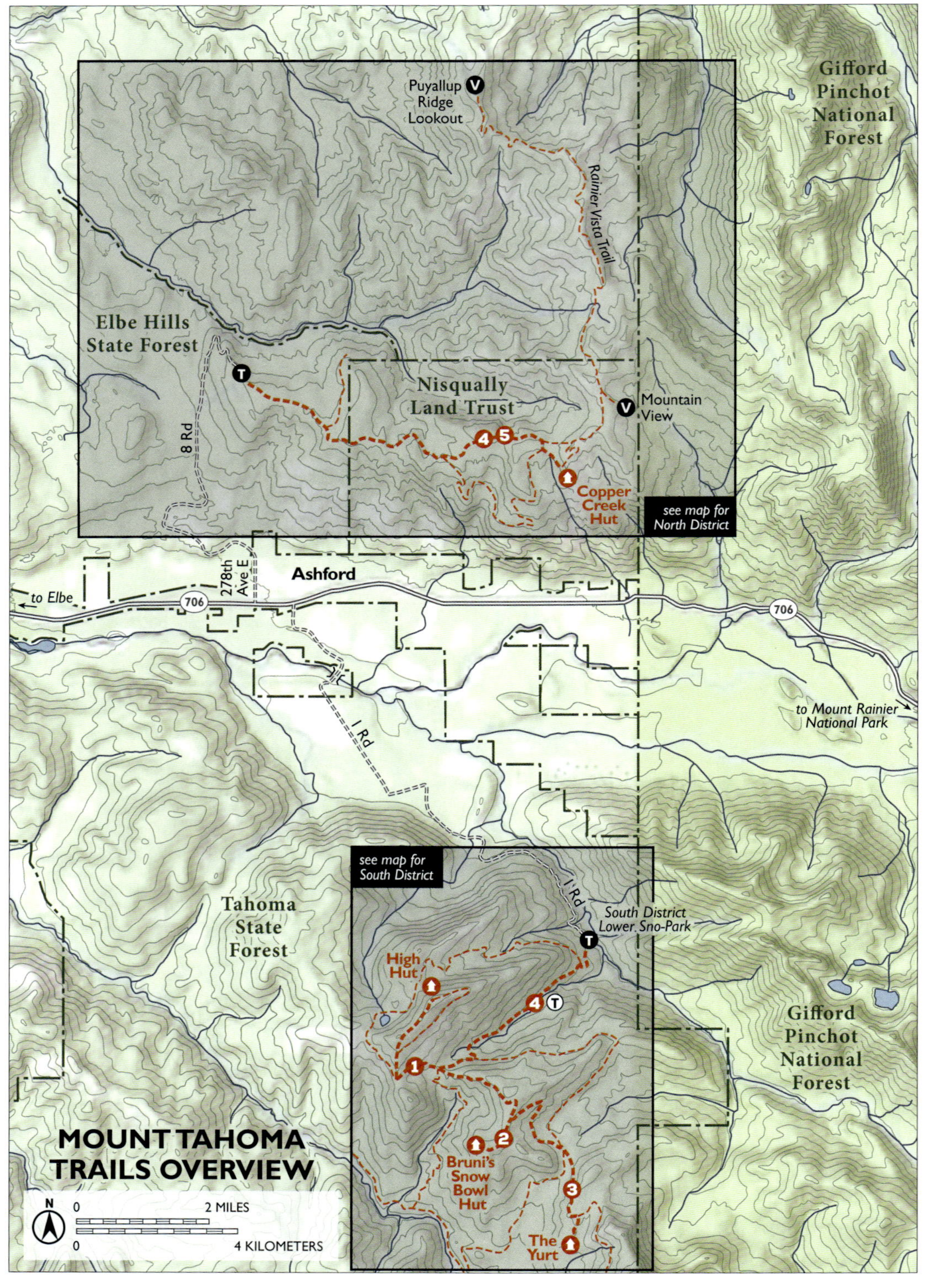
Gifford Pinchot National Forest
Puyallup Ridge Lookout
V
Rainier Vista Trail
Elbe Hills State Forest
T
8 Rd
Nisqually Land Trust
V  Mountain View
4 5
Copper Creek Hut
see map for North District
Ashford
278th Ave E
to Elbe
706
706
to Mount Rainier National Park
I Rd
see map for South District
I Rd
South District Lower Sno-Park
T
Tahoma State Forest
High Hut
4  T
1
Gifford Pinchot National Forest
2
Bruni's Snow Bowl Hut
3
The Yurt
MOUNT TAHOMA TRAILS OVERVIEW
N
0          2 MILES
0          4 KILOMETERS

*High Hut, the first and highest in the system, has a breathtaking view of Mount Rainier.*

retreat dedicated to Judy Scavone, one of the MTTA's most dedicated supporters.

## THE YURT

Nestled in a small forest clearing, this circular structure is the smallest in the system and sleeps six. After settling into the hut, hike a short distance up the Griffin Mountain Trail to catch a glimpse of all three huts in the South District, from the Yurt across to Bruni's Snow Bowl Hut and finally up to High Hut on the ridge.

## COPPER CREEK HUT

The most recent addition to the MTTA system, and separated from the others by a 13-mile drive on logging roads, Copper Creek bears the imprint of lessons learned in good hut design. Enter off a porch into a light-filled mudroom. Then enjoy the main space with defined areas for lounging, eating, and meal preparation. The outhouse takes advantage of the scenic setting, with the "throne" facing a window and views. Copper Creek Hut, with capacity for fourteen guests, is a great one-off destination in the MTTA system. With only 1000 feet of elevation gain from the trailhead via a wide, gradually sloping trail, the hut is the easiest of the four to get to and is a winter-only accommodation. Dogs are not allowed, even on the trail, in keeping with the

Nisqually Land Trust's goal of protecting nesting birds.



**Contact:** www.skimtta.org; (360) 569-2451 (phone staffed by volunteers on weekends from mid-December to mid-April)

**Booking:** Reservation gala held each fall (early November) at REI in Seattle, where an on-site lottery determines the order of reservations; after the gala, check website for availability and to make reservations

**Membership:** Not required; individual and family memberships available

**Rates:** $

**Transportation:** No public transportation to Ashford; personal vehicle required to access the huts and trail network

### MAPS

The MTTA sells its own 1:24,000 map, the best available for navigating this system. Also available is Washington State DNR's recreation map of the Elbe Hills and Tahoma State Forests.

### PACKING TIPS

Bring a sleeping bag. Metal-edged touring skis and skins are recommended (rentals available in Ashford).

### OTHER TIPS

Snowshoes are a popular option on these steep, often wet or icy trails; walk single file along the edge of the groomed trails. Walking, with or without microspikes, is discouraged because of damage to groomed trails and the inevitable post-holing (see "Multiuse Trail Etiquette"). A Washington State Parks Sno-Park Permit is required for overnight trailhead parking and can be purchased online and in many area shops and service stations. Carry chains or auto socks in case of deep snow on the way to trailheads. With the MTTA's porter service, a volunteer will haul gear to the hut in exchange for a donation. Pets are allowed on trails but not in the huts—except at Copper Creek, where dogs are prohibited in order to protect the wildlife preserve.



*25 miles, four days, three nights*

High Hut, Bruni's Snow Bowl Hut, and the Yurt—all in the South District—are very close together. The fourth MTTA hut, Copper Creek Hut in the North District, is accessible from another trailhead about 12 miles from the South District Lower Sno-Park. In the spirit of this guidebook, which focuses on hut systems comprising three or more huts meant to be traveled in sequence, we recommend a ski traverse of all four huts in the system. While skiing is the mode of travel most visitors choose, huts in the South District welcome hikers and bikers during warmer seasons.

The trails follow forest roads; in winter, they are groomed with room for linking turns. The routes are well marked; in addition to large blue-and-white directional signs at junctions, small orange signs posted about every half mile give elevation, GPS coordinates, and mileage to destinations.

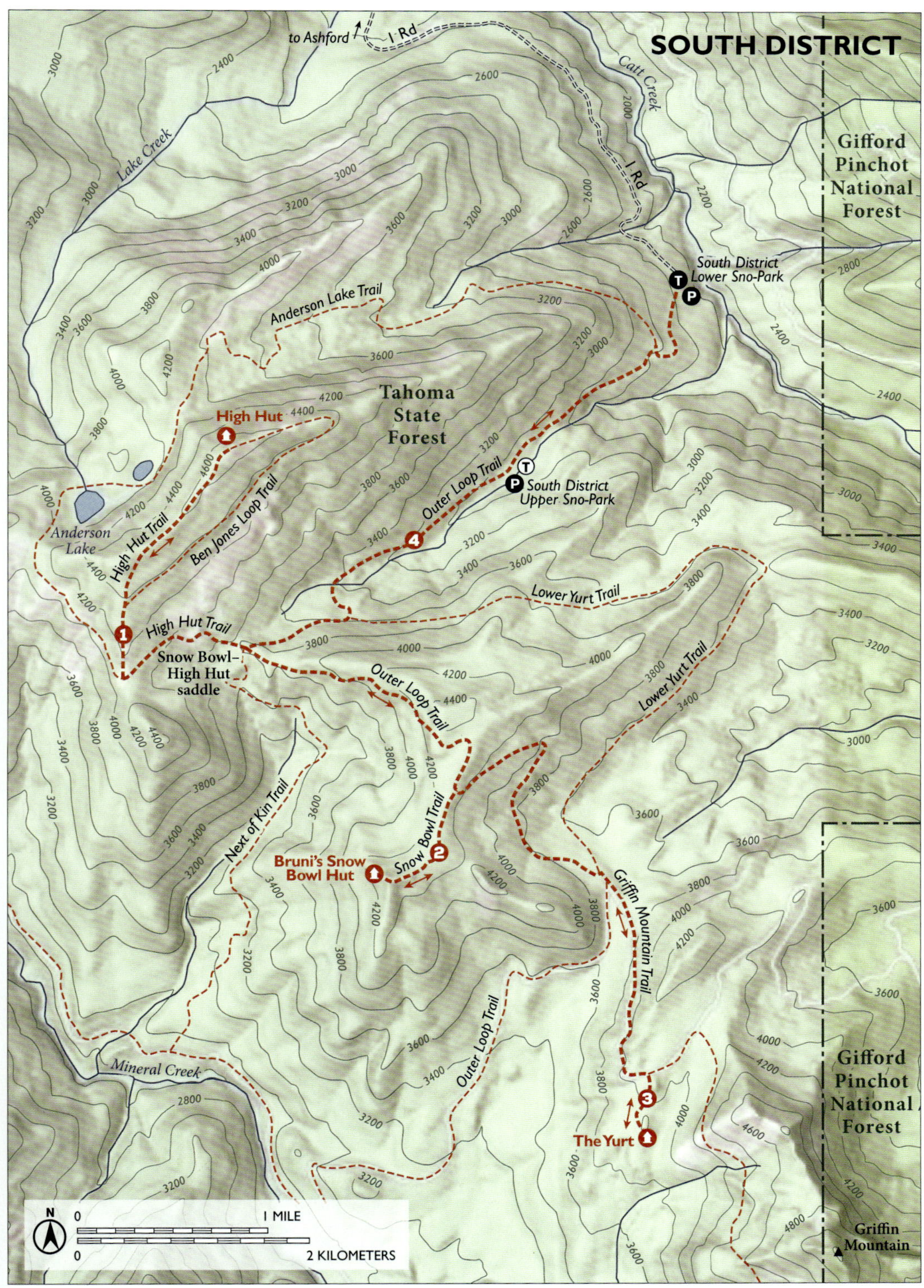
SOUTH DISTRICT
to Ashford
I Rd
Catt Creek
Gifford Pinchot National Forest
Lake Creek
Anderson Lake Trail
Tahoma State Forest
South District Lower Sno-Park
T
P
High Hut
High Hut Trail
Ben Jones Loop Trail
Anderson Lake
High Hut Trail
Snow Bowl–High Hut saddle
Outer Loop Trail
South District Upper Sno-Park
T
P
4
1
Lower Yurt Trail
Lower Yurt Trail
Outer Loop Trail
Next of Kin Trail
Snow Bowl Trail
Bruni's Snow Bowl Hut
2
Griffin Mountain Trail
Outer Loop Trail
Mineral Creek
3
The Yurt
Gifford Pinchot National Forest
Griffin Mountain
N
0          1 MILE
0          2 KILOMETERS

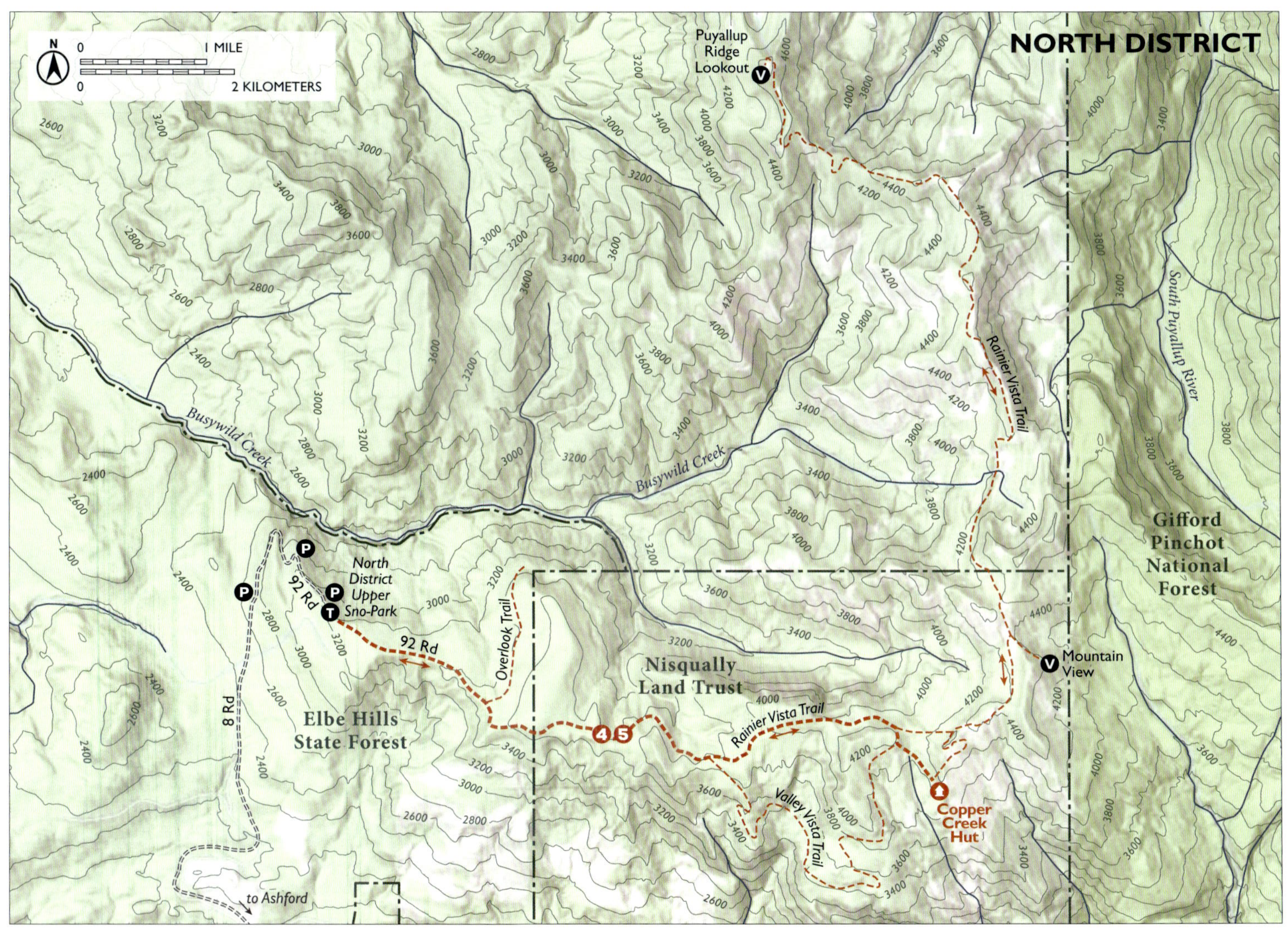
NORTH DISTRICT
N
1 MILE
2 KILOMETERS
Puyallup Ridge Lookout
South Puyallup River
Gifford Pinchot National Forest
Rainier Vista Trail
Busywild Creek
Busywild Creek
North District Upper Sno-Park
92 Rd
92 Rd
8 Rd
Elbe Hills State Forest
Overlook Trail
Nisqually Land Trust
Rainier Vista Trail
Mountain View
Valley Vista Trail
Copper Creek Hut
4 5
to Ashford

Two sno-parks (upper and lower) on 1 Road serve as trailheads in the South District. When snow is abundant, start at the lower sno-park (2360 feet), equipped with an outhouse. In low snow situations, proceed 1 mile farther through the gate to the upper sno-park (3000 feet). The route described below assumes departure from the lower sno-park.

## DAY I: SOUTH DISTRICT SNO-PARK TO HIGH HUT

**Distance:** 4 miles
**Elevation gain/loss:** 2300 feet/0 feet
**Difficulty:** Intermediate
**Hut elevation:** 4760 feet
**Hut GPS:** 46.6966°N, 122.0254°W
**Trailhead:** South District Lower Sno-Park (46.7057°N, 121.9926°W)

### Getting There

From Ashford, head west on State Route 706 and turn left onto 1 Road, just after the First Baptist Church. Follow 1 Road over the Nisqually River, then turn left at the T junction to stay on 1 Road, following it for a total of 6 miles from SR 706 to the South District Lower Sno-Park.

### On the Trail

Use skins to ascend steadily to High Hut on the Outer Loop Trail, passing the junction for the Anderson Lake Trail at 0.3 mile and the Lower Yurt Trail at 2 miles. Reach a Y junction at 2.5 miles and turn right to climb toward High Hut.

In a half mile, at the junction of the High Hut Trail and the Anderson Lake Trail, turn right. Follow the High Hut Trail for 0.9 mile, passing the beginning of the Ben Jones Loop Trail on the right, to arrive at High Hut.

## DAY 2: HIGH HUT TO BRUNI'S SNOW BOWL HUT

**Distance:** 3 miles
**Elevation gain/loss:** 660 feet/1050 feet
**Difficulty:** Intermediate
**Hut elevation:** 4250 feet
**Hut GPS:** 46.7059°N, 121.9927°W

Descend via the High Hut Trail (or try the Ben Jones Loop Trail for variety) to return to the Y junction with the Outer Loop Trail at 1.4 miles. The steep descent to the junction requires extra control in icy conditions. Turn right to ascend (at first steeply) toward Bruni's Snow Bowl Hut via the Outer Loop Trail.

After passing under the prayer flags at a rock quarry, the route levels out, descends slightly, and passes the turnoff for the Yurt on the left; follow the Snow Bowl Trail for the final 0.5 mile to the hut.

## DAY 3: BRUNI'S SNOW BOWL HUT TO THE YURT

**Distance:** 3 miles
**Elevation gain/loss:** 400 feet/550 feet
**Difficulty:** Intermediate
**Hut elevation:** 4100 feet
**Hut GPS:** 46.6616°N, 121.9947°W

Return via the Snow Bowl Trail, descending 0.5 mile to the junction with the Outer Loop Trail, then turn right (northeast), following the Outer Loop Trail toward the Yurt. Descend steadily for 1.3 miles as the trail does a hairpin turn southwest, where the Outer Loop Trail touches the Griffin Mountain Trail.

# OPERATING AN ALL-VOLUNTEER HUT SYSTEM

The Mount Tahoma Trails Association (MTTA) is the only all-volunteer hut system in the US, and it is the least expensive. The casual visitor to the Mount Tahoma slopes may never know that the reservations agent, the webmaster, the snowcat operator, the ski patroller, and the hut master are all volunteers who bring a special enthusiasm and pride to their tasks.

The more than ninety MTTA volunteers are avid skiers deeply committed to this gorgeous place and a common set of values. Some reside in the immediate area, but many live in greater Seattle. Some, including the snowcat operator, began as paid contractors and ended up volunteers. Volunteer staff members, who contribute about eight thousand hours a year to the organization, track their contributions; the monetary value of donated labor becomes a key asset leveraged in grant applications.

The MTTA ski patrol represents the largest number of volunteers. Ski patrollers act as goodwill ambassadors on trails and in huts. Trained in backcountry first aid and winter rescue methods, many ski patrollers also learn to operate the trail grooming equipment. In exchange, they have access to special ski patrol quarters in the huts. Hut managers oversee each of the four lodgings. Although allocated personal quarters, the managers contribute personal touches and bring welcoming cheer to the main hut.

The MTTA remains vital after more than three decades. But the all-volunteer system carries inherent challenges. An economic downturn could disrupt the flow of volunteers. Since many of the most dedicated volunteers are on the verge of aging out, the MTTA's future will depend on recruiting the next generation. Will the all-volunteer model be adopted elsewhere in the US?

Follow the Griffin Mountain Trail for 0.8 mile to the signed turnoff to the Yurt on the right. Continue for 0.25 mile to the yurt.

## DAY 4: THE YURT TO COPPER CREEK HUT

**Distance:** 6.25 miles from Yurt to South District Lower Sno-Park; 4.3 miles from North District Sno-Park to Copper Creek Hut

**Elevation gain/loss:** 680 feet/2420 feet (Yurt to South District Lower Sno-Park); 1040 feet/20 feet (North District Sno-Park to Copper Creek Hut)

**Difficulty:** Novice to intermediate

**Hut elevation:** 4200 feet

**Hut GPS:** 46.7766°N, 121.9966°W

Retrace the 0.25 mile to the Griffin Mountain Trail. Turn left (west) and follow the

Griffin Mountain Trail for 0.8 mile to turn left onto the Outer Loop Trail, following it for 1.3 miles to the junction with the Snow Bowl Trail. Turn right (north) at this junction to continue on the Outer Loop Trail, following it to the South District Lower Sno-Park. Note that 1.25 miles from the junction with the Snow Bowl Trail, the Outer Loop Trail turns sharply right (west) at the clearly signed junction at the Snow Bowl–High Hut saddle, from which it descends 2.5 miles to the South District Lower Sno-Park.

Alternative: If snow conditions are good and you want to ski some ungroomed trail, return to the South District Lower Sno-Park via the woodsy Lower Yurt Trail. This option avoids the climb back up to the Snow Bowl Trail junction but adds a mile to the journey and includes some challenging ups and downs on a very narrow, tree-lined path, as well as a steep downhill at the end.

Drive from the South District Lower Sno-Park to the North District Upper Sno-Park. From the Lower Sno-Park, return to SR 706, turn left, and drive 0.5 mile on SR 706 before turning right onto 278th Avenue East/92 Road (a.k.a. 8 Road and 9 Road). Follow 92 Road for 6 miles to the North District Upper Sno-Park/92 Road Sno-Park (46.7895°N, 122.0671°W) and park your car.

From the North District Upper Sno-Park/92 Road Sno-Park, ascend via the Rainier Vista Trail for 3.9 miles to reach the junction for Copper Creek Hut on the right. This well-signed turnoff is quickly followed by a signed left-hand turn onto the trail leading 0.4 mile to the hut. The easy Rainier Vista Trail has some rolling ups and downs and three climbs, one right before the hut. The trail wends through both commercial forestry holdings and lands managed by the Nisqually Land Trust. On the final approach, views open up toward Ashford, the Nisqually River valley, and beyond.

### DAY 5: COPPER CREEK HUT TO NORTH DISTRICT UPPER SNO-PARK

**Distance:** 4.3 miles
**Elevation gain/loss:** 20 feet/1040 feet
**Difficulty:** Novice

Retrace your steps from the previous day to return to the North District Upper Sno-Park. For a side trip, when you reach Rainier Vista Trail, turn right (east) instead of left (west), and ski a few miles up and back toward Puyallup Ridge Lookout. The lookout is closed, but you can gain fabulous views even if you don't ski the entire 7 miles one way to the lookout.

# THREE SISTERS BACKCOUNTRY



—Finnish proverb

**Location:** Deschutes National Forest near Sisters and Mount Bachelor, Oregon
**Distance:** Huts 7 miles apart; full traverse 21 miles
**Elevation gain/loss:** 1990 feet/3150 feet
**Difficulty:** Intermediate to advanced
**Terrain:** Through mountain forests, frozen lakes, and meadows and across gentle slopes with a few steep climbs
**Mode of travel:** Skiing
**Season:** Mid-December to end of April
**Huts:** Two huts (capacity 8), self-service+, exclusive use on weekends, by the bunk on weekdays

---

**CENTRAL OREGON, CROWNED BY MOUNT** Bachelor (9068 feet), is rich in recreational opportunities. This winter wonderland is known for abundant snowfall, expansive wildlands, and homegrown outdoor enterprises. Three Sisters Backcountry (TSB) invites outdoor enthusiasts into the heart of Three Sisters country, defined by a trio of volcanic peaks in the Cascades south of Sisters, Oregon.

This three-day, two-night backcountry adventure is a great way to sample winter hut-to-hut travel on skis. Show up with your Nordic backcountry skis (snowshoes *not* recommended), proper clothing, and a small pack stuffed with snacks, essential gear, and extra clothing, and TSB takes care of logistics, navigational resources, and hut provisions. Then enjoy the 7-mile trek from the trailhead to the first hut, another 7 miles to the second night's shelter, and then glide out to your waiting vehicle. While the terrain makes for moderate skiing with uphill climbs, weather and a heavy snowpack can pile on extra physical and wayfaring challenges. If your backcountry skills are rudimentary, bring along a few experienced companions!

The TSB hut-to-hut ski traverse debuted in the winter of 2014, catering to nature immersion enthusiasts and hardy friend and family groups. Jonas and Anna Tarlen are hands-on operators; patrons may encounter Jonas stepping off the snowmobile to restock huts and remove trash. The ski traverse is the Tarlens' second enterprise. They also operate the nearby Tam McArthur Rim Alpine Yurts, which are strictly for expert skiers.

*Arriving at the well-stocked Happy Valley Hut where visitors can warm up by the woodstove*

## HUTS AND AMENITIES

Happy Valley Hut and Lone Wolf Hut, while simple and functional, exhibit a few delightful design flourishes. One of the system's founders applied his metalworking talents to decorative doors on the huts and outhouses. Even though the footprint is small (288 square feet), each hut feels roomy because of the high gable and the clerestory, introducing lovely light. Each hut sleeps eight; beds are divided between four singles along the wall and two doubles suspended from the ceiling. The woodstove provides heat and a hot surface to melt snow for drinking water. This vital appliance, opposite a couch and the kitchen island, centers a cozy living space. A hut guitar invites sing-alongs and musical experimentation.

TSB provides plenty to eat and utensils for cooking. A large metal tool cabinet and small cooler for fresh items contain ingredients (all listed on the website) for meals. The provisions are themed Mexican or Italian in each hut. Don't miss the ample beer supply.

Outhouses are a short walk from the huts. Even this brief journey can seem frigid and treacherous at night. Find a headlamp, cram feet back into ski boots, and stumble across sometimes icy snow to the facilities. And then—after gazing skyward to drink in the stars and moon—take a moment to restoke the fire upon your return; huts can turn cold during the long winter nights.

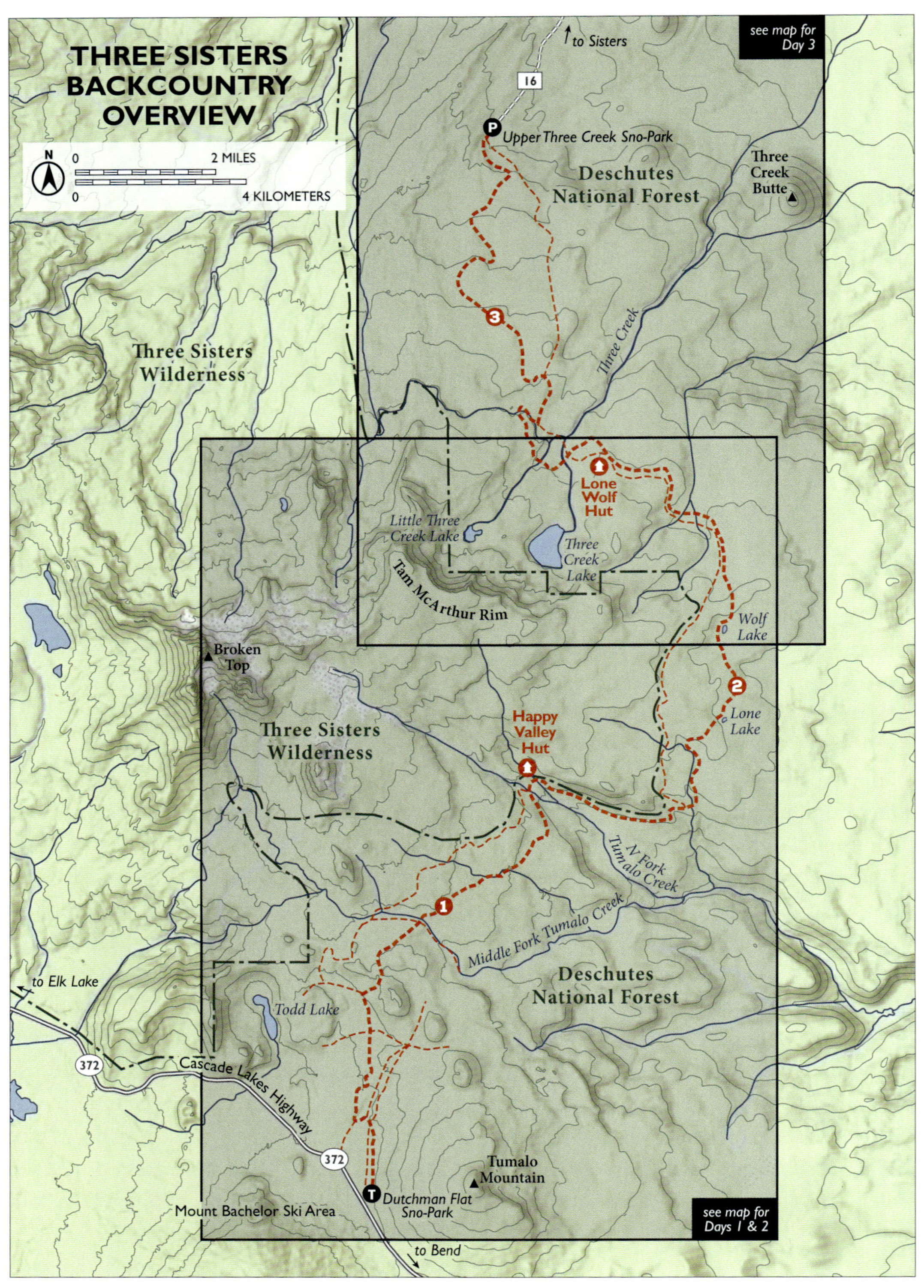
THREE SISTERS
BACKCOUNTRY
OVERVIEW
N
0          2 MILES
0          4 KILOMETERS
see map for
Day 3
to Sisters
16
Upper Three Creek Sno-Park
Deschutes
National Forest
Three
Creek
Butte
Three Sisters
Wilderness
3
Three Creek
Lone
Wolf
Hut
Little Three
Creek Lake
Three
Creek
Lake
Tam McArthur Rim
Wolf
Lake
Broken
Top
2
Lone
Lake
Three Sisters
Wilderness
Happy
Valley
Hut
N Fork
Tumalo Creek
1
Middle Fork Tumalo Creek
Deschutes
National Forest
to Elk Lake
Todd Lake
372
Cascade Lakes Highway
372
Tumalo
Mountain
Mount Bachelor Ski Area
Dutchman Flat
Sno-Park
see map for
Days 1 & 2
to Bend

## PLANNING AND PREPARATION

**Contact:** www.threesistersbackcountry.com; info@threesistersbackcountry.com

**Booking:** Check the online calendar for availability, then complete an online reservation form; owners will respond to reservation requests; weekend reservations (Thursday to Saturday) require booking the entire hut; weekday bookings (Sunday to Wednesday) are by the bunk and require a minimum party of two to reserve

**Membership:** None

**Rates:** $$$; fee includes shuttle service, maps, and access to huts stocked with sleeping bags, food, and beer

**Transportation:** TSB organizes a shuttle service; skiers meet at Upper Three Creek Sno-Park to drop off their vehicles; TSB staff meet the group at this parking lot with maps, safety information, instructions, and up-to-date reports on trail conditions and weather, and then shuttle participants and gear to the starting point at the Dutchman Flat Sno-Park near Mount Bachelor

### MAPS

This route requires a high level of alertness to trail markers and very good map and compass skills. In addition to verbal instructions, TSB provides laminated 1:24,000 topographic maps that can be attached to a backpack for easy consultation and a PDF map of the traverse that can be uploaded to your phone and used with the Avenza Maps app (see the TSB website). Experienced GPS users can request a GPX file to upload to a Garmin or other device.

### PACKING TIPS

Bring a sleeping bag liner. Pack booties or slippers to wear in the hut and to the outhouse. Metal-edged touring skis or telemark skis (with skins) are recommended.

### OTHER TIPS

Split kindling in the evening for a quick fire start in the morning. On trail, take care not to slip into tree wells. Aside from the short sections that use snowmobile trails as a shared corridor, do not ski on snowmobile

*Owner Anna Tarlen checks in on the Happy Valley Hut.* (Photo by Jonas Tarlen)

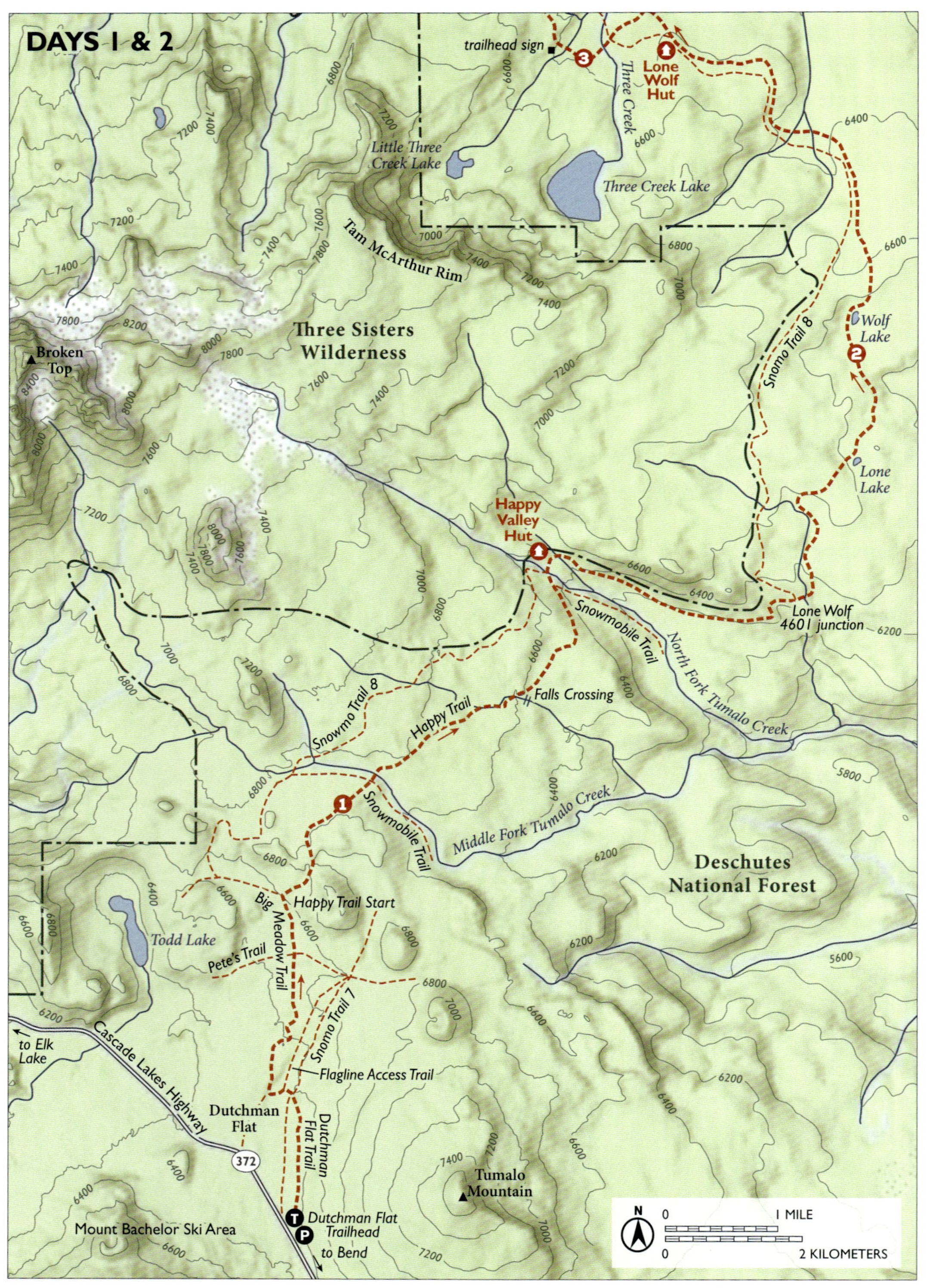

DAYS 1 & 2
trailhead sign
3
Lone Wolf Hut
Three Creek
Little Three Creek Lake
Three Creek Lake
6600
6800
7000
7200
7400
7200
7400
7800
8200
8000
8000
7800
7600
Broken Top
8400
8000
7200
7400
7800
8000
7600
7200
7000
Three Sisters Wilderness
Tam McArthur Rim
Wolf Lake
2
Snomo Trail 8
Lone Lake
Happy Valley Hut
Snowmobile Trail
North Fork Tumalo Creek
Lone Wolf 4601 junction
6600
6400
6200
6600
6400
6200
5800
Snowmo Trail 8
Happy Trail
Falls Crossing
Snowmobile Trail
Middle Fork Tumalo Creek
6400
6600
6800
7000
7200
6800
6600
6400
6200
5600
1
Deschutes National Forest
Todd Lake
6400
6600
6800
6200
Big Meadow Trail
Happy Trail Start
Pete's Trail
Snomo Trail 7
6800
7000
6800
Flagline Access Trail
to Elk Lake
Cascade Lakes Highway
Dutchman Flat
Dutchman Flat Trail
372
Tumalo Mountain
7400
7200
7000
Mount Bachelor Ski Area
6600
6400
6200
T
P
Dutchman Flat Trailhead
to Bend
N
0        1 MILE
0        2 KILOMETERS

trails. To leave a car at the Three Creek Sno-Park, be sure to purchase an Oregon State Sno-Park permit from TSB or a sporting goods store. Cell phones work on most of the route and at both huts, but there are dead spots, especially on day 3. Consider carrying a locator beacon. Slow skiers may wish to book later in the season when the days are longer.

## ITINERARY: DUTCHMAN FLAT SNO-PARK TO THREE CREEK SNO-PARK

*21 miles, three days, two nights*

The route wends across hidden meadows, through magnificent old-growth forests, and under boughs festooned with snow. Deep powder can accumulate into odd sculptural mounds under towering evergreens. From time to time, views open up to the Three Sisters and Broken Top peaks. The track, for the most part, follows the established Metolius-Windigo Trail, and trail junctions are signposted. The most reliable wayfinding method is to follow the blue diamonds at the outset, and then the yellow and orange ribbons tied high in the trees. There are some confusing stretches of the trail, when crisscrossed by other ski and snowmobile trails (marked with orange diamonds). Solid backcountry skiing skills and vigilant attention to trail markers combined with very good map and compass skills are required on this route. Experience using a GPS as a supplement to a map and compass is advisable.

Be fit and flexible: this traverse can be an easy glide over tracks laid by the last group or an aerobic project when new snow requires breaking trail—or if you lose your way and have to consult the map or backtrack. While this backcountry ski journey is full of challenges, it never veers into "extreme sports" territory. Unlike stretches of nearby high country, this particular trail is not in an avalanche zone.

### DAY 1: DUTCHMAN FLAT SNO-PARK TO HAPPY VALLEY HUT

**Distance:** 6.7 miles

**Elevation gain/loss:** 850 feet/760 feet

**Difficulty:** Intermediate

**Hut elevation:** 6489 feet

**Hut GPS:** 44.0631°N, 121.6299°W

**Trailhead:** Meet at Upper Three Creek Sno-Park (44.1599°N, 121.6355°W), start at Dutchman Flat Sno-Park

### Getting There

From Sisters, travel south on Elm Street (a.k.a. Three Creek Lake Road and eventually Forest Road 16) for 11 miles. Park at the Upper Three Creek Sno-Park to meet with TSB staff who will shuttle you to the Dutchman Flat Sno-Park, near the entrance to the Mount Bachelor Ski Area on the Cascade Lakes Highway/Oregon State Route 373.

### On the Trail

Follow the blue-diamond-marked US Forest Service Dutchman Flat Trail along the east side of the meadow. After a mile, at the end of the Dutchman Flat meadow, cross Snomo Trail 7 (40.0149°N, 121.6665°W). After this comes a confusing stretch: first,

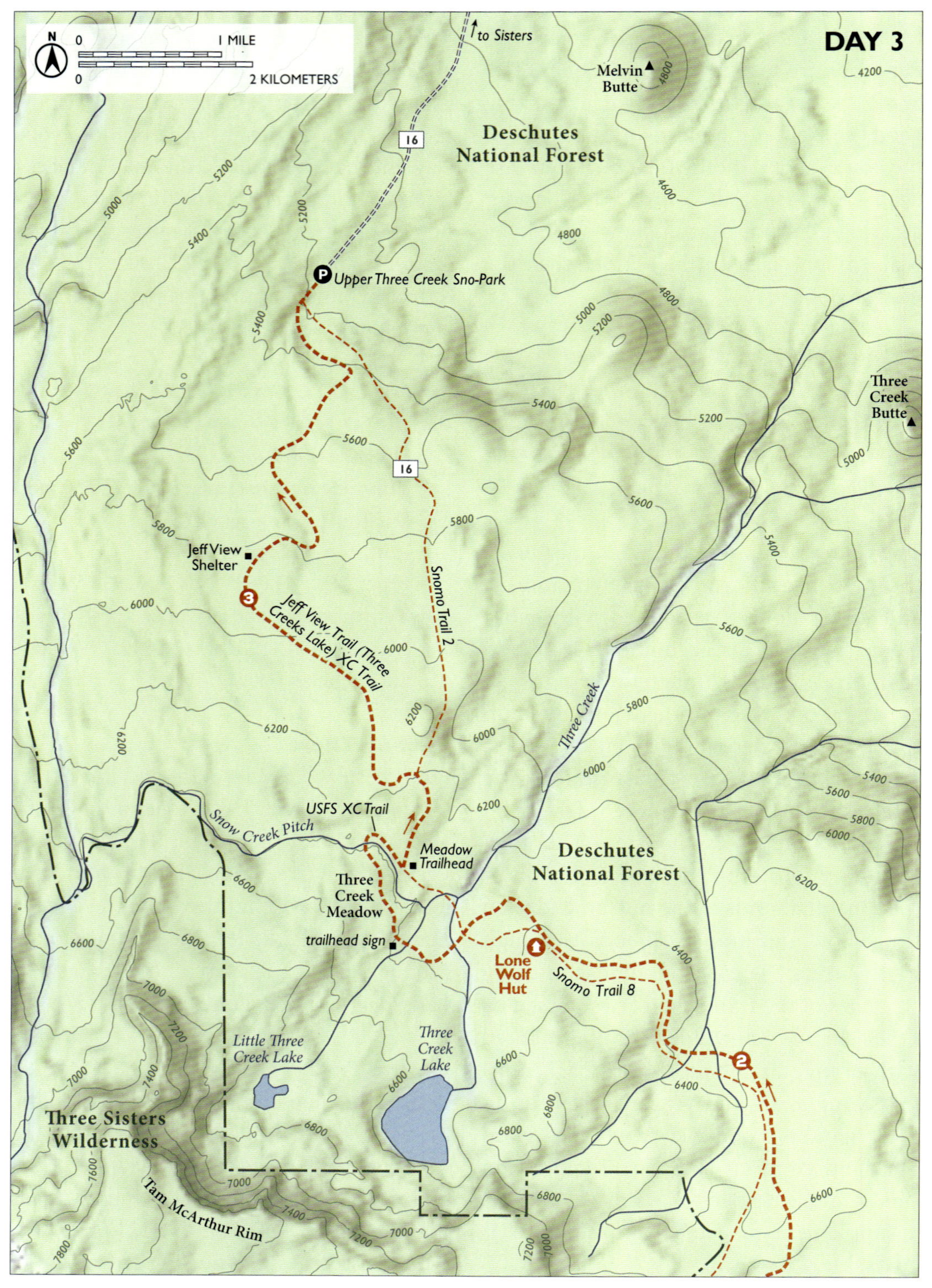
N
0
1 MILE
0
2 KILOMETERS
to Sisters
16
Deschutes
National Forest
Melvin
Butte
4800
4200
4600
4800
5000
5200
5400
5200
5000
Three
Creek
Butte
Upper Three Creek Sno-Park
5200
5400
5600
5200
5400
5600
5000
16
5800
5600
Jeff View
Shelter
3
Jeff View Trail (Three
Creeks Lake) XC Trail
Snomo Trail 2
6000
5800
6000
6200
6000
6200
6200
5800
6000
USFS XC Trail
6200
Snow Creek Pitch
Meadow
Trailhead
Deschutes
National Forest
5400
5600
5800
6000
6200
Three
Creek
Meadow
6600
trailhead sign
Lone
Wolf
Hut
Snomo Trail 8
6400
2
6600
6800
7000
7200
7400
Little Three
Creek Lake
Three
Creek
Lake
6600
6800
6400
Three Sisters
Wilderness
6800
6600
6800
7000
Tam McArthur Rim
7800
7600
7200
7000
7200
7000
6800
6600
Three Creek

DAY 3

take a left onto the Forest Service's Flagline Access Trail and follow it south until you reach the junction with the Big Meadow Trail; now turn right (north) onto the Big Meadow Trail. After about a mile you will cross the junction with Pete's Trail. About 0.25 mile beyond this junction, you arrive at Happy Trail Start; here the blue diamonds end and the Happy Trail is instead marked with yellow and orange flags fastened high in the trees, making navigation is easier. At Happy Trail Start, when the Big Meadow Trail bears left (northwest), you bear northeast to take the Happy Trail. While numerous yellow and orange flags mark the remainder of the traverse, it is advisable to remain vigilant so that you do not lose the trail.

Following the Happy Trail for 2 miles, you will cross two snowmobile trails and go by Falls Crossing (a waterfall hidden by deep snow but exposed in low snow years). Enjoy nice views of Broken Top and the Three Sisters mountains on a clear day. After another steep climb, you enter the Happy Valley drainage, and less than a mile after Falls Crossing, the trail joins Snomo Trail 8 briefly. Follow the double flags (yellow and orange mixed) toward the hut, which is located 200 yards east of Snomo Trail 8, on a ridge between two creeks.

## DAY 2: HAPPY VALLEY HUT TO LONE WOLF HUT

**Distance:** 7.4 miles
**Elevation gain/loss:** 920 feet/940 feet
**Difficulty:** Intermediate
**Hut elevation:** 6451 feet
**Hut GPS:** 44.1123°N, 121.6144°W

Return to Snomo Trail 8 and follow this shared trail corridor east for 1.8 miles as far as Lone Wolf 4601 junction (44.0597°N, 121.5957°W). Yield to snowmobiles on this shared trail.

At Lone Wolf 4601 junction, follow the flags as the trail turns north, reaching snow-covered Lone Lake at 3.2 miles (44.0635°N, 121.6025°W), and continue for another 2 miles to snow-covered Wolf Lake (44.0871°N, 121.5922°W) at 4.3 miles. The

*A chilly outhouse in the Three Sisters Backcountry*

*Back on the trail through the Deschutes National Forest after a lunch break*

flag-marked trail then heads roughly northwest toward the hut, paralleling Snomo Trail 8 and finally crossing it before climbing a short ridge to Lone Wolf Hut.

## DAY 3: LONE WOLF HUT TO UPPER THREE CREEK SNO-PARK

**Distance:** 6.5 miles
**Elevation gain/loss:** 220 feet/1460 feet
**Difficulty:** Novice

The final day is an easy, mostly downhill ski on a well-marked run to the Upper Three Creek Sno-Park. Begin by returning to Snomo Trail 8 and looking for the yellow flags across the road, where you will resume the flagged route. The flagged trail heads west, crosses an intersection with Snomo Trail 8 (FR 16), and continues past a trailhead sign (44.1121°N, 121.6289°W), where it turns northnorthwest. Winding through a burnt forest, it eventually reaches a **T** intersection with the US Forest Service blue-diamond-marked cross-country ski trail at 1.6 miles. Here the yellow and orange flags stop, and the trail is marked with blue diamonds.

Turn right at the **T** intersection and continue southeast 0.3 mile to the Meadow Trailhead (44.1175°N, 121.6287°W) at Snomo Trail 2/FR 16. From the Meadow Trailhead, follow Snomo Trail 2 downhill (north) to its junction with the Jeff View/Three Creeks Lake XC Trail at 2 miles, which you turn onto by turning left (west) at 44.1247°N, 121.6271°W. The Jeff View Trail turns into the Three Creeks Lake XC Trail, on which you follow blue diamonds, passing by the turnoff to the Jeff View Shelter at 4 miles (44.1409°N, 121.6000°W) and continuing downhill for another 2.5 miles to reach the Upper Three Creek Sno-Park. The last section of the trail is low elevation, and in a low snow year, one may need to walk the last stretch (up to 1.5 miles, depending on snowpack).

A quicker, 4-mile alternative route to the Upper Three Creek Sno-Park begins at the junction with the Jeff View/Three Creeks Lake XC Trail. Instead of turning left (west) to follow the Jeff View/Three Creeks Lake XC Trail, continue straight (north) on Snomo Trail 2/FR 16; follow this snowmobile trail all the way to the sno-park.

# YOSEMITE HIGH SIERRA CAMPS

*Climb the mountains and get their good tidings.*
*Nature's peace will flow into you as sunshine into the trees.*

—John Muir, *The Mountains of California*

**Location:** Yosemite National Park, central Sierra Nevada, near Mariposa to the southwest and Lee Vining, California, to the east

**Distance:** Camps 7 to 10 miles apart; full loop 48 miles

**Elevation gain/loss:** 7970 feet/8610 feet

**Difficulty:** Moderate to difficult

**Terrain:** Spectacular mountain terrain encompassing alpine meadows and lakes, rushing streams and many waterfalls, evergreen forests, granite domes, stone-paved staircases, and boulder-strewn mountainsides

**Mode of travel:** Summer hiking, unguided or ranger-led

**Season:** July to August or early September (exact dates depend on weather and snowpack)

**Huts:** Five backcountry tent-cabin camps (capacity 32 to 60), full service, by the bunk; the sixth camp, Tuolumne Meadows Lodge, is a frontcountry facility

---

**YOSEMITE IS AMONG THE OLDEST** and most iconic of America's national parks. Yosemite Valley—a narrow, 7.5-mile slice of meadows with woods flanked by towering granite cliffs and domes—draws the lion's share of the park's more than four million annual visitors. While the valley is crammed with signature spectacles including Yosemite Falls, Bridalveil Fall, Half Dome, and El Capitan, the high country up toward Tioga Pass is simply sublime overall, offering bejeweled lakes, tender alpine meadows, miles of cascading streams, deep forests, and burnished granite slopes too numerous to count. The Yosemite High Sierra Camps—six tent encampments connected by the High Sierra Loop—allow sustained immersion in this enchanted landscape.

Naturalist John Muir, after serving several years in this region as a shepherd and mill-hand in the late nineteenth century, led a successful campaign to preserve Yosemite as a national park. Muir's legacy is kept alive by the park itself, but also by the 211-mile John Muir Trail, which High Camps hikers follow for a portion of their journey.

Step back in time as you spend several days or a week at these distinctive, full-service, seasonal backcountry villages, where beds, meals, and other comforts are provided. During the day, enjoy vigorous hikes between camps, your pack filled with only foul-weather gear, snacks, and a few personal items. The camps, compact collections of tent cabins complemented by a stone-and-canvas dining hall and other outbuildings nestled under towering pines, date back to the early twentieth century. These are living history sites where hospitality is conducted with almost no modern conveniences and supplies are delivered by mule three times a week. Of course, some practices and routines have been updated—most notably in the way waste is handled to mitigate environmental impacts.

Since the beginning, these camps have operated only in the summer. Staff scramble to set up the tent cabins, dining spaces, and bathrooms after the snow melts; some years the camps do not open until mid-July or—in very high snow years—not at all. At season's end, the sleep shelters and most other structures are dismantled. Only the concrete tent pads, old stone cookhouses, and a few modern structures remain during the long, frigid off-season.

Camp staff relish their remote postings, often returning year after year. "It's a real commitment; you are leaving the real world for a dream world," one seasonal worker explained. The eight to nine workers at each camp forge a special bond that translates into warm welcome for overnight visitors. Each camp develops its own personality, shaped by the location and the interests and talents of the crew.

The High Camps were first envisioned by an early park superintendent who tasked the inaugural concessionaire to build three "mountain chalets" in 1916. Camps operated at Tenaya Lake, Tuolumne Meadows, and Merced Lake that year, encompassing canvas tents and a larger wood-and-canvas structure holding a lounge, kitchen, and dining room. The camps then closed until 1923; after a reorganization, the concessionaire restarted hospitality service at Tuolumne Meadows and Tenaya Lake. That same year, superintendent W. B. Lewis sent a park naturalist to scout additional locations in the park's high country. Over the next few years, Glen Aulin opened on the Tuolumne River, May Lake was established under Mount Hoffmann, and Vogelsang offered a high alpine base camp; Tenaya Lake Camp near Tioga Road closed. The chain of camps was finally completed in 1961 with the inauguration of Sunrise between May and Merced Lakes.

The early mission of the High Camps—to attract visitors to the high country and away from Yosemite Valley, to mitigate hikers' environmental impacts, and to provide settings for pilgrims to appreciate conservation efforts—is still relevant. Today, in keeping with tradition, the High Camps present several options to prospective back-country guests. You can make the journey on your own, checking in at night to enjoy the comforts of camp, or opt to join a group guided by a ranger who also offers trail talks and special activities in camp. A third option is to traverse the trails by mule as a member of a saddle trip. Finally, the dining rooms welcome (by reservation) a few hikers staying at nearby backpackers' camps to join the family-style meals; the meals-only guests lighten their daytime loads and contribute conviviality to dining room gatherings.

Yosemite is not only visually spectacular but also one of America's most biologically diverse and unfragmented ecosystems. Graced with remarkable waterfalls, imposing granite cliffs and domes, the Tuolumne and the Merced Rivers, and countless lakes and streams, Yosemite boasts an elevation range from 3000 feet in the valley to peaks more than 13,000 feet high. Yosemite is a naturalist's paradise! We encourage hikers to add John Muir Laws's rather hefty *Laws Field Guide to the Sierra Nevada* to their packs, to help identify some of the more than 300 species of mammals and 1400 plant species.

## HUTS AND AMENITIES

The Yosemite High Sierra Camps include five backcountry tent camps and the frontcountry Tuolumne Meadows Lodge, an encampment of sixty-nine tent cabins accessible by car via Tioga Road. The backcountry seasonal settlements comprise canvas and steel-frame cabins furnished with cots, a woodstove, and a simple table and chairs. Beds are fitted with mattresses, pillows, and multiple wool blankets; guests bring their own sleep sheet or sleeping bag. Most cabins sleep four, but a few fit only two or up to six. The camp manager makes assignments, keeping couples and friend groups together when possible

*Vogelsang Peak serves as a striking backdrop for Vogelsang High Sierra Camp.* (Photo by Rachael Swift)

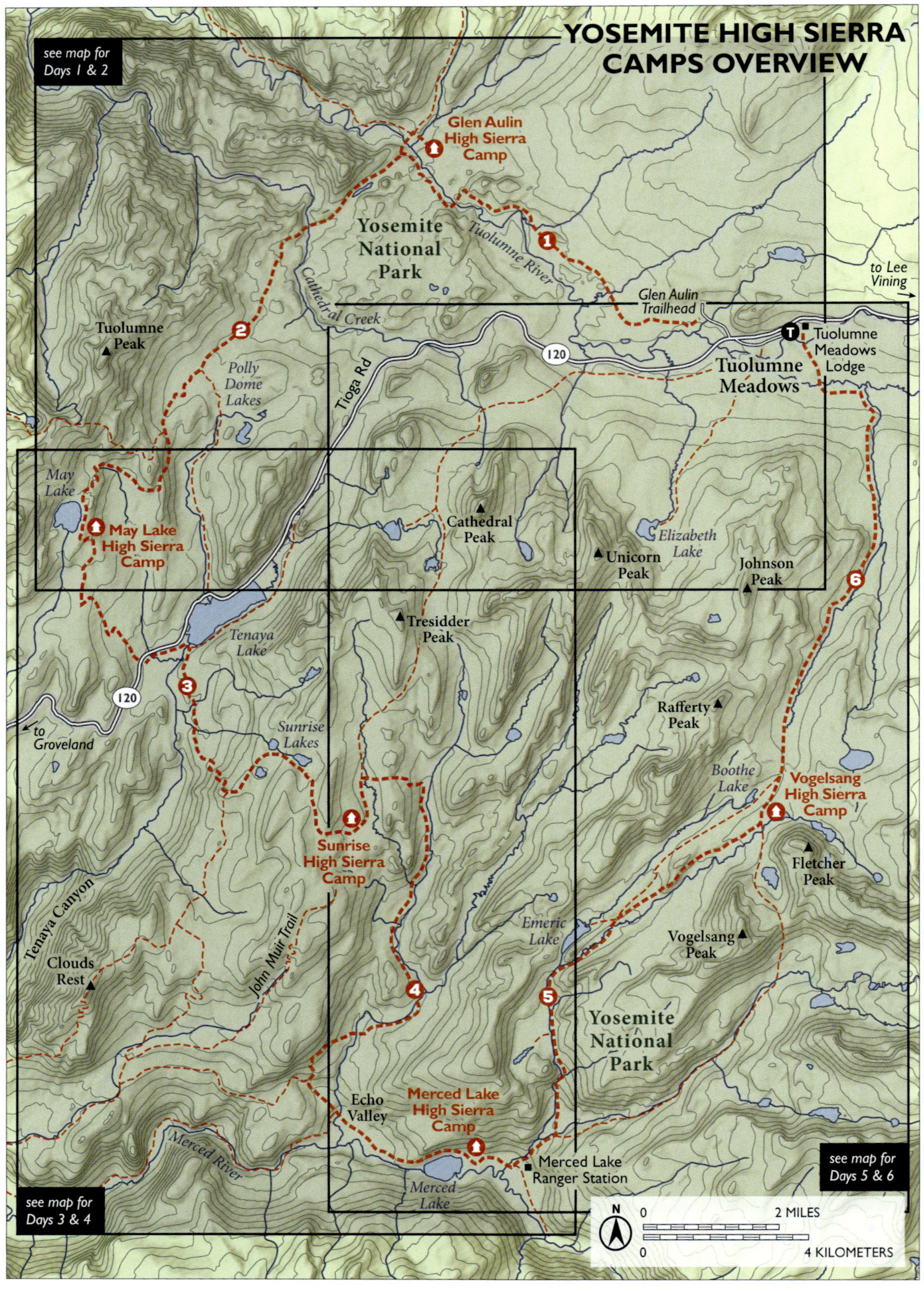
YOSEMITE HIGH SIERRA CAMPS OVERVIEW
see map for Days 1 & 2
Glen Aulin High Sierra Camp
Yosemite National Park
Tuolumne River
1
to Lee Vining
Glen Aulin Trailhead
Tuolumne Peak
T Tuolumne Meadows Lodge
Tuolumne Meadows
2
Cathedral Creek
Polly Dome Lakes
Tioga Rd
120
May Lake
May Lake High Sierra Camp
Cathedral Peak
Unicorn Peak
Elizabeth Lake
Johnson Peak
6
Tenaya Lake
Tresidder Peak
120
to Groveland
3
Sunrise Lakes
Rafferty Peak
Boothe Lake
Vogelsang High Sierra Camp
Sunrise High Sierra Camp
Fletcher Peak
Tenaya Canyon
John Muir Trail
Emeric Lake
Vogelsang Peak
Clouds Rest
4
5
Yosemite National Park
Echo Valley
Merced Lake High Sierra Camp
Merced River
Merced Lake Ranger Station
see map for Days 5 & 6
Merced Lake
see map for Days 3 & 4
N
0
2 MILES
0
4 KILOMETERS

# ALTERNATIVE ITINERARIES

It is not necessary to hike the entire High Sierra Loop to get a satisfying High Camps experience. Instead of a five-camp circuit, choose a shorter loop. The northwest section of the High Sierra Loop—Tuolumne Meadows Lodge to Glen Aulin to May Lake and out at Tenaya Lake—is a good option. Or try the southeast section by starting at Tenaya Lake Trailhead, hiking to Sunrise, Merced Lake, and Vogelsang, and ending at Tuolumne Meadows Lodge.

and allocating single travelers to cabins by gender. Separate buildings house the toilets, sinks, and showers at select camps. Meals are served family style, so guests mingle and chat over breakfast and dinner. Come for a hot drink half an hour before your meal; stay after dinner for games or music. Bag lunches are available by request for an extra charge.

### TUOLUMNE MEADOWS LODGE

This bustling camp, with a capacity for 288 people, gives a taste of the High Camps experience without backpacking and is the ideal place to overnight immediately before and after hiking the High Sierra Loop. After parking your car and stowing foodstuffs in a handy bear-proof box, grab a cart to transport your gear to your assigned tent cabin. Here, you rent an entire tent rather than by the bunk, and linens are provided. The separate bathhouse sits among the many white canvas cabins, just uphill from the dining hall. Treat yourself to breakfast and dinner served by cheerful young staff. Since food is not allowed in the tent cabins, some guests grab a quick bite in the parking lot or drive down to the Lembert Dome parking lot, where outdoor cooking is allowed. Gather in the evening around the campfire, right outside the dining hall, and listen to the Tuolumne River rush by.

### GLEN AULIN

Glen Aulin, meaning "beautiful valley," is an eight-tent camp with capacity for thirty-two located under tall trees near White Cascade on the Tuolumne River. There are no showers at Glen Aulin, but after a hot day's hike, find the small beach near the foaming falls, and slip behind the waterfall to plunge through the falling water and glide downstream. Swim out and do this all over again!

### MAY LAKE

May Lake is nestled at the base of Mount Hoffmann, the geographic center of Yosemite National Park. Overnight visitors to this eight-tent High Camp with capacity for thirty-six will share this beautiful location with many day visitors, who make the 1.2-mile hike from the trailhead to swim, fish, and enjoy the majestic scenery.

## SUNRISE

Sunrise, looking over the expansive Long Meadow and toward Mount Florence and Mount Clark, completed the High Sierra Loop when it opened in 1961. Situated on the flank of Sunrise Peak, this nine-tent camp sleeps thirty-four. The three Sunrise Lakes, which beckon passing hikers to rest or refresh with a swim, are nearby.

## MERCED LAKE

Merced Lake, nearly equidistant from Yosemite Valley and Tuolumne Meadows, is the most remote and lowest-elevation camp. Hikers generally stay at this camp after spending a night at either Sunrise or Vogelsang. Situated on Merced Lake and right next to Fletcher Creek as it slips down a long granite slide and falls, this High Camp of nineteen tents with capacity for sixty is a great place for a rest day. Note there is no woodstove for heat in the tent cabins.

## VOGELSANG

The highest of the camps, Vogelsang on Fletcher Creek is very close to bejeweled Fletcher Lake. This twelve-tent alpine camp sleeps forty-two and can serve as a base for further hikes to Fletcher and Vogelsang Peaks, up to Vogelsang Pass for great views, and to Boothe, Townsley, and Hanging Basket Lakes. Note there are no showers at Vogelsang.

## PLANNING AND PREPARATION

**Contact:** www.travelyosemite.com/lodging/high-sierra-camps; (888) 413-8869; highsierracamp@aramark.com

**Booking:** Reservations are by lottery and highly competitive; submit an online lottery application in October; lottery winners will be notified by email in December; if you fail to get a reservation through the lottery, try during the general availability period starting in March

**Membership:** None

**Rates:** $$$

**Transportation:** Drive and park at one of the trailhead parking lots in the Tuolumne Meadows area or use the Yosemite Area Regional Transportation System (YARTS), which offers transportation to Yosemite from Merced, Fresno, Sonora, and Mammoth Lakes; see www.yarts.com/travel-connections for connections to Amtrak, other bus services, and the airport; the Tuolumne Meadows Hikers Bus circulates once a day and stops at various trailheads (tickets required)

## MAPS

The Yosemite High Country map at 1:63,360 by Tom Harrison Maps covers the High Sierra Loop. National Geographic Maps covers the route on the Yosemite National Park Map at 1:80,000 scale and on two 1:40,000 maps: Yosemite NE and Yosemite SE. This two-map option offers more detail on place names and park features. For the most detailed view at 1:24,000 (informative but not necessary), six USGS quadrangles (Falls Ridge, Tenaya Lake, Merced Peak, Mount Lyle, Vogelsang Lake, and Tioga Pass) are required.

## PACKING TIPS

Bring a water filtration system to resupply drinking water on the trail, which can be hot and dry. Pack a sleep sheet. Bring a

*A mule train hauls supplies to the High Sierra Camps.* (Photo by Rachael Swift)

warm hat or beanie to keep your head warm at night.

## OTHER TIPS

Schedule extra time to acclimate to high elevation. Follow bear safety guidelines (store food and toiletries in bear-proof boxes, not in tent cabins). The Tuolumne Meadows Hikers Bus can be unreliable, so be prepared to wait and adapt your timetable.

If you are staying at Tuolumne Meadows Lodge on your first night, get an early start by skipping breakfast at the dining room. Instead, order a breakfast burrito to go and eat on the trail. At Tuolumne Meadows Lodge, make dinner reservations early to get your preferred seating time. Order trail lunches in advance. Limited supplies are available for purchase at Tuolumne Meadows Lodge.

Packing service (gear haul) is available to High Camps hikers on select days of the week in coordination with the mule supply train. Rates are by the pound. Call (209) 372-8326 to arrange.

Children must be at least seven years old to stay at the backcountry High Camps and at least ten for saddle trips.

## ITINERARY: HIGH SIERRA LOOP

*48 miles, six days, five nights*

We recommend walking the High Sierra Loop counterclockwise, with an easy first day. Alternatively, the clockwise route—with a steep first-day climb to Vogelsang—allows hikers to avoid the extra-strenuous uphill climb from Merced Lake to Vogelsang.

The trails—trampled for over a century by backpackers, High Sierra Camps staff and guests, and horses and mule teams— are well maintained. All trail junctions have signage listing destinations and distances (mileages may be a bit off, and trail names are often omitted). Wayfinding is easy, but there are no trail blazes on trees or rocks. Remain alert to more subtle trail indicators,

*Rock stairs on the trail to May Lake*

including rocks lined up across smooth stone surfaces, cairns, branches drawn across false paths, and carefully crafted water bars, stairs, ramps, and switchbacks. If you go more than 30 paces without clear signs, turn back to find the trail.

### DAY 1: TUOLUMNE MEADOWS LODGE TO GLEN AULIN

**Distance:** 7 miles
**Elevation gain/loss:** 460 feet/1270 feet
**Difficulty:** Easy to moderate
**Hut elevation:** 7884 feet
**Hut GPS:** 37.9086°N, 119.4179°W
**Trailhead:** Tuolumne Meadows Lodge parking lot (37.8776°N, 119.3349°W)

#### Getting There

From Lee Vining, take US Highway 395 south for 0.7 mile, then follow Tioga Road (State Route 120 outside the park) west for 12 miles to the Tioga Pass park entrance; Tuolumne Meadows Lodge is 17 miles into the park on the left. Tioga Road is open only summer through early fall.

From Groveland, take Big Oak Flat Road (SR 120) east 24 miles to the Big Oak Flat park entrance. About 8 miles past the entrance station at the Crane Flat gas station, turn left onto Tioga Road. Continue for about 49 miles to Tuolumne Meadows Lodge, which will be on the right.

#### On the Trail

On this first day, you will follow the Pacific Crest Trail (PCT) and the Tuolumne River. Start at the west end of the Tuolumne Meadows Lodge parking lot, following the PCT west, passing the Wilderness Permits Office

at 0.4 mile and entering Tuolumne Meadows. Alternatively, hop on the hikers bus, or drive 1.9 miles, to start at the Glen Aulin Trailhead at the Lembert Dome parking lot. Once underway, pass Lembert Dome to the north and take in views of Cathedral Peak and Unicorn Peak to the south.

At 2 miles, pass the junction for Soda Springs. If you choose, take the short spur trail to this naturally carbonated spring and a cluster of historic buildings. In the late 1880s, naturalist John Muir and publisher Robert Underwood Johnson camped here and hatched a plan to protect Yosemite as a national park. Today you also find restrooms, and the stone-and-timber Parsons Memorial Lodge, hallowed ground for the Sierra Club. Return to the trail and continue northwest, entering a lodgepole pine forest interspersed with meadows, and cross Delaney Creek at 2.6 miles. Over the next 2 miles, shady banks and sandy beaches beckon hikers to rest or splash around.

At 4.9 miles, the trail emerges into the bright sunlight sweeping across sloping swaths of polished granite. This bedrock, exposed by glaciers and rivers, extends under the river and pops out on the opposite shore. Follow the line of rocks marking the path. At 5.5 miles, the trail ascends briefly under a granite outcropping to reach a flat area. At this point, note the right-hand turn in the trail, then briefly leave the trail, continuing straight a short way onto a promontory with a flat granite floor. Enjoy 360-degree views encompassing the Cathedral Range and, to the south, Little Devils Postpile. After this view, return to where you departed the trail, and descend by means of mammoth, rugged granite steps to the foot of a large cliff on the right. The wooden bridge over the Tuolumne River at 5.6 miles marks the beginning of the long, cascading Tuolumne Falls. Beyond the bridge enjoy the view toward Mount Conness in the northeast and, to the north, Matterhorn Peak up Cold Canyon.

As the river tumbles ever downward through pools and falls, the trail also winds downhill, often on cobblestone steps and over smooth granite stretches. After winding in and out of the forest, at 7 miles arrive at the junction with the trail to May Lake, which you will follow tomorrow. Instead, take the right fork (northeast) toward Glen Aulin High Sierra Camp. Follow the trail 0.3 mile and across two bridges (first over the Tuolumne River and then over Cold Creek) to reach your overnight destination.

### DAY 2: GLEN AULIN TO MAY LAKE

>   **Distance:** 8 miles
>   **Elevation gain/loss:** 2230 feet/760 feet
>   **Difficulty:** Moderate
>   **Hut elevation:** 9334 feet
>   **Hut GPS:** 37.8446°N, 119.4913°W

Retrace your steps 0.3 mile across the two bridges to the junction. Turn right toward McGee Lake and May Lake. The trail ascends slightly through a forest of large conifers, reaching at 0.9 mile the north end of long, narrow McGee Lake, which occupies a saddle between two domes. The trail levels as it passes along the north side of the lake, then descends slightly to cross Cathedral Creek at 2.1 miles.

After crossing Cathedral Creek, the trail begins a long, steady ascent of 1150 feet over the next 4 miles. As you traverse this more open country, enjoy views behind you to the north of Hooper Peak, Wildcat Peak, and Cold Mountain. At 4.5 miles, bear right at the trail junction with the Murphy Creek Trail.

At 4.9 miles, at the next junction, choose the left fork to May Lake instead of right on the Ten Lakes Trail. Walk steadily uphill through a series of well-crafted stone-step switchbacks along the west side of the Murphy Creek drainage. Look down to catch a glimpse of Tenaya Lake to the south. When the trail finally levels off at 6 miles, pause to enjoy views of Polly Dome on the left (east) and, to the northeast, the Grand Canyon of the Tuolumne.

The trail continues south, then gradually turns west, passing tiny Raisin Lake. At 7 miles, begin the final steep ascent as the trail switchbacks upward to the high point at about 7.5 miles. Another 0.25 mile brings you to the north end of May Lake. Continue 0.6 mile along the east shore to reach May Lake High Sierra Camp.

### DAY 3: MAY LAKE TO SUNRISE

>   **Distance:** 8.5 miles
>   **Elevation gain/loss:** 1200 feet/1920 feet
>   **Difficulty:** Moderate

*Striking panoramic view of Yosemite National Park along the High Sierra Loop*

**Hut elevation:** 9380 feet
**Hut GPS:** 37.7947°N, 119.4350°W

Return to the trail, and walk south 1.2 miles, descending to May Lake Trailhead. This trail ends at an asphalt spur road leading from Tioga Road. Turn left, then walk to the north end of the parking lot; pass through an iron gate onto the remnants of the Old Sierra Wagon Road, built for a short-lived mining operation. The trail descends to cross Tioga Road at 2.7 miles.

After crossing Tioga Road, the trail turns sharply left (northeast), paralleling the road for 0.6 mile to reach the trailhead for Clouds Rest and Sunrise Camp (as you walk along, ignore the "Trailhead Junction" sign at 3 miles). At 3.3 miles on the south end of Tenaya Lake, the busy trailhead offers toilets and bear-proof boxes but no potable water.

The trail departs the north end of the trailhead parking lot, heading east to cross a creek issuing from Tenaya Lake. Follow the fairly level trail east, passing the Tenaya Lake Loop on the left. Continue along Tenaya Creek, cross several streams, then at 5.1 miles, ascend the slope above Tenaya Canyon through a series of steep switchbacks. Enjoy the wildflowers on this steep 0.75-mile stretch; look back to catch views of Mount Hoffmann to the northwest.

This ascent ends with a trail junction in a forested saddle, where the trail to Sunrise continues left (east), passing the Clouds Rest Trail junction on the right (south). At the saddle, off the trail to the right of

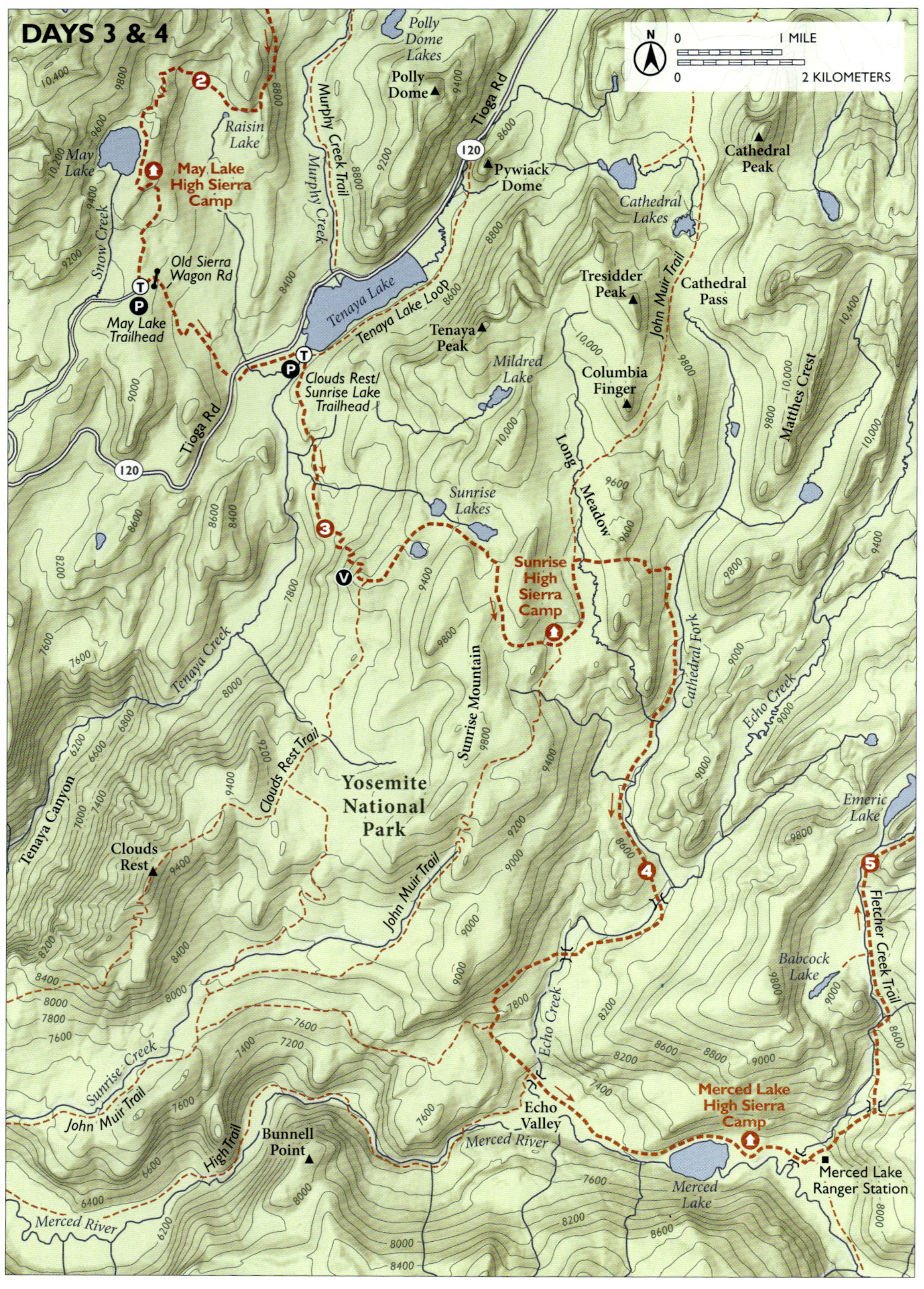
DAYS 3 & 4
N
1 MILE
2 KILOMETERS
Polly Dome Lakes
Polly Dome
Tioga Rd
120
Pywiack Dome
Cathedral Peak
Raisin Lake
Murphy Creek Trail
Murphy Creek
Cathedral Lakes
10,400
9800
8800
9200
8800
8600
9400
10,200
May Lake
May Lake High Sierra Camp
Snow Creek
9400
9200
Old Sierra Wagon Rd
May Lake Trailhead
Tenaya Lake
Tenaya Lake Loop
Tresidder Peak
Cathedral Pass
John Muir Trail
Matthes Crest
9800
10,400
10,000
9800
9800
Clouds Rest/ Sunrise Lake Trailhead
Tenaya Peak
Mildred Lake
Columbia Finger
Tioga Rd
120
8400
8600
8800
9000
8400
8200
Sunrise Lakes
Long Meadow
9600
9800
9400
Sunrise High Sierra Camp
Tenaya Creek
7800
8000
7600
7600
Sunrise Mountain
9800
9400
9200
9000
Cathedral Fork
9000
Echo Creek
9000
9800
9400
Emeric Lake
Tenaya Canyon
7000
6800
6600
6200
7400
9400
9200
9200
Clouds Rest Trail
Yosemite National Park
John Muir Trail
9000
9200
9000
4
8600
8400
Clouds Rest
8200
8400
8000
7800
7600
8000
7600
7400
7200
7600
9000
Echo Creek
8200
7800
7400
Babcock Lake
9000
8600
8800
5
Fletcher Creek Trail
8600
Sunrise Creek
John Muir Trail
High Trail
Bunnell Point
6600
8000
Echo Valley
Merced River
7600
Merced Lake High Sierra Camp
6400
6200
Merced River
8000
8400
8200
8600
Merced Lake
8000
Merced Lake Ranger Station
2
3
V
T
P
T
P

the junction, find a great place to rest with views of Clouds Rest and Half Dome. Back on the main trail, descend northeast to the first of the three Sunrise Lakes, great for swimming. Continue around the first lake, then continue uphill to pass the second lake, barely visible from the trail. Farther along, the trail swerves southeast, and you can spot the largest of these lakes through trees on the left. Continue uphill to a high point with views of the Clark Range to the south, then descend southward across a sandy hillside dotted with pines and hemlock damaged by fire and bark beetles.

The trail switchbacks steeply downhill, past the Sunrise backpackers camp, to the edge of the expansive Long Meadow. Turn left (north) to briefly join the John Muir Trail (JMT) and arrive at Sunrise High Sierra Camp, sheltered in the trees below a rocky outcropping.

## DAY 4: SUNRISE TO MERCED LAKE

**Distance:** 9.8 miles
**Elevation gain/loss:** 660 feet/2730 feet
**Difficulty:** Moderate
**Hut elevation:** 7244 feet
**Hut GPS:** 37.7395°N, 119.4062°W

Leave Sunrise High Sierra Camp for Long Meadow and follow the deeply rutted JMT north (left) along the west side of the open, grassy expanse. At 0.8 mile, turn right (east) at a junction, departing the PCT/JMT. Proceed east to the top of a forested ridge at 1.3 miles, then descend across an open, rocky slope into a valley formed by the Cathedral Fork of Echo Creek.

At 2.1 miles, the trail swings sharply right (south), going deeper into the valley and crossing tributaries to Cathedral Fork at 3.7 miles and 4.2 miles. Enjoy this flat, forested stretch of trail for a mile or so. Cross the bridge below the confluence of Cathedral Creek and Echo Creek at 5.4 miles. At 6.5 miles, cross a second bridge and begin your ascent up the west side of Echo Valley, hugging the base of cliffs as the creek flows far below.

At 7 miles, turn left (southeast), passing the junction on the right to the JMT. Continue 0.7 mile to the junction with the High Trail. The right fork leads to Happy Isles and Yosemite Valley. Take the left-hand choice to Merced Lake and descend southeast into the lush Echo Valley. The trail reaches the valley floor and the Merced River. At 8.3 miles, the trail follows the Merced River upstream. As you ascend, the river pools periodically across wide rocky slabs. Reach the river outlet and the west end of the lake at 9 miles.

Walk along the north shore of Merced Lake for 0.8 mile. About halfway along, a "No Camping" sign marks a forest clearing that is a great access point to the lake; come back for a swim after settling into camp! At the far end of the lake, a short spur trail leads to Merced Lake High Sierra Camp.

## DAY 5: MERCED LAKE TO VOGELSANG

**Distance:** 7.6 miles
**Elevation gain/loss:** 3190 feet/290 feet
**Difficulty:** Difficult
**Hut elevation:** 10,131 feet
**Hut GPS:** 37.7956°N, 119.3454°W

Today involves the greatest elevation gain and extraordinary views. From Merced

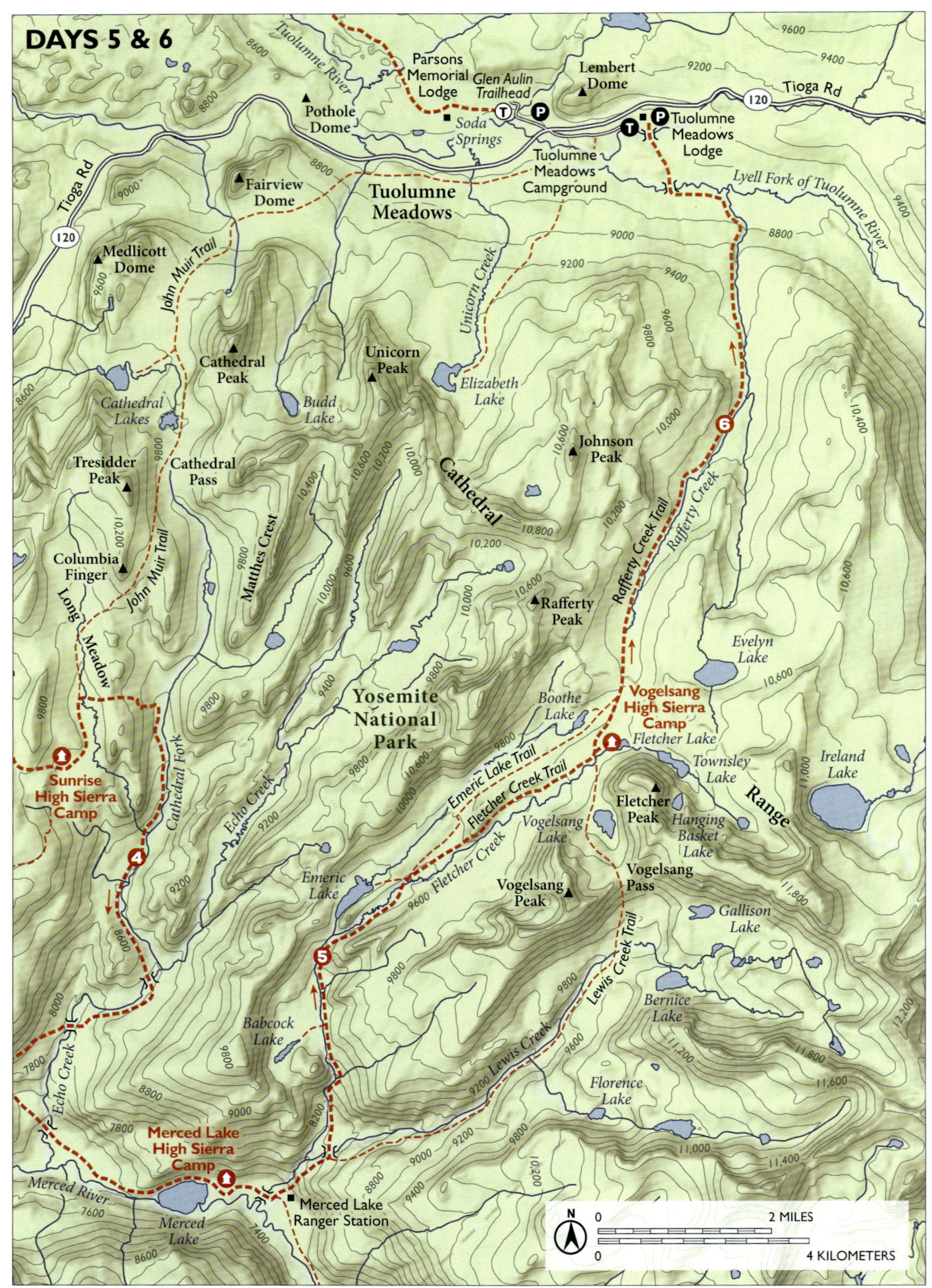
DAYS 5 & 6
Tioga Rd
120
Tuolumne River
Parsons Memorial Lodge
Glen Aulin Trailhead
Lembert Dome
Tioga Rd
120
Pothole Dome
Soda Springs
Tuolumne Meadows Lodge
Fairview Dome
Tuolumne Meadows
Tuolumne Meadows Campground
Lyell Fork of Tuolumne River
Tioga Rd
120
Medlicott Dome
John Muir Trail
Unicorn Creek
Cathedral Peak
Unicorn Peak
Elizabeth Lake
Cathedral Lakes
Budd Lake
Johnson Peak
6
Tresidder Peak
Cathedral Pass
Cathedral
Rafferty Creek Trail
Rafferty Creek
Columbia Finger
Matthes Crest
John Muir Trail
Rafferty Peak
Evelyn Lake
Long Meadow
Yosemite National Park
Boothe Lake
Vogelsang High Sierra Camp
Fletcher Lake
Townsley Lake
Ireland Lake
Cathedral Fork
Echo Creek
Emeric Lake Trail
Fletcher Creek Trail
Fletcher Peak
Hanging Basket Lake
Range
Sunrise High Sierra Camp
Vogelsang Lake
Vogelsang Pass
4
Emeric Lake
Fletcher Creek
Vogelsang Peak
Lewis Creek Trail
Gallison Lake
5
Babcock Lake
Lewis Creek
Bernice Lake
Florence Lake
Merced Lake High Sierra Camp
Echo Creek
Merced River
Merced Lake Ranger Station
Merced Lake
N
0          2 MILES
0          4 KILOMETERS

Lake High Sierra Camp, proceed east on a level trail through mature forest. After crossing three bridges in quick succession, at 1 mile you arrive at the Merced Lake Ranger Station. With a corral and wood stump benches around a fire pit, this 1927 building is worth a quick stop.

At the trail junction by the ranger station, turn left (north) toward Babcock Lake and Vogelsang High Sierra Camp, and begin a 2890-foot ascent over the next 3 miles. The stone-trail switchbacks lead relentlessly upward along tumbling Lewis Creek. Pause to rest and look back toward Merced Lake and up into the Fletcher Creek drainage. At 2 miles, the trail junction sign is a good place to pause and bask in views of Half Dome to the west. Bear left to follow the Fletcher Creek Trail. (Alternatively, bear right on the Lewis Creek Trail to Vogelsang High Sierra Camp. While arguably more scenic, this option is 0.7 mile longer and involves an additional elevation gain and loss of 600 feet.) The Fletcher Creek Trail descends to cross Lewis Creek on a footbridge, then ascends steadily north-northwest.

At 2.7 miles, where the trail nearly touches the creek, scramble off the route up to the broad stone streamed and watch water tumble downward against the backdrop of the Clark Range. As you continue along the trail and resume the steep uphill slog, distract yourself with the music from frolicking Fletcher Creek. Reach the top of the Fletcher Creek gorge at 3.75 miles and admire the panorama.

At 3.4 miles, continue past the turnoff to Babcock Lake on an easy uphill track; at 5.3 miles, enter a broad High Sierra meadow with Vogelsang Peak as the backdrop. The sandy trail traverses the meadow for a mile, passing trail junctions at 5.4 miles to Emeric Lake and to Boothe Lake. Bear right at this junction to continue northeast on the Fletcher Creek Trail. Passing under steep slopes and cliffs on the left, with Fletcher Creek cascading on the right, the trail continues 2.3 miles, passing under Vogelsang Peak to the east. Vogelsang High Sierra Camp is just under Fletcher Peak, rising in the southeast.

## DAY 6: VOGELSANG TO TUOLUMNE MEADOWS LODGE

**Distance:** 7.2 miles
**Elevation gain/loss:** 230 feet/1640 feet
**Difficulty:** Easy

This easy day starts at the signed junction in front of Vogelsang High Sierra Camp, where you begin a long descent on the Rafferty Creek Trail to Tuolumne Meadows Lodge. Head north, passing Boothe Lake on your left at 0.5 mile and then Tuolumne Pass at about 1 mile. The Rafferty Creek Trail continues gently downward and north through open, rocky meadows along the creek and through woods. At 5.25 miles, the descent steepens.

You reach a junction at 5.5 miles; turn left on the JMT/PCT and follow this flat trail as it parallels the Lyell Fork of Tuolumne River for about 0.7 mile. The trails then turns right toward Tuolumne Meadows Lodge, first crossing the Lyell Fork and then the Dana Fork of the river. As you walk the final 0.6 mile, reflect on your High Sierra Loop journey.

# RESURRECTION PASS TRAIL

*Nerve-shaken, over-civilized people are beginning to find out that … wilderness
is a necessity; and that the mountain parks and reservations are useful not only
as fountains of timber and irrigating rivers, but as fountains of life.*

—John Muir, *Our National Parks*

**Location:** Kenai Mountains, Chugach National Forest, near Hope and Cooper Landing, Alaska
**Distance:** Cabins 0.5 to 8 miles apart; full traverse 38.8 miles
**Elevation gain/loss:** 4960 feet/4900 feet
**Difficulty:** Easy to moderate
**Terrain:** Gradual ascent and descent through mixed Sitka spruce, birch, and alder forest;
along watersheds of Resurrection and Juneau Creeks; and across open tundra with expansive
mountain views
**Modes of travel:** Summer hiking and biking
**Season:** July to September
**Huts:** Eight cabins (average capacity 6), basic, exclusive use

---

**THE RESURRECTION PASS TRAIL,** set in moderate mountainous terrain, offers
great opportunities for summer hiking and biking cabin-to-cabin in one of Alaska's
prime recreational areas. About an hour south of Anchorage, the state's most pop-
ulous city, this north–south trail is between Hope, a tiny old mining town on the
Turnagain Arm of Cook Inlet, and Cooper Landing, a thriving resort area spread
along the Kenai River and Kenai Lake. Operated by the US Forest Service (USFS),
the 38.8-mile trail through a section of the country's second-largest national forest
is among the surprisingly few well-maintained multiday treks in this huge state.
Originally conceived for hikers, this route is now also very popular with mountain
bikers out for a vigorous one-day ride and for bikepackers who haul gear in panniers or with a bike trailer into the backcountry for longer stays.

The Resurrection Pass Trail is a satisfying choice for hikers and family groups aiming to immerse themselves in the Alaska backcountry without facing extreme challenges or requiring special equipment. Whether traveling north to south or south
to north, the path ascends gradually, leveling out for several miles before you arrive
at the sign marking Resurrection Pass. While the pass may indeed represent a high
point, the hike in the middle stretch is basically level as you cross from the headwaters of Resurrection Creek to the headwaters of Juneau Creek or from Juneau
to Resurrection Creek. The southern section of the trail, paralleling Juneau Creek,
boasts several mountain lakes and is very popular in summer. With eight cabins

*Juneau Lake at dusk on the Resurrection Pass Trail*

dotted over 38.8 miles, this trail can support various itineraries from quick and strenuous to long and leisurely. We recommend taking your time on the trail and enjoying one or two rest days for day hikes and fishing, swimming, or canoeing.

The limiting factor is availability of cabins, so book early to customize your route. The table below, which provides daily and cumulative mileage between all cabins in both directions, will help you determine an appropriate sequence of cabins.

The trail courses through a pleasantly varied landscape. Trekkers will enjoy thick spruce-birch forest, riotous wildflowers, bustling creeks, stretches of open tundra flanked by mountain peaks, lakes ripe for fishing, and one spectacular waterfall. There's also great blueberry picking here in season! Hikers may encounter any of the typical Alaskan critters including Dall sheep, mountain goats, marmots, beaver, brown and black bears, elk, and birds. Several cabin logbooks recount tales of resident porcupines who entertain guests with regular appearances from under the cabin or outhouse. Plump spruce grouse may wander across your path. The area is also the site of Alaska's first gold rush. Shortly before the more famous 1897 Klondike strike, news of gold discoveries on Resurrection Creek and its tributaries brought thousands to seek their fortunes in this pristine wilderness.

The Resurrection Pass Trail and its cabins are very popular. This is not to say that the trail itself is crowded. Rather, the challenge is to reserve cabins in sequence for

# DISTANCE BETWEEN CABINS IN SUMMER

| NORTH TO SOUTH | | | SOUTH TO NORTH | | |
|---|---|---|---|---|---|
| DAILY MILES | | CUMULATIVE MILES | DAILY MILES | | CUMULATIVE MILES |
| 0 | North Trailhead | 0 | 0 | South Trailhead | 0 |
| 7.1 | Caribou Creek Cabin | 7.1 | 7.9 | Trout Lake Cabin | 7.9 |
| 4.6 | Fox Creek Cabin | 11.7 | 2.2 | Romig Cabin | 9.6 |
| 2.8 | East Creek Cabin | 14.5 | 0.5 | Juneau Lake Cabin | 10.1 |
| 7 | Devil's Pass Cabin | 21.5 | 3.2 | Swan Lake Cabin | 13.3 |
| 4 | Swan Lake Cabin | 25.5 | 4 | Devil's Pass Cabin | 17.3 |
| 3.2 | Juneau Lake Cabin | 28.7 | 7 | East Creek Cabin | 24.3 |
| 0.5 | Romig Cabin | 29.2 | 2.8 | Fox Creek Cabin | 27.1 |
| 1.7 | Trout Lake Cabin | 30.9 | 4.6 | Caribou Creek Cabin | 31.7 |
| 7.9 | South Trailhead | 38.8 | 7.1 | North Trailhead | 38.8 |

an appealing multiday adventure. Prospective users should begin their online booking session armed with knowledge of the eight cabins along the route, distances, and several possible itineraries and with some flexibility in relation to dates. Cabins can be reserved six months in advance; each cabin must be booked separately.

In winter, the trail is open for skiers and snowshoers and—on alternate years—snowmobile users. Skiing the entire traverse is not recommended. The southern end of the trail is more popular in winter and relatively safe if you stay on the hiking trail. Travel from Seward Highway up the Devil's Creek Trail is not recommended due to avalanche hazard.

## HUTS AND AMENITIES

Simple, well-built cabins, with welcoming front porches, provide shelter from weather and insects. Originally built in the 1960s, all eight have been renovated, built, or rebuilt in a style known as Pan Abode, common throughout Alaska. Without many amenities, these are effectively wooden tents and require hikers to carry everything they need. Interiors are a single room organized with counter space for cooking and food preparation, a picnic table and benches for dining and relaxation, and bunk bed platforms for sleeping—double on the bottom and single on top. A woodstove is positioned near the entrance, and expansive windows bring the outside in.

Even though these structures are very basic, clever carpentry details show that they were built with care. With most measuring 12 by 14 feet, and the larger huts at 16 by 16 or 14 by 17 feet, the cabins sleep six comfortably but can accommodate up to eight. Water is available from nearby streams or lakes. Take care to treat water

*Enjoy excellent views of Juneau Lake from the cabin named for it.*

before drinking. Each cabin is accompanied by a large woodshed with saws and a maul. Visitors are expected to "prospect" for dead and downed wood in the nearby forest, and to replenish the fuel supply for the next users. Outside firepits are available. The lakeside cabins offer either a rowboat or canoe with paddles, inviting visitors to stay an extra day or two to fish and swim.

## CARIBOU CREEK CABIN

Set in a clearing by the creek, this homey cabin (941 feet) offers nice woodworking details.

## FOX CREEK CABIN

Perched on a hillside in the woods facing an overgrown meadow, this cabin occupies the site of a long-ago mining camp. Approach by a short spur trail.

## EAST CREEK CABIN

This comfortable cabin (1752 feet) is a short walk to the creekside for water or footbaths.

## DEVIL'S PASS CABIN

At the intersection of the Devil's Creek Trail and the Resurrection Pass Trail, this cabin sits on alpine slopes. Since there is no firewood in the vicinity, the cabin is heated with an oil-burning stove. During chilly months, bring fuel oil or kerosene as recommended on the cabin website.

## SWAN LAKE CABIN

The lakeside setting of this cabin (1473 feet), the oldest along the traverse, feels very private. Anglers enjoy fishing for rainbow trout, lake trout, Dolly Vardens, and sockeye salmon. Swan Lake Cabin, located on

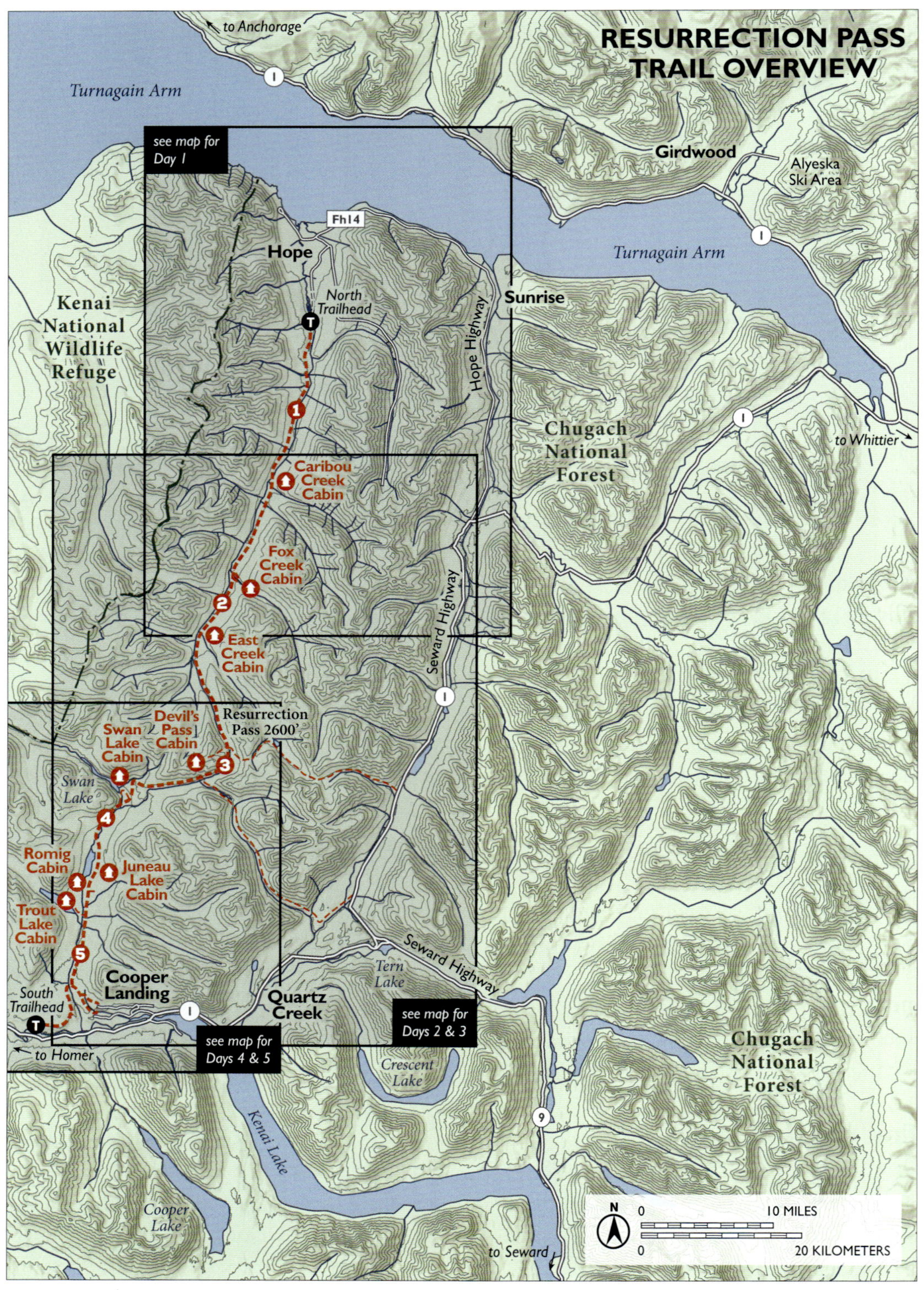
RESURRECTION PASS
TRAIL OVERVIEW
to Anchorage
Turnagain Arm
Girdwood
Alyeska Ski Area
Fh14
Hope
Turnagain Arm
North Trailhead
T
Sunrise
Hope Highway
Kenai National Wildlife Refuge
1
Chugach National Forest
to Whittier
Caribou Creek Cabin
Fox Creek Cabin
2
East Creek Cabin
Seward Highway
Devil's Pass Cabin
Swan Lake Cabin
Resurrection Pass 2600'
3
Swan Lake
4
Romig Cabin
Juneau Lake Cabin
Trout Lake Cabin
5
Seward Highway
Tern Lake
Cooper Landing
South Trailhead
T
I
Quartz Creek
see map for Days 2 & 3
Chugach National Forest
to Homer
see map for Days 4 & 5
Crescent Lake
Kenai Lake
9
Cooper Lake
N
0
10 MILES
0
20 KILOMETERS
to Seward
see map for Day 1

*Looking out over sweeping alpine slopes from Devil's Pass Cabin southwest of Resurrection Pass*

the southeast corner of the lake, is accessible only by floatplane.

## JUNEAU LAKE CABIN

After a steep climb up to this 14-by-17-foot cabin at 1300 feet elevation, enjoy great views of the lake, which is full of rainbow trout, whitefish, burbot, and grayling.

## ROMIG CABIN

This wheelchair-accessible cabin (1265 feet) is close to the shore of Juneau Lake, which is very shallow here. Enjoy watching the mountains reflected on the still water as the light changes.

## TROUT LAKE CABIN

This two-story cabin has a sleeping loft. Down from the front porch, you will find a small dock and gravel beach complete with a boat to simply paddle or to fish for rainbow trout and whitefish.



**Contact:** www.alaska.org/detail/resurrection-pass-trail; (907) 288-3178; Chugach National Forest maintains separate web pages for each of the two districts; visit www.fs.usda.gov/chugach and then look under recreation, hiking, and then backpacking for descriptions of Resurrection Pass Trail

**Booking:** Reservations are required and may be made up to 180 days in advance at www.recreation.gov or by calling (877) 444-6777; each cabin must be reserved separately; to maximize the choice of cabins, book well in advance

**Membership:** None

**Rates:** $

**Transportation:** There is limited public transportation from Anchorage to this area; the Anchorage-to-Homer bus will stop at Wildman's convenience store near Cooper Landing upon request; Wildman's provides a shuttle from the store a short distance to the South

Trailhead; most travelers get to the trail by personal vehicle; use two cars, leaving one at each trailhead, or use a single vehicle and contract with Wildman's to shuttle the car to the end point; learn more at www.wildmans.org/offsite/shuttles

## MAPS

Legible topo maps of the north and south districts downloaded and printed from Alaska.org are adequate. USGS topo maps of Seward B-8, C-8, and D-8 cover the trail at 1:63,360. Seward C-7 covers the side trails mentioned below.

## PACKING TIPS

Bring toilet paper, a stove, fuel, cooking and eating utensils, food, a sleeping pad, a sleeping bag, and a water treatment system.

## OTHER TIPS

Check the Alaska.org and Chugach NF websites for alerts and warnings, such as fire closures and weather events. Wild parsnip (*Pastinaca sativa*) can cause a rash or blisters (no poison ivy or oak in Alaska). Dogs are allowed but must be kept on a leash to protect marmots on the pass. Bring bear spray and follow bear safety guidelines.

## ITINERARY: HOPE TO COOPER LANDING

*38.8 miles, five days, four nights*

In summer, this is an easy to moderate hike on a very well-maintained trail. The track is wide and well graded but can be muddy in spots, and occasionally plants encroach on the pathway. Hikers may ignore the infrequent orange-diamond trail markers; these are primarily placed for winter use when the track takes a slightly different route. Heading out from the North Trailhead at 387 feet, the trail follows Resurrection Creek toward its headwaters, eventually rising to 2600 feet. Resurrection Pass itself, marked with a sign and a stack of stones, falls in the middle of a long stretch of open tundra above tree line, flanked by Kenai Mountain peaks. Enjoy views of wetlands in this high country as you pass the headwaters of Resurrection Creek and then Juneau Creek.

The trail begins a long, gradual descent after Devil's Pass Cabin, which is situated close to the trail's halfway point. This itinerary includes a second night at Devil's Pass Cabin for day hikes on day 3. (You might choose instead, or in addition, to stay an extra night at one or more of the lake cabins.) The trail then follows the Juneau Creek drainage to end at the South Trailhead, elevation 466 feet. Three trails intersect with the Resurrection Pass Trail: the Summit Creek Trail, the Devil's Creek Trail, and the Bean Creek Trail are all well signed.

## DAY 1: NORTH TRAILHEAD TO FOX CREEK CABIN

**Distance:** 11.7 miles
**Elevation gain/loss:** 1940 feet/750 feet
**Difficulty:** Easy
**Hut elevation:** 1618 feet
**Hut GPS:** 60.7299°N, 149.7094°W
**Trailhead:** North Trailhead 60.8673°N, 149.6057°W

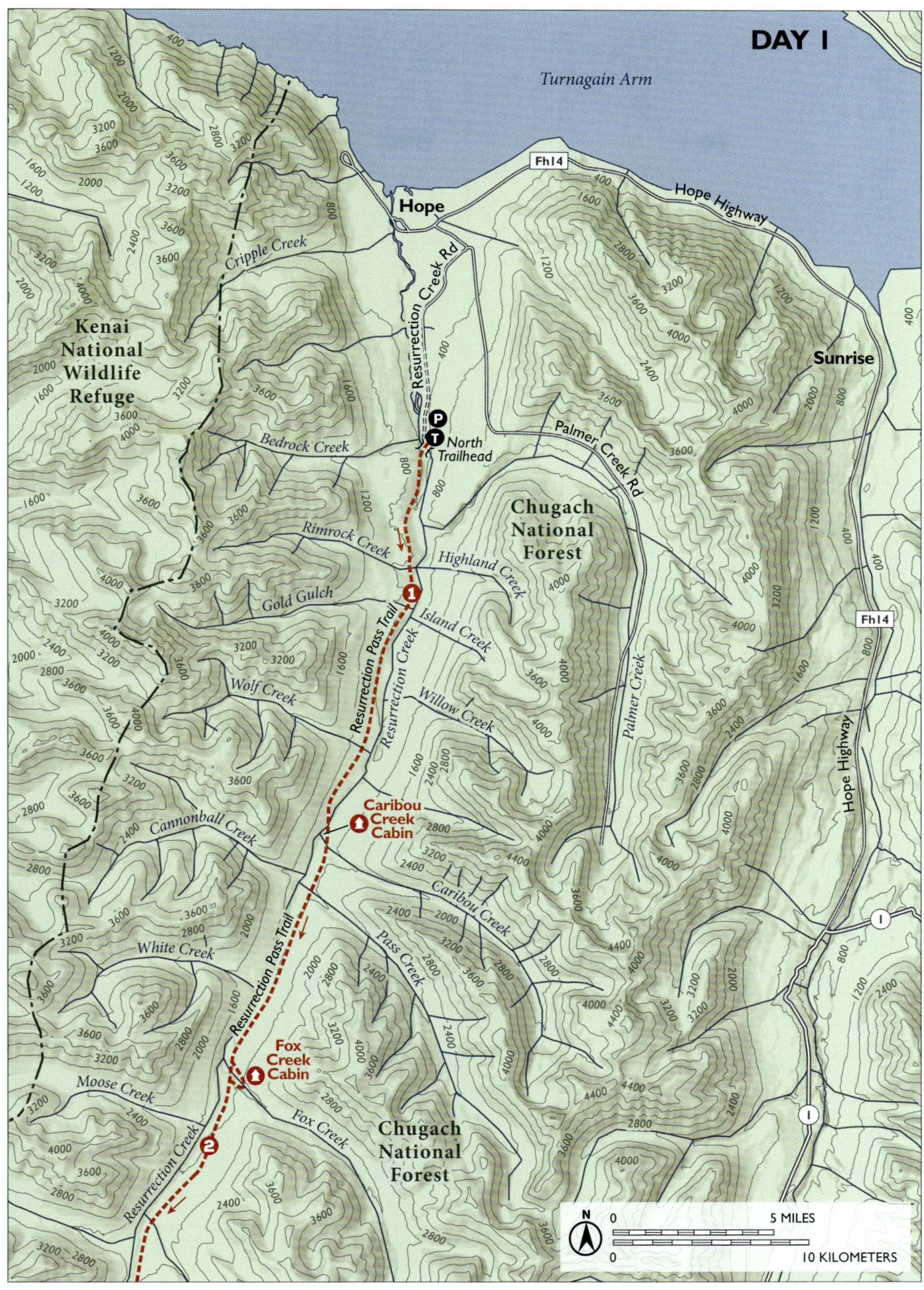

DAY 1
Turnagain Arm
Fh14
Hope
Hope Highway
Resurrection Creek Rd
Sunrise
Cripple Creek
Kenai National Wildlife Refuge
Bedrock Creek
Palmer Creek Rd
North Trailhead
P
T
Chugach National Forest
Rimrock Creek
Highland Creek
Fh14
Gold Gulch
Island Creek
Resurrection Pass Trail
Resurrection Creek
Wolf Creek
Willow Creek
Palmer Creek
Hope Highway
Cannonball Creek
Caribou Creek Cabin
Caribou Creek
White Creek
Pass Creek
Resurrection Pass Trail
1
Moose Creek
Fox Creek Cabin
Fox Creek
Chugach National Forest
Resurrection Creek
2
N
0        5 MILES
0        10 KILOMETERS

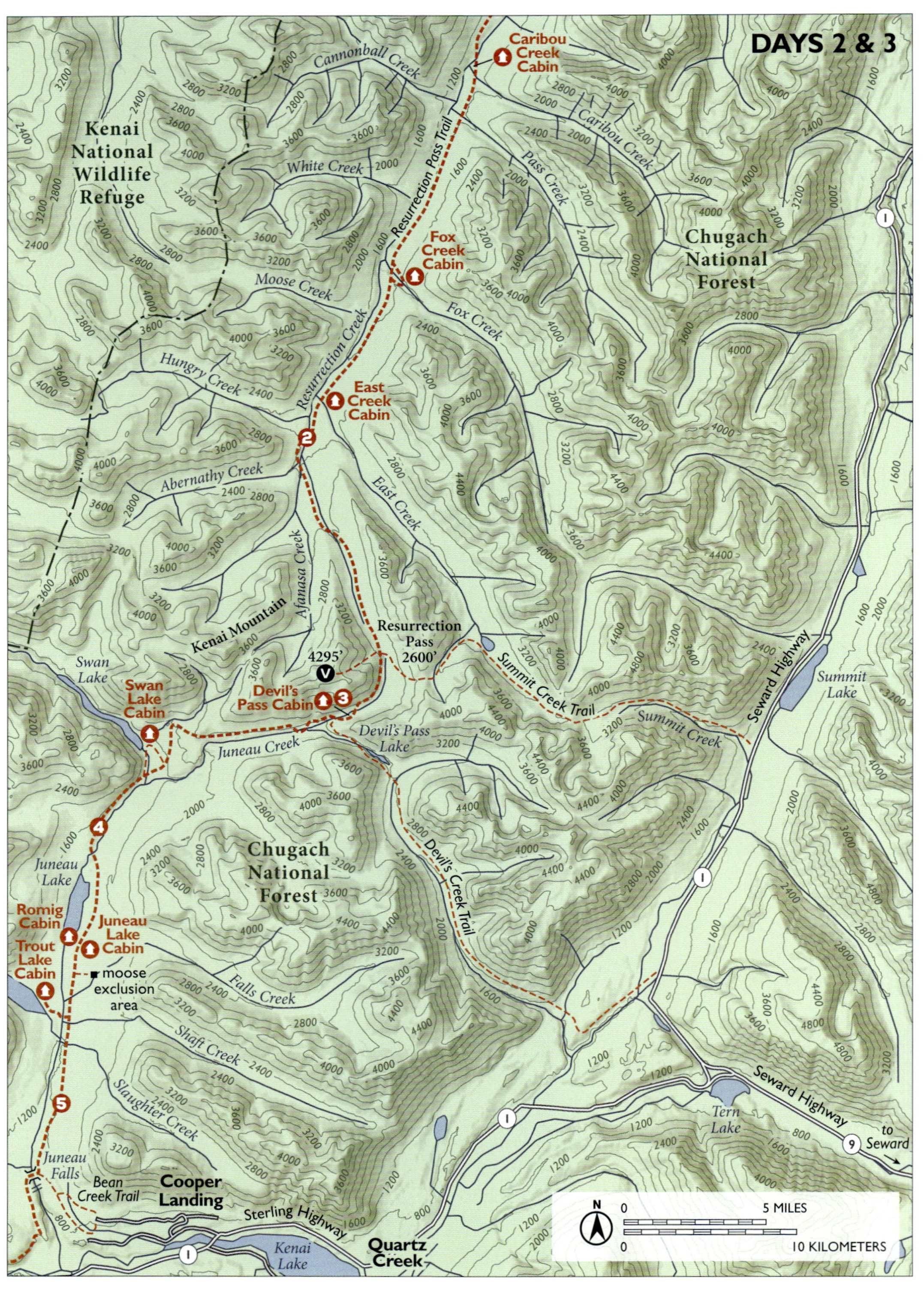

DAYS 2 & 3
Caribou Creek Cabin
Cannonball Creek
Kenai National Wildlife Refuge
White Creek
Caribou Creek
Pass Creek
Chugach National Forest
Resurrection Pass Trail
Fox Creek Cabin
Fox Creek
Moose Creek
Resurrection Creek
Hungry Creek
East Creek Cabin
2
East Creek
Abernathy Creek
Afanasa Creek
Kenai Mountain
4295'
Resurrection Pass 2600'
Summit Creek Trail
Summit Creek
Seward Highway
Summit Lake
Swan Lake
Swan Lake Cabin
Devil's Pass Cabin
3
Devil's Pass Lake
Juneau Creek
Devil's Creek Trail
4
Chugach National Forest
Juneau Lake
Romig Cabin
Juneau Lake Cabin
Trout Lake Cabin
moose exclusion area
Falls Creek
Shaft Creek
5
Slaughter Creek
Seward Highway
Tern Lake
to Seward
9
Juneau Falls
Bean Creek Trail
Cooper Landing
Sterling Highway
Quartz Creek
Kenai Lake
N
0          5 MILES
0          10 KILOMETERS

## Getting There

From Hope, travel east on Hope Highway (Forest Highway 14). After 1.5 miles, turn right (south) onto Resurrection Creek Road and drive 4 miles to the trailhead, which has parking and an outhouse.

## On the Trail

After signing the trail log, cross Resurrection Creek on the footbridge at the northwest corner of the parking lot and follow the wide trail south. Along the way, note signs of restoration work to the creek channel to repair damage from gold mining. The trail runs on the west side of Resurrection Creek; footbridges cross several smaller creeks.

The trail crosses to the east side of Resurrection Creek at 6.5 miles. A footbridge over Caribou Creek at 6.8 miles signals your approach to Caribou Creek Cabin on the right at 7.1 miles. Pass the cabin turnoff and continue another 4.9 miles to the Fox Creek Cabin sign. The 0.2-mile access trail is on the left and winds through trees and an overgrown meadow immediately below the cabin.

## DAY 2: FOX CREEK CABIN TO DEVIL'S PASS CABIN

> **Distance:** 9.8 miles
> **Elevation gain/loss:** 1740 feet/890 feet
> **Difficulty:** Easy
> **Hut elevation:** 2400 feet
> **Hut GPS:** 60.6216°N, 149.7524°W

Return to Resurrection Creek Trail via the cabin access spur, turn left, and continue south, passing the access trail to East Creek Cabin after 3 miles. Climbing steadily, cross back to the west side of Resurrection Creek at 5 miles. The trail levels out for the next 5 miles as you walk through the long, gentle Resurrection Pass. Across this tundra plateau, vegetation changes from thick forest to low shrubs and mosses, lichen, and alpine flowers. The mountains on both sides are covered in patches of white-green reindeer moss and brilliant pink swatches of fireweed. Resurrection Creek narrows and pools in small ponds below the trail.

At about 8 miles, a wooden sign indicates Resurrection Pass at 2600 feet. The Summit Creek Trail branches off here eastward. Continue south on the Resurrection Pass Trail for another 1.8 miles to reach the well-marked, right-hand turnoff to Devil's Pass Cabin, visible from the trail above Juneau Creek. The Devil's Creek Trail (sometimes called the Devil's Pass Trail) joins the Resurrection Pass Trail here from the southeast.

## DAY 3: REST DAY AT DEVIL'S PASS

Here are three hiking options for your rest day at Devil's Pass Cabin.

Hike the Devil's Creek Trail 1.7 miles to pretty Devil's Pass Lake. After the lake, this trail descends steeply for another 8.3 miles to Seward Highway/State Route 1 through a spectacular V-shaped valley; while the entire distance is too far for a day hike, you might wish to taste this terrain by continuing beyond the lake before turning back.

Sample the Summit Creek Trail. Return to the Resurrection Pass sign on the Resurrection Pass Trail and then hike 1.5 to 2 miles between low mountains to a series of saddles. If you are lucky, glimpse the elusive caribou herd in the area.

For stunning 360-degree views, including the Harding Icefield to the southeast and Denali and the Alaska Range to the north, climb the ridge west of Resurrection Pass. From the cabin, return to the Resurrection Pass sign on the Resurrection Pass Trail. Then depart the trail and head upward and west to the ridge 1700 feet above. Adventurers can reach this 4295-foot-high viewpoint in less than a mile with a steep uphill, off-trail scramble.

### DAY 4: DEVIL'S PASS CABIN TO TROUT LAKE CABIN

**Distance:** 9.4 miles
**Elevation gain/loss:** 640 feet/ 1790 feet
**Difficulty:** Moderate
**Hut elevation:** 1274 feet

**Hut GPS:** 60.5512°N, 149.8953°W
Return to the Resurrection Pass Trail and turn right (west), crossing Juneau Creek several times. After 3 miles, the trail swings left (south) and zigzags steeply downhill through lush, head-high meadows and offers simultaneous distant views of Swan and Juneau Lakes. The trail passes the north access trail to Swan Lake Cabin at 3.7 miles, then continues west, passing the south access trail to Swan Lake Cabin at 4.3 miles. Continue southwest for another 2.5 miles to reach the north end of Juneau Lake.

The trail skirts the eastern shore of Juneau Lake, passing below Juneau Lake Cabin perched on the hillside and soon passing Romig Cabin at 7.9 miles. About 0.3 mile after Romig Cabin, opt to take a quick detour on the left. The fenced moose exclusion area shows the difference between landscapes browsed by and protected from moose. The trail continues on a level course through wetlands from Juneau Lake to the Trout Lake Cabin access trail at 9.4 miles from Devil's Pass Cabin. Turn right (west) to follow the access trail 0.5 mile to the cabin, beautifully situated on the southeast end of Trout Lake.

## DAY 5: TROUT LAKE CABIN TO SOUTH TRAILHEAD

   **Distance:** 7.9 miles
   **Elevation gain/loss:** 650 feet/1470 feet
   **Difficulty:** Easy
   **Trailhead:** South Trailhead (60.4845°N, 149.9534°W

Return to the Resurrection Pass Trail and turn right (south), following the wide trail through open woods. At 2.7 miles, stay on the Resurrection Pass Trail when it jogs right (west), following signs to Sterling Highway and Juneau Falls. This is where the signed Bean Creek Trail comes in from the south. The trail soon crosses Juneau Creek on a footbridge, then jogs left (south), following the west side of Juneau Creek.

At about 4 miles, well before the trail veers right (southwest) to parallel Sterling Highway, the traffic noise announces your return from the backcountry. At 4.3 miles, the spectacular Juneau Falls lookout offers a great rest stop. The trail continues high above Juneau Creek, which cuts a deep gorge below. The South Trailhead, with an outhouse, is a few miles west of the resort town of Cooper Landing on Highway 1.

*Mom biking with baby in tow toward Trout Lake*

# BONUS HUT OPPORTUNITIES

**THERE ARE THOUSANDS OF CABINS,** yurts, huts, fire towers, and other amazing front- and backcountry accommodations scattered across the US. Thus far, we have covered backcountry accommodations that form hut-to-hut traverses. But we also wish to share a sampling of other delightful lodging opportunities, including hut systems requiring advanced mountaineering skills, additional hut systems, and a selection of cabins, lodges, and yurts—mostly one-offs but some in clusters—that will appeal to outdoor-loving readers. Organized by categories that highlight origins and operators, the following lists indirectly reveal the organizations, institutions, and individuals that shape this sector. Listings, which are selective rather than exhaustive, are annotated with enough information to jumpstart trip planning. Amenities levels are indicated for backcountry accommodations only.

## HUT SYSTEMS REQUIRING ADVANCED SKILLS

Experienced skiers with avalanche training and skilled mountaineers can enjoy thrilling high mountain ridges, demanding glacier crossings, and very remote landscapes in hut-to-hut journeys in Alaska and Colorado. These systems, recommended only for those with advanced skills, are not suited for folks with mere above-average fitness, but many readers will be ready for these challenges. In Alaska, mountaineering clubs have organized life-saving shelters for adventurous members since the 1960s. The Bomber Traverse, offering the most huts, is

OPPOSITE: *Mint Hut, run by the Mountaineering Club of Alaska, is the first and most accessible hut along the Bomber Traverse in the Talkeetna Mountains.*

# MORE HUT-TO-HUT TRAVERSES

| | STATE | HUTS | BEDS | AMENITIES |
|---|---|---|---|---|
| Bomber Traverse | AK | 5 | 40 | B |
| Delta Range mountaineering huts | AK | 3 | 14 | B |
| Eklutna Traverse | AK | 4 | 40 | B |
| Nancy Lake State Recreation Area | AK | 6 | 36 | B |
| White Mountains National Recreation Area | AK | 10 | 52 | B |
| Sierra Club Donner Pass area huts | CA | 4 | 63 | B |
| Haleakala National Park | HI | 3 | 36 | SS |
| Idaho State University Portneuf Range Yurt System | ID | 4 | 22 | SS |
| AMC Maine Wilderness Lodges | ME | 3 | 197 | FS (winter only) |
| Vermont Huts Association | VT | 4 | 28 | B and SS |

Note: For amenities, B = basic; SS = self-service; FS = full service

the closest of three Alaska mountaineering systems to population centers. The Eklutna Traverse and Delta Range huts are very small, basic refuges located amid glaciers and rugged mountain terrain. Colorado's Alfred A. Braun Hut System is made up of exclusive-use hostelries in steep ski mountaineering terrain with recurring avalanche cycles and unmarked routes.

## ALASKA

**Bomber Traverse.** This traverse, which attracts trekkers in both summer and winter, crosses glaciers and avalanche terrain. Huts in the vicinity of Bomber and Penny Royal Glaciers, affiliated with the Mountaineering Club of Alaska and the American Alpine Club, include Snowbird (sleeps twelve), Bomber (sleeps seven to nine), Mint (sleeps four), Dnigi (sleeps six to eight), and the new Seth Holden Hut (sleeps eight

to ten). Visitors must belong to one of the two clubs to stay in the huts. Utilizing multiple trailheads in the Hatcher Pass region of the Talkeetna Mountains, several two-to-four-night routes—only partially marked—traverse the Hatcher Pass area. Huts are rented by the bunk.

**Delta Range mountaineering huts.** The Alaska Alpine Club has provided shelters for visitors (membership required) to this remote area encompassing Castner Glacier northeast of Wrangell–St. Elias National Park and Preserve. Several routes lead to Thayer Hut, Lower Canwell Hut, and MacKeith Hut, three small huts (capacity for four to five people, all rented by the bunk) that can be strung together for a multiday traverse.

**Eklutna Traverse.** This 38-mile, four-night traverse crosses four glaciers and ventures

| RESERVATION FORMAT | | MODES OF TRAVEL | | | | | DIFFICULTY |
| EXCLUSIVE USE | BY THE BUNK | HIKE | FAT BIKE | SKI | SNOWSHOE | PADDLE | |
| --- | --- | --- | --- | --- | --- | --- | --- |
|  | ✓ | ✓ |  | ✓ |  |  | Difficult, advanced |
|  | ✓ | ✓ |  | ✓ |  |  | Difficult, advanced |
|  | ✓ | ✓ |  | ✓ |  |  | Difficult, advanced |
| ✓ |  |  | ✓ | ✓ | ✓ | ✓ | Novice |
| ✓ |  |  | ✓ | ✓ |  |  | Intermediate |
| ✓ | ✓ | ✓ |  | ✓ |  |  | Easy, intermediate |
| ✓ |  | ✓ |  |  |  |  | Moderate |
| ✓ |  |  |  | ✓ | ✓ |  | Intermediate |
| ✓ | ✓ | ✓ |  | ✓ |  |  | Easy, novice |
| ✓ |  | ✓ |  | ✓ | ✓ |  | Novice to intermediate |

through avalanche terrain in Chugach State Park. Four huts, all rented by the bunk, stand ready to shelter visitors: Serenity Falls Cabin (sleeps thirteen), Pichler's Perch (sleeps eight to ten), Han's Hut (sleeps eight to ten), and Rosie's Roost (sleeps eight to ten). Three of the huts are maintained by the Mountaineering Club of Alaska and one by the Alaska Department of Natural Resources.

## COLORADO

**Alfred A. Braun Hut System.** The oldest US backcountry ski hut system, affiliated with the Tenth Mountain Division Hut System, extends south of Aspen across Pearl Pass between Ashcroft and Crested Butte. These eight huts (seven in the Braun system, plus the allied Friends Hut) offer multiday hut-to-hut opportunities across steep, snowy terrain mostly above tree line in the White River National Forest. Navigation skills are critical for finding the huts, which are about 5 miles apart via unmarked, unmaintained trails. The self-service huts (capacity seven to fourteen; available for exclusive rental by groups of at least four people) are open in winter only.

## MORE HUT SYSTEMS

This section includes additional opportunities for the hut-to-hut enthusiast. Included are systems that don't quite fit the definition used for the sixteen featured systems. There may be fewer huts than specified by our definition of a system, or the system may have multiple cabins or yurts that could be, but almost never are, strung together for a multiday hut-to-hut excursion.

This section also presents a few systems that we missed but want to honor in the book. The Appalachian Mountain Club's Maine lodge-to-lodge ski program came to

*Almost 250 miles of trails connect twelve cozy backcountry cabins in the million-acre White Mountains National Recreation Area north of Fairbanks, Alaska. (Photo by Madi McConnell)*

our attention too late in the research process. We did not get to experience Alaska's public use cabins in the Nancy Lake State Recreation Area or the White Mountains National Recreation Area. This section highlights some systems, including the Vermont Huts Association, that were not yet open as we concluded our research; the Alaska Huts Association's Glacier Discovery Project is still in the dreaming and planning phase.

## ALASKA

**Alaska Huts Association.** The Glacier Discovery Project is an ambitious plan to create a three-hut system in the Kenai Mountains over the next decade. In partnership with the Alaska Railroad and the Chugach National Forest, the Alaska Huts Association (AHA) is working toward building a single hut at Spencer Glacier, a railroad whistle stop, and once the 30-mile Glacier Discovery Trail is finished, two additional lodgings at Bartlett and Trail Glaciers. This future hut system will cater to hikers, skiers, and bikers and will offer a higher level of amenities than most very basic US Forest Service backcountry cabins in the state. Currently, the AHA offers lodging year-round at Manitoba Cabin and two yurts in the Chugach National Forest location on the Kenai Peninsula. These huts are self-service and either by the bunk or exclusive use.

**Nancy Lake State Recreation Area.** This lake-studded recreation area, a summer favorite with paddlers, is also open for winter adventures including a hut-to-hut traverse on skis, snowshoes, or ice blades. The flat, forested landscape across frozen lakes and wetlands (elevation ranges from 120 to 375 feet) in the Matanuska-Susitna Valley near Willow is perfect for a relaxing winter getaway. Among the thirteen rustic cabins (capacity four to six, basic, exclusive use), several can be strung together for a hut-to-hut trip with 3 to 6 miles between venues. Of 40 miles of maintained trails, 10 miles are for nonmotorized travel.

A 13-mile hut-to-hut ski option runs from the trailhead to Rhein Lake Cabin, Lynx Lake Cabins, Bald Lake Cabin, and to a trailhead.

**Pinnell Mountain National Recreational Trail.** Ptarmigan Creek Shelter Cabin and North Fork Shelter Cabin—two small, enclosed backcountry shelters without bunks or other amenities—are found along this 27.3-mile ridgeline route in the Steese National Conservation Area. Designated as a National Recreational Trail in 1971, this is one of the few primitive maintained trails in the Alaska interior north of Fairbanks (off the Steese Highway).

**White Mountains National Recreation Area.** Twelve backcountry cabins and almost 250 miles of maintained trails draw recreationists to this million-acre national recreation area north of Fairbanks, featuring rolling terrain and jagged limestone features, with elevations between about 2000 and 4000 feet. Because of the remote location and distances between cabins (9 to 17 miles), the area is best suited to experienced backcountry winter travelers. Skiers and fat-tire bikers share trails with dogsleds, skijorers, and snowmobiles. Basic, exclusive-use cabins sleep four to six. Hut-to-hut ski options include Colorado Creek Loop (76

miles): Trailhead to Colorado Creek Cabin, Wolf Run, Windy Gap, Caribou Bluff, Colorado Creek, trailhead; and Wickersham Dome Loop (40 miles): Trailhead to Lee's, Eleazar's, Moose Creek, trailhead.

## CALIFORNIA

**Sierra Club Donner Pass area huts.** Four rustic huts, dating from the 1930s to the 1950s, above Clair Tappaan Lodge (accessible by road; open year-round) have welcomed hikers and skiers for decades. Benson, Peter Grubb, and Ludlow are open year-round; Bradley is closed in summer. Reservations (basic, by the bunk, and exclusive use) can be made by phone only.

Hut-to-hut ski option (huts 4.5 to 5 miles apart, full traverse 14 miles; three days, two nights): Donner Pass to Benson to Bradley to trailhead at State Route 89 near Squaw Valley.

## HAWAII

**Haleakala National Park, Maui.** Three backcountry cabins (capacity twelve) are located in the Summit section of the national park. The cabins—built by the Civilian Conservation Corps in 1937 in the rustic National Park Service style—can be hiked in a multiday sequence any time of year with a permit from the National Park Service. They are self-service and exclusive use.

Hut-to-hut option (full traverse 19 miles; four days, three nights): Keonehe'ehe'e (Sliding Sands) Trailhead to the Kapalaoa cabin (5.6 miles); Kapalaoa cabin to Palikū cabin (3.3 miles); Palikū cabin to Hōlua cabin (6.3 miles); Hōlua cabin to the Halemau'u Trailhead (3.7 miles).

## IDAHO

**Idaho State University Portneuf Range Yurt System.** Four yurts (capacity five to six) are operated by the university's Outdoor Adventure Center in winter in the Caribou-Targhee National Forest. Established in 1983 with wall tents, this self-service, exclusive-use system is among the earliest backcountry hut-to-hut ski routes in the country.

Hut-to-hut ski options require the use of the Pebble Creek Ski Area lift to begin and a shuttle vehicle. Trails are not consistently marked, so navigation skills are essential. One option is the Pebble Creek Ski Area to Jackson Creek Yurt to Skyline Yurt and out for a 5.6-mile traverse including a 3840-foot descent. Another is the Pebble Creek Ski Area to Jackson Creek Yurt to Inman Yurt and out for an approximately 11.4-mile traverse with the longest section at 5.3 miles.

## MAINE

**Appalachian Mountain Club Maine Wilderness Lodges.** Three lodges in the AMC Recreation and Conservation Area—Medawisla Lodge and Cabins, Little Lyford Lodge and Cabins, and Gorman Chairback Lodge and Cabins—each comprise multiple buildings, including dorm-style bunk rooms and single-use cabins. The 32 miles of trails in the 100-Mile Wilderness (not a federally designated wilderness), southwest of Baxter State Park, are groomed but not tracked.

The club's lodge-to-lodge ski program incorporates the three lodges and the private West Branch Pond Camps into several itineraries with daily distances between 6 and 9 miles. Baggage transfer and car shuttles are available.

## VERMONT

**Vermont Huts Association.** This young organization, founded in 2016, is working with other organizations and private landowners to stitch together a four-season hut system across the Green Mountain State, which is home to several long-distance walking routes including the Catamount Trail, the Appalachian Trail, and the Long Trail. For a hut-to-hut ski option, consider Camel's Hump to Bolton Valley (20 to 25 miles). This four-hut traverse passes through gentle rolling terrain with a long, gradual uphill toward the end of the journey, mostly following the Catamount Trail. This winter-only route utilizes two private and two Green Mountain Club lodgings, basic and self-service, exclusive-use Triple Creek Cabin, Crow's Nest Yurt, Bolton Lodge, and Bryant Camp.

## WYOMING

**Bear River Outdoor Recreation Alliance.** Lily Lake, a multiuse recreation area in the Uinta-Wasatch-Cache National Forest, 30 miles south of Evanston, Wyoming, and 82 miles northeast of Salt Lake City, Utah, features six yurts (capacity ranges from eight to twelve) and 12 miles of groomed trails (classic and skate), as well as marked nongroomed trails. While seldom attempted, it is possible to link any of the lower yurts (Bear Claw, East Fork, Lily Lake, and Beulah Vista) to one or both of the two upper yurts (Ridge and Boundary Creek) for a multiday winter adventure. All self-service,

*The Lower Canwell Hut in Alaska's Delta Range is strictly for advanced mountaineers. (Photo by Sean Marble, Alaska Alpine Club)*

exclusive-use yurts use the same trailhead; distances are moderate, and the farthest yurt is 6.5 miles from the trailhead.



American outdoor clubs, including those dedicated primarily to hiking, skiing, and mountaineering, and other conservation organizations have long created lodging for members to better enjoy the great outdoors. These cabins and lodges are mostly single structures or encampments—situated either as drive-up base camps or as backcountry destinations. We came across some great examples during our research; even though the following hostelries do not specifically support human-powered hut-to-hut travel, they should appeal to the same audience. The annotated list is not exhaustive. Each listing distills just enough information to encourage further research.

**Adirondack Mountain Club.** This upstate New York organization offers the front-country Adirondack Loj at Heart Lake and Heart Lake Cabins and the backcountry Johns Brook Lodge (capacity twenty-eight), accessed by a 3.5-mile hike in; it operates as full service in summer, and caretaker season is September to late June (i.e., guests bring and prepare their own meals).

**American Alpine Club.** This nonprofit maintains several dormitory-style cabin ranches and one hut in various locations: Grand Teton Climbers' Ranch in Moose, Wyoming (June through September); Hueco Rock Ranch near El Paso, Texas (November through March); and Snowbird Hut in Alaska (see Bomber Traverse above).

**Colorado Mountain Club.** The Boulder Group owns two high-elevation, self-service, by the bunk backcountry huts in the Arapaho and Roosevelt National Forests.

*Chittenden Hut is owned and operated by the Vermont Hut Association, which also coordinates network reservations for privately owned huts. (Photo by Marius Becker)*

Arestua Hut sleeps eight and requires reservations. Brainard Cabin sleeps twelve and is available first come, first served.

**Green Mountain Club.** The frontcountry Bolton Lodge and Bryant Camp are located along the Catamount Trail in the Mount Mansfield State Forest between Montpelier and Burlington, Vermont. The Wheeler Pond Camps (two cabins) are in Barton, near Lake Willoughby.

**The Mountaineers.** This Washington-based nonprofit has three full-service, frontcountry mountain lodges near ski areas: Baker Lodge near Mount Baker in the North Cascades, Stevens Lodge on the Pacific Crest Trail near Stevens Pass, and Meany Lodge near Stampede Pass. Rented by the bunk, the lodges are open weekends and run mostly by volunteers.

**Randolph Mountain Club.** This organization maintains 100 miles of trails, along with two backcountry cabins, Gray Knob and Crag Camp, in the northern Presidential Range of the White Mountain National Forest. The cabins are open year-round and available first come, first served; overflow guests should be prepared to camp. The club also maintains two three-sided shelters: the Perch and the Log Cabin.

**Rocky Mountain Biological Laboratory.** This organization offers self-service, exclusive-use winter accommodations in Gothic, Colorado, an abandoned mining town (elevation 9485), with a 4-mile ski in. Maroon

Hut (sleeps eight to ten) and Crystal Cabin (sleeps six downstairs, eight upstairs) are available from November to April.

**Sequoia Parks Conservancy.** Pear Lake Winter Hut (9200 feet elevation) is a rustic-style granite and timber backcountry hut built in 1939–41 and located in Sequoia National Park. Available for winter use only, the hut sleeps ten, and reservations are by lottery. This self-service, by the bunk hut is recommended for advanced skiers only.

**Sierra Club.** Built by Sierra Club volunteers, the Clair Tappaan Lodge (full service) and backcountry huts (basic), all by the bunk, are located in the Tahoe National Forest near Donner Pass (see above).

**Sierra Club Angeles Chapter.** Mount San Antonio, informally known as Mount Baldy, elevation 10,043 feet, boasts several lodging options from the 1930s maintained by the Angeles Chapter of the Sierra Club: Harwood Lodge (sleeps sixty-four) and Keller Peak Ski Hut (sleeps twenty) are near the base of Mount Baldy, and San Antonio Ski Hut (sleeps sixteen) requires a steep 3-mile hike. The self-service, by the bunk lodges are open all year, with the schedule depending on a volunteer caretaker roster.

**Utah Nordic Alliance (TUNA).** The backcountry Boulder Creek Yurt, located along the Norway Flats Road in the Uinta National Forest, is at an elevation of 8600 feet and sleeps eight. Dogs are allowed with prior permission. The self-service, exclusive-use yurt is open year-round.

**Yosemite Conservancy.** Built in 1941, Ostrander Ski Hut (8500 feet) is a two-story stone building with capacity for twenty-five. Located a 10-mile ski from Badger Pass Ski Area in the southern section of the national park, the hut is usually open from mid-December to the end of March. Online reservations start in mid-November. Hut keeper is in residence. Snowshoes not advisable. This self-service, by the bunk hut is recommended for advanced skiers only.

**Yosemite National Park.** Glacier Point Ski Hut, rebuilt in 1997 as a summer visitors center and winter ski hut, provides meals, indoor bathrooms, and dorm-style bunk beds (capacity twenty). The intermediate 10.5-mile trail departs from Badger Pass Ski Area. This full-service hut is rented by the bunk.

## HUTS OPERATED BY PRIVATE OWNERS AND OUTFITTERS

The US has countless backcountry lodging businesses, some operated by guide services. We present a very selective list. Many long-established businesses operate multiple yurts, tents, or cabins in remote locations; visitors enjoy the base camp experience rather than the more prolonged hut-to-hut journey. Among operators are pioneers who introduced yurts and other innovative structures for intensive backcountry experiences. While this book focuses on human-powered travel, here we mention a few guiding outfits that employ snowmobiles, snowcats, and special tracked vans to ferry visitors to winter backcountry encampments; there is such an operation, for example, in Yellowstone National Park.

## COLORADO

**Hinsdale Haute Route.** Near Lake City in Hinsdale County, this system offers two (sometimes three) self-service, exclusive-use yurts with unique picture-window designs. Open year-round, John Wilson Yurt sleeps up to eight people and can be reached via a 1.25-mile trail. Colorado Trail Yurt is farther into the backcountry.

**Leadville Backcountry Yurts.** Two self-service, exclusive-use yurts, Emma and Marceline (capacity five each), are 5.5 miles from the trailhead and right next to each other; available in winter and summer.

**San Juan Haute Route.** OPUS Hut, a full-service lodge, connects with Thelma Hut to form a high-elevation hut-to-hut itinerary between Telluride and Silverton in the San Juan National Forest. OPUS, short for Ophir Pass Ultimate Ski, sleeps sixteen and is at 11,600 feet. The stylish and comfortable Thelma Hut, opened in December 2018, sleeps eight and features a hut keeper and prepared meals. The hut-to-hut itinerary, which crosses avalanche-prone terrain, requires a car shuttle or two vehicles. Both OPUS and Thelma Huts are open year-round.

**Weston Pass Hut.** At 11,950 feet elevation, Weston Pass Hut is touted as the highest accommodation in Colorado. Opened in 2015, the self-service, by the bunk hut features a unique design with three sides buried in the hillside. It sleeps twenty, with motorized access in summer, and is accessed by ski, snowshoe, and snowmobile in winter.

## IDAHO

**Sawtooth Mountain Guides.** Williams Peak Hut, in the Sawtooth National Forest south of Stanley, features two yurts (from backcountry yurt pioneer Kirk Bachman) located side by side. They are self-service, available only in winter via a 5-mile route. Guided trips are available, and avalanche preparedness training is required.

## MONTANA

**Montana Backcountry Yurts.** YurtSki, located at the base of Mount Morrell in the Swan Mountains, features two backcountry yurts, Alpine (sleeps ten) and Lupine (sleeps eight), which are accessed by an 8-mile ski in and are self-service, exclusive use. Big Belt Hut, with capacity for fifteen, is open year-round and can be reached by a 3-mile route (or longer depending on season). Gear haul is available. Big Belt Hut is self-service and by the bunk.

## OREGON

**Wallowa Alpine Huts.** Camp McCully, the original site for this business, which started in 1980, is located in the Eagle Cap Wilderness and features two yurts, each with capacity for five people. Wing Ridge has two-walled sleeping tents (capacity twelve) and a kitchen yurt. Big Sheep is a large walled tent that sleeps twelve. Norway Basin, a two-story yurt, sleeps eleven. Guided, hosted, and DIY options (with mandatory first-day escort) are available.

*Williams Peak Hut in Idaho's Sawtooth Mountains features two yurts designed and built by Kirk Bachman.* (Photo by Theo Rich)

There are no connecting routes between the four backcountry locations. Big Sheep is appropriate for snowshoers and beginning skiers as well as more advanced skiers. The other three sites are for advanced skiers with avalanche training. Porters and gear haul available.

## UTAH

**Powder Ridge Ski Touring.** This outfitter operates three self-service, winter-use yurts in the Bear River Range north of Salt Lake City. Bunchgrass, with a 3.6-mile trail, sleeps eight. Steam Mill, with a 3.3-mile access, sleeps six. A family-friendly yurt that sleeps twelve, Green Canyon is accessible via 3.5 miles on a groomed road.

## WASHINGTON

**Stehekin Outfitters.** Bridge Creek and Cottonwood Camp, featuring large outfitter tents, connect to form a summer tent-to-tent variation on hut-to-hut travel in this remote valley inaccessible by car. Take the ferry across Lake Chelan to the town of Stehekin, or hike in over Cascade Pass in the North Cascades. Distances between the trailhead and camps are 3.5 and 6 miles.

## WYOMING

**Teton Backcountry Guides.** Founded in 1984 in Alta, Wyoming, this company owns five yurts that each sleep four to six. The four backcountry yurts, about 4 miles in, are available for winter use: Baldy Knoll

Yurt, Teton Canyon Yurt, Plummer Canyon Yurt, and Commissary Ridge Yurt. Rammell Mountain Yurt is accessible by vehicle in summer and fall. These yurts are mostly used for guided trips; DIY rentals are available only for "experienced parties who are proficient in route-finding, avalanche awareness, first aid, bivouac, and evacuation skills." Guide is required for the first day.

## HUTS OPERATED BY COLLEGE AND UNIVERSITY CLUBS

Nineteenth-century ideals cultivating self-reliance in sports and the outdoors found expression in the outing clubs at America's earliest, mostly (formerly) all-male colleges such as Harvard and Dartmouth. Remote cabins in the wilds of New England remind us of this legacy and continue to serve outdoor enthusiasts. The practice of educational institutions providing lodging for outdoor pursuits was reborn in the 1980s in response to the outdoor recreation boom and the growth of extracurricular programs that aim to educate the whole person. Portable and easy to construct, yurts suit these programs perfectly.

Cabins used primarily for backcountry activities, some available only to members of the college community, include the Bowdoin Outing Club Cabin in Maine, the sixteen cabins operated by the Dartmouth Outing Club in New Hampshire (the first collegiate outing club), and the Harvard Mountaineering Club Cabin in New Hampshire.

The following universities have yurts that are mostly seasonal (winter) and located in the backcountry: California State University, Chico; Idaho State University (in Portneuf Range); St. Lawrence University, New York; Utah State University in Logan; and Weber State University in Ogden, Utah (the yurt is in southern Idaho).

## RENTAL CABINS AND YURTS ON STATE AND FEDERAL LANDS

For those seeking backcountry accommodations accessible by foot, ski, bike, or paddle (and remote frontcountry accommodations), do not overlook the thousands of cabins, yurts, fire towers, and other structures offered for rent by federal and state agencies. In fact, the Federal Lands Recreation Enhancement Act encourages and authorizes agencies including the US Forest Service and the Bureau of Land Management to offer some of their architectural inventory to the public for their enjoyment, and to generate revenue. The Pacific Northwest, for example, has a great website to facilitate the search for remote lodgings, including fire towers; search for Pacific Northwest's Forest Service Rental Program online. Alaska boasts hundreds of backcountry cabins, many accessible only in winter, or by boat or plane, and maintained by both federal and state agencies. Spend time with maps and websites and talk to agency staff to put together potential multi-day cabin-to-cabin adventures.

State agencies, including those overseeing parks and forests, are particularly keen to add cabins and yurts to satisfy an enthusiastic public, and for their revenue potential. Yurts are the popular new rustic lodging type, especially in state parks. While most of these are installed in drive-in campgrounds, you can find backcountry yurts in state parks and recreation areas. One notable set of yurts, managed by a state parks and recreation department, is in Idaho City, one and a half hours north of Boise. Idaho City Yurts and Trails comprises six temporary dwellings, each with a capacity of six. Although primarily for skiers, a few of these yurts are open year-round.

## SHELTER SYSTEMS ON LONG-DISTANCE TRAILS

Hikers can travel shelter to shelter on some of the Northeast's long-distance hiking trails. Unlike huts, these shelters are most often three-sided, with a sloped roof and plank floor. Under the first-come, first-served system, hikers must be prepared to pitch a tent or string up a bivvy or hammock when the shelters are full. The Appalachian Trail, stretching more than 2190 miles from Georgia to Maine, offers more

*One of the many cabins operated by the Dartmouth Outing Club in New Hampshire* (Photo by Kevin O'Donoghue, Dartmouth Outdoors)

than 250 shelters, spaced 5 to 15 miles apart. Besides providing rain protection to weary travelers, these simple structures reduce the impact of dispersed camping along this ever more popular route. The 272-mile Long Trail in Vermont offers seventy shelters; twenty of these double as Appalachian Trail shelters where the two trails merge or overlap.

# SAM'S HUT DREAM



**PEOPLE ASK IF I PLAN** to start a hut system. During a glorious forty-two-day hut-to-hut walk in Europe, my trail musings blossomed into vivid hut dreams. Passing over alpine passes and along river valleys, I fantasized about possible roles for huts in the US. This impulse continued through the years as occasional notes dropped into a file labeled "Hut Dreams." It gradually evolved into a passion to seriously explore the present reality and future possibilities of huts in the US, and eventually led to this book. This final section, or caboose—the rolling hut at the end of the train where the crew actually lives—is my way of sharing my hut dream with you. The following, dear reader, is what my hut system would look like.

Imagine a circuit of forty-two huts beginning at the urban edge and looping more than 350 miles into beautiful frontcountry terrain undergoing conservation restoration. About twelve of these huts will actually be camps or lodges—that is, clusters of buildings resembling youth and family camps (the original purpose of some). These will provide meals in a central lodge, indoor and outdoor classroom spaces, bunk rooms, and cabins with options for self-service accommodations. People will participate in workshops and activities at these lodges, often staying for a week or more. The other thirty huts will be simple, self-service accommodations along the trail, linking to

OPPOSITE: *Juneau Creek Falls on the Resurrection Pass Trail in Alaska*

each other and to the lodges. The trails will have a collection of irresistible, handcrafted benches and picnic tables featuring designs from around the world.

All the huts and camps will operate as multigenerational work-study environments, with participants serving as teachers, learners, and workers. Hospitality will be offered by teams of young people and elders who earn their food and lodging by helping to run the enterprise.

These forty-two affiliated huts and camps will operate on principles of dialogue rising above politics and religious denominations and encourage work for the common good. Open-minded people of goodwill from all spiritual traditions, ethnicities, races, political stripes, and socioeconomic classes will be welcomed to live, work, learn, and teach in huts together.

In essence, this hut system will function as a life-cycle environmental pilgrimage. While the forty-two huts and camps along the way may be visited in one long journey, most folks will choose to make the circuit in sections, over years and decades. Traveled in sequence over a lifetime, the experience will support, echo, and inspire one's journey through life. Families, friend groups, and organizations will develop a pattern of retreating for a week annually to hike hut-to-hut for a few days and then stay at one of the camps to participate in "classes." This experience will become a kind of multigenerational rite of passage.

The golden rule—applied equally to human and other-than-human beings—will be the bedrock of the curriculum. Based on interconnectedness, the aim of this hut system

will be to cultivate "the better angels of our nature." Its programs will provide experience and build skills in living a good life, caring for the earth, and caring for each other.

Most of the classes will be outdoors, hands-on, and will teach useful skills, aesthetic appreciation, applications of scientific and cultural lessons to conservation, altruism, and methods of developing one's personal credo and of understanding what is important in life.

Each of the twelve camps or lodges has a theme, listed below, which animates its workshops and programming.

**Natural history.** Teaching and learning about evolution, ecology, and the interconnectedness of all beings, human and nonhuman, will be central to the work of this hut system. Basic natural history knowledge will inform the pilgrimage, and is woven into each of the other forty-one huts and camps.

**Outdoor skills and camp craft.** Workshops and expeditions will be designed to teach essential skills for staying safe, healthy, and comfortable while hiking, camping, and backpacking. For beginners, this will include use of map and compass, selecting proper clothing and gear, first aid, starting a fire, cookery, and Leave No Trace principles. A gear lending library and scheduled outings will support programs building on these basics.

**Hunting, fishing, and foraging.** Meeting novices where they are, programs will help them develop both skills and a personal set of ethics about these hobbies, which are no longer necessary for meeting food needs, but which can foster respectful connection to nature. Programs will explore how these

*Embodying* hygge, *huts evoke a shared sense of comfort, equality, and gratitude, and encourage spontaneity and social interaction among visitors.* (Photo by Marco Volken)

skills can be practiced to advance conservation and economic and social goals.

**Gardening, agriculture, cooking, and food studies.** Programs will foster skills for participation in a food production system, from local to global, that is grounded in reciprocity with the earth to sustain human nutrition and health.

**Arts, crafts, and music.** Programs will focus on the celebration and practice of human capacities to make music, sing, draw, and engage in other creative expressions. Participants will develop skills and pride in handcrafts, to preserve craft traditions and to fashion sustainable solutions for living.

**Folklore, storytelling, writing, poetry, and theater.** Participants will develop confidence and skills in these forms of human expression in service to compassion and harmony between humans and the earth.

**Spirituality, therapy, yoga, forest bathing, and other forms of caring for the mind and body.** Programs will offer techniques for encouraging time-honored practices of realizing the recuperative powers of nature, service to others, self-care, and solitude.

**Community building.** Participants will explore the pursuit of human obligations beyond self-interest and learn strategies for developing the innately good human capacities with which we are hardwired, such as the "social suite" identified by Nicholas Christakis: love, friendship, cooperation (even with strangers), teaching, and social learning.

**Approaches to environmental activism.** Programs will focus on the development and diffusion of strategies for giving the natural world a stronger voice in human affairs and for mobilizing individual, community, and global action to protect the biota and natural earth systems.

**Trail community.** The Benton MacKaye Center for Hut and Trail Studies will explore ways of implementing MacKaye's vision of establishing temporary communities to provide urbanites with outdoor experiences in a folk-school-like setting. Located near a school or university campus, at the junction with one of our long-distance National Scenic Trails, this camp will also study, celebrate, and teach all aspects of huts, trails, and their uses. It will be a stopover for through-hikers and will equip and prepare environmental pilgrims for long and short journeys of all kinds.

**Peace, reconciliation, and environmental studies.** Groups will experiment with ways of finding common cause in use and protection of the land. For example, hunters and hikers, and skiers and snowmobilers will work on strategies for healing the earth, and for getting beyond polarized views to focus on what used to be called "sportsmanship"—that is, honorable, fair, generous, and respectful treatment of each other and of the other-than-human beings with whom we share the earth.

**Preparation for the last phases of life, death, and dying.** For elders and their family and friends, programs will encourage a reflective capacity to learning, teaching, and loving at end-of-life; this will include workshops on writing bespoke health care directives and a nature-based hospice program.

Altogether, the forty-two huts, each a stage on the journey, will comprise a hut-based *school of life studies.* The precise labels, sequences, combinations, and emphases will depend on many factors, not least the people involved in shaping the personality of each station along the way, and the terrain and regional culture. Hardly original, this dream is firmly rooted in Benton MacKaye's vision for the Appalachian Trail, and springs directly from myriad influences in my life, such as the work of educators like Johann Pestalozzi, Maria Montessori, John Dewey, and Rudolf Steiner, who informed my approach to environmental education. It is inspired by elements of existing hut systems, outdoor education programs, retreat centers, folk schools, and centers for healing and learning around the world.

Reactions to my hut dreams over the years—except from a handful of imaginative hut nuts—are mostly indulgent smiles or sighs about the challenges inherent in realizing such "hopelessly" idealistic visions. After studying huts for years, I am more aware than most people of the challenges; but my eccentric little pilgrimage of researching huts over the past seven years has emboldened me. After experiencing most of America's hut systems, getting to know the owners and operators, and talking with the people who stay in huts, I am more convinced than ever that versions of these hut dreams are achievable.

If as a culture we can build thousands of schools, universities, hospitals, museums, libraries, parks, bridges, and concert halls, I believe we are capable of developing a network of hut systems grounded in developing and teaching environmental ethics. Of course, it's possible this is a dream whose time hasn't come. Or perhaps it is fundamentally flawed, or unsuited to the times and the culture in ways I cannot grasp.

In any case, I invite you, dear readers who have read this far, to join me: dream your own hut dreams and share them with others as Americans reinvent the abiding, ancient hut in the twenty-first century.

# ACKNOWLEDGMENTS

The owners, operators, and board members of American hut systems were generous in supporting our research in many ways. In particular, we wish to acknowledge the remarkable croo in the Appalachian Mountain Club (AMC) huts, Bron Austin, Jenifer Blomquist, Morgan Boyles, Bob Brown, Whitney Brown, Cindy Carpenter, Zach Crist, Paul Cunha, Joe Dadey, Ben Dodge, Jack Drury, Lee Girvin, Eric Gotthold, Greg Graves, Bob Jonas, Leighton Jump, Mike Quist Kautz, Kristin Kurtz, Jesse Labenski, Rodney Ley, Doug MacLennan, Drew McElvain, Scott Messina, Ben Nelson, Chuck Ogilby, John and Cynthia Orcutt, Carolann Oulette, John Phelps, Lou Prill, Mare Pyke, Lee Rimel, Samwise Rogers, Joe and Kelly Ryan, Joe and Francie St. Onge, Jonas and Anna Tarlen, Chris Tennal, R. J. Thompson, John Warner, John Wolfe, Charlie and Mary Woodworth, James Wrigley, Eric Yeager, Barbara and Ted Young, and Mike Zobbe.

The incredibly lively and committed community around the Methow Valley was great fun and inspirational to talk with: Eric Burr, Dale Caufield, James DeSalvo, Charlie Hickenbottom, Jay Lucas, and Don Portman.

Our trips were enriched immeasurably by the intrepid friends and family who accompanied us: Perrin Boyd; Mike, Kelly, and Sophie Scheurman; Bill and Rachel Swift; Damon, Lanie, and Xanthe Demas; David Amdur; and Chloe Wardropper.

Through publications and conversations, colleagues from around the world added to our understanding of the international context of huts, notably Mike Abbott, Shaun Barnett, Rob Brown, Brian Dobbie, Kev Reynolds, Geoff Spearpoint, and Marco Volken.

Our work was enriched by editorial comments, technical assistance, and moral support from useful conversations with and inspiring publications by John Barbour, Chris Beck, Kristin Bloomer, Tom Courtney, Theo and Damon Demas, Kevin Keeler, Robert Manning, Jeffrey Marion, Bob Ratcliffe, and Mary Kate Repetski.

We are grateful for expert assistance with procuring photographic files from staff, curators, and individuals. These include R. J.

Thompson, Vermont Huts Association; Matt Krebs, Green Mountain Club; Nina Paus-Weiler and Becky Fullerton, AMC; Jean Tabbert, Glacier National Park Museum and Archives; Gretchen Roecker, Yosemite Conservancy; Kristin Kurtz, San Juan Huts; Travis Campbell, American Prairie Reserve; Niels Meyer, Sawtooth Mountain Guides; Rory Gawter, Dartmouth Outdoors; Neil Stewart, Mountain Bothy Association; Sean Marble, Alaska Alpine Club; and Madi McConnell, Jeffrey Marion, and Robert Manning.

We are especially grateful for the hundreds of hut-to-hut trekkers with whom we shared huts, meals, and camaraderie along the way.

The book and our writing journey were buoyed by Carleton College research funds, and by the support and editorial acumen of the staff at Mountaineers Books, including Kate Rogers, Janet Kimball, and Laura Shauger, and copyeditor Jennifer Zaczek Kepler—a heartfelt thank-you.

# RESOURCES

This list includes publications mentioned in the book as well as other useful resources.

Ambrose, Stephen. *Undaunted Courage: Meriwether Lewis, Thomas Jefferson, and the Opening of the American West.* New York: Simon & Schuster, 1996.

Arnold, Lloyd. *Hemingway: High on the Wild.* Caldwell, ID: Caxton Printers, 1968.

Bachelard, Gaston. *The Poetics of Space.* Translated by Maria Jolas. 1958. Reprint, Boston: Beacon Press, 1969.

Barnett, Shaun, Rob Brown, and Geoff Spearpoint. *Shelter from the Storm: The Story of New Zealand's Backcountry Huts.* Nelson, New Zealand: Craig Potton Pub., 2012.

Bisson, Christian A., and Jamie Hannon. *AMC's Mountain Skills Manual: A Comprehensive Desk Reference for Backpackers of All Skill Levels.* Boston: Appalachian Mountain Club Books, 2017.

Brower, David. *Manual of Ski Mountaineering.* San Francisco: Sierra Club, 1942.

Christakis, Nicholas. *Blueprint: The Evolutionary Origins of a Good Society.* Boston: Little Brown, 2019.

Cline, Ann. *A Hut of One's Own: Life Outside the Circle of Architecture.* Cambridge, MA: MIT Press, 1997.

Courtney, Tom. *Walkabout Northern California: Hiking Inn to Inn.* 2nd ed. Birmingham, AL: Wilderness Press, 2019.

Dawson, Louis. "10th Mountain Division History." Last modified November 14, 2019. www.loudawson.com/ski -mountaineering-history/10th-mountain -division-history/.

———. "History of Huts." Accessed September 19, 2020. www.huts.org/The_Huts /hut_history.php.

Demas, Sam. Hut2Hut. www.hut2hut.info.

Douglas, William O. "Journey to Outer Mongolia." *National Geographic* 121, no. 3 (March 1962): 289–344.

European Ramblers' Association. "E-Paths." Accessed March 20, 2020. www.era-ewv -ferp.org/e-paths.

Fay, Charles E. "The Appalachian Mountain Club." *The Annals of the American Academy of Political and Social Science* 35, no. 2 (March 1910): 177–84.

Johannes, Daniel, and Edward Rolfe. *Hut to Hut on the Appalachian Trail in the White Mountains of New Hampshire: Illustrated Hiking Map and Guide.* 6th ed. Twin Mountain, NH: Wilderness Map Co., 2005.

Johnson, Dianne D. *Hut in the Wild.* Leura, New South Wales, Australia: D. D. Johnson, 2011.

Lanza, Michael. *Winter Hiking and Camping.* Seattle, WA: Mountaineers Books, 2003.

Laughlin, James. "A Plea for Huts in America." In *American Ski Annual, 1941–1942.* Brattleboro, VT: Stephen Daye Press, 1942.

Laugier, Marc-Antoine. *An Essay on Architecture.* Los Angeles: Hennessey & Ingalls, 1977.

Laws, John Muir. *The Laws Field Guide to the Sierra Nevada.* San Francisco: California Academy of Sciences; Berkeley, CA: Heyday Books, 2007.

Leonard, Joe. *The Son of the Madam of Mustang Ranch.* Self-published, Bradenton, FL: BookLocker.com, 2016.

Litz, Brian. *Colorado Hut to Hut.* 2 vols. Englewood, CO: Westcliffe, 2000.

Louv, Richard. *Last Child in the Woods: Saving Our Children from Nature-Deficit Disorder.* 1st ed. Chapel Hill, NC: Algonquin Books of Chapel Hill, 2005.

MacKaye, Benton. "An Appalachian Trail: A Project in Regional Planning." *Journal of the American Institute of Architects* 9, no. 10 (October 1921): 325–30.

Marion, Jeffrey L. *Leave No Trace in the Outdoors.* Mechanicsburg, PA: Stackpole Books, 2014.

Ohlrich, Warren. *10th Mountain Hut Guide: A Winter Guide to Colorado's 10th Mountain and Summit Hut Systems near Aspen, Vail, Leadville, and Breckenridge.* 2nd ed. Woody Creek, CO: People's Press, 2011.

Park, Geoff. *Theatre Country: Essays on Landscape and Whenua.* Wellington: Victoria University Press, 2006.

Pearson, Claudia. *NOLS Cookery.* 7th ed. Guilford, CT: Stackpole Books, 2017.

Rafferty, Michael, and Robert Sprague. *The Last Porcupine Mountains Companion: The Story of Michigan's Porcupine Mountains Wilderness State Park.* N.p.: Back to Nature Store, 2020.

Reifsnyder, William E. *High Mountain Huts: A Planning Guide.* Golden: Colorado Mountain Trails Foundation in cooperation with USDA Forest Service, n.d.

Reynolds, Kev. *100 Hut Walks in the Alps.* 3rd ed. Milnthorpe, Cumbria, UK: Cicerone Press, 2014.

———. *The Mountain Hut Book.* Kendal, Cumbria, UK: Cicerone Press, 2018.

San Juan Hut Systems. *The Bikers' Bible.* Revised March 2015. https://sanjuanhuts .com/images/documents/biker-bible.pdf.

Scott, Jim. *Backcountry Huts and Lodges of the Rockies and Columbias.* Calgary, Alberta, Canada: Johnson Gorman, 2002.

Smith, Steven D., ed. *White Mountain Guide: AMC's Comprehensive Guide to Hiking Trails in the White Mountain National Forest.* 30th ed. Boston: Appalachian Mountain Club Books, 2017.

Todd, John. *Simple Sketches.* Vol. 2. Pittsfield, MA: EP Little, 1845.

Unsworth, Walt, comp. *Encyclopaedia of Mountaineering.* Milnthorpe, Cumbria, UK: Cicerone Press, 1992.

US Forest Service. n.d. *Boundary Waters Canoe Area Wilderness Trip Planning Guide.* Duluth, MN: US Forest Service. www.fs.usda.gov/Internet/FSE_DOCUMENTS/stelprd3799760.pdf.

Volken, Marco, and Remo Kundert. *The Huts of the Swiss Alpine Club.* Zurich: AS Verlag, 2013.

Volken, Martin, Scott Schell, and Margaret Wheeler. *Backcountry Skiing: Skills for Ski Touring and Ski Mountaineering.* Seattle, WA: Mountaineers Books, 2007.

Warne, Kennedy. "Conversation with the Abbott." *New Zealand Geographic.* Accessed February 18, 2021. www.nzgeo.com/stories/conversation-with-the-abbott/.

Waterman, Laura, and Guy Waterman. *Forest and Crag: A History of Hiking, Trail Blazing, and Adventure in the Northeast Mountains.* Boston: Appalachian Mountain Club Books, 2003.

———. *Wilderness Ethics: Preserving the Spirit of Wildness.* 2nd ed. Woodstock, VT: Countryman Press, 2014.

Wilson, Edward O. *Half-Earth: Our Planet's Fight for Life.* 1st ed. New York: Liveright, 2016.

Wivell, Ty. *Passport to AMC's High Huts in the White Mountains.* Boston: Appalachian Mountain Club Books, 2011.

Yule, Leigh Girvin, and Scott Toepfer. *The Hut Handbook: A Guide to Planning and Enjoying a Backcountry Hut Trip.* Englewood, CO: Westcliffe, 1996.

Zahniser, H. *Where Wilderness Preservation Began: Adirondack Writings of Howard Zahniser.* Edited by Ed Zahniser. Utica, NY: North Country Books, 1992.

# INDEX

# ABOUT THE AUTHORS

**Laurel Bradley,** a lifelong hiker and outdoor enthusiast, has trekked hut-to-hut worldwide. Bradley is a Sierra Club Service Trip volunteer leader and accomplished backcountry cook. She trained as an art historian and served as a curator, museum director, and teacher at several colleges and universities.

**Sam Demas**, a leading authority on hut systems, has walked or skied most hut-to-hut routes in the US and all over Europe and New Zealand. His website, www.hut2hut.info, is a go-to resource for outdoor enthusiasts, hut operators, and land management professionals. Demas worked as an academic librarian for many years. He is passionate about conservation, environmental education, and the role of huts in providing nature immersion experiences, as well as fostering and boosting an environmentally conscious mindset among visitors. Bradley and Demas live in Northfield, Minnesota.

*Enjoying one of the Rendezvous Huts in Washington's Methow Valley (Photo by Leyton Jump)*

**MOUNTAINEERS BOOKS**, including its two imprints, Skipstone and Braided River, is a leading publisher of quality outdoor recreation, sustainability, and conservation titles. As a 501(c)(3) nonprofit, we are committed to supporting the environmental and educational goals of our organization by providing expert information on human-powered adventure, sustainable practices at home and on the trail, and preservation of wilderness.

Our publications are made possible through the generosity of donors, and through sales of 700 titles on outdoor recreation, sustainable lifestyle, and conservation. To donate, purchase books, or learn more, visit us online:

**MOUNTAINEERS BOOKS**

1001 SW Klickitat Way, Suite 201 • Seattle, WA 98134

800-553-4453 • mbooks@mountaineersbooks.org • www.mountaineersbooks.org

*An independent nonprofit publisher since 1960*

Mountaineers Books is proud to support the Leave No Trace Center for Outdoor Ethics, whose mission is to promote and inspire responsible outdoor recreation through education, research, and partnerships. The Leave No Trace program is focused specifically on human-powered (nonmotorized) recreation. For more information, visit https://lnt.org.


## YOU MAY ALSO LIKE:

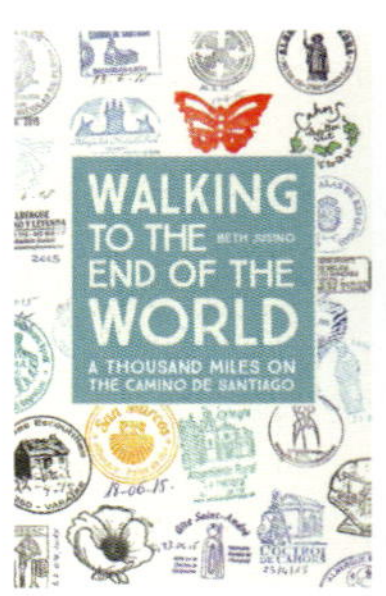